Great Sieges in World History

Great Sieges in World History

Great Sieges in World History

From Ancient Times to the 21st Century

Spencer C. Tucker

BLOOMSBURY ACADEMIC
NEW YORK • LONDON • OXFORD • NEW DELHI • SYDNEY

BLOOMSBURY ACADEMIC
Bloomsbury Publishing Inc
1385 Broadway, New York, NY 10018, USA
50 Bedford Square, London, WC1B 3DP, UK
29 Earlsfort Terrace, Dublin 2, Ireland

BLOOMSBURY, BLOOMSBURY ACADEMIC and the Diana logo
are trademarks of Bloomsbury Publishing Plc

First published in the United States of America by ABC-CLIO 2021
Paperback edition published by Bloomsbury Academic 2025

Copyright © Bloomsbury Publishing Inc, 2025

COVER PHOTO: Panorama of *The Fall of Constantinople*, Military Museum, Istanbul, Turkey.
(Zhanna Tretiakova/Alamy Stock Photo)

All rights reserved. No part of this publication may be reproduced or
transmitted in any form or by any means, electronic or mechanical,
including photocopying, recording, or any information storage or retrieval
system, without prior permission in writing from the publishers.

Bloomsbury Publishing Inc does not have any control over, or responsibility for,
any third-party websites referred to or in this book. All internet addresses given
in this book were correct at the time of going to press. The author and publisher
regret any inconvenience caused if addresses have changed or sites have
ceased to exist, but can accept no responsibility for any such changes.

Library of Congress Cataloging-in-Publication Data
Names: Tucker, Spencer, 1937– author.
Title: Great sieges in world history : from ancient times to the 21st century / Spencer C. Tucker.
Description: Santa Barbara : ABC-CLIO, 2021. | Includes bibliographical references and index.
Identifiers: LCCN 2020023129 (print) | LCCN 2020023130 (ebook) |
ISBN 9781440868023 (hardcover) | ISBN 9781440868030 (ebook)
Subjects: LCSH: Sieges—History. | Military history.
Classification: LCC D25.5 .T77 2021 (print) | LCC D25.5 (ebook) |
DDC 355.4/409—dc23
LC record available at https://lccn.loc.gov/2020023129
LC ebook record available at https://lccn.loc.gov/2020023130

ISBN: HB: 978-1-4408-6802-3
PB: 979-8-7651-4013-0
ePDF: 978-1-4408-6803-0
eBook: 979-8-2160-9196-7

To find out more about our authors and books visit www.bloomsbury.com
and sign up for our newsletters.

*For Robert Keefe,
dear friend, accomplished editor,
and master of print production*

Contents

List of Entries   ix

Preface   xiii

A Brief Introduction to Siege Warfare   xv

Great Sieges in World History   1

About the Author and Contributors   283

Index   285

List of Entries

Siege of Troy (1194–1184 BCE)

Siege of Babylon (539–538 BCE)

Siege of Plataea (428–427 BCE)

Siege of Syracuse (415–413 BCE)

Siege of Veii (404–396 BCE)

Sieges of Tyre and Gaza (332 BCE)

Siege of Syracuse (213–212 BCE)

Siege of Carthage (149–146 BCE)

Siege of Numantia (Numancia) (134–133 BCE)

Siege of Alesia (July–October 52 BCE)

Siege of Jerusalem (April 14–September 8, 70 CE)

Siege of Masada (72–73)

Siege of Ravenna (Autumn 490–February 27, 493)

Siege of Rome (March 2, 537–March 12, 538)

Siege of Damascus (634–635?)

Siege of Constantinople (August 15, 717–August 15, 718)

Siege of Pavia (September 773–June 774)

Siege of Paris (November 25, 885–October 886)

Siege of Jerusalem (June 7–July 18, 1099)

Siege of Acre (August 28, 1189–July 12, 1191)

Siege of Baghdad (January 29–February 10, 1258)

Siege of Xiangyang (March 1267–March 14, 1273)

Siege of Calais (September 4, 1346–August 3, 1347)

Siege of Orléans (October 12, 1428–May 8, 1449)

Siege of Constantinople (April 6–May 29, 1453)

Siege of Granada (Mid-April 1491–January 2, 1492)

Siege of Tenochtitlán (May 26–August 13, 1521)

Siege of Rhodes (July 28–December 21, 1522)

Siege and Battle of Pavia (October 28, 1524–February 24, 1525)

Siege of Vienna (September 24–October 14, 1529)

Siege of Malta (May 18–September 8, 1565)

Siege of Szigetvár (August 6–September 8, 1566)

Siege of Antwerp (July 1584–August 17, 1585)

Siege of Odawara Castle (May–August 4, 1590)

Siege of Breda (August 28, 1624–June 5, 1625)

Siege of La Rochelle (August 1627–October 28, 1628)

Siege of Magdeburg (November 20, 1630–May 20, 1631)

Siege of Candia (May 1, 1648–September 27, 1669)

Siege of Maastricht (June 13–30, 1673)

Siege and Battle of Vienna (July 14–September 12, 1683)

Siege of St. Augustine (November 10–December 29, 1702)

Siege of Isfahan (March–October 23, 1722)

Siege of Cartagena de Indias (March 9–May 20, 1741)

Siege of Fort William Henry (August 3–10, 1757)

Siege of Louisbourg (June 8–July 26, 1758)

Siege and Battle of Quebec (June 26–September 13, 1759)

Siege of Havana (June 6–August 13, 1762)

Siege of Boston (April 19, 1775–March 17, 1776)

Siege of Fort Stanwix, New York (August 2–23, 1777)

Siege of Gibraltar (June 21, 1779–February 6, 1783)

Siege of Charles Town (Charleston), South Carolina (March 29–May 12, 1780)

Siege of Pensacola, West Florida (March 9–May 10, 1781)

Siege of Yorktown (September 28–October 19, 1781)

Siege of Toulon (September 18–December 19, 1793)

Siege of Acre (March 17–May 20, 1799)

Sieges of Zaragoza (June 15–August 17, 1808; December 20, 1808–February 20, 1809)

Siege of Cádiz (February 5, 1810–August 24, 1812)

Third Siege of Missolonghi (April 15, 1825–April 23, 1826)

Siege of Puebla (September 14–October 12, 1847)

Siege of Venice (August 1848–August 27, 1849)

Siege of Sevastopol (October 17, 1854–September 9, 1855)

Siege of Saigon (March 1860–February 1861)

Siege of Fort Sumter (December 26, 1860–April 14, 1861)

Sieges of Vicksburg (May 18–July 4, 1863) and Port Hudson, Louisiana (May 21–July 9, 1863)

Siege of Petersburg (June 15, 1864–April 2, 1865)

Siege of Metz (August 19–October 27, 1870)

Siege of Paris (September 19, 1870–January 28, 1871)

Siege of Pleven (July 19–December 10, 1877)

Siege of Khartoum (March 13, 1884–January 26, 1885)

Siege of Tuyen Quang (November 24, 1884–March 3, 1885)

Siege of Santiago de Cuba (July 1–17, 1898)

Siege and First Battle of Manila (May 1–August 14, 1898)

Siege of Mafeking (October 13, 1899–May 17, 1900)

Siege of Peking (Beijing) (June 20–August 14, 1900)

Siege of Port Arthur (February 8, 1904–January 2, 1905)

Siege of Liège (August 5–16, 1914)

Siege of Qingdao (August 23, 1914–November 7, 1914)

Siege of Przemyśl (September 16, 1914–March 22, 1915)

Siege of Kut (December 7, 1915–April 29, 1916)

Siege of the Alcázar at Toledo (July 21–September 27, 1936)

Siege of Madrid (November 6, 1936–March 31, 1939)

Siege of Dunkirk (Dunkerque) (May 26–June 4, 1940)

Siege of Malta (June 11, 1940–November 20, 1942)

Siege of Tobruk (April 10–December 5, 1941)

Siege of Leningrad (July 10, 1941–January 27, 1944)

Siege of Sevastopol (October 30, 1941–July 4, 1942)

Siege of Singapore (February 8–15, 1942)

Siege of Stalingrad (November 19, 1942–February 2, 1943)

Siege of Imphal and Kohima (April 4–May 31, 1944)

Siege of Budapest (November 3, 1944–February 13, 1945)

Siege of Bastogne (December 20–27, 1944)

Siege of Berlin (April 16–May 2, 1945)

Berlin Blockade and Airlift (June 24, 1948–May 12, 1949)

Siege of Dien Bien Phu (March 13–May 7, 1954)

Siege of Khe Sanh (January 21–April 8, 1968)

Siege of Beirut (June 14–August 21, 1982)

Siege of Vukovar (August 25–November 18, 1991)

Siege of Aleppo (July 19, 2012–December 22, 2016)

Siege of Kobanî (September 27, 2014–January 26, 2015)

Siege of Mosul (October 17, 2016–July 9, 2017)

Preface

This study of 100 great sieges begins with that of Troy (c. 1194–1184 BCE) and concludes with that of Mosul (2017). Obviously, there are thousands of sieges from which one could choose. I have tried to provide a range of sieges throughout history. I endeavored to provide a mix of time periods, and this worked out as follows: 12 from the Ancient period, 10 from the Early Modern period, 4 from the Renaissance, 31 from the Early Modern period, and 43 from the Modern period. Some of these might appear at first glance to be unusual selections, but they all had important repercussions in influencing subsequent policies and events. All my selections are generally accepted by scholars as sieges, although the besieged often received reinforcements and so were not always completely cut off from outside assistance.

The entries are not of equal length. Some of the entries, especially those in more recent times, are longer, in part because of the increased amount of information available about them. I have, however, endeavored to stay out of the "weeds," so to speak, and concentrate on the broader outline as opposed to identifying all units involved and their commanders, which is a temptation in the case of later events where so much more is known.

I have in each case, however, provided background information on the course of events leading up to the siege as well as discussing the siege itself and its consequences. Each siege entry also has a list of books for further reading, and there are 25 sidebars that provide material related to many of the sieges, such as a particular weapons system, innovation, or interesting fact.

I am grateful to distinguished military historians Colonel Jerry Morelock, PhD, U.S. Army Rtd., and Major General David Zabecki, PdD, U.S. Army Rtd. They reviewed my initial entry list and made many helpful suggestions. I am also grateful for the other scholars writing for ABC-CLIO. Of the 100 entries, I have written 85 myself; 6 are shared with another author, and 9 are by other authors. All are identified as such.

Spencer C. Tucker

A Brief Introduction to Siege Warfare

The word "siege" is derived from the Latin word "sedere," meaning "to sit." A siege involves the effort by a military force to blockade a city, fortress, or enemy position with the intent of securing its submission, either by cutting off its food or water supply, thus starving it out, or by taking it by assault. Both methods might be applied simultaneously. It is, however, rare for a besieger to completely cut off some access to friendly forces by the besieged, especially in the present day, given aircraft.

A siege occurs when an attacking force encounters either an enemy population center or military strong point that cannot be taken by an immediate assault and that rejects surrender. The besieging force will endeavor to surround the enemy position, cutting it off from outside communication and reinforcement or resupply but also to prevent the forces in the targeted position from escape. This process is known as an "investment."

Once investment has occurred, the attacking force seeks to reduce the besieged fortifications by means of siege engines in the Ancient and Early Medieval periods or with the advent of gunpowder weapons, by artillery fire. Another tactic, employed into modern times, is by digging mines (also known as sapping) to tunnel into an enemy position or using these to set off powerful explosive charges to destroy part of the enemy defensive wall or position to enable access for attacking infantry, as in the "Battle of the Crater" in the siege of Petersburg (1864–1865) during the American Civil War (1860–1865) and in the siege of the Alcázar in Toledo (1936) during the Spanish Civil War (1936–1939). Deception or treachery have also helped bring victory on occasion for the besieger.

Many sieges have been decided by starvation, thirst, or disease. Weather can also play a role. Such factors can certainly affect the attacking force, as well as the besieged, as in the case of the British siege of Cartagena de Indias in 1741. Starving an enemy force into submission can be a long process, however, and depending on circumstances, it can take months and even, on occasion, years.

If possible, the attacking forces would carry out circumvallation. This is the process whereby the attacking army constructs a line of fortifications facing and circling around a besieged city. Besieging armies used this fortified line to protect themselves against sorties by those in the city as well as to enhance their own blockade. The resulting fortifications were known as lines of circumvallation and were mostly of earthen ramparts and entrenchments.

In contravallation, the besieging forces would build a second fortified line facing outward in order to protect themselves from attacks by forces allied to those of the besieged city and to enhance the blockade. The resulting fortifications were known as lines of contravallation and also usually consisted of earth ramparts and entrenchments paralleling those of lines of circumvallation facing toward the besieged city. This enveloped the city in a double line of fortifications and doubly protected the besiegers, who might, however, then find themselves besieged within their lines of circumvallation and contravallation. Julius Caesar (100–44 BCE) and the Romans were masters of this, with the outstanding example of the double lines being Caesar's siege of Alesia in Gaul, in 52 BCE. Union Army Major General Ulysses S. Grant also employed contravallation in his siege of the Confederate stronghold of Vicksburg in 1863, during the American Civil War.

Ancient cities in the Middle East show archaeological evidence of having had fortified city walls. During the Warring States era of ancient China (481/403–221 BCE), there is both textual and archaeological evidence of prolonged sieges and siege machinery employed against the defenders of city walls. In this early period from 600 to 400 BCE, siege warfare failed to keep pace with fortification. Unless they could be starved out in a protracted siege, or be taken by ruse or betrayal, walled cities were generally safe from an enemy attack.

Siege machinery in the ancient Greco-Roman world became highly developed. The basic weapons here remained the battering ram used to act against the gate or walls of an enemy fortress and the movable wooden tower that protected it. Mantelets, large wooden or wicker shields, helped protect besieging infantry and siege engine operators from enemy missiles, most notably arrows. Diades of Pella, who lived in the fourth century BCE and was known as the Besieger, was one of the great innovators in siege warfare. Accompanying Alexander the Great in his campaigns, Diades came up with several inventions used to attack city walls. One was the mural hook or crow. It consisted of a long, heavy bar or lever suspended from a large wooden frame that could be worked back and forth by men on the ground to act against the upper parapets of a wall. He also invented the telenon, a large basket capable of holding a number of soldiers that was slung from a boom, which was in turn mounted on a large mast or frame. The basket was raised or lowered by means of tackle. The basket could be swung over obstacles like a moat and raised to sufficient height that the soldiers in the basket were above an enemy parapet and able both to fire down on the enemy battlements or be deposited there.

Archimedes (c. 287–c. 212 BCE), the great scientist and engineer of Syracuse in Sicily, is credited with having designed highly efficient siege artillery for the defense of his city against the Romans. Although no precise information on his inventions survives, he certainly refined existing artillery systems and also came up with new types of engines, notably large grappling devices or tongs used to destroy enemy siege towers or to seize ships next to the sea walls of the city.

The Romans were great masters of military engineering and drew on the work of the Greeks. Julius Caesar followed Alexander the Great as one of the two preeminent practitioners of siege warfare in the ancient world. Roman siege warfare included the use of mantelets and movable gallery sections to protect workers and soldiers from missiles, the construction of redoubts, and the use of circumvallation and contravallation.

One Roman innovation to siege warfare came in the assault phase, after siege engines and battering rams had breached the city walls. A cohort of soldiers would then charge the wall, their shields held not from the back but by the sides. The first rank would place their shields in front of them to cover the formation's front, while the others would place their shields over their heads to protect from above, balancing the shields on their helmets and overlapping them. This formation generally protected against attack from light missiles, such as arrows and javelins. The primary problem with the formation was that it was so tight that the soldiers had difficulty engaging in hand-to-hand combat.

No major tactical innovations occurred in the early to mid–Middle Ages. The large number of fortifications, including castles, led to a premium on siege warfare. Types of siege engines and techniques of siege warfare were well known, even among the Vikings, and here too there were no major changes but merely the application of techniques practiced by the Romans—although only the Byzantines approached the Romans in effectiveness. The sole important military manual of the time, read and followed by those in command who could read, was *De Re Militari* written by Publius Flavius Vegetius Renatus in the late Roman Empire.

In the late Middle Ages, fortifications reached the peak of their development with powerful castles, patterned after those of the Byzantine Empire and the Crusader states in the Middle East, appearing throughout Europe. Such structures were generally impervious to the siege engines of the day, and unless a besieger had the time and resources to starve out the defenders, they could withstand almost any attacker. Unlike the Huns or the Vikings, the Mongols were adept at military engineering and at siege warfare, including the construction of such artillery pieces as the trebuchet.

During the Renaissance and the early modern period, siege warfare dominated the conduct of war in Europe. Leonardo da Vinci (1452–1519) gained as much of his renown from the design of fortifications as from his artwork. Siege warfare underwent considerable refinement with the introduction of gunpowder weapons.

During the course of the seventeenth century, fortifications, as well as the tactics of defense and offensive, became highly sophisticated. Complicated star-shaped fortresses that permitted enfilading fire from gunpowder weapons dominated the European landscape, and capturing them became the principal form of warfare. The goal for the attacker was to be able to advance one's own artillery forward to where it would be able to blast an opening in the enemy fortification and allow attacking infantry to mount a successful assault. The defender's challenge was to prevent this.

If attacking infantry were not able to carry a fortification by assault, most likely because of the defender's artillery, the attacker's first task was to dig a trench, called a "parallel" because it paralleled the defensive line, some 600–700 yards from the fortification at the approximate maximum effective range of contemporary artillery. Heavy siege artillery would be in place at selected points in the parallel. The direction of the trench precluded the defender's artillery being able to fire down it. The besiegers would also throw up significant earthworks in front of the parallel to defend their guns against enemy fire.

Then, in part protected by their artillery, the attacking military engineers would begin digging toward the objective small trenches known as "saps"—the origin of the term "sapper" for military engineer. The saps advanced in zig-zag fashion to preclude the enemy from firing down their entire length. This is credited to the preeminent practitioner of seventeenth-century siege warfare Marshal of France Sébastien Le Prestre de Vauban (1633–1707). Gabions (wicker structures covered with earth, frequently on wheels so they could be pushed forward) helped protect those digging the saps from enemy fire.

When the besiegers were about 300 yards from the objective, the saps were linked by the digging of a second parallel, to which the attacker's artillery would be advanced under cover of darkness. At this range the artillery could be employed to actually batter down a section of the defender's walls.

To counter this, the defenders might attempt a sortie in which they would raid the attacker's trenches and endeavor to capture or "spike" their opponent's guns. Spiking involved driving a metal wedge or spike into the cannon's touchhole located at the breech of the gun, thus rendering the piece useless until the hole could be drilled out. In order to prevent such attacks and protect the guns, the besiegers maintained large numbers of infantry in the forward parallel.

If it still proved impossible to breach the walls from the second parallel, a third parallel might be dug at the very walls of the fortress, enabling one's own artillery to fire point-blank and facilitating mining operations that might collapse the walls of the fortification and create the desired breach. The defenders would dig countermines to defeat such efforts.

Despite the appearance of new weapons and transportation systems that have aided both defenders and attackers, some of these techniques continued into the modern era. Certainly, sieges continue to be employed in contemporary warfare, often at great cost in terms of human casualties and physical destruction.

Spencer C. Tucker

Great Sieges in World History

Siege of Troy (1194–1184 BCE)

The chief source on the siege of Troy is Homer's great epic, the *Iliad*. Its 24 chapters treat the last year of the siege; however, it was composed two or three centuries after the siege. Modern archaeological excavations have revealed a series of strata, identifying a number of different cities built on the site. The one associated with the siege is the seventh stratum (from the bottom); it bears traces of a fire, and according to Homer, a great fire ended the siege. Scientific experts agree that the fire in the seventh stratum occurred in 1184 BCE. Homer tells us that the siege of Troy by the Mycenaeans (the mainland Greeks) went on for 10 years, hence the starting date of 1194 BCE.

The siege was undoubtedly motivated by economics. Located at the southern entrance to the Hellespont (the Dardanelles today), Troy controlled the important trade between East and West—that is, from the Black Sea to the Mediterranean. Along this route flowed such commodities as grain, precious metals, and timber to construct ships. Troy was allied with a number of other neighboring city-states, and the Mycenaeans saw this as a threat to their position in the Mediterranean. Homer tells us that the cause of the conflict was the rape of Helen, wife of Menelaus, king of Sparta, by Paris, the son of Priam, king of Troy. Helen fled to Troy with Paris, possibly taking part of Menelaus's treasure. Another account has the Trojans turning an official visit to Sparta into a raid of revenge for something done to them by the Greeks.

In any case, according to Homer, the city states of Greece were outraged and provided both contingents of troops and 1,200 ships, which then came under the command of Agamemnon, king of Mycenae and the brother of Menelaus. Homer tells us that on the Greek side, the greatest heroes of the fighting were Achilles, son of the Nereid Thetis and Peleus, king of Phthia, and Ulysses, king of Ithaca. On the Trojan side, there were Hector, son of Priam, and Aeneas, son of Venus and Anchises.

Following an unsuccessful effort to take Troy by assault, the Greeks settled in for a siege, which apparently was not complete. The Trojans were able to communicate by land to the interior most of the time. Homer indicates that the ships were brought up on land, where they were protected by entrenchments. Quarreling between Agamemnon and Achilles served to divide the Greeks, allowing Hector and the Trojans to attack and destroy a number of the beached Greek ships. Following the deaths of a number of prominent figures on each side (including Hector and Achilles), the Greeks found themselves in desperate straits. Both sides, however, were exhausted by the long siege.

At this point, Ulysses came up with the ruse of an enormous wooden horse. Left on the field, it contained Ulysses and a number of other Greek warriors. The remaining Greeks got in their ships and sailed away. The Trojans, believing that the Greeks had given up, thought the trophy had religious significance and brought it inside the city. At night Ulysses and his warriors climbed down out of the horse, signaled to the fleet offshore, and opened the city gates. The Trojans were taken by surprise, and the city burned.

Some have suggested that the "Trojan horse" that ended the siege was rather a great movable siege tower of wood, covered by horse hides for the protection of those working it, which the Greeks set against the western, and weakest, part of the great wall that protected the fortress. Others believe the wooden horse refers to some type of battering ram or to the image of a horse painted on one of the gates of the city, which was opened by a Trojan traitor. In any case, as a consequence of their victory, the Greeks secured control of the important trade through the Dardanelles and Black Sea.

Spencer C. Tucker

Further Reading
The Iliad of Homer. Translated by Alexander Pope. New York: The Heritage Press, 1943.
Melegari, Vezio. *The Great Military Sieges.* New York: Crowell, 1972.

Siege of Babylon (539–538 BCE)

Having absorbed Lydia, it was natural that King Cyrus II (the Great) of Persia would eventually move against Lydia's ally, Babylon. King Nabonidus's authority in Babylon was weak because he had secured the throne as a successful general rather than by right of inheritance, and he had further alienated his people by advancing the worship of Sin, the moon goddess, over Marduk, the national deity. He had also spent years away from his capital, campaigning in distant lands, including Harran, where he established a temple to Sin. In Arabia, he secured a number of oases, and his journey reached as far as Medina.

Cyrus, meanwhile, seems to have established contact with Babylon's alienated religious leaders, assuring them of his support for their traditional religious practices. Too late, Nabonidus embraced Marduk and ordered all statues of the god to be assembled at Babylon to fortify it spiritually.

There are two very different accounts of how Cyrus secured Babylon. One has him defeating the Babylonians at Opis, the former capital of Akkadia, and then destroying that city. Learning this, the city of Sippar surrendered to Cyrus, whereupon Nabonidus fled Babylon and Cyrus made a peaceful entry into the city in October.

The second account is put forward by the Greek historian Herodotus and supported by the books of Daniel and Jeremiah in the Bible—although Daniel incorrectly identifies Darius as king of Persia and Belshazzar as king of Babylon. (The latter was the son of Nabonidus and ruled the city while his father was away on campaign.) This version tells of a great siege during 539–538 BCE.

In it, Cyrus arrived and quickly encircled the city with his army under the walls, cutting off Babylon from assistance. Riding on horseback, Cyrus personally inspected the troop dispositions and concluded that the city could not be taken by direct assault. He then ordered his troops to institute a siege.

Cyrus either advised or came up on his own with a stratagem to take Babylon. He ordered the construction of a circular system of trenches around the city and ditches to be dug sufficient to accommodate the water of the Euphrates River, which bisected Babylon through a break in the city walls. This work went

Cyrus the Great

From early 538 BCE, Cyrus styled himself "king of Babylon and king of the countries" (i.e., of the world). Known for his toleration of the religions of the peoples he conquered, Cyrus was welcomed by the peoples of Syria and Palestine. In 538 BCE, he permitted the Jews who wished to do so to leave Babylon, where they had been removed during 597, 587/586, and 582/581 BCE, and to return to Jerusalem to rebuild the city and its temple that had been destroyed by the Babylonians in 586 BCE. Thus ended the "Babylonian captivity of the Jews." Cyrus also returned temple vessels that had been removed by the Babylonians.

Cyrus was killed or mortally wounded during an expedition to the East against the nomadic Massagetae in 530 BCE. In a very short span of time, he had built the mighty Persian empire, reaching from the Indus and Jaxartes Rivers west to the Aegean Sea and the Egyptian frontier. A great warrior, Cyrus was also a benevolent ruler and humane in his treatment of the conquered, a rarity in the ancient Middle East and which probably explains a good deal of his military success.

Spencer C. Tucker

---

forward into the winter, supervised by Persian engineers. The Euphrates was separated from the ditches by only a simple dam that could be easily opened. The Persians also constructed towers made of palm trees, which led the Babylonians to believe that their enemies intended to starve them out. The authorities in the city were not worried though, as they had gathered sufficient food stocks to last for many years.

Early in 538 BCE, Cyrus was ready to unleash his attack, which he timed to coincide with the beginning of an important Babylonian festival. That evening, with the Babylonian rituals underway and the inhabitants distracted, Cyrus ordered the dam broken and the Euphrates diverted. Normally the river was so deep that the breaks in the walls where it flowed through Babylon did not represent a serious threat from outside enemies. When the river was diverted, however, the flow was so low that it was possible for Persian infantry and even cavalry to traverse the newly formed river banks into Babylon itself.

The Persian attack caught the Babylonians by surprise, and the city was soon taken. Cyrus was known for sparing the lives of kings he had defeated, and this may have been the case with Nabonidus, who is said to have been sent into exile. Reportedly Belshazzar and his principal followers were slain. Cyrus ordered that Babylon be destroyed. As the prophet Jeremiah notes in the Bible (51:29 and 51:37): "And the land shall tremble and sorrow: for every purpose of the Lord shall be performed against Babylon to make the land of Babylon a desolation without an inhabitant. . . . And Babylon shall become heaps, a dwelling place for dragons, an astonishment, and an hissing, without an inhabitant."

Following the reduction of Babylon, Cyrus took Jerusalem. He allowed those Jews of Babylon who wished to do so to return home to Jerusalem, ending the "Babylonian captivity of the Jews."

Spencer C. Tucker

Further Reading

Cook, J. M. *The Persian Empire*. New York: Schocken Books, 1983.

Herodotus. *The History of Herodotus*. Edited by Manuel Komroff. Translated by George Rawlinson. New York: Tudor Publishing Co., 1956.

Lamb, Harold. *Cyrus the Great*. Garden City, NY: Doubleday, 1960.

Melegari, Vezio. *The Great Military Sieges*. New York: Crowell, 1972.

Xenophon. *Cyropaedia*. Translated by Walter Miller. Cambridge, MA: Harvard University Press, 1979.

Siege of Plataea (428–427 BCE)

The long Second Peloponnesian War (431–404 BCE) between the Greek city-states was marked by cruelties and breaches of honor on both sides, particularly for the small states caught between the major powers in the conflict. The historian Thucydides, a contemporary, provides ample record of this in his chronicling of the war and especially his telling of the Spartan reduction of Plataea.

In 428 BCE, having already laid waste to Attica and fearing infection from the great plague that had swept Athens, the leaders of Sparta decided to attack Plataea. This Athenian ally and small Boeotian city-state was of no strategic value and had done nothing to invite attack. The invasion was undertaken instead on the insistence of Thebes, Sparta's ally.

Plataea had been the only other Greek city-state to aid Athens during the Battle of Marathon against Persia in 490 BCE. Following the Battle of Plataea in 479 BCE that ended the Greco-Persian Wars, as Thucydides reported, the Spartans had administered an oath to all the Greeks who had taken part by which they restored to the Plataeans "their land and their city, holding them in independence," and swore to see to it "that no one should march against them unjustly or for their enslavement; if any one did the allies who were present should defend them with all their might" (qtd. in Kagan, *The Peloponnesian* War, p. 88). Thus, the Spartan attack on Plataea was a considerable embarrassment to and stain on the honor of the Spartans. King Archidamos of Sparta offered the Plataeans the choice of abandoning their alliance with Athens and joining Sparta or at least pledging neutrality. But Spartan promises rang hollow, for Thebes was determined to acquire Plataea.

The Plataeans asked for a truce so that they might request permission to surrender from Athens. Plataea hoped that Athens might allow it to strike some arrangement with the Spartans, since the city could not be rescued without an infantry battle that Athens could not win. Athens refused, urging the Plataeans to remain true to their alliance and promising assistance. Plataea therefore refused the Spartan demands; whereupon, Archidamos announced that Plataea was responsible for what would ensue because it had rejected a reasonable offer.

A series of Spartan attempts to take Plataea by storm failed. Plataea was defended by only 400 of its own men and 80 Athenians, with 110 women to cook for them. The remainder of its citizenry, including all the children and the elderly, had been sent to Athens for safety. Despite the small number of defenders, Plataea's walls were formidable and were sufficient to hold off a large enemy force.

Thus, in September 428 BCE, the Spartans laid siege, building a palisade around the city and manning it with troops. Archidamos ordered construction of an embankment behind the palisade that would equal the walls in height. During a 70-day period, the Spartans created the embankment with earth, stones, and logs sufficient to support siege machines. During this time, however, the Plataeans used wood to add to the height of their own walls that faced the embankment. Most materials for the construction came from structures in the city, but at least some were secured from the enemy by means of a tunnel. The defenders also built a second wall inside the first so that if the latter was breached the attackers would have to begin the process anew.

The Spartans sent their battering rams against the outer wall but were unsuccessful; the defenders damaged a number by dropping large chained beams on the long metal-tipped rams. Archidamos then tried filling the short space between the embankment and wall with combustible materials and setting them afire. The Plataeans thought that the walls were lost, but a providential rain extinguished the flames.

In September 428 BCE with winter coming on, Archidamos had his men build a more substantial double wall around the city and then ordered half his force home for the winter. That winter on a stormy night, 200 of the Plataeans managed to get across the Spartan wall by means of ladders without being detected. After a brief skirmish, they broke free and made their way to Athens.

The remaining defenders were simply starved into surrender in the summer of 427 BCE. The Spartans might easily have taken the city earlier by force, but they did not do so because if peace was to be concluded with Athens, Sparta could hold on to Plataea by claiming that defenders had gone over of their own free will.

The Spartans therefore promised that each of the defenders would receive a fair trial by a panel of five Spartan judges. The question put to each defender, however, was whether he had rendered assistance to Sparta or its allies in the war. All had to answer no. At least 200 Plataeans and 25 Athenian men were subsequently put to death. All of the women were sold into slavery.

Eventually the Spartans turned Plataea over to Thebes, which leveled it entirely and divided the land among its own citizens. Thereafter, Thebes considered what had been Plataea to be part of its own territory. The siege of Plataea offered plenty of embarrassment for all sides. The Athenians might have released their loyal ally to conclude reasonable terms with the Spartans or rendered the military assistance promised but did neither. Granting Athenian citizenship to the surviving Plataeans was hardly adequate compensation.

Spencer C. Tucker

Further Reading

Hanson, Victor Davis. *A War Like No Other: How the Athenians and Spartans Fought the Peloponnesian War.* New York: Random House, 2005.

Kagan, Donald. *The Peloponnesian War.* New York: Viking, 2003.

Melegari, Vezio. *The Great Military Sieges.* New York: Crowell, 1972.

Thucydides. *History of the Peloponnesian War.* Translated by Rex Warner. New York: Penguin, 1984.

Siege of Syracuse (415–413 BCE)

The siege of the city-state of Syracuse, in Sicily, by Athens and its allies during 415–413 BCE initiated the final phase of the Second Peloponnesian War (431–404 BCE). Alcibiades, a nephew of Pericles, convinced the Athenians that securing Sicily would provide Athens with the resources necessary to defeat their enemies. The grain of Sicily was immensely important to the people of the Peloponnese, and cutting it off could turn the tide of war. The argument was correct, but securing Sicily was the problem.

The Athenians put together a formidable expeditionary force. Thucydides, a contemporary historian, described the expeditionary force that set out in June 415 BCE as "by far the most costly and splendid Hellenic force that had ever been sent out by a single city up to that time" (qtd. in Finley, *The Greek Historians*, 314). The naval force consisted of 134 triremes (100 of them from Athens and the remainder from Chios and other Athenian allies), 30 supply ships, and more than 100 other vessels. These carried, in addition to sailors, rowers, and marines, some 5,100 hoplites and 1,300 archers, javelin men, and slingers, as well as 300 horses. In all, the expedition numbered perhaps 27,000 officers and men. Command was vested in three generals—Alcibiades, Lamachus, and Nicias.

The original plan was for a quick demonstration in force against Syracuse and then a return of the expeditionary force to Greece. Alcibiades considered this a disgrace, however. He urged that the expeditionary force stir up political opposition to Syracuse in Sicily. In a council of war, Lamachus pressed for an immediate descent on Syracuse while the city was unprepared and its citizens afraid, but Alcibiades prevailed.

The expedition's leaders then made a series of approaches to leaders of the other Sicilian cities; all ended in failure, with no city of importance friendly to Athens. Syracuse, however, used this time to strengthen its defenses. Alcibiades, meanwhile, was recalled to stand trial in Athens for impiety.

Nicias and Lamachus then launched an attack on Syracuse and won a battle there, but the arrival of winter prevented further progress, and they suspended offensive operations. What had been intended as a lightning campaign now became a prolonged siege that sapped Athenian efforts elsewhere.

Alcibiades, fearing for his life, managed to escape Athens and find refuge in Sparta. There he not only betrayed the Athenian plan of attack against Syracuse but also spoke to the Spartan assembly and strongly supported a Syracusan plea for aid. The Spartans then sent out a force of their own, numbering some 4,400 men and commanded by Gylippus, one of their best generals.

In the spring of 414 BCE, the Athenians renewed offensive operations at Syracuse. Despite Syracuse's work during the winter, the Athenians captured the fortifications at Euryalus close to Syracuse and drove the Syracusans behind their city's walls. The Athenians then constructed a fortification known as "the circle" along with other protective walls. They also destroyed several Syracusan counter-walls. Unfortunately for the Athenians, Lamachus was killed in the fighting, and leadership devolved on the ineffective Nicias.

Syracuse was now in despair though, with the city on the brink of defeat. At this point, a Corinthian ship made it into the harbor with news that help was on the way. Fortified by this development, the leaders of Syracuse vowed to fight on. Gylippus's expeditionary force then landed in northern Sicily and marched to Syracuse. Nicias failed to challenge it en route, and Gylippus's men were able to strengthen the defenses of Syracuse. In the spring of 413 BCE, they won a stunning victory over the Athenian Navy, capturing its base.

Rather than lose prestige by abandoning the siege—the wise course under the circumstances—the Athenians decided to send out a second expedition. Led by Demosthenes, one of Athens's most distinguished generals, it consisted of 73 triremes carrying 5,000 hoplites and 3,000 bowmen, slingers, and javelin throwers—in all some 15,000 men—and arrived at Syracuse in July 413 BCE.

Demosthenes attempted to destroy one of the Syracusan counter-walls; when this proved unsuccessful, he mounted a night attack. It caught the defenders by surprise, and the Athenians took Euryalus and much of the Epipolaen plateau. Enough of Gylippus's troops held fast though, and the Syracusans mounted an immediate counterattack that caught the Athenians disorganized and inflicted heavy casualties. Cut off from supplies and prey to enemy cavalry, the Athenians attempted a breakout from the harbor of Syracuse in September 413 BCE with 110 ships—both fit and unfit for action—but were contained by a great boom of block ships across the mouth of the Great Harbor as well as some 76 Corinthian and Syracuse ships. The naval battle ended in Athenian defeat, with Athens losing 50 ships to its enemy's 26.

The Athenians still had 60 triremes to their enemy's 50, and the generals wanted to try another breakout. The crews refused and demanded a retreat over land. Instead of setting out at once in the midst of Syracusan victory celebrations, the Athenians paused for 36 hours because of a false report (which had been spread to gain time until the victory celebrations had ended) that the retreat route was blocked.

Once the retreat was underway, a group of 6,000 Athenian men under Demosthenes was offered freedom if they would desert. They refused and fought on until the situation was hopeless. On receiving a guarantee that his men's lives would be spared, however, the Athenian commander surrendered. The other group of 1,000 men was also forced to surrender. Nicias and Demosthenes were butchered, against the will of Gylippus. The 7,000 Athenians who had surrendered—out of 45,000–50,000 who had taken part in the expedition on the Athenian side—were sent off to the stone quarries of Syracuse. The expedition also cost Athens some 200 triremes. Thucydides concluded, "This was the greatest Hellenic achievement of any in this war, or, in my opinion in, Hellenic history; at once most glorious to the victors, and most calamitous to the conquered" (qtd. in Finley, *The Greek Historians*, 379).

Had the advice of Lamachus been followed at the outset, there is little doubt that Syracuse would have fallen and that the main Sicilian cities would also have submitted to Athens. Once grain to the Peloponnese had been cut off, Sparta and Corinth would have been forced to give up, despite Athens's inferiority in manpower.

The annihilation of the Athenian fleet and army in Sicily shook the Athenian Empire to its core. The islands of Euboea, Lesbos, and Chios now revolted against Athens. Sparta built 100 warships; and Persia set out to regain her lost Ionian dominions.

The Athenians might have had peace in 410 BCE, but its people were buoyed by a naval victory that year and rejected Spartan overtures. In 405 BCE an Athenian fleet of 170 ships was taken while beached in the "Battle" of Aegospotami at the Hellespont while securing supplies. Lysander, the Spartan naval commander, then captured the remaining Athenian garrisons at the Hellespont and severed Athenian access to Ukrainian wheat supplies. The Spartans permitted their Athenian prisoners to return to Athens in order to increase the strain on its scant food stocks. Pausanias, the second Spartan king, then brought a large land force to Athens and laid siege to the city from the land, while Lysander arrived with 150 ships and blockaded it from the sea. Starved into submission, Athens surrendered in 404 BCE. Corinth and Thebes urged that the city should be utterly destroyed and its people sold into slavery. To their credit, the Spartans rejected these proposals, insisting that the city's Long Walls and fortifications all be demolished. Athens also had to give up all its foreign possessions and its fleet, and the city was forced to enter into alliance with Sparta and accept its leadership. The Peloponnesian Wars were over. So too was the period of Athenian supremacy.

Spencer C. Tucker

Further Reading

Finley, M. I., ed. *The Greek Historians: The Essence of Herodotus, Thucydides, Xenophon, Polybius.* New York: Viking, 1959.

Green, Peter. *Armada from Athens.* Garden City, NY: Doubleday, 2003.

Kagan, Donald. *The Peloponnesian War.* New York: Viking, 2003.

Siege of Veii (404–396 BCE)

In the fifth century BCE, Veii was an important Italian city. Located in central Etruria and situated on high ground about two and a half hours' march from Rome, this rich and powerful republic was well protected with high walls. Veii's territory reached the Tiber River, blocking Roman expansion to the north.

The Romans regarded Veii as the most important threat to their expanding power. Both Veii and Rome claimed the town of Fidenae (Castel Giubileo) on the south (Latin) bank of the Tiber. The hill on which Fidenae stood controlled the lowest river ford above Rome and apparently changed hands a number of times. Apparently, Veii broke a truce with Rome to seize Fidenae.

Believing conflict inevitable and desiring the Veii lands for farming, Rome carried out governmental reforms to prepare for war and then captured Fidenae. The inhabitants of Veii meanwhile worked to strengthen their city's defenses against an anticipated Roman attack. Where possible, the cliffs on which the city stood were cut back to make them steeper, and around other portions of the periphery of the 480 acres of the city, the inhabitants built earthen ramparts with a stone breastwork.

Renewed warfare began between the two cities in 404 BCE on Roman initiative. Veii appealed in vain for assistance to the Etruscan confederation, which blamed it for the renewal of fighting. The war marked a number of firsts for Rome. It was the first conflict for Rome beyond the area occupied by the original Latin people, the first time the Romans campaigned year-round without interruptions for the harvest, and the first occasion on which Roman soldiers received regular pay. It was also perhaps the most important war in Roman history, as the city's survival depended on a successful outcome.

The Romans soon placed Veii under siege. The fighting went on for eight years, from 404 to 396 BCE. At one point, a Veientine force sortied from the city at night and destroyed siege works that had taken the Romans months to build. This only strengthened Roman resolve.

The Romans succeeded, during the course of the siege, in occupying the northern neck of land that provided the only level access to Veii. This contained one of the large tunnels used for irrigation purposes. The tunnel went under the city walls and opened into Veii itself. Marcus Furius Camillus set a large number of sappers to work, in shifts of six hours at a time, to enlarge the tunnel. Camillus, who was made dictator of Rome and directed the latter stages of the operation, was so confident of victory that he requested a decision by the Senate on how to divide the spoils. The Senate decided to allow the troops to take what they could. This brought out a large portion of the population of Rome to participate in the final assault in 396 BCE.

While the vast majority of his forces loudly assaulted Veii's walls, Camillus sent a force of handpicked shock troops through the tunnel into the city's center. This smaller force did its work well and managed to open the gates. Not until the city was entirely in Roman hands did Camillus issue orders to spare the defenseless and begin the pillage. Once the city was sacked, the Romans partially destroyed it, razing its defenses and forcing many of the inhabitants to leave.

Rome's elimination of the independent existence of another city-state was both a radical departure and an ominous precedent, an indication of the importance of the conflict. The Romans also took over the city's deity of Juno, the symbol of vitality and youthfulness, as one of their own. Now she watched not over Veii but instead over Rome.

Spencer C. Tucker

Further Reading
Grant, Michael. *History of Rome*. New York: Scribner, 1978.
Melegari, Vezio. *The Great Military Sieges*. New York: Crowell, 1972.

Sieges of Tyre and Gaza (332 BCE)

Alexander the Great's sieges of Tyre and Gaza in 332 BCE are two of the great military operations in history. In the summer of 334 BCE, Alexander (353–326 BCE), ruler of Macedon and master of all Greece, led some 35,000 men across the Hellespont in an invasion of Asia Minor. Alexander defeated the Persian army on the Granicus River and conquered much of Asia Minor. In 333 BCE he defeated Persian king Darius III at Issus, then turned south to conquer Egypt. This secured his southern flank prior to resuming his eastward march to the extremities of the Persian Empire. Securing the Phoenician coastal city-states of Syria would also open those ports for his own triremes and deny them to the Persian fleet, preventing a Persian naval descent on Greece.

Tyre was the most important of the Phoenician coastal city-states. Ruled by King Azemilk and located in present-day Lebanon, Tyre was actually two cities. Old Tyre was located on an island about three miles in circumference, separated from the mainland city by a half mile of water. The channel between the island and mainland was more than 20 feet deep. The island citadel was protected by massive walls up to 150 feet high on the land side that were reputedly impregnable. Alexander wanted to bypass Tyre, but he had to reduce it before he could move against Egypt, lest it be used as a base for Darius's fleet. Alexander predicted that once Tyre fell the Phoenician ships, deprived of their bases, would desert to the winning side.

Determined to hold out, the Tyrians rejected Alexander's overtures. They were confident in their defenses and believed that a protracted siege would purchase time for Darius to mobilize a new army and campaign in Asia Minor. Alexander had second thoughts about the task ahead and sent heralds to the Tyrians to urge a peaceful resolution. The Tyrian leaders, however, saw this as a sign of weakness; they killed the heralds and threw their bodies over the walls. This foolish act cemented Alexander's resolve and won him solid support from his generals.

Alexander took mainland Old Tyre without difficulty and initiated siege operations against the island in January 332 BCE. He ordered Dyadis the Thessalian, head of the Macedonian army's corps of engineers, to construct a great mole, about 200 feet wide, out from the land and to reach the island and bring up siege engines. The Macedonians secured wood from the forests of Lebanon for the piles of the mole, while the structures of mainland Tyre were demolished for the fill. Alexander reportedly worked alongside his men on the project.

The Tyrians sent ships from the island filled with archers to attack the Macedonians working on the mole. To counter such forays, Alexander ordered his men to construct two great siege towers, each 150 feet in height. As the mole advanced, the towers moved with it. One night with a favorable wind, the Tyrians sent an old horse transport rigged as a fireship and laden with combustibles against the towers and causeway. The towers caught fire and were destroyed. At the same time, a flotilla of smaller Tyrian craft arrived; men from them attacked Alexander's men on the mole and destroyed other siege equipment that had escaped destruction in the fire. They then withdrew.

Alexander responded by ordering construction of two more towers. Leaving operations at Tyre in the hands of trusted lieutenants, he then traveled to Sidon to secure ships to operate against the island and protect those working on the mole. Soon he had gathered 223 ships from Sidon, Cyprus, Rhodes, and other eastern Mediterranean city-states. Alexander placed in them some 4,000 hoplites recruited from the Peloponnese by Cleander. This flotilla then sailed for Tyre. Alexander commanded its right wing, and Pinitagoras commanded its left wing.

The Tyrians learned of Alexander's activities and planned to give battle at sea, but noting the size of the approaching fleet, the Tyrian admiral changed his mind; he chose instead to protect the two narrow entrances to the island's harbor. A number of ships sunk side by side were sufficient to block both. Alexander concentrated offensive actions against Sidonian Harbor, the smaller of these entrances and about 200 feet wide, but he was unsuccessful. Subsequently, the Tyrians substituted heavy iron chains for their block ships.

Thanks to the presence of Alexander's flotilla, it was no longer possible for the Tyrians to attack the mole with their ships. Instead, they employed catapults against both it and the Macedonian siege towers as the latter came within range. Alexander's catapults replied. Although the Macedonians suffered setbacks, the mole gradually advanced and ultimately reached the island. Under the protection of the towers, the Macedonians employed battering rams against the citadel's walls, but the Tyrian defenses stood firm.

Alexander had also ordered construction of naval battering rams. Each was mounted on a large platform lashed between two barges. Other barges carried catapults. Finally, this naval assault opened a breach in the walls; unfortunately, a gale then arose. Some of Alexander's vessels were sunk, and others were badly damaged.

During this respite, the Tyrians demolished a number of buildings and dropped the masonry over the walls to keep Alexander's naval rams at a distance. They also devised drop beams, which could be swung out against the ships by derricks, and, at the end of lines, grappling irons or barbed hooks known as crows that could be dropped on the Macedonians, hooking and hoisting them up to a tortured death in front of their colleagues.

Alexander's men now had to remove the debris in the water around the walls, allowing the assault craft to close on the island. The Tyrians replied by tipping bowls of red-hot sand onto the attackers. Finally, Alexander's naval rams broke down a section of the wall. Infantry were sent into the breach on boarding ramps as the defenders continued their resistance in the city center.

Tyre fell at the end of July. Frustration regarding the length and ferocity of the siege gave way to rage, and the Macedonian troops extended no quarter to the inhabitants. Reportedly 8,000 Tyrians died during the siege; the Macedonians slew another 7,000 afterward as the city became one large abattoir. Another 30,000 inhabitants, including women and children, were sold into slavery.

With Tyre destroyed, the Macedonian army set out on foot in July or early August for Egypt. Some 160 miles from Tyre, the army encountered the fortress city of Gaza, situated on a rocky hill on the sole route between Egypt and Syria. The city's governor, Batis, rejected calls for surrender. Siege operations were quite difficult, as the siege engines sank in the sand. On occasion, the defenders sallied to destroy the Macedonian siege equipment. On one such foray, Alexander was badly wounded in the shoulder by an arrow.

Alexander again called on Dyadis, this time to build an earthen rampart around the city. In two months, the Macedonians had built an earthen rampart topped by a wooden platform encircling Gaza, a mammoth undertaking. A breach was finally made in the walls, and Macedonian troops entered the city. The Macedonians had also carried out mining operations, and another group went in by a tunnel.

After heavy fighting, the city fell. Reportedly the Macedonians slew 10,000 defenders, and the women and children were all sold as slaves. Batis was among the captured. Alexander ordered him lashed by his ankles behind a chariot and dragged around the city walls until he was dead.

Although it was fortunate for Alexander that during these operations Darius III did not move against the Macedonian lines of communication, the successful sieges of both Tyre and Gaza thoroughly demonstrated Alexander's mastery of this type of warfare and greatly added to his mystique of invincibility. In 1627 Cardinal Richelieu of France drew inspiration from Alexander's tactics at Tyre for his own reduction of La Rochelle.

Spencer C. Tucker

Further Reading
Green, Peter. *Alexander of Macedon, 356–323 B.C.: A Historical Biography*. Berkeley: University of California Press, 1991.
Kern, Paul Bentley. *Ancient Siege Warfare*. Bloomington: Indiana University Press, 1999.
Sekunda, Nick, and John Warry. *Alexander the Great: His Armies and Campaigns, 332–323 B.C.* London: Osprey, 1988.

Siege of Syracuse (213–212 BCE)

The siege of Syracuse (213–212 BCE) occurred during the Second Punic War, also known as the Hannibalic War (218–212 BCE). Following his great victory in the 216 BCE Battle of Cannae in southern Italy, Carthaginian general Hannibal Barca appeared to have the military advantage. The Romans avoided pitched battle with him unless on favorable terms, however, and Hannibal lacked the resources to take the Roman cities and to protect those cities that rallied to him. Not until 214 BCE did he receive significant reinforcements, when a Punic fleet managed to land men, elephants, and supplies at Locri in Calabria, Italy. Consul Marcus Claudius Marcellus defeated Hannibal's repeated efforts to take Nola in the interim and then sailed with a Roman army to the island of Sicily, where Propraetor Appius Claudius Pulcher was attempting to keep Syracuse from joining with Carthage in the war.

Sicily was effectively divided in two. Rome controlled the west and north, while the staunchly pro-Roman tyrant of Syracuse, Hiero, controlled the remainder. Hiero died in late 216 or early 215 BCE, however. His young grandson Hieronymus succeeded him and immediately opened negotiations with Carthage. After little more than a year Hieronymus was murdered in a coup, and Syracuse became a democratic republic where the Carthaginian faction dominated. Hippocrates and Epicydes, two brothers of Syracusan extraction but natives of Carthage, led the pro-Carthage group and hoped to make all Sicily a Carthaginian stronghold. The government therefore sent Hippocrates and

4,000 men, many of them deserters from the Roman army, to garrison the city of Leontini. From there, Hippocrates began to raid the Roman portion of the island.

On his arrival in Sicily, Marcellus immediately seized Leontini and ordered all Roman deserters taken prisoner there to be beaten with rods and then beheaded. Hippocrates and Epicydes, who had joined his brother at Leontini, escaped and subsequently spread the story that the Romans had massacred all inhabitants of the city, including women and children. They exploited this lie to bring Syracusan soldiers over to their side and seize power in Syracuse.

Marcellus commenced military operations against Syracuse, probably in the spring of 213 BCE, supported by Appius Claudius Pulcher. The latter led troops against the city from the land side, while Marcellus utilized 68 quinqueremes to blockade and attack Syracuse from the sea. The Roman land force may have numbered 16,000 men.

Both sides employed a number of novel devices. For instance, Marcellus had four pairs of galleys specially prepared. He ordered removal of the starboard oars from one side and the port oars from the other. The two ships were then lashed together. Solid scaling ladders were mounted in their bows. These could be raised by means of ropes attached to pulleys at the tops of masts in the center of the ships. The resulting craft was known as a *sambuca* because it somewhat resembled a harplike instrument of the same name. The *sambuca* enabled troops in the ships to reach the top of the city walls.

On the land side, the Romans employed *tolleni*. These assault machines consisted of a boom and counterweight mounted on a mast. A large wicker or wooden basket was attached to the far end of the boom. This basket, loaded with men, could be lifted by soldiers pulling down the other end of the boom by means of ropes wound around a capstan.

The Syracusans, on the other hand, had a formidable asset in the celebrated geometrician Archimedes. Then in his seventies, he developed a number of innovative military devices. To attack the Roman ships, Archimedes arranged catapults and ballistae situated in batteries according to required range. He also came up with a type of crane that extended over the walls and employed a grapple, known as a claw, to hook onto a ship. A counterbalance enabled the crane to lift the ship. Letting it go again would dash the vessel to pieces. Another technique was to drop heavy stones on the ships that would crash through their hulls and sink them. A number of these boulders, one of which was said to weigh 10 talents (670 pounds), were dropped on the *sambucas*, destroying them. Archimedes also used smaller shorter-range catapults, known as Scorpions, to hurl boulders and stones at the attackers. The most controversial story of the siege concerns Archimedes's supposed invention of "burning mirrors," whereby the sun's rays were reflected to set fire to the Roman ships.

All Roman attempts to overcome the city, by land and by sea, were failures, including a night attack from the sea against a section of the wall that seemed to offer maximum protection from the Syracusan war machines. With only heavy casualties to show for his efforts, Marcellus settled in for a siege and blockade. In the meantime, he sent some Roman troops to defeat the other rebel

Illustration of the Roman siege of Syracuse during 213–212 BCE. The cranes protruding from the walls were used to drop grapples, known as "claws," into the Roman ships. The ships could then be lifted up and then suddenly released, destroying them. (Photos.com)

Sicilian cities, in one instance surprising a force under Hippocrates near Acila and inflicting 8,000 casualties. Reportedly, only Hippocrates and 500 cavalry escaped.

Both sides reinforced in Sicily. The Romans built their strength up to three or four legions in addition to the allied troops. The Carthaginians sent an expeditionary force of 25,000 men, 3,000 cavalry, and 12 war elephants under the command of Himilco. They also broke through the blockade with 55 galleys commanded by Bomilcar.

The siege continued through the winter, and early in 212 BCE, Marcellus decided on a surprise attack. Outside Syracuse near a tower known as Galeagra while negotiations over prisoner exchange were under way, one of the Romans carefully calculated the height of the tower based on its even blocks of stone. Shortly thereafter, taking advantage of the distraction of a major festival in Syracuse dedicated to the goddess Artemis, Marcellus sent at night 1,000 men with scaling ladders against the Galeagra tower. The ladders proved to be the correct height, and the assaulting troops took the defenders by surprise.

Before the night was over, the Romans had opened the Hexapylon Gate to other troops and captured much of the city. Other portions of the city continued to hold out but suffered greatly from the ravages of disease, which seems to have hit the Romans less hard. Carthaginian ships continued to penetrate the blockade, but Marcellus confronted and turned back a massive Carthaginian convoy of 700 merchantmen protected by 150 warships.

With all hope gone, Epicydes fled the city. (Hippocrates had earlier died of disease.) In the summer of 212 BCE, Roman forces took the remainder of Syracuse. The Romans then gave the city over to pillage and fire. Although Marcellus had ordered that Archimedes be taken alive, he died with his city. Reportedly he was working on a mathematical problem when the Romans burst in upon him. The soldiers were ignorant of the identity of the old man who demanded that they not disturb his "circles" in the dirt, whereupon a soldier dispatched him with a single sword thrust.

Spencer C. Tucker

Further Reading
Craven, Brian. *The Punic Wars.* New York: Barnes and Noble, 1992.
Goldsworthy, Adrian. *The Punic Wars.* London: Cassell, 2000.
Melegari, Vezio. *The Great Military Sieges.* New York: Crowell, 1972.

Siege of Carthage (149–146 BCE)

After the defeat of its forces by the Romans in the Battle of Zama in 202 BCE and end of the Second Punic War, Carthage observed the terms of its treaty with Rome and abstained from any provocation. Hannibal Barca, the legendary Carthaginian general, put Carthaginian finances in good order and paid off the heavy indemnity Rome had imposed. When Carthage began to prosper again, Roman fears and hatred were again aroused. No Roman could forget that it had taken 25 legions to subdue Hannibal.

Roman leaders therefore schemed with Masinissa, the ruler of neighboring Numidia, encouraging him to encroach on what remained of Carthage's territory. Finally, after many vain appeals to Rome, Carthage was goaded into an attempt at self-defense. In 150 BCE Carthage declared war, sending an army under Hasdrubal

---

War Galleys

The trireme was a galley, the predominant warship of the ancient Mediterranean world for almost 5,000 years. The galley was a long, narrow wooden ship with a shallow beam and low freeboard. It was propelled by rows of oars and almost always sailed on one or two masts. Originally galleys had a single bank of oarsmen. Two banks made it a bireme, while a trireme had three banks of superimposed oars.

The war galley was effective because it could move quickly to an enemy vessel for boarding. In the eighth or ninth century BCE, the ram—a massive, pointed bronze projection set at the waterline—was introduced in war galleys. It was used to punch a hole in an opposing ship in order to sink it.

Originally each oar was pulled by one man, but later several men were put to each oar. Although some galleys had four or five superimposed banks of oars (the latter known as quinqueremes) and carried crews of up to 500 men, by the first century CE, the Romans had returned to the trireme as their main battleship.

Spencer C. Tucker

against Masinissa. This was a violation of the peace that had ended the Second Punic War whereby Carthage could declare war only with Roman consent. The Roman Senate agreed that Carthage had to be destroyed and dispatched a sizable force to Utica in North Africa. This city had been Carthage's most important ally but rallied to Rome just before the war. This provided Rome with an important base less than 30 miles from Carthage.

The Roman expeditionary force to North Africa was under two consuls, Manius Manilius, who had command of four legions of some 40,000–50,000 men, and Lucius Marcius Censorinus, who had charge of the fleet with 50 quinqueremes. Thus began the Third Punic War (149–146 BCE), which was basically the siege of Carthage. The Romans fully expected a short, profitable, and virtually bloodless campaign.

The Carthaginians opened negotiations with the two consuls and were informed that they must surrender their fleet, arms, and missile weapons. The Roman position was that since Carthage would pass under Roman protection, the city would have no need of weapons. The Carthaginians agreed. They surrendered their fleet, which was burned in the harbor, as well as a reported 200,000 sets of infantry weapons and 2,000 catapults. The Roman consuls then announced that the inhabitants would have to leave the city, as they intended to destroy it. The Carthaginians would be allowed to rebuild at any location so long as it was at least 80 stades (10 miles) from the sea.

The Carthaginian envoys returned to the city with the Roman demand. Following initial shock and despair, the Carthaginian Council rejected the Roman demand,

The ruins of Carthage in present-day Tunisia. Following their victory in the siege of 149–146 BCE, the Romans plundered and then completely destroyed the city, selling its surviving inhabitants into slavery. (Itanart/Dreamstime.com)

declared war on Rome, shut the gates of the city, and commenced the manufacture of weapons. The Romans were surprised, having assumed that with Carthage virtually disarmed its leaders would have no choice but to accept their demands.

The Romans then mounted an assault on the city, led by Manilius from the land side and Censorinus from the sea. Carthage had excellent defenses, being surrounded by three walls that were almost 50 feet high and sufficiently wide to contain stalls for elephants and horses as well as troop quarters. The Carthaginians easily repelled the first two assaults. When the Romans sent troops to find timber to build additional catapults, they were surprised by Carthaginian forces under Hamilcon who had been harassing their base camps. In one engagement, a cavalry force led by Himilco Phameas inflicted some 500 casualties on the Romans and seized a number of weapons.

Despite this setback, the Romans located the timber to build a number of new siege machines, including two large ones equipped with battering rams. The Romans employed these to make a breach in the wall, but the Carthaginians quickly repaired it and then mounted sorties from the city, setting fire to and destroying both machines. Scipio Aemilianus, tribune of the Fourth Legion, distinguished himself in the fighting both by rescuing some trapped legionnaires and in subsequent engagements against Hasdrubal.

In the spring of 148 BCE, Himilco defected, bringing over a reported 2,200 Carthaginian cavalry to the Romans. Two new Roman consuls, L. Calpurnius Piso Ceasonibus for the army and Lucius Hostilius Mancinus for the navy, arrived at Carthage. They concentrated their resources against minor cities close to Carthage and destroyed most of them. Piso then retired for the winter to Utica.

Meanwhile in Rome, Scipio was elected at age 37 as consul and set sail for Africa with additional forces in 147 BCE. He landed at Utica and then proceeded to Carthage, rescuing Mancinus and a number of his men who had been cut off by the Carthaginians. Mancinus returned to Italy, and Scipio undertook the construction of extensive siege works.

The Carthaginians secretly built 50 triremes. Instead of using the element of surprise to launch an attack on the unprepared Roman fleet, the Punic admiral paraded his ships (to give his crews practice) and returned to port. When he sallied out to do battle several days later, the Roman fleet was ready, and the Carthaginians were soundly beaten.

At the beginning of the spring of 146 BCE, Scipio launched his major offensive. Employing Carthaginian deserters as guides, the Romans managed to overcome the three lines of Carthaginian defenses and penetrate the city itself, with vicious fighting in the narrow streets and in the six-story buildings along them. Fighting was house to house and room to room, and the Romans laid plank bridges from houses already taken to the remainder, eventually reaching the slopes of the Byrsa, where the citadel was situated. Once the buildings had been taken, Scipio ordered that the city be fired. The flames raged for six days and nights. Many Carthaginians were trapped in the buildings and died. Roman engineers then leveled what remained of the structures.

The Carthaginian leaders at Byrsa appealed to Scipio to spare the lives of those who wished to leave. He agreed except for any Roman deserters. Reportedly

50,000 people departed the Byrsa, to be held under guard. This left only some 900 Roman deserters and Hasdrubal and his wife and sons. Hasdrubal turned traitor, however, opening the gates to the Romans and begging Scipio for mercy. Hasdrubal's wife then came out on the roof of the temple, which the defenders had set on fire; she denounced Hasdrubal for his treachery and leapt with her sons into the flames.

The Romans plundered the city (Scipio took nothing for himself) and utterly demolished it. The 50,000 survivors of Carthage, all that remained of a pre-siege population of 500,000, were sold as slaves. The terrible destruction gave rise to the term "Carthaginian Peace." Africa now became a Roman province.

Spencer C. Tucker

Further Reading
Craven, Brian. *The Punic Wars.* New York: Barnes and Noble, 1992.
Goldsworthy, Adrian. *The Punic Wars.* London: Cassell, 2000.

Siege of Numantia (Numancia) (134–133 BCE)

The siege of Numantia (Numancia) marked the end of the decade-long Numantine or Third Celtiberian War fought during 143–133 BCE between the forces of the Roman Republic and the people of Numantia in Iberia. Numantia (now Garray) was the principal Celtiberian urban center. Founded on the site of earlier settlements by Iberians who penetrated the Celtic highlands about 300 BCE, it was centered on a hill known as Cerro de la Muela some four miles north of the modern-day city of Soria on the upper Douro (Duero) River in Soria Province, Spain. Numantia became the epicenter of Celtiberian resistance to Rome and had withstood a number of Roman attacks.

Rome had secured the Carthaginian holdings in Spain as a result of its victory in the Second Punic War in 206 BCE. In 181 BCE the first Celtiberian War began, lasting until 179 BCE. The first, second (154–151 BCE), and the third (143–133 BCE) Celtiberian Wars were all major rebellions by a loose confederation of Celtic tribes in east central Hispania against Roman rule. It should be noted here that the third Celtiberian War of 143–133 BCE, also known as the Numantine War (Bellum Numantinum, from Roman historian Appian's account of the conflict) is sometimes conflated into the second Celtiberian War as a 20-year conflict known as the Numantine War of 154–133 BCE.

In 154 BCE there was yet another revolt beginning in Numantia of the tribes of Hispania Citerior against Roman rule. The first phase of the war, which occurred at the same time as the Lusitanian War in Hispania Ulterior, ended in 151 BCE, but in 143 BCE an unexpected Roman defeat led the Celtiberians to renounce their treaty with Rome, and yet another insurrection began in Numantia. Rome then sent out a succession of generals to subdue the Numantines.

In 143 BCE Quintus Caecilius Metellus Macedonicus managed to subdue all the other tribes of the Arevaci except the Numantines. He besieged Numantia but failed to take the city. His successor, Consul Quintus Pompeius Aulus was sent out with 30,000 legionnaires, but his campaigning went badly and, in 140 BCE, after having suffered major defeats by the Numantines, reached a secret understanding with their leadership agreeing to abide by the previous treaty with Rome. However, in 139 BCE, a new Roman general, Marcus Popillius Laenas, arrived on the scene and disavowed his predecessor's peace treaty. The issue was referred to the Senate in Rome for a decision, and it opted to scrap the agreement reached by Pompeius.

In 137 BCE the Senate ordered out Gaius Hostilius Mancinus as consul to resume hostilities. On several different occasions, he ordered assaults against Numantia, but all failed. Ultimately, his army of some 20,000 men was surrounded, and he was forced to surrender and accept a peace settlement negotiated on the Roman side by a young Tiberius Gracchus in which the Numantines were treated as equals. Recalled to Rome, on his return to Rome, the Senate placed Mancinus on trial and refused to accept the treaty. Indeed, it ordered Mancinus to be taken back to Spain and handed over bound and naked to the Numantines as a sign of its repudiation. Reportedly, the Numantines refused to accept him, and he later found his way back to Rome. Mancinus's successors, Lucius Furius Philus and Gaius Calpurnius Piso, reportedly avoided conflict with the Numantines.

Fed up with the situation in Spain, in 134 BCE the Roman Senate elected Scipio Aemilianus as consul, waiving the law to allow him to serve as consul a second time, and sent him to Spain. Scipio was well known for his destruction of Carthage in 149 BCE. Reportedly, he commanded 20,000 legionnaires and some 40,000 allied troops, including Numidian cavalry and a dozen war elephants under Jugurtha, later a Roman adversary.

Rather than engage the Numantines in open combat or attempt to assault their city, Scipio planned to starve it into submission. The nearby fields were picked clean of their crops and what was left was burned. Scipio then encircled the city (circumvallation) with a 10-foot tall wall reportedly some six miles in length with seven separate towers, on which were mounted various siege engines and from which his archers were able to fire arrows down into parts of the city. He also caused another outer wall to be built (contravallation) that protected his five camps from outside attack. Scipio also cut off the city from access to the swift-flowing Duero, which he also blockaded with logs moored to the shore that had swords and spear heads embedded in the wood. No opportunity was to be given to the Numantines for combat.

The Numantines attempted several breakouts, but these were repulsed. One of their leaders, Rhetogenes, then managed to escape the city with a small number of others, and they attempted to recruit assistance from other cities. Reportedly, they were betrayed to Scipio by the leaders of Lutia. Scipio then marched there and arrested him and some 400 young men who had agreed to join him against the Romans. Scipio ordered their hands cut off. On Scipio's return to Numantia, its leader Avarus commenced negotiations.

Scipio rejected an appeal from the Numantine negotiators that those surrendering be treated moderately as they had only fought for their families and country. Scipio insisted on *deditio*, or complete submission. The people of the city chose not to believe this and killed their emissaries on their return, convinced that they had betrayed them.

With the failure of negotiations, starvation, and disease took their toll. Cannibalism occurred and some whole families, sensing the inevitable, committed suicide. Weapons were destroyed, and those who remained finally surrendered Numantia in the late summer of 133 BCE after setting their city on fire. Scipio chose some of the survivors for his triumph in Rome and the others were sold as slaves. He then had the city's ruins leveled. The siege had lasted at least eight months.

Numantia was later rebuilt under Emperor Augustus but had little importance thereafter and was abandoned in the fourth century CE. The destruction of Numantia reportedly brought to an end all major resistance to Roman rule in Celtiberia, until the Sertorian War of 80–72 BCE.

Spencer C. Tucker

Further Reading
Appian. *Appian's Roman History.* Translated by Horace White. Cambridge, MA: Harvard University Press, 1964.
Curchin, Leonard A. *Roman Spain: Conquest and Assimilation.* New York: Routledge, 2015.
Keay, Simon J. *Roman Spain.* Berkeley: University of California Press, 1988.
Polybius. *Polybius: The Histories.* Vol. 6. Translated by W. R. Paton. Cambridge, MA: Harvard University Press, 2005.
Richardson, J. S. *Appian: Wars of the Romans in Iberia.* Liverpool, UK: Liverpool University Press, 2000.
Richardson, J. S. *Hispaniae.* Cambridge, UK: Cambridge University Press, 2009.

Siege of Alesia (July–October 52 BCE)

The Roman First Triumvirate (60–51 BCE) gave Julius Caesar the consulship in 59 BCE and then a military command for 5 years (later increased to 10 years) in Illyricum (area of the former Yugoslavia) and in Gaul on both sides of the Alps (France and northern Italy). During 58–57 BCE, Caesar reduced the disunited tribes of northern France and Belgium. He also undertook amphibious operations along the Atlantic seaboard in 56 BCE. In June the next year, Caesar caused a great bridge to be built across the Rhine near present-day Bonn and marched his army over it into Germany. After receiving the submission of several German tribes, Caesar returned to Gaul and destroyed the bridge.

After campaigning for three months in Britain, Caesar returned to Gaul again in 55 BCE. He planned to split up his legions and station them in different parts of Gaul for the winter. Gaul was by no means subjugated, as Caesar soon discovered, for a formidable coalition of central Gallic tribes developed against Roman rule. The uprising began in the area of present-day Orléans, a particularly important area as a meeting place of the Druids who dominated affairs throughout Gaul. This was followed by outbreaks elsewhere, including the Belgae in the northern part of Gaul. Caesar faced the distinct possibility that his legions might be destroyed piecemeal; indeed, one of his garrisons (more than a legion in size) was massacred. Another legion at Samarobriva (Amiens) was narrowly saved from destruction.

In 53 BCE Caesar held a series of conferences with the Gallic chiefs at Samarobriva and elsewhere in an effort to end disaffection. In 52 BCE, however, the tribes of Gaul rose in general revolt. They selected as their leader the only talented military commander produced by the Gauls in the wars against Rome, young Vercingetorix of the Arverni tribe in central Gaul. He adopted a scorched-earth strategy, destroying all Gallic settlements that might aid the Romans. A series of battles and sieges followed. Caesar proved to be a master of both siege warfare and rapid offensive movement and showed himself to be one of the greatest military commanders in history.

The culmination of the fighting in Gaul came in the great siege of Alesia in 52 BCE. Caesar concentrated his efforts against the principal Arverni stronghold of Gergovia but was obliged to break off the siege with the revolt of the Aedui, the other principal tribe of the region. Caesar therefore recalled his deputy Labienus, whom he had sent to the north, and the two of them mounted a siege of Alesia (present-day Alise-Sainte Reine, France), where Vercingetorix had retired following a defeat. Alesia was situated on the top of Mount Auxois near the source of the Seine.

The siege of Alesia lasted from July to October 52 BCE. Vercingetorix commanded more than 90,000 men. Caesar had only 55,000 men, and of this number some 40,000 were legionnaires, with the remainder Gallic cavalry and auxiliaries. Caesar ordered his legionnaires to construct both a wall of contravallation and one of circumvallation; each was roughly 10 miles in circumference and incorporated a ditch 20 feet wide and deep, backed by two additional trenches 15 feet wide and deep. Behind these the Romans constructed ramparts with 12-foot-high palisades and towers every 130 yards. The Romans placed sharpened stakes facing outward in front of and in the ditches.

Caesar's foresight in having a defensive works facing outward as well as inward was soon manifest. Responding to appeals from Vercingetorix, a vast Gallic relief force numbering as many as 250,000 men and 8,000 cavalry gathered around Alesia and besieged the besiegers. Caesar had laid in considerable stocks of food and had an assured water supply, so he calmly continued his own siege operations, repulsing two relief attempts and a breakout sortie with heavy losses.

To win time Vercingetorix tried to send out the women and children from Alesia, but Caesar refused to allow them through the lines. With the situation hopeless, Vercingetorix surrendered. Taken to Rome for Caesar's triumph, Vercingetorix was then executed.

The defeat at Alesia broke Gallic resistance to Rome. The Gauls' failure to unite had cost them dearly. At least a third of their men of military age had been killed in the fighting, and another third were sold into slavery. The vast majority of Gauls hastened to renew their fealty to Rome. After a few mopping-up operations the next year, the Gallic Wars were over. Gaul would be an integral part of the Roman Empire for the next 500 years. The newly conquered territories, with a population of perhaps five million people, proved immensely important to Rome because of their vast resources of agriculture, stock breeding, mining, and metallurgy as well as the production of pottery and glass. During the conquest of Gaul, however, Caesar's army had grown from 2 to 13 legions, making Caesar a threat to Rome itself.

Spencer C. Tucker

Further Reading

Caesar, Gaius Julius. *Seven Commentaries on the Gallic War.* New York: Oxford University Press, 1996.

Grant, Michael. *Julius Caesar.* New York: M. Evans, 1992.

Siege of Jerusalem (April 14–September 8, 70 CE)

The siege of Jerusalem was the decisive event in the First Jewish-Roman War (66–73). The siege began in the spring of 70 and ended that September, effectively ending the war, although pockets of resistance continued until 73. Following his victory in the War of Four Emperors in 69, Roman Emperor Vespasian ordered his son Titus, then Roman commander in Judaea and future emperor, to take Jerusalem, providing the Flavian dynasty with the victory against foreign enemies believed necessary to establish its legitimacy. Jerusalem was held by three competing factions led by Eleazar Ben Simon, John of Gischala, and Simon bar Giora.

Titus and his second-in-command Tiberius Julius Alexander surrounded Jerusalem with four legions (V Macedonica, X Fretensis, XII Fulminata, XV Apollinaris) in the spring of 70. The defenders of the city were handicapped in that they were divided among the three factions, which were only sometimes able to cooperate against the Romans. Food became a major problem for the defenders, especially with the city having been packed with Jews for the celebration of Passover.

The Romans concentrated their efforts at the western portion of the third city wall north of the Jaffa Gate, which they breached in May. By the beginning of the summer, the Romans had also breached the second city wall. This left the defenders in possession of the Temple and the upper and lower city.

By the summer, the Jews were running very low on food. Factionalism also hindered defense efforts. Members of John of Gischala's faction murdered rival faction leader Eleazar Ben Simon, whose men were defending the Temple. Peace between the factions was secured only when the Romans began to construct ramparts preparatory to moving against the Antonia Fortress that overlooked the Jerusalem Temple and the Temple Mount. In surprise sallies, however, the Jews were able to hinder the Romans and destroy their siege equipment. Tightened security and a wooden wall ordered by Titus built around Jerusalem stopped these assaults and also prevented food from reaching the city inhabitants.

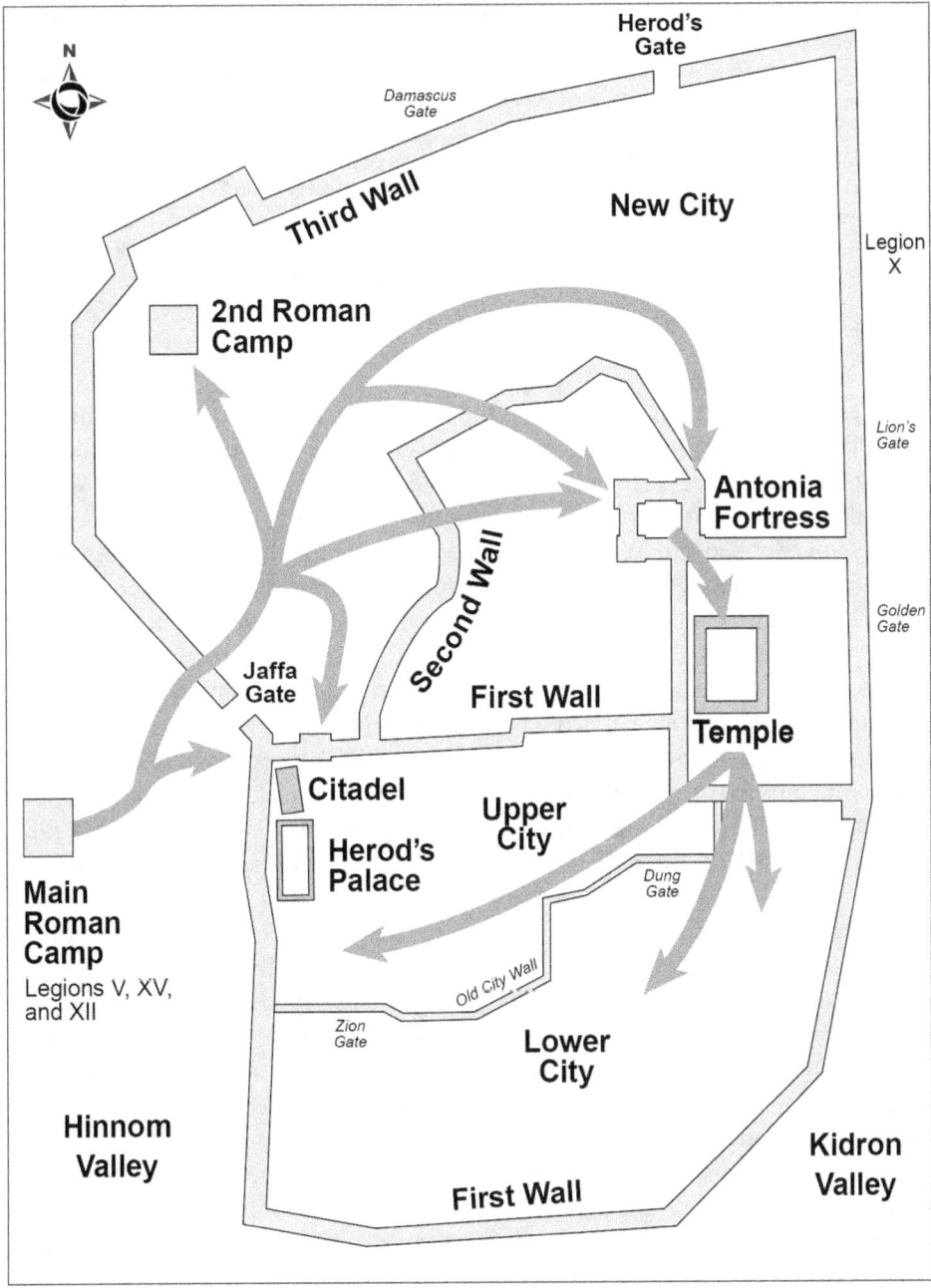

A diagram of the siege of Jerusalem by the Romans during April 14–September 8, 70 CE. (ABC-CLIO)

> **Battering Rams**
>
> Battering rams were siege engines utilized to break apart the masonry walls of fortifications or to splinter wooden gates. Battering rams might be as simple as a large, heavy log carried by a number of men and forcefully propelled by them against the targeted location. More sophisticated, later rams saw the log suspended by ropes or chains within an arrow-proof frame mounted on wheels to move it against the enemy structure with the log then repeatedly swung back and forth against the targeted area. Later the log was given iron bands to keep it from splintering from the shock of the blow as well as a metal cap or helmet, often shaped as a ram's head, hence the name "battering ram."
>
> Stone and brick walls were vulnerable to the rams, which could crack the wall and eventually create a breach, allowing attacking infantry to force their way inside. Rams and other siege engines gave way in the late Middle Ages to heavy gunpowder siege artillery.
>
> **Spencer C. Tucker**

After repeated efforts, by late July the Romans had captured the Antonia Fortress. Titus then sent Josephus, the Jewish historian to negotiate with the defenders. This ended when Josephus was wounded by an arrow and another Jewish sally almost captured Titus. It was only a matter of time, however. The Antonia Fortress overlooked the Temple itself and was thus ideally situated from which to launch an attack. Although Roman battering rams were not successful, fire reportedly from a burning stick thrown by a Roman soldier burned down one of the walls and then spread rapidly, eventually consumed virtually the entire Temple itself on Tisha B'Av (August 30). (The ninth day of Av is an annual fast day in Judaism, on which occurred both the destruction of the First Temple by the Babylonians and the Second Temple by the Romans.) Josephus absolves Titus of any complicity in the destruction of the Temple. Josephus has Titus ordering that the 500-year-old Temple be spared, as he had planned to turn that considerable complex into a Roman temple dedicated to the emperor and Roman pantheon of gods.

Following destruction of the Temple, the Romans moved into the rest of the city. Some of the Jews managed to escape through tunnels or the sewers, while others fought to the end in the Upper City. Herod's Palace fell on September 7, and the Romans secured the city a day later. The Romans either killed or enslaved most of the surviving inhabitants. The sack of the city was terrible. Josephus provides a figure of 1.1 million for the number of those who died in the siege, the vast majority of whom were Jews.

After the Romans had killed all those Jews who had borne arms and the elderly, they enslaved the remaining Jews, reportedly some 97,000. Both John of Gischala and Simon bar Giora were captured. The former was sentenced to life imprisonment and the latter was executed. Titus returned to Rome in 71 for a triumph, bringing with him large numbers of slaves and considerable treasure. Among the items brought back to Rome and paraded through its streets were the Menorah and the Table of the Bread of God's Presence, both of which had only been seen by the Temple High Priest before they were taken.

Nathan Schumer and Spencer C. Tucker

Further Reading

Furneaux, Rupert. *The Roman Siege of Jerusalem*. New York: D. Mackay, 1972.

Josephus, Titus Flavius. *The Works of Josephus, Complete and Unabridged New Updated Edition*. Translated by William Whiston. Peabody, MA: Hendrickson Publishers, 1987.

Price, Jonathan J. *Jerusalem under Siege: The Collapse of the Jewish State, 66–70 CE*. Leiden: Brill, 1992.

Siege of Masada (72–73)

The term "masada" is a Latin transliteration of the Hebrew name Metzada, meaning "fortress." Masada refers to a rock mesa overlooking the Dead Sea in the eastern Judean Desert near Ein Gedi atop which a splinter group of Jewish Zealots stood against a Roman siege (72–73) during the First Jewish-Roman War (66–73), also known as the Herodian Jewish Revolt or the Great Jewish Revolt.

Masada's eastern cliffs rise some 1,350 feet (150 feet above sea level) above the Dead Sea, with the more vertical western cliffs rising 300 feet above the floor of the Dead Sea Valley. The rhomboid-shaped flat plateau comprised an area some 1,200 feet by 900 feet. Access was limited to four very difficult and quite steep approaches: the Snake Path from the east, still used by some tourists today; the White Rock ascent from the west; and one approach each from the south and north. Three large cisterns hewn from the rock mesa collected rainwater. Numerous storehouses also dotted the site.

The Zealot defenders and their families were housed in barracks-like quarters and in the remains of a last century BCE Herodian palace. The plateau was ringed by a watchtower-studded stone casement wall 4,200 feet long and 12 feet thick that incorporated the walls of the living quarters and storehouses.

King Herod the Great was a pro-Roman ruler and appointed Pompey as regent of Palestine in 47 BCE. Herod first fled with his family to Masada in 40 BCE when the Jews joined the Parthians in a rebellion against Rome. Herod then fled to Rome but was restored to his position in 37 BCE after the Romans under Mark Antony crushed the rebellion. Fearing another Jewish rebellion and possible war with Cleopatra of Egypt, during 37–31 BCE, Herod fortified Masada to include an extensive and lavish palace.

Roman soldiers were garrisoned at Masada when in 66 CE when it was captured at the beginning of the Great Jewish Revolt by Jewish Zealots led by Menahem ben Judah. Eleazar ben Ya'ir, nephew of Menahem, assumed command of Masada soon after rival Jews killed Menahem in Jerusalem that same year. Except for the Zealots at Masada, Jewish resistance ended when the Romans captured Jerusalem and destroyed its Temple in September 70 CE.

Lucius Flavius Silva, the Roman governor of Palestine, laid siege to Masada in 73 with a force of 10,000–15,000 men consisting of the Roman Tenth Legion, its support troops, and Jewish prisoners of war who were used as construction slaves. The Jewish defenders and family members numbered as many as 1,500 people, although the generally accepted figure is 960.

Ruins of the ancient Jewish fortress of Masada, scene of the Roman siege of 72–73 CE. (VanderWolfImages/Dreamstime.com)

After surrounding the fortress with eight military camps and a three-foot-high circumvallation wall, the Romans oversaw during the construction during a period of as much as nine months by some 15,000 Jewish slave laborers of an assault ramp against the western face of the plateau that reached to the top of Masada. This entailed moving thousands of tons of rock and earth. It was during this time that the Jewish defenders reinforced the stone wall with an earthen and wooden wall. It is not clear whether there were any attempts by the Sicarii to counterattack the besiegers during the period when the ramp was built.

In the spring of 73, the Romans worked a battering ram up the ramp to breach the stone wall and then succeeded in burning the wooden wall. As the Romans prepared to exploit the breach the next day, Eleazar exhorted the Zealot defenders and their families to a final act of defiance. They burned their personal belongings and selected by lot 10 defenders to kill the general population. These 10 then killed each other in turn, leaving only a final defender to commit suicide. The contents of the storehouses were not burned so as to demonstrate to the Romans that the defenders and their families chose to die rather than suffer defeat by siege and assault. These details and the personal exhortation of Eleazar to his followers were related to the Romans by two women and five children who survived by hiding in one of the cisterns. Their accounts were recorded by the first-century Jewish historian Josephus. The generally accepted date for the Roman capture of Masada is April 16, 73.

Masada emerged as a symbol of Jewish and Zionist resolve and courage and became a widely visited pilgrimage site for many Zionist youth groups and the Haganah in the years prior to the formation in 1948 of the State of Israel. The Star of David flag of Israel was raised over Masada following the end of the Israeli War of Independence in 1949, and the site continues to be used by various units of the Israel Defense Forces (IDF) and contemporary youth movements for swearing-in ceremonies that conclude with the oath that "Masada shall never fall again." Masada is accessible today both by foot on the arduous Snake Path and by aerial tramway.

Richard M. Edwards

Further Reading

Ben-Yehuda, Nachman. *Sacrificing Truth: Archaeology and the Myth of Masada.* Amherst, NY: Humanity Books, 2002.

Campbell, Duncan B. "Dating the Siege of Masada." *Zeitschrift für Papyrologie und Epigraphik* 73 (1988): 156–158.

Cotton, Hannah M. "The Date of the Fall of Masada: The Evidence of the Masada Papyri." *Zeitschrift für Papyrologie und Epigraphik* 78 (1989): 157–162.

Josephus, Titus Flavius. *The Works of Josephus, Complete and Unabridged New Updated Edition.* Translated by William Whiston. Peabody, MA: Hendrickson Publishers, 1987.

Miklowitz, Gloria D. *Masada: The Last Fortress.* Grand Rapids, MI: Eerdmans, 1999.

Richmond, I. A. "The Roman Siege-Works of Masada, Israel." *Journal of Roman Studies* 52 (1962): 142–155.

Yadin, Yigael. *Masada: Herod's Fortress and the Zealots' Last Stand.* New York: Welcome Rain, 1998.

Siege of Ravenna (Autumn 490–February 27, 493)

The siege of Ravenna (490–493) lasted nearly two and a half years, from the autumn of 490 to February 27, 493, and was part of the war of 489–493 fought in northern Italy between the forces of Ostrogoth leader Theodoric the Great and Odoacer, the king of Italy.

Having crossed over the Julian Alps, in August 489 Theodoric arrived in Venetia in northeastern Italy and defeated Odoacer in the Battle of the Sontius (Isonzo) on August 28, 489, with the result that the Ostrogoth leader then controlled all Venetia. Theodoric was again victorious, farther south, in the Battle of Verona (September 30). Odoacer then withdrew into the heavily fortified and easily defended city of Ravenna.

Theodoric laid siege to Ravenna but, with the arrival of reinforcements from south Italy, Odoacer sortied and defeated Theodoric in the Battle of Faenza in 490. Theodoric withdrew back to Pavia, where he constructed heavy fortifications. Odoacer laid siege to that place but was then forced to send some of his forces to meet an invasion of Liguria by the Burgundians and Visigoths. This enabled Theodoric to defeat Odoacer in the Battle of the Adda on August 11, 490. Odoacer again withdrew into Ravenna.

Ravenna was considered impregnable, and for nearly three years Theodoric besieged Odoacer there. Gradually support for Odoacer in Italy melted away until his power was limited to Ravenna itself. Still, the siege dragged on. Ravenna may have been impregnable, but the effects of the siege on the city's population were severe. The price of grain reached astronomical heights, and many people died of starvation and disease. Theodoric established a fortified camp in the Pineta, and his men ravaged the countryside in order to prevent food or reinforcements from reaching Ravenna. Sometime in 491, Odoacer attempted a sortie but, in desperate fighting, his men were rebuffed and forced back into Ravenna itself.

In 492 Theodoric captured Rimini and from there brought ships to the Porto Leone, some six miles from Ravenna, cutting the fortress city off from the sea. Following the institution of this naval blockade, Odoacer finally entered into negotiations with Theodoric giving his son Thelane as a hostage as a gesture of good faith.

The importance of Ravenna, judged impregnable, may be seen in the generous surrender terms, for the two men agreed to share the rule of Italy. The siege of Ravenna officially ended on February 27, 493. On March 15, however, Theodoric murdered Odoacer during a banquet, held to celebrate the conclusion of the treaty, reportedly raising a toast to Odoacer and then killing him with his sword. Theodoric now united the peninsula under his sole rule, beginning the Ostrogothic kingdom of Italy (493–553). Theodoric died in 526 and was interred in a mausoleum in Ravenna, but his bones were scattered and the mausoleum converted to a church after Byzantine Empire general Belisarius conquered the city in 540.

Spencer C. Tucker

Further Reading
Arnold, Jonathan J. *Theodoric and the Roman Imperial Restoration.* Cambridge, UK: Cambridge University Press, 2014.
Heather, Peter. *The Goths.* Oxford, UK: Blackwell, 1996.
Moorhead, John. *Theoderic in Italy.* Oxford, UK: Oxford University Press, 1992.

Siege of Rome (March 2, 537–March 12, 538)

The year-long siege of Rome, during March 2, 537–March 12, 538, occurred during the war between the Ostrogoths and the Byzantine (Eastern Roman) Empire. Known to the Italians as the Gothic War, the conflict was fought during 535–554.

After having secured northern Africa, the Byzantine (Eastern Roman) emperor Justinian I turned his attention to Italy, which had passed under Ostrogoth control in 493. Although the Ostrogoths had recognized Byzantine sovereignty, this was in name only as the kingdom was for all intents and purposes independent. With Italy in some turmoil after the death in 526 of Theodoric I, founder of the Ostrogothic kingdom, Justinian decided to move. The excuse to reunite Italy with the Byzantine Empire came in the murder by the courtier Theodatus of Amalasuntha, queen of the Ostrogoths, who had acknowledged Justinian's suzerainty.

In 535 Byzantine general Belisarius arrived in Sicily at the head of a force of some 8,000 men, half of them heavy cavalry. The only real opposition was at the port city of Palermo. Belisarius brought his ships into the harbor and had archers in their tops fire arrows down into the citadel, which then surrendered. Distracted in 536 by the mutiny of Byzantine forces in North Africa, Belisarius sailed there with only 1,000 men and put down the rebellion. Theodatus, now Goth king of Italy, offered to surrender Italy to the Byzantine Empire, but the defeat of another Byzantine force under General Mundas with 4,000 men in battle at Salona near Split in Dalmatia by a far larger Goth force led Theodatus to withdraw his offer.

Belisarius then crossed to southern Italy, taking the city of Naples after a siege of less than a month. With a Frankish force allied with Emperor Justinian preparing to invade Italy from the north across the Alps, the Goths, angered at the inaction by Theodatus, deposed and killed him. Vitiges, elected to replace Theodatus, immediately came to terms with the Franks by ceding Provence to them.

After having taken Naples, Belisarius proceeded north to Rome. The people of Rome quickly embraced Belisarius, with Pope Silverius and a delegation of eminent citizens leaving the city to treat with him. Realizing their situation was hopeless, the 4,000-man Goth garrison simply abandoned the city. On December 9, 536, Belisarius entered Rome through its Asinarian Gate just as the Goths were departing through the city's Flaminian Gate.

With new Goth ruler Vitiges gathering a large army in north Italy, and possessing only 5,000 troops himself, Belisarius prudently decided to delay any further advance until he was reinforced. After sending an urgent appeal to Justinian in Constantinople for additional manpower, Belisarius set about preparing Rome for a siege. He ordered repairs to the long-neglected city walls, had heavy chains stretched across the Tiber, strengthened the fort of the Mausoleum of Hadrian, and laid in as many supplies as possible. He also recruited some 20,000 Romans to assist in the city's defense.

On March 2, 537, Vitiges arrived at Rome at the head of a large force, estimated by some chroniclers at 150,000 men. While this figure is no doubt inflated, the Goths certainly greatly outnumbered Belisarius's field force. The Goths crossed over the Anio River when the Romans defending the Salarian Bridge simply decamped on the Goth arrival. The next day, Vitiges almost succeeded in cutting off Belisarius, who was unaware of what had transpired and was outside the Flaminian Gate of Rome. A fierce fight ensued, but Belisarius and his men managed to fight their way through the Goths to safety.

Despite the Goth numbers, Rome was too large for them to encircle, so the siege was never quite complete. The Goths set up seven camps, each overlooking the main gates and routes to the city. Much of the southern side of the city was left open, and thus Belisarius was able to receive some supplies and even reinforcements.

The Goths set about trying to starve the city into surrender, and toward that end they blocked the aqueducts that supplied the city with its water. The aqueducts not only gave drinking water but also operated the gristmills that provided the city with most of its bread. Belisarius then had floating gristmills built on the Tiber. Nonetheless, the situation for the citizens of Rome grew increasingly difficult. Vitiges tried to persuade Belisarius to surrender, promising his army safe passage if he would do so, but the Byzantine general refused.

Soon after the rejection of his offer, Vitiges ordered an assault on March 21, 537, with four siege towers pulled by oxen. Belisarius ordered his men to hold their fire until the Goths were within bow range, then used his skilled archers to kill the oxen, immobilizing the towers away from the walls. A second assault in early 538 was also repulsed. Meanwhile, Belisarius sent his subordinate John "the Sanguinary" and some 2,000 men to raid the east coast of Italy.

A victory outside the city by the Goths against a sally by Belisarius decided nothing and, with his own men suffering from disease and famine, Vitiges offered to surrender Sicily and southern Italy (which were already under Byzantine control) in exchange for a withdrawal from Rome.

Finally, the realization that he could not starve the city into submission and the arrival of a large imperial fleet in the Tiber with 5,000 additional Byzantine troops led Vitiges to end the siege and march east after John the Sanguinary, whom he besieged at Rimini. Belisarius then crossed the Apennines, forcing Vitiges to raise his siege of Rimini and withdraw to Ravenna, which Belisarius then besieged.

In 538 Theodebert, the Frankish king of Austrasia, sent a small force across the Alps to operate in connection with the Goths in the vicinity of Milan in northern Italy. Taking advantage of the chaos in north Italy, in 539 Theodebert led a much larger Frankish force into Italy and attacked both Goth and imperial forces alike, ravaging much of north Italy in the process. Preoccupied with the siege of Ravenna, Belisarius was able to negotiate a treaty with Theodebert whereby the latter, whose forces were severely weakened by pestilence, withdrew from Italy. Justinian, meanwhile, alarmed by incursions into the Byzantine Empire by Bulgars and Slavs, and the threat of renewed war with Persia, offered to negotiate peace with Vitiges in Italy, but Belisarius refused to transmit this message.

With the effects of the siege now apparent, the Goths offered to support Belisarius as emperor in the West, and he pretended to agree to this. When the Goths surrendered Ravenna in late 539, though, Belisarius, who remained loyal to Justinian, took Vitiges prisoner and sent him off to Constantinople.

Fighting continued, however, with Goth fortunes reviving under their new king Totila. He besieged Rome again, in 546, and took it. The Byzantines retook it soon thereafter, only to have it besieged and again lost in 549. In 551, however, another great Byzantine general, Narses, arrived in Italy. In July 552, he defeated the Goths in the Battle of Taginae, in which Totila was slain. This battle signaled the end of Ostrogothic power in Italy.

Spencer C. Tucker

Further Reading
Bury, John Bagnell. *History of the Later Roman Empire*. Vols. 1 and 2. New York: Macmillan, 1923.
Hughes, Ian. *Belisarius: The Last Roman General*. Yardley, PA: Westholme, 2009.

Siege of Damascus (634–635?)

The siege of Damascus was part of the Muslim conquest of Syria during the Arab-Byzantine Wars. Dates for the siege vary widely. Some sources say it lasted for six months and the city fell to the Arabs in January 635; others give a far shorter period of August 21 to September 19, 634.

Abu Bakr, the first Rashidym caliph, was determined to expand Muslim control beyond the Arabian Peninsula. In 634 he sent four armies totaling perhaps 20,000 men into Syria, then controlled by the Byzantine Empire. These forces proving inadequate, Abu Bakr dispatched reinforcements under his capable general Khalid ibn al-Walid. These forces captured Bosra and then won a notable battle at Ajnadayn (July 30). Having secured his flank, Khalid then proceeded against the key city of Damascus. The city was heavily fortified with much of it surrounded by a 36-foot-high wall.

The Byzantine army commander of Damascus was an officer named Thomas, son-in-law of Byzantine emperor Heraclius. The senior civilian official was Mansur Ibn Sarjan, a Christian Arab. The Arabs had no siege equipment and so, reportedly on August 21 (again, dates for the siege differ), they surrounded the city with the intention of starving it into submission. Lacking sufficient manpower to surround the city completely, Khalid concentrated his men at the six city gates, sufficient in numbers to repulse any Byzantine sorties. He also sent detachments to cut the Byzantine lines of communication to Damascus and dispatched cavalry to Thaniyat al-'Uqab ("Eagle's Pass"), some 20 miles northeast of the city on the Emesa to Damascus road in order to provide warning of the approach of the anticipated Byzantine relief force and defeat it if possible.

Heraclius was at the city of Antioch when the siege of Damascus commenced, and he ordered a relief force sent there. Numbering only about 12,000 men, it encountered the Arabs at Eagle's Pass and was on the brink of defeating them, when Khalid arrived with reinforcements and turned the tide of battle. The Byzantine relief force then withdrew northward.

The besiegers had been greatly weakened by the removal of Arab forces to meet the Byzantine relief column, and if the defenders had attempted a major sortie at that time, it probably would have broken through. The opportunity soon passed, however, as after his victory at Eagle's Pass, Khalid hurried back to Damascus.

Realizing that relief was now unlikely, Thomas concentrated manpower for a breakout attempt from Thomas Gate. The attempt by infantry covered by archers on the walls failed, and the infantry was driven back into the city. Thomas, who led the attack in person, was wounded in the eye by an arrow. Undaunted, he tried again that evening, this time in an attempt from four of the city gates, with three of these designed to draw off Muslim forces from the main assault from the East Gate, again led by Thomas in person. The fighting was heavy, but the Byzantine breakout attempt was unsuccessful, and Thomas ordered it ended.

There are several versions of how Damascus actually fell. Reportedly an informant told Khalid about a celebration planned in the city for the night of September 19, and Khalid ordered a surprise attack to occur then when the walls were likely to be lightly held. That night the Arabs entered the city from two directions. Khalid's troops were first into the city, reportedly using ropes to get some men over the undefended wall at the East Gate and breaking through there, while another force, under Abu Ubaidah, breached Jabiyah Gate on the west.

Although it was traditional Arab practice to slay all the inhabitants of a city that had refused to surrender, Khalid's terms were generous in that only the Rumi or Byzantines of Greek origin were excluded from a general amnesty. Damascus, largely Christian in population, now became the capital city of Islamic Syria.

Spencer C. Tucker

Further Reading
De Goeje, M. J. *Memoire sur le conquête de la Syrie*. Leiden: Brill, 1900.
McGraw Donner, F. *The Early Islamic Conquests*. Princeton, NJ: Princeton University Press, 1981.

Siege of Constantinople (August 15, 717–August 15, 718)

The chief Muslim goal throughout the seventh and eighth centuries remained the acquisition of Constantinople. That great city controlled the Bosporus and thus access between the Mediterranean and the Black Sea. It also guarded the entrance to Southern and Central Europe. The Muslims first attempted to take the city in 655, when Caliph Othman (r. 644–656) sent out a naval expedition. Although the Byzantine fleet met decisive defeat, the subsequent assassination of Othman and war of succession provided a respite. In 669 the Muslims mounted a second attempt, and thereafter Constantinople came under intermittent attack. Several attempts in the 670s were turned back when the Byzantines defeated the attackers at sea.

The greatest threat to the city, and to Byzantium, came in the siege of 717–718. Caliph Suleiman (r. 715–717) prepared a major effort to attack the city, ending the short reign of Byzantine emperor Theodosius III (r. 716–717) and bringing to the throne a successful general, Leo the Isaurian (Isauria is in Asia Minor, today's Konia). Leo (r. 717–741), who had been born a poor peasant, took the title of Leo III. He immediately ordered the granaries of Constantinople restocked and repairs made to the city's walls. He also secured weapons and ordered siege engines installed.

Constantinople was secure as long as its sea communications remained open. The city was built on a promontory flanked on the north by the so-called Golden Horn, an inlet of the Bosporus forming a natural harbor, and on the south by the Sea of Marmara. The city was protected on its western, or landward, side by both inner and outer walls; the inner wall had been built under Emperor Constantine the Great. The outer wall was constructed under Emperor Theodosius II and was some four miles in length. Normally the city population numbered about half a million people, but in 717 it must have swelled from refugees.

Until the invention of gunpowder, the only practical way to take a strongly held city was by blockading and starving its population. This meant closing both the Bosporus and the Dardanelles, a difficult feat because Constantinople flanked the Bosporus from the south. Everything depended on the Byzantine fleet, which was markedly inferior in numbers to that of the attackers.

Maslama, brother of the caliph, commanded the operation against Constantinople. He took personal command of the land force of some 80,000 men and gave command of the 1,800-ship fleet transporting another 80,000 men to Suleiman the General (not to be confused with the caliph of the same name). The attackers also had some 800 additional ships preparing in African and Egyptian ports, while the caliph was assembling a reserve army at Tarsus.

Maslama crossed over the Dardanelles to Europe, probably in July 717, and then moved overland to Constantinople, arriving there on August 15. Maslama ordered his troops to entrench before the city. He attempted a land attack, but the Byzantines beat it back. Maslama then ordered his men to surround his camp with a deep ditch and decided to reduce the city by blockade. He therefore instructed Suleiman the General to divide his fleet into two squadrons, one to cut off supplies from reaching Constantinople via the Aegean and Dardanelles and the other to move through the Bosporus and sever communications with the city from the Black Sea.

In early September, the second fleet got under way to sail north of the Golden Horn, where Leo III had his fleet. The entrance to the harbor was protected by a great chain suspended between two towers that could be raised or lowered. When the blockading squadron approached, the strong current in the Bosporus threw the leading ships into confusion. Leo immediately ordered the chain lowered, stood out with his galleys, and attacked the broken Muslim formation with Greek fire, destroying 20 ships and capturing others before retiring to the Golden Horn on the approach of the main body of Suleiman's fleet.

Suleiman the General made no further attempt to force the strait, and Leo was thus able to bring in supplies and prevent Constantinople's surrender through starvation. To add to Maslama's difficulties, his brother, Caliph Suleiman, suddenly died, and his successor, Omar II, turned out to be a religious bigot but no soldier. Omar continued the siege by land, but then winter set in and was unusually severe with snow. Many of the besiegers died in these conditions, among them Suleiman the General.

In the spring of 718, an Egyptian squadron of 400 ships arrived. Passing Constantinople at night, it closed the Bosporus. The Egyptian squadron was followed by a squadron from Africa of 360 ships and the reserve army to reinforce the land troops, who had reportedly been reduced to cannibalism. Although the closure of the Bosporus would have, in time, forced Constantinople to surrender, a large number of the crewmen on the Egyptian ships were impressed Christians, and many were able to desert and provide accurate intelligence.

Choosing an opportune time when his enemy was unprepared, Leo again ordered the boom lowered and came out of the Golden Horn to engage and defeat the Egyptian ships. The Christian crewmen deserted en masse. Many Muslim vessels were destroyed by Greek fire, and others were captured. This gave Leo control of the Bosporus. He followed it up by ferrying over to the Asiatic side a sizable land force, which trapped and routed a number of Muslim troops.

Leo was also active diplomatically. He arranged an alliance with Terbelis, king of the Bulgars, who then marched against Maslama and defeated him, probably in July 718, somewhere south of Adrianople. Some 22,000 Muslim troops are said to have been killed. Leo made adroit use of disinformation as well, scattering reports that the Franks were preparing to send large forces to the aid of Constantinople.

The caliph finally recalled Maslama, who raised the siege on August 15. It had lasted exactly one year. The fleet embarked the army, landing them on the Asiatic shore of the Sea of Marmara. The ships then sailed for the Dardanelles, but en route they encountered a great storm. Reportedly only 5 galleys out of some 2,560 in the siege returned to Syria and Alexandria. Of the land forces, which some estimates place at more than 200,000 men, no more than 30,000 made it home. In 739 Leo won a land victory that compelled the Muslims to withdraw from western Asia Minor. Leo's leadership was key to the Byzantine victory.

Spencer C. Tucker

Further Reading

Gibbon, Edward. *The History of the Decline and Fall of the Roman Empire*. Vol. 6. Edited by J. B. Bury. London: Methuen, 1912.

Runciman, Steven. *Byzantine Civilization*. New York: Barnes and Noble, 1994.

Vasiliev, Alexander Alexandrovich. *History of the Byzantine Empire, 324–1453*. Madison: University of Wisconsin Press, 1990.

Siege of Pavia (September 773–June 774)

Following his victory over Muslim forces of the Umayyad Caliphate from Spain in the Battle of Tours in 732, Charles Martel became king of the Franks in all but name. His son Pepin the Short (Pepin III) was the first of the Carolingian line (751–987) to assume the title "King of the Franks." In 751 Pepin sent the last of the Merovingian rulers, Childeric III, off to a monastery.

Pepin was a highly effective ruler. Implacable in war and a wise and effective administrator, he prepared the foundation upon which his son Charles built. Recognizing the importance of the church, Pepin restored its property and brought religious relics to France. He also rescued the papacy from Lombard control. Pepin died in 768, bequeathing the throne jointly to his two sons, Carloman II and Charles.

Charles, born in 742, became the greatest of all medieval kings, recognized by both the French and Germans as Charles the Great (Charlemagne; Karl der Grosse). In 770, on the advice of his mother, Charles divorced his first wife and married Desiderata, daughter of Lombard king Desiderius. Desiderata returned to Lombardy a year later possibly because she was infertile, greatly straining the off-and-on relations between the Franks and Lombards.

In 771 Charles became sole king on the death of his brother. Carloman's wife Gerberge then also departed for Lombardy. Pope Stephen III, who had criticized Charles's marriage to Desiderata, drew closer to the Lombards and appointed a number of Lombard nobles to important posts in Rome. When Stephen died in 772, his successor Adrian I removed the Lombards from their positions, leading Desiderius to send troops into the northern papal territories. Adrian then appealed to Charles for assistance.

> **Charlesmagne**
>
> Physically impressive, charismatic, and highly intelligent (although not well educated), Charlemagne was one of history's great military commanders and rulers. As a general he was bold, resourceful, and imaginative. He believed passionately in God, his strategic plan, and in himself. He planned his campaigns carefully and had excellent mastery of logistics. As a ruler, he was wise and just. A superb administrator, Charlemagne shifted the center of European power from the Mediterranean, which had been the center of Greek and Roman civilizations, to the Rhine, locating his imperial capital at Aachen (Aix-la-Chapelle).
>
> Charlemagne was keenly interested in advancing education and the arts. At Aachen, he established a palace school under the monk Alcuin in order to train individuals for state service. Among the accomplishments of the school was the creation of a more efficient way of writing, known as "Carolingian minuscule."
>
> **Spencer C. Tucker**

While he readied his army, Charles sent letters to both Adrian and Desiderata urging peaceful settlement. In the summer of 773, having received confirmation of Desiderius's invasion of papal territory and refusal of a large monetary settlement to evacuate territories taken, Charles sent his army to northern Italy. The size of Charles's army has been estimated at 10,000–15,000 men. He divided it in half for the passage through the Alps. His uncle Bernard led one part of the army through the St. Bernard Pass, while Charles led the remainder through the Dora Susa via Mount Cenis.

As they descended the Alps, Charles's contingent found their way blocked by Lombard fortifications. An assault failed, but Charles found a way to attack the Lombards in the flank. The Lombard defenders then fled to Pavia, perhaps motivated by news that Bernard was moving in from the east.

In September 773, Charles's combined force arrived before the walled city of Pavia. The Frankish force was sufficiently large to enable them to surround the city. The siege of Pavia lasted for the next 10 months. Although Charles did not have siege engines, the defenders had not anticipated the need, and their city was but poorly provisioned. Desiderius was among those trapped at Pavia, although his son Adelchis had fled to the stronger walled city of Verona, there to watch over Gerberge and her children.

Charles's force was sufficiently large that he was able to subdue the area around Pavia while also sending part of his army to march on Verona. It succumbed without a fight. Adelchis then fled to Constantinople, and Charles secured Gerberge and the children. Meanwhile, Desiderius was content to stay on the defensive and mounted no major sally against the besiegers of Pavia. Finally, with famine taking hold and no other city attempting its relief, Desiderius surrendered Pavia in June 774.

Having captured Pavia and other Lombard cities, Charles absorbed the Lombard kingdom into his rising Frankish Empire, naming himself king of both the Franks and the Lombards. He sent Desiderius off to France to enter a monastery. Charles's victory at Pavia made him supreme in northern Italy. He also reached accommodation with Pope Adrian. While Charles recognized Adrian's claim to much of Italy, he failed to oblige the pope by actually conquering it.

Adrian I died in 795, and Leo III succeeded him. Leo proved unpopular and fled to Charles's capital of Aachen (Aix-la-Chapelle), where he demanded that Charles restore him to power. Charles sent Leo back to Rome with troops, following himself in December 800. On Christmas Day in Rome at St. Peter's Basilica as Charles knelt in prayer, Leo produced a jeweled crown and placed it on Charles's head, proclaiming him "Charles the Augustus, crowned by God the great and peace-bringing Emperor of the Romans." It might not have been to Charlemagne's liking to receive the crown from the pope, opening a long debate as to the relative authority of the pope and Holy Roman emperor.

Charlemagne went on to expand Frankish power significantly. He already had won part of northeastern Spain, and in the 780s he pushed his authority to the east, invading the old German lands and converting them to Catholicism. Ultimately, his territory extended to the Elbe and then south along the Danube to below Vienna. Once more the west was united. Charlemagne established his capital at Aachen near the mouth of the Rhine. He died in 814 and was succeeded as emperor by his son, the ineffectual emperor Louis I (r. 814–840), also known as Louis the Pious. On Louis's death, full-scale civil war involving his three sons broke out almost immediately, and the territory was divided among them in the Treaty of Verdun of 843. From these territories emerged modern France and Germany.

Spencer C. Tucker

Further Reading

Bachrach, N. *Charlemagne's Early Campaigns (768–777): A Diplomatic and Military Analysis.* Leiden: Brill, 2013.

Durant, Will. *The Age of Faith.* New York: Simon & Schuster, 1940.

Riché, Pierre. *The Carolingians.* Translated by Michael I. Allen. Philadelphia: University of Pennsylvania Press, 1993.

Winston, Richard. *Charlemagne: From the Hammer to the Cross.* Indianapolis: Bobbs-Merrill, 1954.

Siege of Paris (November 25, 885–October 886)

The siege of Paris of November 25, 885–October 886 resulted from a Viking raid up the Seine River. It was the most important event in the reign of Charles III, also known as Charles the Fat, king of West Francia (r. 884–887) and Holy Roman emperor (881–887), who had briefly in 1885 reunited under his rule all of his great-grandfather Charlemagne's territorial holdings, save Provence. The siege is generally acknowledged to have marked the high point of Viking influence in western Europe as well as being an important turning point in the fortunes of the Carolingian dynasty and of France.

Mid-ninth-century Paris was centered then, as today, on the Isle de la Cité, the island in the Seine. The Vikings had previously attacked Paris with success, sacking it in 843. Three more Viking raids against the city occurred in the 860s, and each time the raiders were bought off with bribes. In 864 the Paris government ordered two bridges—one of stone and another of wood—to be built connecting the island to both banks of the Seine. These were foot bridges and sufficiently low that they blocked ships from proceeding further upriver. As such, they came to play a key role in the siege of 885–886, as they could block even the shallow Viking ships from proceeding past Paris. Odo (Eudes), Count of Paris, learning of the Viking progress, ordered construction of two towers to guard each of the bridges, one at each end. He also laid in what supplies he could.

On November 25, 885, the Vikings reached Paris. Contemporaries claimed that 700 ships carried as many as 30,000–40,000 Vikings, led by Siegfried and Sinric. While these numbers are believed to be greatly exaggerated (modern scholars put these numbers at less than half), it was nonetheless a significant force. On their arrival at the Isle de la Cité, the Vikings were confident of success, given their superior number of fighting men and past experiences. Nonetheless, Odo rejected their demands, whereupon the Vikings laid siege to the city.

Odo faced a daunting task. Assisted by Gozlin, bishop of Paris, who is widely regarded as the first medieval fighting bishop, as he actually took part in the fighting, Odo could at first count on only several hundred men-at-arms. The Vikings first assaulted the towers overlooking the bridges but were driven back by hot wax and pitch. The Parisians continued to strengthen their defenses, as the Vikings tried a variety of schemes, including mining, battering rams, and fire, with no success.

With the failure of their initial attacks, the Vikings withdrew and built a stone encampment on the right side of the Seine. They also built a number of siege engines, which they used to attack the city and the towers. These attacks continued for some two months.

In January 886, the Vikings attempted to fill the river with debris near the tower and then set several of their ships on fire and sent them against the wooden bridge. The burning ships sank before they could destroy the bridge, but the structure was weakened. On February 6, heavy rains caused the debris-filled river to overflow and the bridge supports to give way. With the bridge gone, the northeast tower was now cut off with 12 men inside. The Vikings demanded the men surrender. They refused and were subsequently all slain.

Having failed in their efforts to take the city by storm, the Vikings then called off their attacks and settled in for a prolonged effort to starve the city into surrender. While maintaining a sizable presence at Paris, most of the Vikings proceeded further to pillage such places as Le Mans, Chartres, Evreux, and the Loire region.

In February a relief force sent by Charles and commanded by Henry, Count of Saxony, arrived. Weakened by their winter march, the men mounted only one, unsuccessful, attack before withdrawing. Although the besieged were able to secure some supplies, nonetheless morale in Paris was low. In May 886, disease spread in Paris, with Bishop Gozlin among those dying. Odo then slipped through Viking-controlled territory to personally petition Charles for more support. Charles agreed, and Odo fought his way back into Paris. There were two relief forces: one under Count Henry and the other under Charles. Charles dallied; Henry arrived but was captured and killed.

In the summer of 886, the Vikings made a final effort to take Paris by storm before Charles arrived. It failed and Charles arrived with his army in October, but much to the disappointment and anger of the Parisians who had held off the attackers for so long, the king made no effort to do battle with the Vikings. Indeed, he acted shamefully, agreeing to pay them a ransom of 700 livres (1,543 pounds) of gold and encouraging them to raid Burgundy, which had refused to acknowledge his authority.

The failure of the siege solidified the strategic importance of Paris in France. The Vikings went on to lay siege to Sens southeast of Paris for six months during 886–887 but were again unsuccessful and then withdrew from France. Charles's shameful bargain with the Vikings at Paris and general incompetence, as well as the ambition of his nephew Arnulf, finally provoked a rising among the nobles against Charles and brought an end to the Carolingian Empire. In November 887, at Frankfurt, the East Frankish nobles removed Emperor Charles. Arnulf was elected king of the East Franks. The West Franks, Burgundy, and Italy refused to recognize Arnulf, however, and elected new kings from their own nobility. Odo of Paris became king of the West Francia on February 29, 888, and ruled until January 1, 898.

Spencer C. Tucker

Further Reading

Abbo Cernuus. *Viking Attacks on Paris: The Bella Parisiacae Urbis of Abbo of Saint-Germain-des-Prés*. With introduction, editing, and translation by N. Dass. Paris: Peeters, 2007.

Bradbury, Jim. *The Medieval Siege*. Woodbridge, Suffolk, UK: Boydell Press, 1992.

Hooper, Nicholas A., and Matthew Bennetew. *The Cambridge Illustrated Atlas of Warfare: The Middle Ages, 768–1487*. Cambridge, UK: Cambridge University Press, 1996.

Logan, F. Donald. *The Vikings in History*. London: Routledge, 1991.

MacLean, Simon. *Kingship and Politics in the Late Ninth Century: Charles the Fat and the End of the Carolingian Empire*. Cambridge, UK: Cambridge University Press, 2003.

Norris, John. *Medieval Siege Warfare*. Stroud, Gloucestershire, UK: Tempus, 2007.

Siege of Jerusalem (June 7–July 18, 1099)

At the end of the eleventh century, Latin Christendom took the offensive against Islam with the Crusades, a series of wars designed to free the Holy Land from Muslim control. A number of factors were behind the Crusades. In 1070 the Ottomans took Jerusalem from Egypt, and accounts began to reach the West of persecution of Christians visiting the holy places. The schism of 1054 dangerously weakened the Byzantine Empire, which had traditionally barred Turkish expansion into eastern Europe, and certain Italian cities (including Genoa, Pisa, and Venice) sought to secure the lucrative trade of the eastern Mediterranean. The final decision rested with Pope Urban II, who in 1095 preached the First Crusade at Clermont. He envisioned it as a holy war to save Europe and the Byzantine

Empire from Islam but also as a means to end feudal strife between Christians in a grand war against the infidel. Urban hoped that the result would be a unified West under the leadership of the Catholic Church.

The First Crusade lasted from 1096 to 1099. Urban called for the Christian armies to depart in August 1096, but the peasants would not wait. Stirred by religious fervor and a plenary indulgence, some 12,000 peasants set out from France, and another 9,000 set out from Germany. The peasants made their way to Constantinople, where Byzantine emperor Alexius I provided ships to transport them across the Bosporus. He urged them to wait there until the armed knights could arrive, but the peasant soldiers set out alone and were slaughtered in large numbers by Sultan Kilij Arslan's Turkish archers on October 21, 1096, at Dracon.

Meanwhile, the feudal knights assembled in France. No king was among them, and the most notable figure was Godfrey of Bouillon, Duke of Lorraine. The knights and supporting infantry then made their way to Constantinople, where Alexis, fearful of their presence, hurried them across the straits in early 1097. Fortunately for the Crusaders, their opponents were even more divided, and most Turkish forces were off conducting operations to the east.

The Crusaders moved south along the Mediterranean coast so that they might be resupplied from the sea. On their way, they were joined by Italian-Norman forces under a certain Taticius. On May 6, Godfrey and his men reached Nicea. Raymond of Saint Giles, Count of Toulouse and Marquis of Provence, joined the force, as did Bohemond of Taranto, uncle of Taticius; Robert, Duke of Normandy (the son of William the Conqueror); and Stephen, Count of Blois and Chartres. On May 21, the Crusaders defeated Turkish forces under Arslan, which then withdrew.

The Crusaders then besieged Nicea. Operations included unsuccessful mining under one of the main towers. Only the appearance of a Byzantine fleet off Nicea induced the leaders to surrender on June 19, 1097, but to the Byzantines. The Crusaders were bent on plunder, but Emperor Alexis plied their leaders with gold and the soldiers with food.

Two weeks later, the Crusaders resumed their southward progression in two separate armies under Bohemond and Raymond of Toulouse. At dawn on July 1, the Turks attacked Bohemond's camp on the plains of Dorylaeum (present-day Eskişehir). Bohemond held off the Turks for six hours until Raymond could arrive, whereupon the combined Christian forces utterly defeated the Turks, capturing their camp and Arslan's treasury.

In November 1097, the Crusaders arrived at the rich, well-fortified city of Antioch, governed by Yaghi Siyan. The Crusaders secured the nearest port, Saint Simeon, thanks to the arrival of 13 ships from Genoa bringing men and supplies. The Crusaders then defeated a Muslim relief force coming from Syria. In early February, with defections mounting and conditions fast deteriorating, the Crusaders defeated a second Turkish relief force. Early in March, English ships arrived at Saint Simeon from Constantinople with siege machines. With yet another Turkish relief force en route, however, they were able to capture Antioch only on June 3. The Ottomans arrived several days later, only to discover the Christians in possession of the city. After an unsuccessful effort to take the city by storm, the Ottomans settled in to starve the Christians out. The situation seemed dire, but on June 28 in a bold strike the entire Christian army sortied from Antioch and defeated the Ottomans.

Following six months' respite, the Crusaders resumed their advance in mid-January 1099. Their objective was Jerusalem, the most holy city for Christians, who believe it to be the site of Christ's death and resurrection. Jerusalem had passed under Muslim control in 638; in 1099, it was ruled by the Fatimid Caliphate of Cairo. Following a 400-mile march south from Antioch along the eastern Mediterranean coast through Sidon, Acre, and Caesarea, the Crusaders arrived at Jerusalem on June 7, 1099.

During the siege of Jerusalem, Duke Godfrey commanded some 13,000 men, including 1,300 knights. The Fatimid governor of Jerusalem, Emir Iftikhar ad-Dawla, could count on 20,000 men. The defenders had poisoned nearby wells and cisterns, and the heat was oppressive. The Crusaders knew that they would have to work quickly. As early as June 12, they attempted an assault, but lacking sufficient scaling ladders and war machines, they were easily repulsed. This material arrived on June 17 when six supply ships sailed into the port of Jaffa, which had been abandoned by the Egyptians. Within several weeks the Crusaders had constructed a large number of mangonels and scaling ladders and two large wooden siege towers.

On the night of July 13–14, the Crusaders braved defensive fire to push the towers against the city walls. On the morning of July 15, Duke Godfrey led attackers in one of the towers over a wooden drawbridge; other Crusaders employed scaling ladders in a well-coordinated attack. Many of the Muslims sought refuge in the El Aqsa Mosque. Tancred, one of the Crusader leaders, promised that their lives would be spared and gave them his banner as proof.

Once the Christian forces had taken the city, they embarked on an orgy of destruction, slaughtering all Muslims who could be found regardless of location, including those within the El Aqsa Mosque. The victims included women and children. Some Muslims were beheaded, others were slain with arrows or forced to jump from the towers, and still others were tortured or burned to death. Estimates of the number slain reach as high as 70,000 people.

Jews fared no better; the Christians herded them into a synagogue and burned them alive. Their blood lust at last spent, the victors proceeded to the Church of the Holy Sepulcher, the grotto of which they believed had once held the body of the crucified Christ, and there gave thanks to the God of Mercies for their victory.

On August 2, 1099, in the Battle of Ascalon (Askelon), Duke Godfrey led 10,000 Crusaders against a relief force of 50,000 Egyptians under Emir Al-Afdal. Unlike the Turks, who relied primarily on mounted archers, the Egyptian Fatimids counted on fanaticism and shock action. They were thus at great disadvantage against the heavily armored and well-armed Crusaders. A cavalry charge gave the Christians an overwhelming victory.

The Latin Kingdom of Jerusalem lasted only 50 years, from 1099 to 1148. Its decline was in part due to the death of Godfrey of Bouillon, who was known as Defender of the Holy Sepulcher. He refused to take the title of king in a city where Christ had worn a crown of thorns. Godfrey's successors were far less capable men. The Crusades continued for more than another century with at least seven separate efforts, all of which ultimately failed. By the end of the twelfth century, the Muslims again controlled the Holy Land.

Spencer C. Tucker

Further Reading

Armstrong, Karen. *Jerusalem: One City, Three Faiths.* New York: Knopf, 1996.

Asbridge, Thomas. *The First Crusade: A New History.* New York: Oxford University Press, 2005.

Baldwin, Marshall W., ed. *A History of the Crusades.* Vol. 1, *The First Hundred Years.* Edited by Kenneth M. Setton. Madison: University of Wisconsin Press, 1969.

Riley-Smith, Jonathan, ed. *The Oxford Illustrated History of the Crusades.* New York: Oxford University Press, 1997.

Tyerman, Christopher. *Fighting for Christendom: Holy War and the Crusades.* New York: Oxford University Press, 2005.

Siege of Acre (August 28, 1189–July 12, 1191)

One of the great sieges in history, the two-year-long operation by Christian Crusaders against the port city of Acre in Palestine during 1189–1191 halted the reconquest of the Holy Land by Egyptian sultan Saladin (Salan-al-din) and helped ensure the survival of a truncated Crusader kingdom there for another century.

In the months following Saladin's great victory over the Crusaders in the Battle of Hattin on July 4, 1187, the Muslims reconquered much of the territory of the Latin Kingdom of Jerusalem. Acre surrendered without a fight on July 10; Jerusalem followed on October 2 after resisting for less than two weeks. Saladin had taken as prisoner King Guy, ruler of the Latin Kingdom of Jerusalem since 1186, but had freed Guy on the promise that he would not again fight against the Muslims. Although Guy was able to secure a ruling from the Catholic Church that the oath he had taken in captivity was null and void, he was without a kingdom.

The fall of Jerusalem prompted the Third Crusade, however, and brought Christian reinforcements under Archbishop Ubaldo of Pisa as well as Sicilian mercenaries. On August 28, 1189, Guy began an ineffectual siege of Acre. An assault

The Trebuchet

The primary heavy siege weapon of the Middle Ages was the counterweight trebuchet. Trebuchets could be very large; some had throwing arms of up to 50 feet in length and could hurl stone shot 300 yards. Repeated hits in the same area could breach even the stoutest fortifications. The counterweights consisted of large wooden hoppers up to 9 feet across and 12 feet deep, holding as much as 10 tons of stone, lead, earth, or sand. Because of their size, trebuchets were usually constructed on site with local materials. Metal fittings and rope were hauled in by wagons. Large trebuchets required crews of 50 or more men. Often, they operated in batteries in order to be able to concentrate fire on a particular point in an enemy fortification.

Spencer C. Tucker

several days later failed, and Guy appealed to the Christian states for additional assistance. A Danish fleet arrived in September and placed Acre under blockade from the sea. Ships from other European states joined this effort, and Conrad of Montferrat, who had established a kingdom at Tyre, lent troops. In October, the Crusaders assaulted Acre again but were halted in bitter fighting.

Saladin sought reinforcements from Muslim powers as far away as Spain. With this support, in both October and December, he was able to pass ships through the Christian naval blockade and bring supplies and men into Acre. He also began a land countersiege of King John's forces. Both sides built extensive trench systems and fortifications, with those of the Crusaders facing in two directions. Conrad was nevertheless able to get vital supplies to Guy by sea.

Using these supplies, during the winter of 1189, the Christians built three large siege towers and moved them against the city walls on May 1, 1190. On May 11, Saladin launched an attack on the Christian siege lines. The fighting was intense, and Saladin's attacks forced the Crusaders to fight on both fronts, allowing the defenders of Acre to burn the Crusaders' siege towers.

During the summer of 1190, more Christian reinforcements arrived, chiefly from France. The most important figure among the new Crusaders was Henry of Troyes, Count of Champagne, who took command of siege operations. In October, Germans from the army of Holy Roman Emperor Frederick Barbarossa arrived but without Frederick, who had drowned in June. The besieging Crusaders constructed both rams and trebuchets for another assault on Acre, but the defenders were again able to destroy the siege engines with inflammatory devices, beating back several major assaults.

In November, the Crusaders succeeded in opening a land supply route. That winter, however, Saladin was able to close it off and isolate the Crusaders again. The winter of 1190–1191 was especially severe and hard on the Crusaders, now suffering from disease and famine. Among the victims were Guy's wife Sybelle and their daughters. The Christians would have broken off the siege had it not been for the hope of English and French reinforcements that spring.

As promised, additional Christian manpower, ships, supplies, and money arrived under French king Philippe II Augustus on April 20, 1191, and English king Richard I (the Lion-Hearted) on June 8. Their arrival created a new sense of hope and enthusiasm among the Crusaders. With additional warships, the Crusader forces were able at last to cut off Acre entirely from the seaborne resupply. On land, the Crusaders constructed a large number of trebuchets and other artillery pieces and a large siege tower. The Crusaders concentrated their attacks on one tower, known as "The Accused."

With Acre in dire straits, Saladin attempted to draw off the Crusaders on July 3. This attack, led by his nephew, failed. The Crusaders had now opened a number of breaches in the city walls. Although the defenders repulsed three assaults, the city finally surrendered on July 12, 1191.

Acre served as the chief military base for King Richard I and his reconquest of much of the coast of Palestine to Jaffa thereafter. Almost exactly 100 years later, there was another siege of Acre. This time the Crusaders defended the city against

Image from an illustrated manuscript depicting the surrender of Acre to Christian Crusaders on July 12, 1191, following a two-year siege. The Crusaders' victory temporarily arrested the Muslim recapture of the Holy Land. (Library of Congress)

a Muslim Turkish attack. The Ottomans were victorious, capturing this last Christian enclave in Palestine in May 1291. The victors then filled in the harbor. Acre was again the site of a famous siege in 1799, when Napoleon Bonaparte and his Army of Egypt tried unsuccessfully to take the city. Failure here forced Napoleon to retreat back to Cairo.

Spencer C. Tucker

Further Reading
Gillingham, J. *Richard I.* 2nd ed. New Haven, CT: Yale University Press, 2000.
Lyons, M., and D. Jackson. *Saladin: The Politics of Holy War.* Cambridge, UK: Cambridge University Press, 1982.
Rogers, R. *Latin Siege Warfare in the Twelfth Century.* Oxford, UK: Clarendon Press, 1992.

Siege of Baghdad (January 29–February 10, 1258)

In 1258 the Ilkhanate Mongol army under Hulegu Khan moved against Baghdad. The city of Baghdad had served as the center of the Islamic world for almost 500 years. Even though the once united Abbasid Caliphate had entered its twilight, Baghdad remained an important intellectual, cultural, and religious center.

Beginning in the 1220s, the Islamic world faced a grave threat from the east as the Mongol hordes of Genghis Khan conquered Central Asia and part of Persia. In 1251 the Great Khan Mongke resolved to extend his authority to the Abbasid Caliphate. He gave his brother Hulegu command of a considerable army and tasked him with extending Mongol power into western Asia. Hulegu's army was drawn from various parts of the Mongol Empire and included military contingents from Georgia, Armenia, and engineers from China.

In 1256 Hulegu directed his men against the infamous sect of Assassins (Hashashin) who had terrorized much of the Middle East since the eleventh century. After destroying Alamut, the Assassins' stronghold, he then advanced on Baghdad. Abbasid Caliph al-Mustasim (r. 1242–1258) refused to recognize the nature of the threat posed by the Mongols and failed to make proper preparations to meet the invasion. Indeed, he sent a sarcastic defiant note to Hulegu.

In January 1258, the Mongols reached the Tigris River and approached Baghdad. Al-Mustasim then sent out a force of some 20,000 cavalry in an effort to engage them, but the attempt failed abysmally near Baghdad when the Mongols broke the dikes and flooded the Muslim camp, drowning many of the Muslims and slaying the survivors. By January 29, the Mongols had taken positions on both sides of the river, placing the city under siege.

The Chinese engineers with the Mongol army constructed siege engines and began bombarding Baghdad in early February. Lacking stone projectiles, the engineers improvised with stumps of palm trees and foundations from the occupied suburbs of Baghdad. Al-Mustasim tried to negotiate and offered to swear fealty to Hulegu, but it was too late. The Mongol leader would accept only unconditional surrender.

On February 10, with Baghdad's walls having been breached, the city surrendered. What followed remains one of the most tragic examples in history of wanton destruction of human lives and property. For days, the Mongols and their Christian auxiliaries murdered and plundered. They destroyed Baghdad's famous Grand Library with its priceless books and manuscripts on such subjects as medicine and astronomy, as well as hospitals, palaces, and mosques. Abdullah Wasaaf, a Persian historian, lamented, "They swept through the city like hungry falcons attacking a flight of doves, or like raging wolves attacking sheep, with loose reins and shameless faces, murdering and spreading terror" (qtd. in Mikaberidze, *Conflict and Conquest in the Arab World,* vol. 1, p. 175). None of the invaders set about their task with greater relish than the Georgian contingent, which was determined to avenge centuries of harassment at the hands of the caliphs.

Probably some 100,000 people died in Baghdad, although some accounts claim 800,000 to one million. Caliph al-Mustasim watched his citizens being slaughtered and then was killed on February 15. Out of respect for his position as a religious leader, Al-Mustasim's blood was not shed visibly, but instead he was sewn up in a carpet and trampled to death by horses. Thus, after more than 500 years, the Abbasid Caliphate came to an end, even though Abbasid shadow-caliphs survived in Egypt until 1517. Baghdad never recovered from this wholesale destruction and continued to linger in the shadow of its former glory for centuries to come.

Alexander Mikaberidze

Further Reading

Chambers, James. *The Devil's Horsemen: The Mongol Invasion of Europe.* New York: Atheneum, 1979.

Curtin, Jeremiah. *The Mongols: A History.* Westport, CT: Greenwood Press, 1972.

Grousset, René. *The Empire of the Steppes: A History of Central Asia.* Translated by Naomi Walford. New Brunswick, NJ: Rutgers University Press, 1970.

Mikaberidze, Alexander, ed. *Conflict and Conquest in the Arab World: A Historical Encyclopedia.* 2 vols. Santa Barbara, CA: ABC-CLIO, 2011.

Morgan David. *The Mongols.* Oxford, UK: B. Blackwell, 1986.

Spuler, Bertold. *History of the Mongols.* Berkeley: University of California Press, 1972.

Siege of Xiangyang (March 1267–March 14, 1273)

The successful siege of the city of Xiangyang (Hsiang-yang) by the Mongols led to the fall of the Song dynasty of China. Although the battle actually involved the cities of Xiangyang and Fancheng, it is usually only known as the siege of Xiangyang.

Mongol leader Ögödei (1185–1241), the third son of Genghis Khan and second Great Khan of the Mongol Empire, succeeded his father in 1229. In 1234 Ögödei conquered the Jin Empire, comprising present-day northern China. At the time, the Mongols and the Song, who ruled southern China, were allies, and the conquered territory was to have been divided between them. But Ögödei refused to do this, leading the Song to unilaterally seize the former Jin province of Henan.

A protracted war (1234–1279) then developed between the Mongols and the Song. In 1235 Ögödei called a conference of key Mongol leaders and there discussed options for future conquests. He laid down four areas for simultaneous military operations: Song China (where the campaign was already underway), Korea, Southeast Asia, and Europe.

Ögödei died in 1241, and his nephews Möngke Khan (r. 1241–1259) and Kublai Khan (r. 1260–1294) undertook the war against the Song. Operating at first under the authority of his older brother, Kublai conquered Yunnan during 1252–1253, and a subordinate took Tonkin, capturing Thang Long (present-day Hanoi in northern Vietnam) in 1257. Möngke himself directed a series of highly effective campaigns against the Song during 1257–1259, but his death from dysentery produced a dynastic struggle in the Mongol Empire and a temporary lull in fighting the Song, allowing the latter a chance to rejuvenate. Not until 1268 was Kublai, having undergone a power struggle, again able to direct full attention to the Song.

Song China territory extended from present-day Manchuria southward to northern Vietnam and westward from the China Sea for a thousand miles. The Song city of Xiangyang in present-day northwestern Hubei province of the People's Republic of China was of vast strategic importance. Situated on the Han River (a major tributary of the Yangtze) and surrounded on the other three sides by mountains, it was the key to southern China. If the Mongols could take Xiangyang and the equally formidable city of Fancheng directly across the Han they would have easy access to the Yangtze River Valley, necessary to access the southern Song cities to include the Song capital of Hangzhou.

The Song leaders understood the importance of Xiangyang and Fancheng and treated their defense as if it was their capital. The cities were well fortified with high walls and towers on all sides, and the Song stored massive amounts of supplies there in order that the city could withstand a long siege. Each entrance to the fortress was protected by two separate walls, and this might be used to trap an enemy.

Xiangyang surrendered without resistance to a Mongol army in 1236, but the Mongols voluntarily left the city two years later. In 1257 the city defeated a Mongol assault, luring a large Mongol force into the city and then trapping the attackers between the double walls and slaughtering them. In 1259 the sudden death of Möngke Khan led to the temporary withdrawal of Mongol forces from Song territory.

In 1260 Kublai Khan became ruler of the Mongols and established the Yuan dynasty. Eager to consummate his grandfather's conquest of all China, in 1267 he ordered Aju and the Song defector Liu Zheng to attack and take Xiangyang and Fancheng. Lü Wenhuan had charge of the defense with some 8,000 soldiers and 200,000 city residents.

The attackers, who numbered some 100,000 Mongols and Han Chinese, arrived at Xiangyang and Fancheng in March 1268 and soon had established a ring of forts around the cities. The Mongols had brought some 100 trebuchets. These weapons had been highly effective earlier in reducing the Jin fortresses. The trebuchets were siege engines that employed a swinging arm to hurl a projectile of slightly more than 100 pounds some 100 yards.

Anticipating such a bombardment, the defenders of Xiangyang had expanded the city moat to some 150 yards, placing the city walls beyond effective trebuchet range. They also had reinforced the walls with clay and had covered them with netting to lessen the impact of projectiles. These defensive measures proved highly effective.

With their initial plans stymied, the Mongols resorted to starving out the defenders. They established camps along the roads leading into the city and created a fleet said to number 5,000 ships on the Han as well as a series of stone platforms capped by large crossbows known as arbalests, in order to prevent Song supplies from reaching Xiangyang. All Song efforts to reach the city from the south failed, the Song forces being no match for the Mongol cavalry. A sortie by the defenders in early December fared so badly that no other such attempts were made.

Although the Song had taken extensive efforts to stockpile food within Xiangyang, by 1271 these were running low. A Song resupply effort in August 1269 failed with some 3,000 Song killed. Finally, in September 1272, another Song force of 3,000 men was able to break through the Yuan naval blockade on the Han and get some supplies to the city. News of this success failed to reach the Song court, however. It assumed that the attempt had failed and undertook no relief efforts thereafter. Meanwhile, Aju appealed to Kublai Khan for additional Chinese infantry, and he dispatched there another 20,000 men.

The siege of Xiangyang ended the next year, in 1273, owing to the introduction of the powerful counterweight trebuchet. Because the Han Chinese commander Guo Kan had fought with the Mongols in the Middle East, he was aware of these, and experts at their construction were dispatched by Abagha, the Ilkhan of Persia. By March 1273, they had constructed some 20 of these powerful mangonels. They were much more accurate than their predecessors, had an effective range of 500 yards, and could launch projectiles weighing more than 650 pounds.

The attackers first assaulted Fancheng. Under the cover of bombardment, they were able to fill in the moat and take the walls, after which there was a cavalry assault. Fancheng fell within a few days. Lü Wenhuan sent a messenger to Song emperor Duzong requesting immediate reinforcements, but on learning of the success of the new powerful trebuchets, Duzong considered Xiangyang lost and no reinforcements were sent.

It was now only a matter of time as the bombardment began to collapse buildings within the city as well as its walls. Lü Wenhuan realized Xiangyang could not long survive and surrendered it under uncharacteristically generous terms on March 14, 1273. As a part of these terms, he became governor of Xiangyang and Fancheng under Yuan rule.

With the fall of the strongest fortresses of the Song dynasty, Yuan forces were free to conquer what remained of China. The Song cities easily fell to the counterweight trebuchets and, later, gunpowder cannon. The Song dynasty came to an end on February 4, 1276, with the capture of its capital of Hangzhou and abdication of Song emperor Duzong. It took three additional years of fighting, however, before the Mongols established complete control over the entire vast Song Empire.

Spencer C. Tucker

Further Reading

Brent, Peter. *Genghis Khan: The Rise, Authority, and Decline of Mongol Power.* New York: McGraw Hill, 1976.

Hartog, Leo. *Genghis Khan, Conqueror of the World.* Reprint, New York: I. B. Taurus, 1999.

Juvayni, 'Ala' al-Din, 'Ala Malik. *Genghis Khan: The History of the World Conqueror.* Seattle: University of Washington Press, 1997.

May, Timothy. *The Mongol Art of War: Chinggis Khan and the Mongol Military System.* Yardley, PA: Westholme, 2007.

May, Timothy. *The Mongol Conquests in World History.* London: Reaktion Books, 2011.

Morgan, David. *The Mongols.* 2nd ed. Hoboken, NJ: Wiley-Blackwell, 2007.

Ratchnevsky, Paul. *Genghis Khan: His Life and Legacy.* Malden, MA: Blackwell, 1991.

Rossabi, Morris. *Kublai Khan: His Life and Times.* Berkeley: University of California Press, 1988.

Rossabi, Morris. *The Mongols: A Very Short Introduction.* New York: Oxford University Press, 2012.

Saunders, J. J. *The History of the Mongol Conquests.* Philadelphia: University of Pennsylvania Press, 2001.

Turnbull, Stephen. *Genghis Khan and the Mongol Conquests, 1190–1400.* New York: Routledge, 2003.

Siege of Calais (September 4, 1346–August 3, 1347)

The siege of Calais (September 4, 1346–August 3, 1347) occurred early in the series of wars between England and France known as the Hundred Years' War (1337–1453). Tensions could be traced back to 1066 and the conquest of England by William Duke of Normandy. The chief cause of the war was the desire of the English kings to hold on to and expand their territorial holdings in France (limited roughly to Aquitaine in southwestern France), while the kings of France sought to "liberate" territory under English control. King Edward III of England (r. 1327–1377) believed that he had a better claim to the French throne than did its occupant, the first Valois dynasty king of France, Philippe VI (r. 1330–1350). Other factors were the struggle for control both of the seas and international trading markets. Finally, the English sought retribution for French assistance to the Scots in their wars with the English.

The first phase of the war lasted from 1337 to 1396. It began with Edward dispatching raiding parties from England and Flanders to attack northern and northeastern France. In 1339 Edward invaded northern France but then withdrew before Philippe's much larger army. Philippe VI planned to turn the tables and invade England, ending Edward III's claim to the French throne. Toward that end, French admiral Hughes Quiéret assembled some 200 ships, including four Genoese galleys, off the Flemish coast in June 1340. But Edward staged a preemptive strike and secured an overwhelming victory in the naval Battle of Sluys off the coast of Flanders on June 24, 1340. This most important naval engagement of the war gave England command of the English Channel for a generation, making possible the English invasions of France and the English victories on land that followed.

Edward then landed troops and besieged Tournai, but the French forced him to raise the siege and to conclude a truce that same year. During 1341–1346, a dynastic struggle occurred in Brittany in which both Edward III of England and Philippe VI of France intervened. Edward landed at La Hogue near Cherbourg in mid-June with perhaps 15,000 men, including a heavy cavalry force of 3,900 knights and men-at-arms and a large number of archers. Most were veterans of the Scottish wars, probably the most efficient and effective military force for its size in all Europe.

The fleet returned to England, and Edward marched inland. The English took Caen on July 27 following heavy resistance. Edward ordered the entire population

---

Rodin's Sculpture The Burghers of Calais

The siege of Calais was the inspiration for an important work of art. The bronze sculpture entitled *The Burghers of Calais* is one of the best-known works by acclaimed French sculptor Auguste Rodin. Executed for the city of Calais during 1884–1889 and first cast in bronze in 1895, it stands in front of the city hall. This life-size work was controversial at the time, as it depicts the six leaders of Calais, ropes around their necks, but in pained and anguished aspects in the expectation of execution. Rodin, however, saw the men as heroic in that they were prepared to sacrifice themselves for the good of the city.

Spencer C. Tucker

killed and the town burnt. Although he later rescinded the order, perhaps 3,000 townsmen died during a three-day sack of Caen. His act set the tone for much of the war.

Edward III then moved northeast toward the Seine, pillaging as he went. Only after the English had crossed the Seine and were headed north did Philippe VI attempt to intercept. At last forced to stand and fight, Edward chose an excellent defensive position.

In one of the most important land battles of the entire war, Edward with scarcely more than 11,000 men at Crécy-en-Ponthieu on August 26, 1346, defeated an attacking French force estimated at 30,000 and 60,000 men, including 12,000 heavy cavalry of knights and men-at-arms, 6,000 Genoese mercenary crossbowmen, and a large number of poorly trained infantry. The French dead included some 1,500 knights and men-at-arms, and between 10,000 and 20,000 crossbowmen and infantrymen. Philippe VI was among the many Frenchmen wounded. English losses were only about 200 dead and wounded.

Crécy made the English a military nation. Europe was unaware of the advances made by the English military system and was stunned at this infantry victory over a numerically superior force that included some of the finest cavalry in Europe. Crécy restored the infantry to first place. Since this battle, infantry have been the primary element of ground combat forces.

After several days of rest, Edward III headed for the English Channel port of Calais and there instigated a siege. He planned to secure the port, then turn it into a secure base through which his forces could be easily supplied from England. The fact that Calais was well defended with two walls and a moat enhanced its attractiveness to Edward but also made it more difficult for the English to take. The French defense of the port was led by the capable Jean de Vienne.

The siege commenced on September 4, 1346. In November, having received siege equipment, including cannon, from England, Edward attempted an assault, which failed. Calais had been receiving some supplies by sea, and the English now closed this off completely. Not wishing to destroy the port's defenses, Edward opted for simply starving Calais into submission. In the spring, both sides received reinforcements, but the marsh land around Calais protected the English attackers from French forces attempting to raise the siege.

To ease the strain on the city of some 5,000 people, Vienne sent out 2,000 of the citizens, mostly women and children. They were considered *bouches inutiles*, useless mouths. Edward let them pass through his lines. But in June, with food and water running out, Vienne endeavored to send out another 500 children and elderly. This time Edward refused to permit passage into the English lines, and they died of starvation under the city walls. This has been contradicted by French chronicler Jean Le Bel, however, who praised Edward for his charity in feeding the expelled and providing each a small monetary gift.

Only in July 1347 did French king Philippe VI make a half-hearted attempt to relieve Calais, but his army reached only as far as Boulogne. Philippe's decision to withdraw brought the surrender of Calais on August 4. According to French chronicler Jean Froissart, Edward offered to spare the people of the city if six of its leaders would surrender themselves, presumably to be executed. Edward demanded that they walk out wearing nooses around their necks and carrying the keys to the city gates and citadel. Six prominent citizens volunteered. Froissart claimed that the burghers' lives were spared through the intervention of Edward's wife, Philippa of Hainault, who persuaded her husband that the execution of the men would be a bad omen for her unborn child. (Her son, Thomas of Windsor, lived only one year.)

Calais was the sole English territorial gain of the campaign, actually of the entire Hundred Years' War. Edward made the port of Calais an entrepôt for trade with Flanders and the empire, the only port through which English wool, lead, tin, and later cloth, could pass to continental European markets. With its defenses repaired and strengthened, Calais remained in English hands until 1558.

On September 28, 1347, the two sides concluded a truce, which, under the impact of the Black Death (plague) lasted until 1354.

Spencer C. Tucker

Further Reading
Bourne, Alfred H. *The Crécy War*. Reprint, Westport, CT: Greenwood Press, 1976.
Clowes, William Laird. *The Royal Navy: A History from the Earliest Times to the Present*. Vol. 1. London: Sampson Low, Martson, and Co., 1897.
Froissart, Jean. *Froissart's Chronicles*. Translated and edited by John Jolliffe. New York: Modern Library, 1968.
Seward, Desmond. *The Hundred Years' War: The English in France, 1337–1453*. New York: Atheneum, 1978.
Sumption, Jonathan. *The Hundred Years' War: Trial by Battle*. Philadelphia: University of Pennsylvania Press, 1988.

Siege of Orléans (October 12, 1428–May 8, 1449)

The relief of the siege of Orléans by a French army under Jeanne d'Arc (Joan of Arc) was the decisive event of the Hundred Years' War (1337–1453) between the French and the English. The course of the war had to that point constantly shifted. On October 25, 1415, King Henry V of England defeated the French in the Battle of Agincourt. Five years later, French king Charles VI agreed to the Treaty of Troyes, whereby his daughter Catherine was to marry Henry V. Charles VI also repudiated the dauphin, his son Charles, as illegitimate and acknowledged Henry as his heir. Henry V then campaigned successfully against French forces loyal to the dauphin until his untimely death in August 1422 reopened the matter of succession. The English named Henry's nine-month-old son as king of France and England. Charles VI died that October, and many French supported his son Charles, the former dauphin, as the rightful king. Charles, however, was weak, degenerate, vacillating, and utterly incapable of leadership.

In these circumstances, the regent for the young Henry VI, the Duke of Bedford, allied England with the powerful Duchy of Burgundy and on July 21, 1423, defeated the French at Cravant, establishing English rule over all of France north of the Loire River. On August 17, 1524, Bedford annihilated a French force at

Verneuil. In the autumn of 1428, English-Burgundian forces launched an offensive to secure the crossing of the Loire River at Orléans to campaign in Armagnac, the heart of Charles's territory.

Orléans was a large city and one of the strongest fortresses in France. Three of its four sides were strongly walled and moated, and its southern side rested on the Loire. The city walls were well defended by numerous catapults and 71 large cannon, and stocks of food had been gathered. Jean Dunois, Comte de Longueville, commanded the city's garrison of about 2,400 soldiers and 3,000 armed citizens.

English troops under the Earl of Salisbury arrived at Orléans on October 12, 1428. Because he had only about 5,000 men, Salisbury was not able to invest Orléans completely. Nonetheless, on October 24, the English seized the fortified bridge across the Loire, although Salisbury was mortally wounded in the attack. In December, William Pole, Earl of Suffolk, took over command of siege operations. The English constructed a number of small forts to protect the bridge as well as their encampments.

Jeanne d'Arc (Joan of Arc) played a key role in the liberation of the French city of Orléans on the Loire during the siege of October 12, 1428–May 8, 1449. (Library of Congress)

Although the French in Orléans mounted several forays and were able to secure limited supplies, by early 1429 the situation in the city was desperate, with the defenders close to starvation. Orléans was now the symbol of French resistance and nationalism. Charles was considering flight abroad, but the situation was not as bleak as it appeared. French peasants were rising against the English, and only a leader was lacking.

That person appeared in the young illiterate peasant girl, Jeanne d'Arc. She informed Charles that she had been sent by God to raise the siege of Orléans and to lead him to Reims to be crowned king of France. Charles allowed Jeanne, dressed in full armor, to lead (as *chef de guerre*) a relief army of up to 4,000 men and a convoy of supplies to Orléans. The Duc d'Alençon had actual command, however.

Jeanne's fame quickly spread far and wide, and her faith in her divine mission inspired the French. As the relief force approached Orléans, Jeanne sent a letter to Suffolk demanding surrender. Not surprisingly, he refused. Jeanne then demanded that the army circle around and approach the city from the north. The other leaders agreed; the French army was ferried to the north bank of the Loire and entered the city through a north gate on April 29.

Jeanne urged an attack on the English from the city, assuring the men of God's protection. On May 1, Jeanne awoke to learn that a French attack against the English at Fort St. Loup had begun without her and was not going well. She rode out in full armor and rallied the attackers, who were then victorious. All the English defenders were killed, while the French lost only two dead. Jeanne then insisted that the soldiers confess their sins and ban all prostitutes from the army and promised the men that they would be victorious in five days. Another appeal to the English to surrender met with derisive shouts.

On May 5, Jeanne led an attack out of the south gate of the city. The French avoided the bridge over the Loire, which the English had captured at the beginning of the siege. The French crossed through shallow water to an island in the middle of the river and from there used a boat bridge to gain the south bank. The French captured the English fort at St. Jean le Blanc and then moved against a large fort at Les Augustins, close to the bridge. The battle was costly to both sides, but Jeanne led a charge that left the French in possession of the fort.

The next day, May 6, Jeanne's troops assaulted Les Tournelles, the towers at the southern end of the bridge. Jeanne was hit by an arrow and carried from the field, but the wound was not major; by late afternoon she had rejoined the battle. On May 7, a French knight took Jeanne's banner to lead an attack on the towers. She tried to stop him, but the mere sight of the banner caused the French soldiers to follow it. Jeanne then joined the battle.

Using scaling ladders, the French assaulted the walls, with Jeanne in the thick of the fight. The 400–500 English defenders attempted to flee on the bridge, but it was soon on fire and collapsed. On May 8, the remaining English forces abandoned the siege and departed.

In his official pronouncements, Charles took full credit for the victory, but the French people attributed it to Jeanne and flocked to join her. In successive battles, most notably at Patay on June 19, the French routed the English from their Loire strongholds. In July, the French took Reims from the Burgundians, and there, on July 16, Charles was anointed king, with Jeanne in attendance in full armor and with banner in hand. The moral effect of this coronation was vast. Given the circumstances, few could doubt that Charles VII was the legitimate ruler of France.

Jeanne called for an immediate advance on Paris. Charles, however, wanted only to return to the Loire. Jeanne's attempt to capture Paris failed, and Charles signed a truce with the Duke of Burgundy. Charles ordered Jeanne to cease fighting and had her army disbanded. In May 1430, Jeanne was taken prisoner by the Burgundians. When Charles refused to ransom her, Duke Philip of Burgundy sold Jeanne to the English, who put her on trial at Rouen for heresy and sorcery and executed her in May 1431.

Although the Hundred Years' War continued for another two decades, the relief of the siege of Orléans was the turning point in the long war. Jeanne's death checked for a time the uprising of French nationality, but peace between France and Burgundy in 1435, Charles VII's effective advisers (he became known as

"Charles the Well-Served"), and military reforms in France that provided for a standing army and infantry militia finally brought the expulsion of the English. The Hundred Years' War ended with the fall of Bordeaux to the French in 1453.

Spencer C. Tucker

Further Reading
Gies, Frances. *Jean of Arc: The Legend and the Reality.* New York: Harper & Row, 1981.
Seward, Desmond. *The Hundred Years' War: The English in France, 1337–1453.* New York: Atheneum, 1978.
Sumption, Jonathan. *The Hundred Years' War: Trial by Battle.* Philadelphia: University of Pennsylvania Press, 1988.
Warner, Marina. *Joan of Arc: The Image of Female Heroism.* New York: Knopf, 1981.

Siege of Constantinople (April 6–May 29, 1453)

The successful 1453 Ottoman Turk siege of the city of Constantinople marked the end of the Byzantine Empire. Throughout the course of the fourteenth century, the Ottomans had expanded their power over Anatolia. In 1352 Ottoman forces crossed the Bosporus from Asia and established a foothold in Europe in Rumelia. From there, the Ottomans moved into Thrace. Soon they controlled the land around Constantinople, although this great Christian city on the Bosporus, the capital of the once-great Byzantine Empire, remained free of their control.

Mehmed II (Muhammad II), who became sultan in 1451, made it his principal goal to take Constantinople. In 1452 he completed construction of the Rumili Hisar (Castle of Europe) at the eastern outlet of the Bosporus on the European shore, opposite the older Anadolu Hisar (Castle of Asia) in Anatolia. These two fortresses assured Mehmed control of the passage across the straits from Anatolia to Rumelia and gave him the ability to block shipping from the Black Sea to Constantinople. In addition, artillery at Rumili Hisar could bombard Constantinople. In June 1452, Mehmed's action brought war with Byzantine emperor Constantine XI.

In addition to a highly trained Janissary corps comprised of Christian boys taken as slaves, Mehmed could call on substantial mercenary and irregular troops. The force he took to Constantinople has been variously estimated at between 100,000 and 200,000 men. He also brought some 70 artillery pieces. Many of the Ottoman guns were cast by an experienced Hungarian cannon founder and renegade named Urban. They included a dozen large bombards and one bronze gun nearly 27 feet in length with a 2.5-foot-diameter barrel that fired a 1,300-pound projectile.

During the winter of 1452–1453, Mehmed ordered the assembly of some 125 naval vessels of various types. He was well aware that previous sieges of Constantinople had failed because they were from the land only. In the spring of 1453, his fleet sailed from Gallipoli into the Sea of Marmara. With a naval force five times that of the Byzantines, Mehmed was confident he had command of the sea and could block any relief attempt. At the same time, he began moving his vast land force from Thrace. The army arrived before the walls of Constantinople on

Siege of Constantinople, Apr 6–May 29, 1453

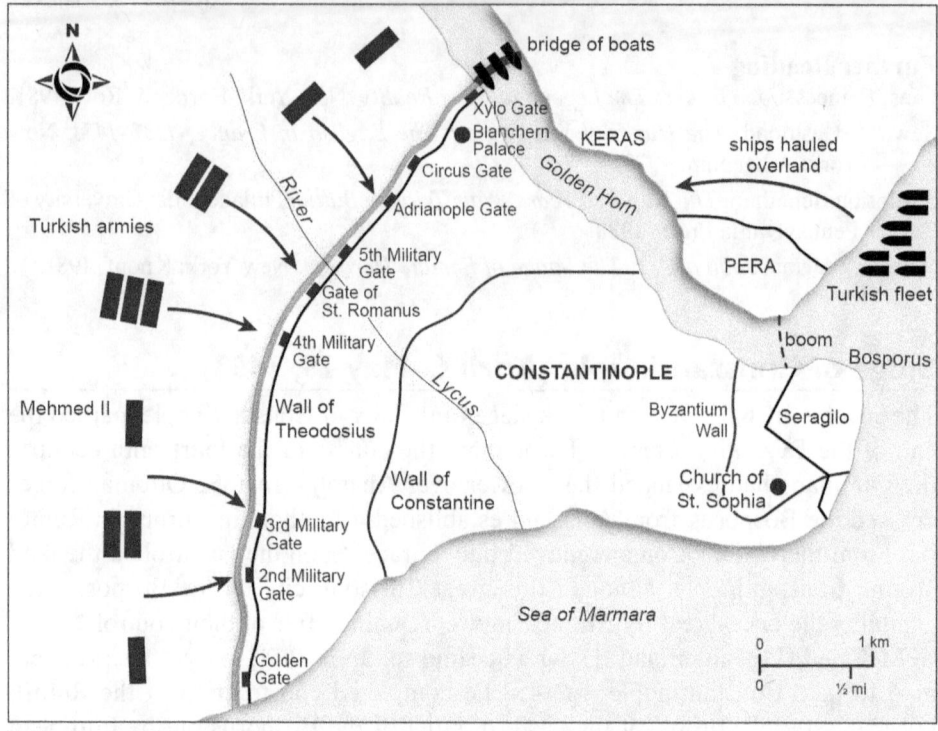

The successful Ottoman siege of Constantinople (now Istanbul) during April 6–May 29, 1453, was one of the most important events in world history, for it marked the end of the Byzantine Empire and led to the expansion of Islam into southern Europe. (ABC-CLIO)

April 2, 1453. Mehmed then sent messengers to offer the inhabitants freedom of life and property under Ottoman protection if they would surrender. These terms were rejected, and on April 6, Mehmed's heavy guns commenced fire.

Constantinople received limited aid from Venice and Genoa. To defend the city, Constantine had only 26 ships guarding the sea approaches and a small regular force of fewer than 10,000 men, 2,000 of whom were foreigners. The city's chief defense was its 14 miles of nearly impregnable walls, but this translated into one defender per 7.5 feet of wall. Actual command of the defense fell to the leader of the Genoese mercenaries and an expert in siege warfare, Giovanni Giustiniani. With news of the Ottoman approach, Constantine ordered the gates to the city closed, bridges over the moat demolished, and a great chain stretched across the mouth of the city harbor, known as the Golden Horn.

The Ottoman artillery bombardment of the western walls of the city continued for six weeks without letup, but each time there was a breach the defenders managed to fill it in and drive back the Ottoman infantry. Superior Byzantine seamanship and armaments enabled them to repulse attacks by the Ottoman fleet, but Mehmed had 70 galleys hauled overland to the Golden Horn on great greased rollers, bypassing the closed harbor entrance. When these were launched in the Golden Horn, the defenders knew that the battle was lost. Still, the Ottomans might have been repulsed had the major European powers made an effort to help defend the Christian city, but they did nothing.

By May, food in Constantinople was in short supply, and the population was starving. Toward the end of that month the Ottomans managed to create a breach in the wall that the defenders could not completely block, and early on the morning of May 29, the Ottomans launched a great assault, accompanied by trumpets, drums, and war cries. Following human wave assaults, the Ottoman troops forced an entry. Although many of the defenders took refuge in the ships, Constantine refused to flee. He removed his insignia, plunged into battle with the oncoming Janissaries, and was promptly slain.

After a disciplined march into Constantinople, the conquerors broke ranks and for three days subjected the city to an orgy of slaughter and pillage, carrying off not only the contents of palaces and houses but also their attractive young inhabitants as well. Mehmed entered the city on horseback with a guard of Janissaries the evening it was taken and made his way to the great church of Hagia Sophia, which he ordered transformed into a mosque.

Regarded as a seminal event in the history of the West, the fall of Constantinople was a great psychological and strategic blow to the European powers. It ended the Byzantine Empire, which had been the last buffer between Europe and the Ottomans. Mehmed II, now known as Mehmed the Conqueror, renamed the city Istanbul and made it his capital. The city faced both Asia and Europe, and over the next several decades Mehmed directed from it the extension of Ottoman power to include Serbia, Greece, Albania, the Aegean, and even Otranto in southern Italy. Mehmed died in May 1481. Over the next two centuries, his successors mounted repeated offensives to push Ottoman control west into the Mediterranean and north into Central Europe.

Spencer C. Tucker

Further Reading
Browning, Robert. *Byzantine Empire.* New York: Scribner, 1980.
Gibbon, Edward. *The Decline and Fall of the Roman Empire, 1185–1453.* New York: Modern Library, 1983.
Kinross, Lord [John Patrick]. *The Ottoman Centuries: The Rise and Fall of the Turkish Empire.* New York: William Morrow, 1977.
Norwich. John Julius. *Byzantium: The Decline and Fall.* New York: Knopf, 1996.

Siege of Granada (Mid-April 1491–January 2, 1492)

The Arabs first raided southern Spain in 710. The next year Taraq, a freed Berber slave, mounted a true invasion across the Strait of Gibraltar, beginning the rapid Arab conquest of Spain. The Muslim expansion northward was halted in the Battle of Tours in France in 732, but the Moors (as the Spanish Muslims were known) ruled in Spain for the next seven and a half centuries. In the far north of

Spain, a few Christian fortresses held out, and in the late eleventh century the Christian Spanish began the Reconquista (the long Christian effort to reconquer Spain) under Rodrigo Díaz de Bivar, known as El Cid (from the Arabic *al-sayyid*, or "chieftain"), who took Valencia in 1094. King Alfonso VIII of Castile was victorious at Navas de Tolosa in 1212.

From the middle of the thirteenth century, the two sides faced one another in established positions, the Christian kingdoms in the north and the only remaining Moorish territory, the Kingdom of Granada, on the southern coast of Spain. At the end of the fifteenth century, the marriage of Queen Isabella of Castile and Ferdinand II of Aragon united Christian Spain, and the Reconquista recommenced in earnest.

Muhammad XI, born Abu Abdullah and known to the Spanish as Boabdil, ruled the Kingdom of Granada from the famous Alhambra Palace in the beautiful fortified city of Granada. Under pressure from the powerful Christian kingdoms to the north, Muhammad had agreed to give over Granada to Ferdinand and Isabella if they could conquer Baza, Cádiz, and Almería. Thus, the siege of Granada was part of general operations throughout Granada.

By early 1488, the forces of Ferdinand and Isabella had conquered the western half of Granada. In June, Ferdinand advanced with his forces from his headquarters at Loja to Vera, which promptly surrendered. He then advanced on Almería, which, according to secret agreements, was also to surrender to him without a fight. This did not happen, and Ferdinand then withdrew with his forces. He recommenced operations in the spring of 1489 and laid siege to Baza with 13,000 cavalry and 40,000 infantry. With Baza resisting and Ferdinand's resources nearing exhaustion, Queen Isabella pawned her own jewels to enable the continuation of operations and joined her husband before the city, which capitulated on December 4, 1489. After taking Baza, Ferdinand and Isabella moved against Almería, which promptly surrendered. The monarchs then entered the city and received the fealty of its inhabitants. The same occurred at Cádiz. Ferdinand then sent emissaries to Muhammad to demand that he fulfill the agreement. The Moorish king replied that it was impossible for him to fulfill the pact's conditions immediately. However, Muhammad's true response became clear when his forces occupied the Christian fortress of Padul near Granada. He intended to fight.

In the spring of 1490, Ferdinand ordered all the trees cut down and crops destroyed in the fertile plain around the city of Granada in preparation for operations against the Moorish stronghold. Although Muhammad's cavalry carried out attacks on the Christian forces engaged in this activity and killed many of them, this did not prevent the operations from being completed. A belt of destruction now extended around the city of Granada. In reprisal, Muhammad's forces attacked and captured the Christian fortress of Alhendin, leading to a revolt of Moors in the surrounding area. Moorish forces also moved against other locations, especially the coastal city of Salobreña, to allow regular resupply from the Muslim Kingdom of Barbary in North Africa. The Christian garrison managed to hold out, however, and word that Ferdinand was arriving with a relief force caused the Muslim besiegers to withdraw to Granada.

In September, Ferdinand ordered destruction of the grain crop around Granada and then withdrew his forces to Córdoba. Muhammad then stirred up revolt against the Christian rulers in Almería, Baza, and Cádiz. Ferdinand then moved against Cádiz, his presence there restoring calm. In order to be certain of the security of his new territory, Ferdinand ordered all Moorish inhabitants of fortified cities to leave them and live in open cities or sell their property and relocate to Barbary.

In the spring of 1491, Ferdinand and Isabella finally began serious military operations against Granada. Ferdinand dispatched the Marquis of Villena with 3,000 cavalry and 10,000 infantry to destroy fortifications in the Lecrin Valley. Fearing that Villena might be ambushed, Ferdinand followed close behind with the rest of the army. Villena was successful, however, and Ferdinand then ordered the destruction of everything of value in the valley. Muhammad occupied the Tablate and Lanjaron passes, hoping to ambush Ferdinand's forces on their return. This failed, however, and Catholic forces drove the Moors from the passes. Ferdinand's entire army then assembled on the plain before Granada.

On April 26, 1491, Ferdinand opened the siege of Granada, establishing his headquarters in the nearby village of Atqa. Isabella remained in the field with her husband to observe events and inspire the troops. Granada was situated on two hills, with the Alhambra crowning one and the Alcazaba fortress the other. The Darro River ran between the two hills, and a long wall with numerous watchtowers and strong points surrounded the city. There were few major confrontations. One occurred in July, which the Spanish won, and the Moors attempted a number of small sorties, but all were beaten back.

By September, the inhabitants of Granada were in desperate straits, the population of the city having swelled just prior to the siege. Realizing that relief from Muslim forces in North Africa would not be forthcoming and that there was no hope of reversing the situation, Muhammad entered secret negotiations with King Ferdinand. On November 25, 1491, Muhammad agreed to generous terms. The Muslims were to surrender all their artillery and fortresses but were able, for the time being, to continue practice of their religion, to keep their own language and customs, to be governed by their own laws, and to dispose of their property as they wished. They would also be exempt from royal taxation for a period of three years. Muhammad received the small territory of Alpujarras but would govern as a vassal of Castile. These terms were to go into effect in 60 days, but with opposition to Muhammad protesting this arrangement, the surrender was moved forward, and Ferdinand received the keys to the city from Muhammad's own hand on January 2, 1492.

The capitulation marked the end of the long Muslim rule in Spain and the consolidation of the Spanish kingdoms into one state. This long religious Crusade also resulted in Spanish nationalism being closely identified with the Catholic Church. Despite the terms granted in the capitulation of Granada, the militant Catholicism of Spain soon led to the persecution of people of both the Islam and Jewish faiths.

Spencer C. Tucker

Further Reading

Fernández-Armesto, Felipe. *Ferdinand and Isabella*. New York: Taplinger, 1975.

Harvey, L. P. *Islamic Spain, 1250 to 1500*. Chicago: University of Chicago Press, 1990.

Hillgarth, J. N. *The Spanish Kingdoms, 1250–1516*. 2 vols. Oxford, UK: Clarendon Press, 1976–1978.

Melegari, Vezio. *The Great Military Sieges*. New York: Crowell, 1972.

Siege of Tenochtitlán (May 26–August 13, 1521)

The siege and capture of the Aztec capital of Tenochtitlán during May 26–August 13, 1521, was the most important event in the Spanish conquest of Mexico. The Aztecs, or people from Aztlan in the north (they were also known as the Mexica), came to dominate much of the region. Their society was highly developed, with a complex governmental structure and long-distance trade, but they had limited scientific knowledge and no modern weaponry.

In the mid-fourteenth century, the Aztecs established their capital in the city of Tenochtitlán (present-day Mexico City) on an island on the western side of Lake Texcoco connected to the shore by long causeways. The Aztecs worshiped Huitzilopochtli (the god of the sun and war) and other deities. Believing that daily human sacrifices were necessary to keep the sun healthy and shining, they built altars to Huitzilopochtli and the other gods in the form of great pyramids that dominated the city. On special days thousands of prisoners might be sacrificed. This practice did not endear the Aztecs to their conquered peoples and created ready allies for the Spaniards. Ultimately, Tenochtitlán came to be a large and wealthy city of approximately 60,000 buildings and 200,000 people, perhaps one-fifth of the total Aztec population. A million or so Aztecs ruled a subject population of perhaps 5 million.

In 1519, 34-year-old Hernán Cortés landed on the west coast of Mexico from his base in Cuba under orders to establish a coastal trading post. Cortés, however, was determined to explore the mysterious land of the west, which was rumored to abound in gold. Cortés commanded a small force of 550 men with some 17 horses and 10 small cannon. In August, he began his march to the interior, and during the next month he defeated the Tlaxcalan people in a series of battles and captured their capital of Tlaxcala. The Tlaxcalans then allied themselves with the Spaniards.

In November 1519, Emperor Montezuma II received Cortés at Tenochtitlán with all possible honors. The Spaniards, who were dazzled by the gold and wealth of the capital, soon made clear their intention to rule. Cortés was able to capitalize in part on the Aztec belief in a great white god, Quetzalcoatl, whose return had been prophesied. With their horses, metal armor, and firearms, the Spaniards could play the part.

Following the death of some Spanish soldiers on the coast near Veracruz, Cortés seized Montezuma and began to rule through him. This worked until Cortés sought to introduce Christianity. In the spring of 1520, Cortés departed Tenochtitlán to do battle with a rival Spanish force sent by his superior, Cuban governor

Siege of Tenochtitlán, May 26–Aug 13, 1521

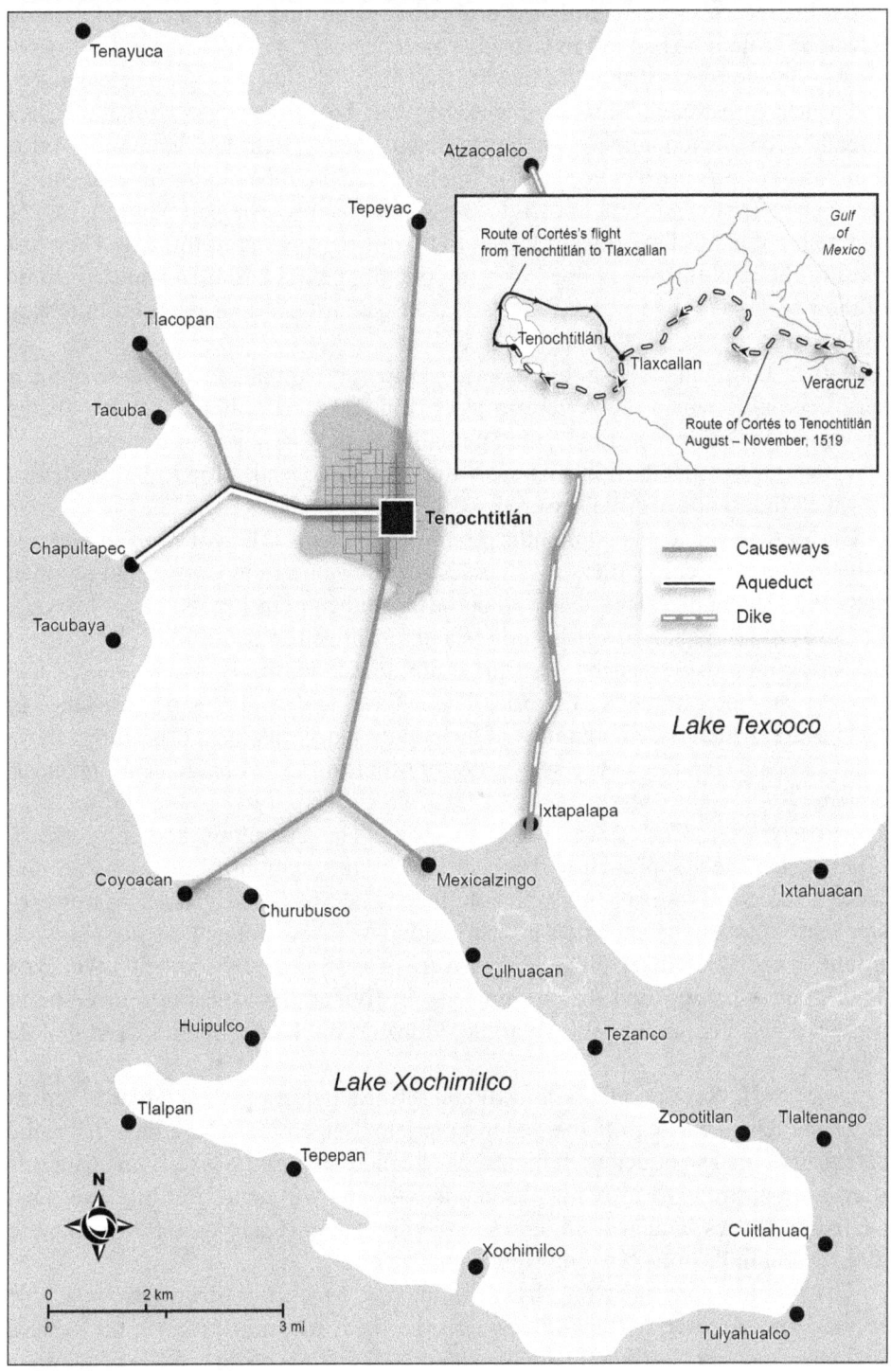

The successful siege of the Aztec capital city of Tenochtitlán (today Mexico City) by Spanish conquistadors and allied native forces during May 26–August 13, 1521, marked the end of the Aztec Empire and the Spanish conquest of Mexico. (ABC-CLIO)

Diego Velázquez, to punish Cortés for disobeying orders. Cortés defeated that force and added the men he captured to his own forces.

On his return to Tenochtitlán, Cortés discovered that his lieutenant Pedro de Alvarado, whom he had left in charge, was under siege by the Aztecs. While Cortés was able to reestablish his authority, the situation in the city soon deteriorated, and warfare resumed. Montezuma was killed, but his brother Cuitláhuac had already been elected emperor by chiefs determined to fight the Spaniards. Aztec numbers now prevailed over Spanish firepower, and on the night of June 30–July 1 (La Noche Triste as it was known to the Spaniards, or "The Sad Night"), Cortés and many of his followers were forced to fight their way out of the city. They lost most of the gold they had hoped to bring out along with 600 men and two-thirds of their 68 horses. The Aztecs harassed the Spaniards in their retreat all the way to Tlaxcala.

Rather than pursue a guerrilla war, Emperor Cuitláhuac chose to fight a set-piece battle where the Aztec warriors came up against horse cavalry for the first time. At Otumba on July 7, the Spaniards used their 28 horses to great advantage, driving against the conspicuously dressed Aztec leadership to win a victory in which thousands of Aztecs were killed.

Cortés then spent several months rebuilding his force. He sent ships to Jamaica to fetch replacement artillery and horses. At the same time Cortés had his men construct 13 small brigantines to approach Tenochtitlán across Lake Texcoco. Each vessel carried 25 Spanish soldiers and 12 native rowers.

Cortés was also aided by a surprise ally, for unwittingly the Spaniards had brought smallpox to the New World. The natives had absolutely no resistance to the disease, which wiped out much of the population. Cuitláhuac was among those who perished. Cuauhtémoc, a son-in-law of Montezuma, succeeded Cuitláhuac as emperor.

In early 1521, Cortés was ready to move. The Spaniards and their native allies began their approach to Tenochtitlán by taking control of towns around Lake Texcoco. By April, this was complete. The Spaniards had 184 harquebusiers, crossbowmen, and men-at-arms along with 86 horsemen, perhaps 700 infantry, and 18 artillery pieces. They were greatly aided by some 50,000 allied Tlaxcalans who opposed Aztec rule. Cortés divided his forces into three main groups under his lieutenants Alvarado, Gonzalo de Sandoval, and Cristóbal de Olid.

On May 26, forces under Sandoval and Alvarado destroyed the great aqueduct at Chapultepec, cutting off the water supply to Tenochtitlán. Five days later, the Aztecs mounted an attack with hundreds of canoes across the lake. The Spaniards used cannon fire to destroy most of the canoes and win control of the lake. That same day Cortés launched an attack on Tenochtitlán. Some crossbowmen were able to land in the city, but they were soon driven out.

The fighting continued for 10 weeks, during which the Spaniards were able to view the sacrifice by the Aztecs atop the great pyramid of those the Aztecs had taken prisoner. At night, the defenders made fresh breaks in the causeways providing access to the city, but the Spaniards and their allies were able to repair them. The Aztecs mounted human wave attacks, which the Tlaxcalans defeated at high cost. Finally, on August 13, Cortés launched an assault that brought victory the next day. Only a few Aztec survivors escaped in canoes. Reportedly, 150,000 people died in the city. One Spanish eyewitness said that it was impossible to walk in Tenochtitlán without stepping on corpses.

Following the capture of Tenochtitlán, Cortés set about completely dismantling Aztec society and replacing it with Spanish civilization. He was assisted in this by the continued ravages of smallpox that may have wiped out 90 percent of the native population. Within a generation, both the Aztec language and religion had disappeared. Spain would be the dominant power in the region for the next 300 years.

Spencer C. Tucker

Further Reading
Carrasco, David. *Montezuma's Mexico.* Niwot: University of Colorado Press, 1992.
Diaz del Castillo, Bernal. *The Discovery and Conquest of Mexico, 1517–1521.* Translated by A. P. Maudslay. New York: Harper, 1928.
White, Jon Manchip. *Cortés and the Downfall of the Aztec Empire.* London: Hamish Hamilton, 1971.

Siege of Rhodes (July 28–December 21, 1522)

Rhodes is the largest of the Dodecanese islands in the eastern Mediterranean and lies about 10 miles from Anatolia. The Knights of St. John (Hospitallers) controlled Rhodes in the sixteenth century, the last Christian holding in the eastern Mediterranean. The siege of Rhodes during July 28–December 21, 522, pitted the Knights of St. John against a large invading Ottoman force commanded by sultan Suleiman I (Süleyman I).

The Knights of St. John had been in possession of Rhodes since 1310, and over the years they fortified both its harbor and its high ground. The knights used the island, astride major Ottoman shipping lanes, to raid Muslim shipping throughout the eastern Mediterranean. This led Sultan Mehmed II (Mehmed the Conqueror) to mount an unsuccessful three-month siege of the island in 1480.

Continued raiding from Rhodes induced Ottoman sultan Suleiman I to plan a major effort against the island. In 1522 Suleiman assembled some 400 ships, 100,000 men, and siege artillery. On Rhodes, the grand master of the Knights of St. John Auguste de Villiers de L'Isle-Adam commanded only about 5,700 men: 700 knights drawn from all over Christendom, 500 mercenaries from Crete, 500 Genoese, 50 Venetians, and 4,000 men-at-arms from other places. The knights did what they could to prepare for the attack. They closed off the entrance to the port with great chains, laid in supplies, and even demolished some buildings to create better fields of fire. Each of the principal defensive positions on the island was held by a particular language grouping.

The Ottoman host arrived off Rhodes on June 26 and anchored off Parambolino in the north, where the Ottoman troops landed uncontested. Among the artillery brought ashore were 40 bombards and 12 large basilisks. The

> **Ottoman Sultan Suleiman I, the Magnificent (r. 1520–1566)**
>
> Suleiman I was probably the greatest of Ottoman rulers. At war almost constantly throughout his 45-year reign, Suleiman greatly expanded Ottoman power. Not only a great military leader, Suleiman also accomplished a great deal domestically. He reformed the Ottoman administrative structure, improved education, codified and simplified laws (leading to the appellation of Suleiman the Lawgiver), and carried out a major building program in Istanbul. His rule saw the height of Ottoman influence, but decline set in soon thereafter.
>
> **Spencer C. Tucker**

Ottoman engineers took about a month to position their ordnance, opening fire on July 28. The Ottomans fired explosive shell, the first recorded use in battle in history. When this shelling failed to have the desired effect, at the end of August the Ottomans commenced mining operations. The defenders were well aware of this and dug countermines, setting off explosions against the Ottoman tunnels and venting them to disperse the blasts. Attempts to take the principal Christian stronghold, commanded by the grand master in person, were unsuccessful. The knights also launched a number of effective counterattacks.

Suleiman's forces had suffered heavily, and morale among them was low; Suleiman is said to have lost upward of half his force. In recognition of both the tremendous costs of the siege and the heroic Christian defense, on December 10, he offered to discuss a Christian surrender on honorable terms. The onset of winter, their own precarious position, dwindling numbers and supplies, and unrest among the civilian population all prompted the knights to negotiate. On December 21, agreement was reached. Suleiman allowed the knights to depart the island with the full honors of war, their arms, their religious relics, and the treasury of the Order. Such civilians as wished to leave could also depart and take with them portable possessions.

The knights departed Rhodes on January 1, 1523. The siege had lasted 145 days. At least temporarily, Suleiman had removed the last serious threat to Ottoman naval power in the eastern Mediterranean and Aegean. For five years, the knights were homeless, but they eventually took up residence in Malta, from which they continued to harry Ottoman shipping. This induced Suleiman in 1565 to order military operations against that island, although these operations were unsuccessful.

Spencer C. Tucker

Further Reading

Brockman, Eric. *The Two Sieges of Rhodes: The Knights of St. John at War, 1480–1522.* New York: Barnes and Noble, 1995.

Kinross, Lord [John Patrick]. *The Ottoman Centuries: The Rise and Fall of the Turkish Empire.* New York: William Morrow, 1977.

Prata, Nicholas C. *Angels in Iron.* Huntingdon Valley, PA: Arx Publishing, 1997.

Siege and Battle of Pavia (October 28, 1524–February 24, 1525)

The siege and Battle of Pavia (October 28, 1624–February 24, 1525) were part of the Italian War of 1521–1526. In 1515 King François (Francis) I of France had invaded northern Italy and taken Milan. In 1521 François and Holy Roman Emperor (and king of Spain) Charles V began formal hostilities. François claimed Navarre and Naples, while Charles laid claim to Milan and Burgundy. Although some fighting occurred in northeastern France and north of the Pyrenees in Navarre, the chief battleground became northern Italy. Fighting began with French invasions of first Luxembourg and then Navarre, but in late November 1521, in a surprise attack, imperial forces captured Milan.

In April 1522, in the Battle of Bicocca near Milan, imperial troops under Italian condottiere Prosper Colonna defeated a larger French and Swiss force. The battle demonstrated the superiority of gunpowder small arms, the Spanish harquebus, against attacking Swiss infantry. Bicocca brought the expulsion of the French from Lombardy.

On September 28, François, at the head of 40,000 French troops, raised the imperial siege of Marseille and then pushed into northern Italy, retaking the city of Milan. Leaving a small force to garrison the city, François moved the bulk of his army to Pavia, 21 miles south of Milan on the lower Ticino River near its confluence with the Po. The French arrived there on October 28, 1524. Some 5,000 German mercenaries along with 1,000 other mercenary troops and Italian levies defended the city.

Since no moat protected the city outside the walls, François immediately ordered artillery fire opened. The heavy French guns created a breach, but a following infantry attack encountered an interior moat full of water and came under heavy musket fire. François then decided to invest the city. Several weeks of work to divert the Ticino River from Pavia were wiped out by a sudden storm,

---

The Harquebus (Arquebus)

The harquebus (arquebus) was the term for any type of early long individual firearm. In the late fourteenth and early fifteenth centuries, a wide variety of individual firearms appeared. These were unwieldy and heavy, difficult to load, and usually were fired from a simple forked rest.

To fire the weapon, the soldier would pour a set amount of gunpowder down the muzzle, then ram a round ball (usually of lead) wrapped in a cloth wad to hold the ball tightly against the powder charge at the bottom of the bore. The charge was ignited by means of a slow-burning match applied to the small hole (touch hole) in the top of the breech end of the barrel. Shoulder stocks appeared around 1470, and by the early 1500s hand-held firearms with new ignition mechanisms had arrived on the battlefield to stay.

Although early gunpowder weapons were difficult to handle and wildly inaccurate, infantrymen with them could kill or maim knights on horseback. Such weapons in the hands of well-trained individual infantrymen eventually ended the primacy of horse cavalry and knights on the battlefields of Europe.

Spencer C. Tucker

so François decided to starve out the city. At the same time, however, he detached John Stuart, Duke of Albany, and a force of 15,000 men from his army to conquer Naples. This left him 26,000 men (2,000 of them cavalry) to maintain the siege of Pavia.

Meanwhile, some 20,000 imperial troops of Charles de Bourbon and a force under Georg Frundsberg, a south German knight in imperial service, gathered at Lodi before moving to Pavia on January 24. Viceroy of Naples Charles de Lannoy had nominal command, with the actual field command apparently exercised by the Spaniard Ferdinando Francisco d'Avalos, Marquis of Pescara. François detached part of his army to meet the imperial forces, digging defenses along the most likely route, while the bulk of his army continued the siege. During much of February, the two armies faced one another across an unfordable stream and exchanged artillery fire. François further diminished the size of his army when he detached 6,000 Swiss to strengthen his lines of communication back to Switzerland, which were being harassed by imperial forces. This left him with fewer than 20,000 men.

During the stormy night of February 23–24 under cover of an artillery bombardment and leaving only a small detachment behind to fool the French, the imperial forces disengaged and marched several miles to their right, crossed the brook, and turned the French left to attack the principal French camp, located in a large park at Mirabello north of Pavia. By dawn on February 24, the imperial forces had broken through the park wall and were drawn up in battle line about a mile north of the French camp.

To win time for his army to shift position and come up, François personally led a charge by his heavy cavalry against the imperial left flank. This caught the imperial forces by surprise and temporarily scattered their cavalry. Over the course of several hours the Spanish infantry used harquebus fire to halt first the French cavalry and then the infantry. With few harquebuses and crossbowmen, the French side was unable to silence the opponents' fire. To make matters worse, about a third of their forces, under Duke Charles d'Alençon, were never engaged, and some 8,000 Swiss defected.

François led dwindling cavalry charges until his horse was killed, and he was badly wounded and taken prisoner. The Duke d'Alençon then led the remaining French forces in a retreat westward. The French sustained about 8,000 killed or wounded, including many prominent nobles. Most of the casualties were the result of Spanish harquebus fire. Among the hardest hit were 5,000 German mercenaries in French service who died without retreating when attacked by two squares of imperial pikemen (each square containing 6,000 pikes). Imperial troops killed or wounded came to only about 1,500 men. François remarked of the battle, "Tout est perdu, hors l'honneur" ("All is lost, except honor").

The Battle of Pavia gave the imperial side temporary advantage in the long Valois-Habsburg Wars (1494–1559). It also marked the beginning of the decline of heavy cavalry and the predominance of infantry with firearms as decisive in warfare. François I, held prisoner in Madrid, was obliged to sign the Treaty of Madrid of January 14, 1526, by which he gave up all claims in Italy and surrendered Burgundy, Artois, and Flanders to Charles V.

Spencer C. Tucker

Further Reading

Casali, Luigi, and M. Galandra. *La battaglia di Pavia: 24 Febbraio 1525.* Pavia: Luculano, 1984.

Giono, Jean. *The Battle of Pavia, 24 February 1525.* London: Peter Owen, 1965.

Knecht, R. J. *Renaissance Warrior and Patron: The Reign of Francis I.* Cambridge, UK: Cambridge University Press, 1994.

Konstam, Angus. *Pavia, 1525: The Climax of the Italian Wars.* London: Osprey, 1996.

Siege of Vienna (September 24–October 14, 1529)

Bitter struggles between the major European powers in the 1520s presented the perfect opportunity for outside military intervention. The rivalry between King François I of France and Holy Roman Emperor Charles V divided much of Europe, allowing Ottoman sultan Suleiman I (Süleyman I) to open a campaign to restore his authority north of the Danube River and capture Vienna. Strategically located on the Danube, the city of Vienna was both the capital of the Habsburg Empire and a bastion of Germanic civilization and Christian Europe against the Slavs, the Magyars, and then the Ottomans.

On August 29, 1526, Ottoman forces had won a great but sanguinary victory at Mohács that gave them control of Hungary. Ottoman military forces were in fact as advanced as those of the West European powers, especially in heavy siege artillery and in heavy infantry. The Janissaries, formed of Christian children converted to Islam, were a particularly well-disciplined force.

In 1526 Suleiman took Buda. János Zápolya (Szapolyai) then claimed the Hungarian throne. Archduke Ferdinand of Austria (who was also king of Bohemia) contested this, and a rebellion broke out in Hungary, with Ferdinand ousting Szapolyai. This situation was unacceptable to Suleiman, and in the summer of 1529, he returned to Hungary at the head of a large army, determined to reverse the situation there and take Vienna. During September 3–8, the Ottomans stormed Buda, massacred most of its defenders, and swept aside Ferdinand's advance posts. The Ottomans then moved along the Danube River to the chief prize of Vienna.

As soon as Archduke Ferdinand learned of Suleiman's plans, he had called on his brother monarchs in Europe for assistance, but few responded with troops. Meanwhile, authorities in Vienna oversaw preparations to resist an Ottoman assault. They gathered in food, ammunition, and other stores; removed many of the women and children from the city to ease the strain on supplies; positioned the 72 pieces of artillery available to them; cleared fields of fire; and effected such interim repairs as were possible under the circumstances to the relatively low 250-year-old city walls. Philip, Count Palatine of Austria, had charge of the defense, ably assisted by Count Nicholas zu Salm-Reifferscheidt and Field

Marshal Wilhelm von Roggendorff. The defending troops numbered some 22,000 infantry and 2,000 cavalrymen.

Suleiman, however, commanded a vast force. Counting the garrisons that he had gathered en route, the Hungarian levies under King Szapolyai allied to him, and camp followers, Suleiman's force may have numbered as many as 350,000 people, although the actual Ottoman fighting force at Vienna was probably on the order of 120,000 men. The first Ottoman skirmishers arrived at Vienna on September 23, although the main army did not come up and surround the city until four days later, when the siege officially began. Some 400 ships of the Ottoman Navy meanwhile controlled the Danube.

The weather turned out to be a key factor aiding the defenders. It was a rainy autumn, and winter set in early. This delayed the Ottoman supply trains and prevented Suleiman from bringing up his heavy artillery. Although he had 300 guns immediately available, they were too small to effect serious breaches in the city's walls.

Suleiman sent emissaries to demand the defenders' surrender. If they failed to do so, he promised that he would destroy the city so completely that nothing of it would remain. Receiving no reply, Suleiman began daily artillery fire against Vienna and commenced mining operations to blow holes in the walls and utilize his superior numbers of infantry. Made aware of Suleiman's plans by a deserter, the defenders commenced countermining, resulting in a number of underground battles. The defenders also made several sorties from the city to disrupt Ottoman siege operations but with little effect.

On October 12, the Ottomans managed to breach the city wall with a mine, but the hole was not sufficiently large, and the defending pikemen were able to hold the Janissaries at bay, killing 1,200. That same night Suleiman met with his principal lieutenants and surveyed the situation. Supplies were insufficient to sustain his vast force. Suleiman's was basically a summer army, and winter was approaching.

Suleiman decided on one last attempt. On October 14, the Ottomans again exploded a mine under the city walls, but the section of wall fell outward, creating problems for the attackers. Despite hard fighting, the defenders again held.

On October 15, Vienna awoke to find that the sea of tents pitched before the city had disappeared. The Ottomans had struck camp, massacred their prisoners (except those young enough to qualify for the slave market), and departed. The harsh winter took a heavy toll on the army as it slowly withdrew southward to Istanbul, harassed also by Christian cavalry. The bells of Vienna peeled out in celebration amid salvos of gunfire.

Had Suleiman taken Vienna in 1529, he could have spent the winter there and then resumed campaigning in the spring in an invasion of Germany. It is by no means clear what France might have done in those circumstances. Suleiman returned to Austria in 1532, but a spirited imperial defense at Güns (Köszeg) and Emperor Charles V's success in assembling a substantial European force dissuaded him from further advance. Suleiman returned to Hungary in 1541, however, to recapture it from an invasion mounted by Ferdinand.

Spencer C. Tucker

Further Reading
Bridge, Anthony. *Suleiman the Magnificent: Scourge of Heaven.* New York: Dorset, 1987.
Clot, Andre. *Suleiman the Magnificent.* London: Saqi Books, 1992.
Kinross, Lord [John Patrick]. *The Ottoman Centuries: The Rise and Fall of the Turkish Empire.* New York: William Morrow, 1977.

Siege of Malta (May 18–September 8, 1565)

In 1522, following a six-month Ottoman siege of Rhodes in the Dodecanese Islands, the Christian Knights of St. John of Jerusalem (Hospitallers) were forced to surrender to the Ottomans. With his forces having sustained heavy casualties and impressed by the knights' valor, Ottoman emperor Suleiman I (Süleyman I) spared the defenders' lives, a decision he would have cause to regret.

In 1530 Holy Roman Emperor Charles V gave the knights his possession of Malta. This island, strategically located in the narrows of the central Mediterranean, controlled east-west access and allowed the knights to raid to the east. At the same time, the Ottomans were conquering much of the North African coast and even raiding out into the Atlantic. Malta was the only barrier to Ottoman control of the entire Mediterranean Sea.

Supposedly Suleiman's influential daughter Mihrimah encouraged him to undertake the campaign on religious grounds. Suleiman's trusted military adviser and commander of his galleys, Dragut Torghoud, agreed. A competent artillerist, Dragut had taken Tripoli from the knights for the sultan and became its governor. There was popular support for such an operation, particularly after the knights captured a large Ottoman merchant ship on its way from Venice to Istanbul.

Suleiman was then 70 years old and did not attempt to lead the expedition in person. He appointed Piale Pasha to command the naval force and his old general Mustafa Pasha to head the land operations. Suleiman also sent along as advisers Dragut and Uluj Ali, insisting that his two commanders consult with them. The Ottoman naval force consisted of some 150 galleys, while the land force numbered 28,000 men, including 7,000 Janissaries.

About 5,000 men, most of them Spaniards, defended Malta. They were led by the grand master of the Knights of St. John, Jean Parisot la Valette. La Valette had been born in the same year as Suleiman and fought against him in the siege of Rhodes. La Valette combined effective military leadership with Christian fanaticism. Aware of Ottoman preparations, he sent out a call for assistance from all the knights in other countries, and a number responded. The people of Malta remembered what had happened at the hands of the Ottomans in 1551. The Ottomans had invaded with 10,000 men but then withdrew after only several days to move on to the neighboring island of Gozo. Its citadel surrendered after several days of bombardment, whereupon the Ottomans sacked Gozo and made slaves of virtually its entire population of 5,000 people. Now in 1565, the people of Malta were determined to resist the invaders. Galleys from Malta also ferried in supplies from Sicily.

Two main forts, St. Angelo and St. Michael, guarded the city of Malta. A brief raid by Dragut convinced the defenders to add a new fort, St. Elmo, to protect the entrance to the Grand Harbor and a parallel inlet, the Middle Harbor or Marsa Muscet, north of it. Just before the Ottomans arrived, the knights also placed a great chain across the Grand Harbor of the city of Malta.

The great Ottoman force arrived off Malta on May 18, 1565. The Ottomans were confident of an easy victory. The Ottoman naval and land commanders had decidedly different views on how to proceed, however. Ultimately Piale Pasha's views prevailed, and the Ottomans decided to first take the Marsa Muscet as a fleet anchorage. To accomplish this, they would have to reduce Fort St. Elmo.

The Ottomans were well equipped with artillery, including three cannon especially cast for this undertaking. One gun reputedly weighed 40 tons and fired 200-pound round shot, and the other two guns weighed 20 tons each and fired 90-pound shot. After coming ashore, the Ottomans opened a bombardment of Fort St. Elmo, where the knights were heavily outnumbered. In heavy fighting, the Ottomans captured the ravelin, or outer earthworks, but the knights used their own artillery to good advantage and repulsed successive attacks, inflicting heavy losses. Dragut then supervised erection of an additional siege works but was mortally wounded by a rock splinter from a shell burst. He lived long enough to learn, in mid-June, that the Ottomans had taken the fort. Only nine knights were taken alive in its remains.

Forts St. Angelo and St. Michael were the next Ottoman targets. Mustafa, with Rhodes as precedent, offered the remaining knights the chance to surrender, but La Vallette refused. The Ottomans attempted to destroy the boom but were met by Maltese swimmers, who were armed to the teeth and prevented the Ottomans from carrying out their design. For two months, the Ottomans made land assaults on the Maltese forts without success. Both sides were now exhausted. Christian corsairs had taken a heavy toll of Ottoman supply ships, and the attackers were short of supplies. Many of their men were also sick with fever and dysentery.

In early September, with the defenders down to as few as several hundred men and about to be overwhelmed, a relief force of some 10,000 Spaniards under Don Garcia de Toledo arrived from Syracuse and made landfall on the northern part of the island. This reinforcement, the threat of additional Spanish aid, low morale (some 24,000 Ottomans had been casualties thus far), and the approach of winter without a fleet anchorage all led the Ottomans to raise the siege on September 8 and return home. Little more than a quarter of the original Ottoman force had survived. The defenders suffered more than 5,000 dead, including 240 knights. His rebuff at Malta ended Suleiman's efforts to control the Mediterranean.

Spencer C. Tucker

Further Reading
Bradford, Ernie. *The Cruel Siege: Malta, 1565*. London: Wordsworth Editions, 1999.
Ellul, Joseph. *The Great Siege of Malta*. Siggiewi, Malta: Ellul, 1992.

Kinross, Lord [John Patrick]. *The Ottoman Centuries: The Rise and Fall of the Turkish Empire*. New York: William Morrow, 1977.

Prata, Nicholas C. *Angels in Iron*. Huntingdon Valley, PA: Arx Publishing, 1997.

Sire, H. J. A. *The Knights of Malta*. New Haven, CT: Yale University Press, 1996.

Siege of Szigetvár (August 6–September 8, 1566)

The siege of Szigetvár or Battle of Szigeth (August 6–September 8, 1566) saw Ottoman forces under the nominal command of sultan Suleiman the Magnificent (Süleymān) lay siege to the Kingdom of Hungary fortress of Szigetvár blocking Suleiman's line advance to Vienna.

On August 29, 1526, King Louis II and his Hungarian forces were defeated by Ottoman forces under Suleiman in the pivotal Battle of Mohács. Louis was killed in the battle. As he had no direct heir, this brought an end to the independent Kingdom of Hungary. Both Hungary and Croatia were now disputed territories claimed by both the Austrian Habsburgs and the Ottomans. Ferdinand, the brother of Holy Roman Emperor Charles V, married Louis II's sister and was then elected King Ferdinand I by the nobles of both Hungary and Croatia. Nonetheless, John Zápolya of Transylvania disputed Ferdinand's claim to the Hungarian throne. Suleiman supported Zápolya and promised to make him ruler of all Hungary. Seeking to reinforce his claim to Hungary, Ferdinand I invaded and captured the city of Buda from Zápolya in 1527, only to relinquish his hold following Ottoman military successes in 1527 and 1528. Then in 1529, Suleiman laid siege to Vienna itself. This siege of September 23–October 15, 1529, marked the farthest expansion of Ottoman territory in Europe.

The Ottoman effort to take Vienna was unsuccessful, and in 1530 Ferdinand attempted to take Buda again, but his forces were driven off by Zápolya. Ferdinand did manage to capture Gran (Esztergom) and other fortresses along the Danube River, which became a Habsburg frontier. In 1541, the Hapsburgs again tried and failed to take Buda by siege. Fighting seesawed back and forth. With casualties in the long-running warfare heavy, the fighting largely ended in 1552 until Suleiman launched a final effort to try to take Vienna.

In 1566 Suleiman again took the field for the last time. He had ruled the Ottoman Empire for 46 years. Then 72, he was not in the best of health and had to be transported by litter. On August 6, 1566, the Ottoman army arrived at Szigetvár in south central Hungary. Hungarian forces holding its fortress were commanded by a Croat, Miklós Zrínyi (in Hungarian Zrínyi Miklós). Zrínyi had fought at Vienna during Sultan Suleiman I's siege of that city in 1529 and in October 1539 had murdered the traitor Johann Katzianer, who tried to persuade him to defect to the Ottoman side. Zrínyi led 400 men to help save the imperial forces from defeat in the siege and assault of Pest (September 26–October 5, 1542), for which he was named bán (viceroy) of Croatia in 1542 and received significant land holdings in Hungary from Ferdinand I.

As one of Hungary's largest landholders, Zrínyi was committed to keeping the Ottomans out of the country. He led the relief of Szigetvár on July 22, 1556, but resigned the governorship of Croatia in 1561. The same year, Zrínyi was appointed captain of Szigetvár but soon resigned because of the lack of financial support from the court for the restoration of the damaged fortress. Zrínyi again defeated Ottoman forces at Segesd in 1564.

When Suleiman resumed warfare against Austria in 1566 and moved north with his large army in his campaign to take Vienna, Zrínyi carried out attacks against the Ottoman flanks, destroying several Ottoman detachments at Siklós in July. He also accepted reappointment as captain of Szigetvár. Suleiman halted his progression north to move against Szigetvár, reportedly committing 90,000 men and 399 cannon for the purpose.

The Ottoman advanced force arrived at Szigetvár on August 2 and the main army with Suleiman on August 5. The siege commenced on August 6. Suleiman had his tent pitched on Similehov Hill, which provided him a good view of the ensuing siege operations and where he received battle reports and issued orders. Grand Vizier Sokollu Mehmed Pasha held actual field command. Zrínyi had assembled a force of only 2,300 Croatian and Hungary soldiers, with a majority of them Croats. There were also some 2,000 civilians in the fortress.

Suleiman ordered an assault on August 6, but it was beaten back. Szigetvár held out for a month, despite no imperial reinforcements being sent there from Vienna. Suleiman offered Zrínyi the rule of Croatia under Ottoman influence for his surrender, but Zrínyi refused. On September 7, the defenders abandoned the outer walls for the citadel after the former had been reduced by the Ottoman heavy guns and mining. On September 8, the Ottomans were advancing on a narrow bridge toward the citadel when the gate to the citadel suddenly opened and a large gun charged with scrap metal was fired at the attackers, killing hundreds. Zrínyi then led out a desperate sortie with some 600 men, dying in it at the head of his troops. Although some were able to return to the citadel, almost all of those with him were also slain.

A great number of Ottoman soldiers then raced into the citadel in the expectation of finding valuables there, and some 3,000 died in the explosion of the last cannon powder, touched off by a slow match. Grand Vizier Sokollu Mehmed Pasha was saved by a member of Zrínyi's personal household. The grand vizier was in the citadel when he was told of the powder and slow match. He and some of his officers were able to escape just before the blast. In all, the battle claimed some 20,000–35,000 Ottoman dead. Almost all of the 2,300 defenders were also dead, a few having been spared as a tribute to their courage.

Suleiman was among the dead. He had died of natural causes on September 6, only two days before, but the truth was deliberately concealed from his troops for a full 48 days to avoid panic. Suleiman's death nonetheless led to the Ottomans abandoning their effort to take Vienna. They soon returned south. Vienna was not again threatened until a new Ottoman siege in 1683.

The month-long siege may well have saved Vienna. French statesman Cardinal Armand Jean du Plessis, 1st Duke of Richelieu and Fronsac, was said to have called it "the battle that saved civilization." It is still widely remembered in

Croatian and Hungarian literature and music, and the Hungarian National Defense University, now merged with the National University of Public Service in Budapest, was named for Zrínyi.

Spencer C. Tucker

Further Reading

Fine, John Van Antwerp. *The Late Medieval Balkans: A Critical Survey from the Late Twelfth Century to the Ottoman Conquest.* Ann Arbor: University of Michigan Press, 1994.

Hanák, Péter, ed. *The Corvina History of Hungary: From Earliest Times until the Present Day.* Budapest: Corvina Books, 1991.

Oman, Charles W. C. *A History of the Art of War in the Sixteenth Century.* London: Greenhill Books, 1999.

Wheatcroft, Andrew. *The Enemy at the Gate: Habsburgs, Ottomans, and the Battle for Europe.* New York: Basic Books, 2009.

Siege of Antwerp (July 1584–August 17, 1585)

The Spanish siege of the Dutch city of Antwerp was one of the major military events of the Dutch Wars of Independence (1568–1648). Antwerp, located on the Scheldt River that connected the city with the North Sea, had a population of about 100,000 people and was Northern Europe's most important economic center.

Fernando Álvarez de Toledo, Duke of Alva and Spanish commander in the Netherlands, combined skillful military operations with a reign of terror against the civilian population. In October 1576, mutinous Spanish troops who had not been paid captured and ravished Antwerp. This atrocity united the Netherlands against Spain in the Pacification of Ghent of November 1576. In 1578 Spanish king Philip II replaced Alva with Alessandro Farnese.

Farnese negotiated a peace settlement with the southern provinces of the Netherlands while continuing the war against the Protestant north. In 1582 he went on the offensive and the next year took both Diest and Westerlo, cutting communications between Antwerp and Brussels. In 1584 Farnese decided to take Antwerp, and Spanish forces captured a series of strategic positions that cut the city from the sea. For operations against Antwerp, Farnese had at his disposal some 60,000 men, while Philippe de Marnix, Lord of Sainte-Aldegonde and commander of the Antwerp garrison, had about 20,000 men. Antwerp's defenses were strong, however, leading Farnese to believe that it would be next to impossible to take the city by storm. He decided to starve it into submission.

To isolate Antwerp, Farnese built a series of strong points and a blockading pontoon bridge on the Scheldt that would cut seaborne supply. Completed in February 1585, the 800-yard bridge was an impressive engineering feat. Farnese is said to have designed it himself, while two Italian engineers, Giambattista Piatti and Properzio Boracci, supervised the construction. The bridge had a road running its entire length with parapets on either side to protect against musket fire. Thirty-two barges moored side by side in the Scheldt supported the center of the bridge, and each mounted two large cannon, one at bow and one at stern. The two wings of the bridge, each about 180 yards long, rested on pilings. Twenty galleys in the river constituted a mobile defense force, and two powerful forts with 10 cannon each guarded the ends of the bridge.

The Dutch were not idle. They employed an Italian engineer, Federico Giambelli (or Gianibelli), and a Fleming named den Bosche to develop the means to attack the bridge. Devices sent against the bridge included floating casks known as porcupines, which had sharp metal points on the outside and inflammables within. These and a raft filled with cannon powder to be ignited from the bank when it hit the bridge all failed. Den Bosche then came up with an armed craft filled with 1,000 men and mounting cannon, but Spanish artillery drove it ashore and destroyed it.

In the spring of 1585, Giambelli designed large flat-bottomed barges with reinforced sides. These were filled with explosives and covered with shrapnel, the charges to be set off by clockwork devices. On April 5, he sent four of these against the bridge. Only one worked, but its explosion blew out nearly 100 yards of the span. Eight hundred Spaniards died, and Farnese narrowly escaped death. The Dutch failed to exploit their temporary advantage, and the Spanish soon repaired the bridge and came up with a system whereby one or more of the pontoon barges could be moved to let any floating incendiary device pass through.

With starvation now taking hold in Antwerp, the Dutch attempted sorties from the city and relief expeditions, but Farnese's forces easily defeated these and launched their own attacks. Early in August, the Spanish captured the city's citadel, whereupon Antwerp surrendered on August 17, 1585. The successful siege was the highpoint of Farnese's military career. The next year, on the death of his father who had held the title, he became Duke of Parma. The Dutch, who still controlled both banks of the Scheldt estuary, closed off the river to commerce. This led to Antwerp's decline and the exodus of more than half its population.

Spencer C. Tucker

Further Reading
Melegari, Vezio. *The Great Military Sieges.* New York: Crowell, 1972.
Parker, Geoffrey. *The Dutch Revolt.* Rev. ed. London: Penguin Books, 1990.
Rady, Martyn. *From Revolt to Independence.* London: Hodder & Stoughton, 1990.

Siege of Odawara Castle (May–August 4, 1590)

Sixteenth-century Japan was marked by a weak central authority and near constant warfare among the clans. In the second half of that century, however, there emerged a group of "great power" warlords, who with superior military organizations were able to substantially expand their territories at the expense of their weaker neighbors. Examples of such powerful daimyo houses were the Uesugi, Takeda, and Go-Hōjō clans in the east, and the Mori, Shimazu, and Otomo clans in the west. These warlords all had important roles in the unification campaigns of the last three decades of the sixteenth century.

The unification campaigns were driven by three key warlords: Oda Nobunaga (1534–1582), Toyotomi Hideyoshi (1536–1598), and Tokugawa Ieyasu (1542–1616). From 1568 until 1582, Oda Nobunaga fought relentlessly against the Takeda, Uesugi, and Mori clans, the Ikko ikki, and several smaller clans. Ultimately, he controlled most of central Japan. As a commoner, Oda Nobunaga could not become shōgun (short for Sei-i Taishōgun or "commander in chief of the expeditionary force against the barbarians," the individual governing Japan at various times until 1867 when Tokugawa Yoshinobu relinquished the office to Emperor Meiji), but he established Yoshiaki Ashikaga in that position and ruled Japan through him.

Oda Nobunaga was assassinated in 1582, however. He was succeeded by another capable military leader in Hideyoshi Toyatomi. Interested in projecting Japanese power beyond the home islands, he first had to unify Japan. Having defeated the Shimazu in 1587, the only formidable force was the Hōjō clan.

In July 1589, Hideyoshi arbitrated a long-standing dispute between the Hōjō clan and the Sanada clan of Ueda in Shinano dealing with Numata castle and the Azuma Valley area in Kozuke Province. Hideyoshi awarded most of the land to the Hōjō, but assigned the Sanada the Azuma district and Nagurumi castle, located north of Numata. That November, however, Hōjō forces from Numata seized control of Nagurumi castle and killed its commander. Hideyoshi then declared war on the Hōjō.

The culmination of Hideyoshi's military efforts came in 1590 when he moved against Odawara castle, the stronghold of the Hōjō clan. Aware of Hideyoshi's determination to invade and the likely superior strength of his force, after some debate the Hōjō clan decided not to oppose him in open battle but to concentrate their resources at Odawara castle, one of the strongest fortifications of its day in all Japan. The castle now held some 82,000 people. Hōjō leader Hōjō Ujimasa laid in supplies and did what he could to strengthen the castle's defenses. The Hōjō leaders put their trust in the strength of its defenses and the immense logistical difficulties that Hideyoshi would face in maintaining his large invading army for an extended period.

Hideyoshi arrived at Odawara in May 1590 with a massive force of some 220,000 men and immediately surrounded the castle. Given their considerable numerical disadvantage, the Hōjō were reluctant to challenge the besiegers in sorties and as a result the siege saw little fighting. The siege was highly unconventional, as it saw the presence with the besiegers of a great many concubines, prostitutes, and even musicians and acrobats to entertain the soldiers. The few skirmishes that did occur included an effort by the besiegers to dig under the castle walls that enabled some of the attackers to enter the castle but not in sufficient numbers to carry the works.

The besiegers were able to stymie efforts to get food and other supplies to the castle from other satellite Hōjō strong points, with food finally in short supply and given the numbers against them the Hōjō surrendered on August 4, 1590.

Hideyoshi then went on to take other Hōjō strong points. He gave the Hōjō lands to Tokugawa Ieyasu, who had spearheaded the effort against Odawara castle. These territorial gains turned out to be an immense assist in Tokugawa's subsequent rise to power.

Hideyoshi established his capital at Edo (later named Tokyo). Having secured his base, he dreamed of making Japan the dominant power in East Asia. Toward that end, he set the ambitious goal of conquering Ming Dynasty China. Such an effort would also have the advantage of diverting the energies of the ever-ambitious Japanese warlords from domestic affairs. To get at China, Hideyoshi planned to first invade and secure control of Joseon (Chosŭn) Dynasty Korea, then a tributary state of China. That effort, generally referred to as the Imjin War (1592–1598), failed, and with Hideyoshi's death in September 1598, any plans to conquer Korea were shelved.

Spencer C. Tucker

Further Reading
Berry, Mary Elizabeth. *Hideyoshi*. Cambridge, MA: Harvard University Press, 1982.
Hane, Mikiso. *Modern Japan: A Historical Survey*. Boulder, CO: Westview Press, 1992.
Jansen, Marius B. *The Making of Modern Japan*. Cambridge, MA: Harvard University Press, 2000.
Lorimer, Michael James. *Sengokujidai: Autonomy, Division and Unity in Later Medieval Japan*. London: Olympia Publishers, 2008.
Sansom, George. *A History of Japan, 1334–1615*. Stanford, CA: Stanford University Press, 1961.
Turnbull, Stephen. *Battles of the Samurai*. New York: Arms and Armour, 1987.
Turnbull, Stephen. *The Samurai: A Military History*. New York: Macmillan, 1977.

Siege of Breda (August 28, 1624–June 5, 1625)

The successful Spanish siege of the city of Breda in the Netherlands, during August 28, 1624–June 5, 1625, was one of the major military events of the Dutch Wars of Independence (1568–1648). In 1622 the struggle between Spain and the Dutch became part of the wider conflict of the Thirty Years' War (1618–1648). In July of that year, Spanish general Ambrosio de Spinola laid siege to Bergen-op-Zoom, but a force of Dutch and German Protestants led by Prince Maurice of Nassau, stadtholder of Holland, raised the siege. Prominent officials in the Spanish court of King Philip IV, most notably the king's prime minister Gaspar Guzmán, Duke of Sanlucar and Count of Olivares, were jealous of Spinola's military successes and may have attempted to set him up for failure. In any case, they now persuaded Philip IV to order Spinola to lay siege to the fortified city of Breda, a Dutch stronghold in northern Brabant that many considered unassailable.

Spinola moved against Breda with some 60,000 men in his Army of Flanders. Prince Maurice had garrisoned Breda with about 9,000 troops, supported by artillery. The Dutch had also improved its defenses with moats, trenches, and revetments. Unlike previous Spanish sieges of Dutch towns except that of Jülich during 1621–1622, Spinola opted to starve out the city. While the siege lasted, the relief of the city was the focus of Dutch military efforts.

Spinola made his preparations carefully, mounting his artillery on raised platforms to secure maximum effectiveness. He ordered construction of barricades

The Surrender of Breda by Diego Velázquez (1635). The painting depicts the Spanish surrender of this important city in the Netherlands to Dutch forces on June 5, 1625, after a siege that lasted more than nine months. (Photos.com)

that blocked major egress points from Breda so that his troops could defeat any sorties. Spinola also held back most of his cavalry and infantry in a mobile reserve to meet anticipated Dutch relief operations.

The Dutch did attempt sorties from the city, and Prince Maurice of Nassau attempted to get supplies into the city. All met rebuff, including several efforts by Count Peter Ernst von Mansfeld, a German mercenary serving under Prince Maurice. At the same time, Maurice refused Spinola's efforts to draw him into a pitched battle.

The winter of 1624–1625 was severe, and both sides suffered, especially the Spanish in their field shelters. With the arrival of spring, the Dutch, reinforced by German troops, mounted several unsuccessful attempts to break the siege. Maurice died on April 23, 1625, and was succeeded as stadtholder of Holland by his younger brother Prince Frederick Henry, who continued to refuse a decisive battle with Spinola. By early May, Spinola had some 80,000 men at Breda: 25,000 in the actual siege, 25,000 along the supply corridor, and 30,000 as general reserves.

Frederick Henry continued efforts to relieve Breda, sending Mansfeld and 12,000 men on a fifth attempt to reach the city with supplies. On May 12, to distract the besiegers, 2,000 Dutch sortied from Breda against what they thought was a weak point in the line. Mansfeld approached the city from the opposite direction at the same time. Spinola beat back both efforts, with the attackers sustaining heavy losses. Spinola had increased his artillery and was able to largely silence the guns of the fortress. He then brought up battering guns, effecting breaches in the walls.

On June 5, 1625, with all hope of relief gone and with Spanish troops inside Breda, Governor Justinius van Nassau surrendered Breda under favorable terms. The defenders were allowed to leave the city with their personal weapons, four artillery pieces, and such personal possessions as they could carry. Four thousand departed Breda, leaving behind 5,000 of their fellow soldiers dead along with 8,000 civilians who died of disease and hunger.

The Spaniards' success at Breda actually proved a detriment to their overall plans. The city had little strategic value, and the siege had been costly in financial terms. Its heavy drain on troop resources also prevented the Spaniards from pursuing other goals. Dutch forces finally retook Breda in 1637.

Spencer C. Tucker

Further Reading

Geyl, Pieter. *The Netherlands in the Seventeenth Century: Part One, 1609–1648.* London: Ernest Bern, 1966.

Israel, Jonathan I. *The Dutch Republic and the Hispanic World, 1606–1661.* Oxford, UK: Clarendon Press, 1982.

Parker, Geoffrey. *The Dutch Revolt.* Rev. ed. London: Penguin Books, 1990.

Siege of La Rochelle (August 1627–October 28, 1628)

The Protestant Reformation, especially the radical version preached by Frenchman John Calvin (né Jean Cauvin), who set himself up in Geneva, spread to France soon after it began. Calvinism was particularly appealing to the French middle class and nobles. As the nobles were often the chief source of opposition to the Crown, French kings naturally took alarm. In the 1550s, the government of Henri II persecuted adherents of the new faith, who came to be called Huguenots, and burned a number of them at the stake. Despite this persecution, Calvinism continued to make inroads, especially in southwestern France.

During 1562–1598, France experienced a series of costly religious wars during which the Huguenots established a number of fortified cities, including La Rochelle on the southwestern Atlantic coast. The wars were settled when the Huguenot champion, Henri de Navarre, became king of France as Henri IV. Because the great majority of Frenchmen were still Catholic and because Henri IV wished to secure the Catholic stronghold of Paris, he converted to Catholicism ("Paris is well worth a mass," he is supposed to have said). To mollify his former coreligionists, he issued the Edict of Nantes in 1598 that granted religious toleration and full civil rights to the Huguenots. The edict also allowed them to fortify some 100 towns where the Huguenot faith was in the majority.

Unfortunately for France, Henri IV's reign was brief; he was stabbed to death in Paris by a religious fanatic in 1610. His son, Louis XIII (r. 1610–1643), was then only nine years old. Louis grew up to be weak and indecisive, but he had a capable chief minister in Armand Jean du Plessis, Cardinal de Richelieu, who was the virtual ruler of France during 1624–1642. This born administrator made raison d'état (reason of state) the dominant consideration in all his policies. Although he

> **Armand Jean du Plessis, Cardinal Richelieu**
>
> Richelieu's wise judgment was apparent in his amendment of the Edict of Nantes. This cardinal of the Catholic Church allowed the Protestants to maintain the practice of their religion and civil rights. French Protestants continued to practice their religion and live in relative peace and harmony in France for nearly six decades until the reign of Louis XIV (1643–1715) when, seeking to bend all to his will and considering unity of religion a national necessary, he revoked the Edict of Nantes entirely in 1685.
>
> It was probably the greatest mistake Louis XIV made, for during the next two decades between 200,000 and 900,000 French Protestants emigrated. Their loss cost France dearly, as the Huguenots were disproportionately represented in commercial and artisan enterprises. Indeed, some historians claim that Louis XIV's decision may have been the single most important factor in allowing Britain to best France in the race for world commercial supremacy.
>
> **Spencer C. Tucker**

was a sincere Catholic, Richelieu never let religion get in the way of strengthening the state.

To Richelieu, the Huguenot-fortified towns formed a state within a state and were thus unacceptable. Alarmed by Richelieu's stance, the Huguenots rebelled under the leadership of the dukes de Rohan and Soubise. Richelieu responded by declaring the suppression of the rebellion his first priority in 1625. Protestant, rich, and looking toward England, La Rochelle relished its independence. The city itself lay at the end of a channel. Off it were two islands: the closest, Île de Ré, and the more distant Île d'Oléron. La Rochelle was the strongest of the Huguenot fortresses and the center of resistance to royal rule.

In 1626 La Rochelle had been forced to accept a royal commissioner, to agree not to arm its ships, and to accord full rights to Catholics. In March 1627, France formed an alliance with Spain that solidified its position. Six months later, Richelieu's forces initiated a siege of the city and exchanged artillery fire with its Huguenot defenders. Because La Rochelle was a port, it could receive aid by sea, and in June 1627 King Charles I of England sent 120 ships and 6,000 soldiers there under his favorite, George Villiers, Duke of Buckingham.

The English fleet arrived at Île de Ré on July 10. If the people of La Rochelle welcomed the troops, Buckingham was to place them under command of the Duc de Soubise, who arrived with him. If not, the men would return to England. Soubise went to La Rochelle to negotiate with its leaders, but they feared the consequences of welcoming English troops. Buckingham therefore ordered his men ashore to secure Fort St. Martin on Île de Ré, which was controlled by the royalists, as a base for future operations. His men, most of whom had been pressed, were poorly trained, and many refused to go ashore. Others bolted on the first gunfire with the royal garrison on the island. Buckingham was thus unable to take the fort; instead, he resorted to a blockade.

Richelieu was certain that if Buckingham took Fort St. Martin, his siege operation would fail. Richelieu therefore sent French ships to supply the fort, called up

Siege of La Rochelle

Illustration depicting French king Louis XIII and his entourage at the French royalist forces siege of the Huguenot stronghold coastal city of La Rochelle in southwestern France during August 1627–October 28, 1628. (Antonio Abrignani/Shutterstock.com)

feudal levies, and sent about 20,000 men toward La Rochelle. The brother of the king, Gaston d'Orléans, had nominal command, but field command was held by the Duc d'Angoulême. As it worked out, Richelieu actually retained direction of affairs.

In August, Angoulême closed off the city from the land side, and the city fathers voted to call on Buckingham for arms and assistance. The royal garrison on the Île de Ré continued to hold out, although on October 1 its commander Jean de St. Bonnet de Toiras sent word that his men were almost out of food and that without relief he would have to surrender on the evening of October 8. Therefore, on the night of October 7, Richelieu sent a relief force of 47 vessels under an adventurer named Beaulieu-Persac. That night a battle took place off Île de Ré between the French and English warships. Although he was eventually forced to surrender, Beaulieu-Persac succeeded in distracting the English long enough for his 29 supply ships to beach themselves on the island.

A few days later King Louis XIII arrived in the vicinity of La Rochelle. Richelieu then personally led 9,000 reinforcements to the Île de Ré and Île d'Oléron from northern French mainland ports. Running short of supplies himself, in desperation Buckingham and 2,000 men launched a last attempt to storm Fort St. Martin on November 5. The English took the outer works but were then driven back and shortly thereafter came under heavy attack from the French relief force. On November 8, Buckingham sailed away with the half of his force that remained.

With Île de Ré secure, Richelieu could concentrate on La Rochelle. In November, the French constructed a powerful siege line more than seven miles long with 11 forts and 18 redoubts. The French lacked the means to blockade the city completely from the sea, but after reading how Alexander the Great had built a great causeway to end the siege of Tyre, Richelieu ordered construction of a great stone dike at the end of the bay to close La Rochelle off from the sea. Jean de Thirot, architect to the king, and Clément Métezeau, the king's master builder, had charge of construction.

Work began in October and for all practical purposes was complete by January 1628, with the jetty and 56 ships chained together and armed to form a floating wall. In addition, Richelieu assembled 36 galleys and pinnaces in the roadstead to attack any expedition launched from La Rochelle to destroy the dike.

In March, an English ship made it to La Rochelle with supplies and promised assistance from Charles I. The people of La Rochelle took heart and elected Jean Guiton as mayor. He infused new life in the defense. Moreover, in early May, an English fleet under Lord Denbigh arrived. The English ships briefly bombarded the dike but without effect. Then, learning that a Spanish fleet was at sea, Denbigh sailed away on May 18. On September 28, a larger English fleet under Count Lindsey appeared off the dike, transporting 11 regiments and food for many months, but the troops were disaffected, and it departed without landing either men or supplies.

With this final disappointment and virtually no hope of resupply, on October 28, the La Rochelle garrison finally surrendered. During the siege, largely as the consequence of famine and disease, the population of the city went from 27,000 to only 5,000 people. Richelieu entered the city in triumph, and French troops immediately began the destruction of La Rochelle's walls and fortifications. Richelieu then amended the Edict of Nantes in the Peace of Alais, which formally ended the siege. The Huguenots lost the right to maintain fortified towns and military formations independent of the Crown. They did, however, retain full religious and civil rights until 1685, when King Louis XIV, much to the detriment of his kingdom, annulled the Edict of Nantes altogether.

One reason the siege had been so lengthy was that France did not have much of a navy. Richelieu may be regarded as the father of the French Navy, for he ordered construction of a force of 38 warships for the Atlantic and 10 for the Mediterranean.

Spencer C. Tucker

Further Reading

Holt, Mack P. *The French Wars of Religion, 1562–1629*. Cambridge, UK: Cambridge University Press, 1995.

O'Connell, D. P. *Richelieu*. New York: World Publishing, 1968.

Sutherland, N. M. *The Huguenot Struggle for Recognition*. New Haven, CT: Yale University Press, 1980.

Wood, James B. *The Army of the King: Warfare, Soldiers, and Society during the Wars of Religion in France, 1562–1676*. Cambridge, UK: Cambridge University Press, 1996.

Siege of Magdeburg (November 20, 1630–May 20, 1631)

The siege of the German city of Magdeburg, during November 20, 1630–May 20, 1631, resulted in what is considered the worst atrocity of the Thirty Years' War (1618–1648). Located on the Elbe River in Lower Saxony, Magdeburg was then one of the largest cities in Germany and had been strongly Protestant since 1524.

Magdeburg had been a target for the Catholic forces for some time in the war as the city had rallied to Swedish king Gustavus II Adolphus, a Protestant Lutheran, who had joined the Thirty Years' War by invading northern Germany in July 1630. Late that same month, Magdeburg's former leader Christian Wilhelm von Brandenburg had returned to the city and seized power there, immediately declaring his allegiance to Sweden, seeing in Gustavus a Protestant champion against Catholic Holy Roman Emperor Ferdinand II. Gustavus commanded an expeditionary force of some 36,000 men, which was undoubtedly the most efficient military force of his generation. In November, he had promised Magdeburg his protection, dispatching there one of his lieutenants, Dietrich von Falkenberg, to direct its military affairs with the title of commandant. Falkenberg did what he could, strengthening the city's defenses and recruiting additional manpower.

A Catholic operation to seize Magdeburg had been planned by Imperial general Albrecht von Wallenstein, but Ferdinand II had dismissed him before he could carry it out, and the operation was now implemented by Imperial forces under general Count Gottfried H. zu Pappenheim. His forces arrived at the city in November and instituted a loose blockade. Well-supplied and fortified, Magdeburg resisted Imperial attacks and, indeed, fared better than the besiegers. Then, on April 3, 1631, a large Catholic League army under Johan Tserclaes, Count Tilly, arrived and joined the siege operations. Tilly had a powerful siege train with artillery and the attackers now numbered some 25,000 men. The defenders counted only some 2,400 trained soldiers with another 5,000 conscripts (2,000 of them children).

Gradually the besiegers reduced the city's outer defenses. With Magdeburg's situation now precarious, Gustavus, who had seen his efforts in northern Germany handicapped by the attitude of the Protestant German princes who feared his intentions and refused to allow him access to their territories, had instead concentrated on securing eastern Pomerania. He now carried out a brilliant surprise march against the city of Frankfurt (Frankfurt on der Oder), capturing it on April 13. Gustavus hoped that this would cause Tilly to raise the siege of Magdeburg, but Tilly held on there and Gustavus now prepared to march against him.

The Catholic besiegers of Magdeburg were determined to take the city before Gustavus could arrive. Tilly's men captured the Magdeburg suburbs of Sudenburg and Neustadt on April 21 and April 23 respectively, and on April 24 Tilly demanded the city surrender. The city council was in favor and urged Falkenberg to accept honorable terms, but he resisted, insisting that Gustavus and his army would arrive in time. By May 1, the besiegers had taken all of the city's outer defenses, but the defenders beat back assaults on May 17 and 18. On the 18th, with the Swedes then some 56 miles distant, Falkenberg again rejected Tilly's surrender demands.

At 7.00 a.m. on May 20, supported by artillery fire, some 18,000 Imperial and League troops stormed the city from five different directions and within two hours their infantry had breached part of the city walls along the Elbe. The infantry was quickly followed by cavalry. Falkenberg was shot and killed while trying to organize a counterattack. The Imperialists set fire to a house held by musketeers and that fire soon spread, followed by others, some apparently set by the defenders.

The soldiers had not been paid for some time, and they quickly took out their frustrations on the townspeople. All order collapsed as they rampaged through the city, looting, raping, and slaying. With several dozen fires soon raging, Tilly, Pappenheim, and some of their men, tried to fight the flames, but to no avail. Magdeburg, built largely of wood, was burnt to the ground, with only the cathedral left standing. Tilly thus lost all the supplies that he had hoped to secure. Some 25,000 of the 30,000 inhabitants perished in that one day of May 20. Most of the 5,000 survivors had taken refuge in the cathedral. Losses for the attackers were on the order of 300 dead and 1,600 wounded.

Order was not restored until May 24, with a Catholic mass celebrated in the cathedral the next day. The massacre at Magdeburg shocked most of Europe, although Pope Urban VII expressed his satisfaction that "the nest of vipers" had been wiped out. Indeed, the city never recovered its former prominence. Fear and anger now combined to move Protestant sentiment in Germany sharply in support of Gustavus of Sweden and against Emperor Ferdinand II. The siege and its aftermath thus had an important impact on the course of the war.

Spencer C. Tucker

Further Reading

Parker, Geoffrey. *The Thirty Years' War*. New York: Routledge, 1997.

Wedgewood, C. V. *The Thirty Years' War*. London: Pimlico, 1992.

Wilson, Peter H. *Europe's Tragedy: A New History of the Thirty Years War*. Cambridge, MA: Harvard University Press, 2009.

Wilson, Peter H. *From Reich to Revolution: German History, 1558–1806*. New York: Palgrave MacMillan, 2004.

Siege of Candia (May 1, 1648–September 27, 1669)

Touted as perhaps the longest siege in military history, the siege of Candia (present-day Heraklion) in Crete extended from May 1, 1648, to September 27, 1669, and was part of the Cretan War of 1645–1669. Venice had acquired Crete in the distribution of spoils following the Fourth Christian Crusade that had been redirected against Constantinople in 1204. The island was sometimes referred to as the Kingdom of Candia, for its port city and capital, situated on the north coast of Crete near the ruins of the palace of Knossos, which in Minoan times was the largest population center on the island.

The long siege of Candia war was precipitated by the Knights of Malta, who in 1644 captured a number of ships in an Ottoman convoy sailing from Alexandria to Constantinople and that included part of Sultan Ibrahim I's harem returning from a pilgrimage to Mecca. The raiders then put into their base at Candia. Responding to this action, in 1645 a large Ottomans expeditionary force, said to number 60,000 men and commanded by Yussut Pasha, invaded Crete. In an effort to cut off the Ottoman forces there, the Venetians attempted to blockade the

Dardanelles. This in turn led to a series of naval engagements there and off Crete, in which the two sides traded victories.

Meanwhile on Crete, after some four months, the Ottomans took and occupied both La Canea (present-day Chania) and Rettimo (Rethimno). They then went on to expand their control over the entire island save the capital of Candia.

The Ottomans commenced their siege of Candia on May 1, 1648. During a three-month span, they invested the city and cut off its water supply. For the next 16 years, they carried out sporadic bombardment and siege operations without being able to take the city. The Venetians enjoyed victory in two naval battles on June 21, 1655, and August 26, 1656, and were thus able to prevent Ottoman resupply of their forces in Crete, but the Ottomans scored a major sea victory during July 17–19, 1657, and were then able to send reinforcements to the island. In 1666, Ottoman grand vizier Fazil Ahmed Köprülü went in person to the island to direct siege operations.

Following the conclusion of peace between France and Spain in the Treaty of the Pyrenees of 1659, King Louis XIV of France agreed to send a French land force to Crete to assist the besieged. At the same time, the Ottomans benefited from the Peace of Vasvár in 1664 between themselves and the Habsburgs.

A Venetian attempt in 1666 to recapture La Canea was a failure, and the next year, Andrea Barozzi, a Venetian military engineer, defected to the Ottoman side and provided them with important information on Candia's defenses. On July 24, 1669, a French expeditionary force failed to raise the Ottoman siege, and the French also lost their 58-gun ship of the line *La Thérèsa* to a magazine explosion. Apparently chastened by their failure, the French departed Crete that August. Left with only some 3,600 able-bodied men to defend the fortress, General Francesco Morosini, commander of the Venetian forces at Candia, surrendered to Grand Vizier Ahmed Köprülü on September 27, 1669.

Under the terms of capitulation negotiated by Morosini, all Christians were allowed to depart with what possessions they could carry. In addition to losing all Crete, Venice also lost most of its Aegean islands, retaining only Grambusa, Souda, and Spinalonga. Venice did, however, receive some compensation in Dalmatia, where there had also been fighting between the Venetians and Ottomans, and the Venetians had registered some successes.

Spencer C. Tucker

Further Reading

Detorákis, Theócharis E. *History of Crete*. Translated by John C. Davis. Iraklion: Detorákis, 1994.

Freese, John Henry, and P. W. Clayden. *A Short Popular History of Crete*. London: Jarrold & Sons, 1897.

Siege of Maastricht (June 13–30, 1673)

The siege of Maastricht of June 13–20, 1673, occurred during the Dutch War of (1672–1678), which resulted from the efforts of King Louis XIV of France (r. 1643–1715) to acquire a natural frontier for France in the northeast by securing

Sébastien Le Prestre de Vauban

Vauban was responsible for a number of important innovations in siege warfare. At Maastricht, he introduced the digging of parallel trenches, each succeeding trench being dug slightly closer to the fortress. The trenches were connected to each other by zig-zag communication trenches. During the War of the League of Augsburg (1688–1697), Vauban carried out several more successful sieges. At Philippsburg (captured October 29, 1688), he came up with ricochet fire to bounce shot along the parapets and maximize the destructiveness of artillery fire.

Named marshal of France in 1703, Vauban conducted some 50 sieges in his long career. He also designed and oversaw the construction of more than 160 French fortresses, most of which were in the northeast to protect territory acquired there in Louis XIV's many wars. Vauban is also usually credited with having invented the socket bayonet, which enabled soldiers to fight at the same time with their muskets and a thrusting edged weapon.

Spencer C. Tucker

---

the Netherlands for France. The Netherlands was then divided between the United Provinces or Dutch Republic in the north and the southern provinces (present-day Belgium) controlled by the Spanish Crown.

In the so-called War of Devolution, on May 24, 1667, Louis had sent his army of some 120,000 men, then the largest in Europe, into the Spanish Netherlands. By October, with his army under Marshal Henri de la Tour d'Auvergne, Vicomte de Turenne, having enjoyed considerable success and, in effect, controlling the Spanish Netherlands, Louis sent forces into the adjoining Habsburg territory of Franche-Comté in 1668. Alarmed at these incursions, England, Sweden, and the United Provinces formed the Triple Alliance to support Spain against France in 1668. This powerful international coalition gave the French king pause and led him to conclude the Treaty of Aix-la-Chapelle that May, in which he conceded most of his gains.

This setback did not lessen Louis's determination to secure a natural frontier for France in the northeast. Having concluded an alliance with England against Spain in the secret Treaty of Dover (June 1, 1670), Louis tried again in what became known as the Dutch War or Franco-Dutch War (1672–1678). This new French invasion, however, would raise up Louis's great adversary of William, Prince of Orange, stadholder of Holland, Zeeland, Utrecht, Gelderland, and Overijssel in the Dutch Republic from 1672 and king of England (as William III), Ireland and Scotland from 1689 until his death in 1702. William managed to forge an alliance with Holy Roman Emperor Leopold I and Austria, Spain, Denmark, and Brandenburg against France.

France declared war in March 1672. In what is known in Dutch history as the Rampjaar (Disaster Year), the Dutch Republic found itself at war with France, England, and three German Bishoprics simultaneously. Its navy was able to prevent the English and French navies from reaching its western shores with a planned joint landing. On land, however, the Dutch Republic was almost taken over by the advancing French and German armies.

A French army of 130,000 men commanded personally by Louis moved down the Meuse. In May, feinting a march on the cities of Ghent and Brussels, the French marched past the fortress city of Maastricht, a condominium stronghold of the Dutch and the Bishopric of Liège, and went on to occupy Düsseldorf.

The Dutch were quite unprepared for the war. With the French invasion imminent, William had only 27,000 men. By the time the French had invaded, however, William had put together an army of 80,000 men.

Three separate armies invaded the Netherlands. Turenne led more than 50,000 French troops down the left bank of the Rhine. Marshal Louis II de Bourbon, Prince de Condé, commanding an army of equal size, moved down the right bank of the Rhine. At the same time, Marshal François Henri de Montmorency-Bouteville, Duc de Luxembourg, commanding a force primarily of German soldiers from states allied to France (Köln [Cologne] and Münster), moved from Westphalia toward Overijssel and Groningen.

William's Dutch forces attempted to hold the French along the Ijssel and Rhine Rivers, but the French forced the line at Tolhuis on June 12. Advancing rapidly, they then took Nijmegen and Gorinchem. A French cavalry raid into the central Netherlands captured Utrecht. The French also moved against Amsterdam, but the Dutch saved that city by flooding the countryside. The Dutch were also able to halt the Duc de Luxembourg at Groningen.

Dissatisfaction with French military success led to a political revolution in the Dutch Republic. The States General revived the Stadtholdership and, on July 8, 1672, William was declared stadtholder, captain-general, and admiral for life. Now greatly alarmed by the threat posed by French military successes, Holy Roman Emperor Leopold I, Elector Frederick William of Brandenburg, and Charles II of Spain all agreed to aid the Dutch. Ignoring the advice of his marshals, King Louis XIV now dispersed his forces to deal with the additional powers arrayed against France.

In the winter of 1672–1673, with only some 20,000 men, Turenne outmaneuvered and outgeneraled his opponents, Imperial General Count Raimondo Montecuccoli and Elector Frederick William of Brandenburg in the area of the middle Rhine. Indeed, the latter was so discouraged by events that he concluded a separate peace with France in the Treaty of Vossem of June 6, 1673.

The French hoped for success in the winter, when the flooded areas would be frozen. A sudden thaw, however, forced Luxembourg, then threatening both Leyden and The Hague, to withdraw to Utrecht, while Condé, who appeared poised to take Amsterdam, was also forced to withdraw on December 29 in order to avoid being trapped by the water.

In mid-1673, his supply lines eastward threatened, and at the head of what was then his largest field army, Louis decided to take Maastricht. He moved his men up the Scheldt River in a feint toward Ghent, then turned eastward to threaten Brussels but bypassed it and proceeded to Maastricht, where the French arrived on June 11. At the same time Turenne sent some of his army to approach the city from the east and prevent reinforcements from that direction.

The operation to take Maastricht commenced on June 13 and was directed by then colonel Sébastien le Prestre de Vauban, who would come to be acknowledged as one of history's master practitioners of siege warfare. The French had some 40,000 men: 24,000 infantry and 16,000 cavalry, along with 58 artillery pieces. Jacques de Fariaux had command of the Maastricht garrison of only 6,200 men: 5,000 infantry, and 1,200 cavalry.

Vauban concentrated his activities before the Tongre Gate, laying the first parallel for his artillery. On June 18, 26 French heavy siege guns commenced firing at Maastricht. Here Vauban introduced one of his most important innovations, the digging of parallel trenches. Zig-zag communication trenches were advanced forward toward the objective. These became a feature of siege warfare and were specifically designed so as to prevent a cannon ball or shell explosion in the trench from impacting the whole of it. The communications trenches were advanced a set distance with a new parallel trench then laid and the artillery brought forward.

By June 24, Vauban had completed the investment by parallels of Maastricht to a point where an assault might be mounted. That being the feast day of Saint John the Baptist with Louis XIV having expressed his desire to celebrate it in the Maastricht cathedral, the assault went forward. It was led by the King's Regiment and the Company of the Gray Musketeers commanded by Charles de Batz de Castelmore d'Artagnan (the source for the character of the fourth musketeer in the writings of French novelist Alexandre Dumas).

The fighting was fierce as the French attackers proceeded through the counterscarp before the moat and then across the moat itself, and then were able to enter one of the crescent fortifications protecting the city walls. Although the Spanish troops here defeated most of the force, some 30 men under the Marquis de Villars held their position here throughout the night.

The next morning James Scott, duke of Monmouth and son of King Charles I of England, sent his men to take the embarkment covering the moat, but they were driven back with some 300 casualties. The Spaniards then placed a mine under the crescent and, following its explosion, recaptured it from the French. Monmouth then sent his men in yet another unsuccessful attack, during which d'Artagnan was fatally wounded.

With the failure of the allied assault, the besiegers recommenced artillery fire. Realizing that it was now only a matter of time, Fariaux secured terms and surrendered Maastricht on June 30. The defenders marched out of the city under the honors of war with their arms and proceeded to the nearest Dutch garrison.

Following the capture of Maastricht, Louis moved his army into the Rhineland and took Trier (Treves). He also secured Franche-Comté. The war continued into 1678, with the cities taken becoming bargaining chips in the Treaties of Nimwegen (Nijmwegen, Nimeguen) of August and September 1678. Thus, although Louis XIV secured Franche-Comté and additional holdings in the Spanish Netherlands (including the town of Saint-Omer and the remaining northwestern part of the former Imperial County of Artois; the lands of Cassel, Aire, and Ypres in southwestern Flanders; the Bishopric of Cambrai; and the towns of Valenciennes and Maubeuge in the southern County of Hainaut), he ceded Maastricht and the Principality of Orange to Dutch stadtholder William. The French also withdrew from several occupied territories in northern Flanders and Hainaut.

Although Louis XIV was unable to secure all he wanted, he did not give up and plunged his country into two more costly struggles. The Dutch War was followed by the War of the League of Augsburg (1689–1697) and the great War of the Spanish Succession (1702–1713). Although France recovered from these wars, the Dutch Republic never was able to regain its former glory and underwent a general decline in the eighteenth century under economic competition from England and the long-standing internal rivalry between those supporting a republic and those backing the stadtholder.

Spencer C. Tucker

Further Reading
Duffy, Christopher. *The Fortress in the Age of Vauban and Frederick the Great, 1660–1789.* New York: Routledge, 2016.
Lynn, John. *The Wars of Louis XIV.* New York: Longman, 1999.
Sonnino, Paul. *Louis XIV and the Origins of the Dutch War.* New York: Cambridge University Press, 1988.

Siege and Battle of Vienna (July 14–September 12, 1683)

The great 60-day siege of Vienna during July–September 1683 was the second effort by the Ottomans to take the capital city of the Habsburg Empire, their most powerful European rival. The siege captured the attention of all Europe as did no other event of the century, and in Catholic countries funds were raised as if for a crusade.

While Ottoman power was not what it had been in the first siege of Vienna in 1529, Habsburg ruler and Holy Roman Emperor Leopold I was under attack from several sources. In the west, King Louis XIV of France was endeavoring to add chunks of the Holy Roman Empire to his holdings. In Royal Hungary (the Habsburg portion of Hungary), Hungarians incited and financed by the French and the Ottomans had rebelled. When the Habsburgs moved to put the insurgency down, the Hungarians appealed to the Ottomans for assistance.

Sultan Mehmed IV responded by leading a large army up the Danube to take Vienna. Actual field command was in the hands of Grand Vizier Kara Mustafa Pasha. Mehmed IV called upon and was assisted by Transylvania, his vassal state. Louis XIV did not positively assist the Ottomans but at least declined to join the proposed crusade against them.

With the addition of Transylvanian units, the Ottomans advanced up the Danube with perhaps 200,000 men. Ahmed detached part of his army to besiege Györ and then continued the advance toward Vienna. On July 7, 1683, the first Ottoman troops reached the gates of the city. On their approach, Emperor Leopold I and the court as well as about 60,000 inhabitants fled. Charles V, Duke of Lorraine, with an Austrian army of some 20,000 men, also retired, to Linz.

This left Vienna defended by a garrison of perhaps only 15,000 men commanded by Count Ernst Rüdiger von Starhemberg. The Viennese had had ample time to prepare, and they demolished houses around the city walls and cleared away the debris to provide clear fields of fire for their artillery, which was both more numerous and more modern than that of the Ottomans. The Ottomans had only a few heavy pieces, sent up the Danube by barge.

On July 14, the main Ottoman force arrived at Vienna and encircled the city. Siege operations commenced on July 17. Starhemberg sought to keep the Ottomans off guard by frequent sorties, while the small imperial forces under Duke Charles tried to contain Ottoman raiding.

The vastly superior Ottoman numbers soon began to tell nonetheless. The Ottomans undertook mining operations and made a number of breaches in the city walls through which they launched assaults. The defenders contained the penetrations by throwing up makeshift fortifications, but by the beginning of September Starhemberg's force was down to about half of its original strength and running short of critical supplies.

At this point a Polish army arrived in present-day Wiener Neustadt, on the other side of a small mountain range from Vienna. The Polish Force was under the personal command of King John III Sobieski, who was honoring a mutual defensive pact made in late March with Leopold I. Sobieski made the forced march of 220 miles from Warsaw in only 15 days. He now assumed command of an allied force of some 70,000 men: 30,000 Poles; 18,500 Austrian troops led by Duke Charles; 19,000 Bavarians, Swabians, and Franconians under Prince Georg Friedrich of Waldeck; and about 9,000 Saxons commanded by Elector John George III of Saxony. As the relief force approached Vienna, scouting reports spread terror among the allied troops, but Sobieski managed to keep them moving forward.

Sobieski's arrival surprised Grand Vizier Kara Mustafa, who nonetheless continued siege operations in an effort to take Vienna before battle could be joined. The Battle of Vienna began early on the morning of September 12, 1683, when at 4:00 a.m. the Ottomans attacked in an effort to interfere with the allied deployment. Fighting raged all day. The battle was decided by a surprise allied cavalry charge at about 5:00 p.m. led by Sobieski in person from the hills near the city directly on Kara Mustafa's headquarters. The remainder of the Viennese garrison sallied to join in. During the fighting, a cloud caused the crescent moon to fade from the sky, an omen that is said to have produced consternation among the Ottomans.

By nightfall, the Ottomans had been defeated and were in full flight, although they found the time to execute thousands of Christian prisoners, including children, taken in their march against Vienna. Sobieski suspended the pursuit that night, fearing an ambush. The battle itself claimed some 2,000 killed and 2,500 wounded on the allied side. The Ottomans lost some 10,000 dead and 5,000 wounded as well as 5,000 prisoners taken along with all their cannon. Sobieski is said to have paraphrased Julius Caesar when he said, "Veni, vidi, Deus vicit" ("I came, I saw, God conquered").

Sobieski's victory was the last great military effort of the dying Kingdom of Poland. The next month Sobieski pursued the Ottomans into Hungary and inflicted a serious defeat on them before dysentery forced an end to the pursuit. The Polish contribution was not appreciated, as Sobieski noted with some bitterness. It certainly did not save Poland. Indeed, it strengthened the Habsburgs at the expense of Poland. In the late eighteenth century, Austria took part in two partitions of

Poland. The relief of Vienna in 1683 did put an end to the Ottoman dream of further European conquest.

Spencer C. Tucker

Further Reading

Barker, Thomas M. *Double Eagle and Crescent: Vienna's Second Turkish Siege and Its Historical Setting.* Albany: State University of New York Press, 1967.

Hoskins, Janina. *Victory at Vienna: The Ottoman Siege of 1683, a Historical Essay and a Select Group of Readings.* Washington, DC: Library of Congress, 1983.

Kinross, Lord [John Patrick]. *The Ottoman Centuries: The Rise and Fall of the Turkish Empire.* New York: William Morrow, 1977.

Siege of St. Augustine (November 10–December 29, 1702)

The abortive English siege of Spanish-held St. Augustine (Florida) occurred at the beginning of the War of the Spanish Succession (1702–1713, known in America as Queen Anne's War) and lasted from November 10 to December 29, 1702. The conflict was sparked by the death without heirs of Spanish king Charles II in 1700. The Spanish throne then passed to the grandson of King Louis XIV of France, who became king as Philip V and began the Bourbon dynasty in Spain. This Spanish-French alliance left Britain dangerously isolated. The English feared encirclement of their North American colonies by the Spanish to the south and French to the north and west and were therefore determined to destroy St. Augustine, the only substantial Spanish military base in North America.

In September 1702, Governor James Moore of Carolina launched an expedition made up of between 800 and 1,200 (sources disagree) colonists and Native Americans to take St. Augustine. Most of the men traveled by sea in 14 vessels, but a small contingent led by Colonel Robert Daniel marched overland to attack St. Augustine from the west.

St. Augustine proved a challenging objective, as its strategically placed, well designed, and strongly built fort, the Castillo de San Marcos, provided an effective defense for the city. Spanish governor and captain general (who had been made a field marshal during the fighting in the Netherlands) José de Zúñiga y la Cerda commanded the defenders. His strong leadership proved a major factor in enabling the defenders to endure a prolonged siege.

Moore mistakenly launched an unnecessary attack against a Spanish position on Amelia Island during the voyage to St. Augustine. This action deprived the English of the element of surprise. When their vessels arrived in St. Augustine a week later, Zúñiga was well aware of the English intentions. He had also been able to dispatch a ship with a plea to Spanish authorities in Havana, Cuba, for reinforcements.

Zúñiga did what he could to prepare for the expected arrival of the English forces. He ordered his soldiers to round up cattle, and he opened the fort to the 1,500 inhabitants of St. Augustine. There they joined 323 soldiers. Zúñiga also ordered all structures within musket range of the Castillo to be razed in order to deprive the English of cover and allow the defenders clear fields of fire. On

November 10, Colonel Daniel arrived from the west at the same time the Spanish soldiers were returning with a herd of 163 cattle. The Spanish were able to move the herd into the moat of the fort before the English could stop them.

When Moore's fleet arrived on November 10, the sand bar that lay at the entrance of the harbor prevented his larger vessels from approaching the Castillo. The distance prevented their cannon from firing on the fortress. Moore then dispatched an appeal to English authorities in Jamaica for additional troops and sea mortars, which could lob shells (known as bombs) over the fort's walls.

Knowing he was badly outnumbered and determined to endure the siege until reinforcements arrived, Zúñiga never attempted to engage the English in open battle. Although the Castillo de San Marcos was badly overcrowded, Zúñiga's firm discipline and his rationing of provisions would allow the defenders to resist for some time. If Moore could not starve the Spaniards out in the short term, his only hope of victory was to receive reinforcements himself before the Spanish also might reinforce.

On December 26, 1702, lookouts at the fort spotted ships' masts on the horizon. This sighting turned out to be four Spanish warships bearing supplies and reinforcements, enabling the Spaniards to bring an end to the 50-day siege.

Now facing superior force, Moore ordered the town of St. Augustine burned and his ships also destroyed. His forces then withdrew overland.

Both Moore and Zúñiga endured censure from their own governments. Moore had lost the element of surprise and, without effective artillery, his vastly superior manpower counted for little. Rather unfairly, Zúñiga came under criticism for failing to mount anything more than a defensive action to the English assault and allowing them to raze the settlement. An official Spanish inquiry, however, cleared Zúñiga of any wrongdoing and indeed praised him for his leadership during the siege.

Dorothy A. Mays

Further Reading

Arnade, Charles W. *The Siege of St. Augustine in 1702*. Gainesville: University Press of Florida, 1959.

Moore, Gregory A. "The 1702 Siege of St. Augustine: English Miscalculation or Spanish Good Fortune?" *Escribano* 39 (2002): 16–28.

Waterbury, Jean Parker, ed. *The Oldest City: St. Augustine, Saga of Survival*. St. Augustine, FL: St. Augustine Historical Society, 1983.

Siege of Isfahan (March–October 23, 1722)

By 1700, the Safavids had lost much of their sway in Afghanistan. As a consequence, in 1704, Safavid Shah Sultan Husayn dispatched a Georgian-Iranian army, led by Georgian king Giorgi XI (Gorgin Khan), to subdue the rebellious Afghani tribes. Gorgin Khan defeated the Afghans and forced them to accept Safavid rule. However, his heavy-handed and oppressive governorship in Afghanistan prompted an Afghani revolt in the spring of 1709, led by Ghilzai tribe chief Mir Vays (Mir Ways). The Afghans defeated the Georgian contingents and expelled the Persians from Afghanistan. The loss of capable generals and elite troops left Persia exposed to attack. After the death of Mir Vays, his son Mahmud assumed the leadership of a loose coalition of Afghani tribes and in 1722 he invaded Iran and routed the Safavid army near Gulnabad on March 8, 1772.

The destruction of the Safavid army took the Ghilzai leader by surprise, and he did not immediately realize the full extent of his victory. Concerned about ambushes, he spent three days on the battlefield before cautiously advancing to Isfahan, which he could have easily captured had he pursued the Persians immediately after his victory. Mahmud captured Farahabad, Sultan Husayn's favorite castle, without a fight, and he then plundered Julfa, Isfahan's suburb populated by Armenian merchants.

The Afghans then laid siege to the city itself, while the Safavid leadership continued to show indecision and lack of resolve. The shah retained counselors whose advice had contributed to the Persian defeats and dismissed those who could have helped him. Persian attempts to negotiate revealed to the Afghans the full gravity of situation facing the Safavids.

Sultan Husayn failed to evacuate the civilian population of Isfahan and instead imposed a general ban on leaving it. Most important, he decided to remain inside the capital instead of escaping to provinces to raise fresh troops. Meanwhile, the Georgians, who had played such a prominent role in the Safavid state and could probably have defeated the Afghans on their own, refused to come to Sultan Husayn's help, based on his earlier mistreatment of them.

In April, the Ghilzai captured a bridge in the Abbasabad quarter and established a bridgehead into Isfahan. While the Afghans could not completely surround the city owing to the size of their army, Mahmud skillfully deployed his men at crucial points making it virtually impossible to get in or out of it. Life inside the city quickly deteriorated as supplies run out and desperate residents turned against each other; within weeks, cannibalism became rife. By August, hundreds of people were dying each day from starvation and diseases, their corpses piling up in the city streets. After six months of siege, Sultan Husayn realized that further resistance was futile, and he surrendered the city to Mahmud on October 23. At a meeting in the castle of Farahabad, the shah announced his abdication in favor of Mahmud, presenting him with the bejeweled tuft of heron's feathers (jiqa), the symbol of monarchy. Two days later Mahmud entered Isfahan in triumphant procession.

The fall of Isfahan marked the twilight of the Safavid dynasty. In 1726 most Safavid princes were massacred and Shah Sultan Huseyn himself executed. The Ghilzai supremacy in Iran lasted seven years, but this period was full of domestic turmoil and foreign threats. In the 1730s, Nadir Khan expelled the Afghans and briefly restored the Safavid dynasty to the throne before claiming it for himself.

The city of Isfahan itself, once the crown jewel of Iran, suffered greatly during the siege, its infrastructure was damaged or destroyed and its population decimated. The city never recovered from this destruction and was later eclipsed by Shiraz, Mashhad, and finally Tehran.

Alexander Mikaberidze

Further Reading

Floor, Willem, ed. *The Afghan Occupation of Safavid Persia, 1721–1729*. Paris: Association pour l'avancement des études iraniennes, 1998.

Lockhart, Laurence. *The Fall of the Safavi Dynasty and the Afghan Occupation of Persia*. Cambridge, UK: Cambridge University Press, 1958.

Siege of Cartagena de Indias (March 9–May 20, 1741)

The British siege of the Spanish city Cartagena de Indias in modern Colombia during March 9–May 20, 1741, was part of the War of Jenkins' Ear (1739–1743), which itself was subsumed by the War of the Austrian Succession (1740–1748). As a consequence of the 1713 Treaty of Utrecht ending the War of the Spanish Succession (1702–1713), the British had secured certain limited trading rights in Spanish America. This so-called Asiento was a 30-year contract that allowed the British to supply an unlimited number of slaves and 500 tons of goods to the Spanish colonies per year. Understandably, the Spanish sought to enforce this concession very narrowly, while the British sought to pry open the lucrative Spanish imperial market for their finished goods.

In 1731 in the West Indies, a Spanish patrol vessel *La Isabela* stopped a British merchant ship the *Rebecca* to search for contraband. Finding the ship engaged in illegal trading, the Spaniards plundered it, and the Spanish captain cut off the ear of its master, Robert Jenkins. This incident created little concern at first, but in 1738 with war fever against Spain stoked by British merchants increasing, Jenkins appeared before the House of Commons and reportedly displayed the scarred stump of his ear and its shriveled remains. Members of the House of Commons then expressed their outrage.

Apparently, the Spanish government sought to resolve the issue without recourse to war, but the British government succumbed to mercantile demands and asserted claims to "freedom of the seas," which the Spaniards rejected in a defense of their right to search suspicious vessels. On October 23, 1739, with much popular support, Britain declared war on Spain in what became widely known in Britain as the War of Jenkins' Ear.

The British objective in the war was to capture and retain control of the four major Spanish port cities in the Americas: Puerto Bella, Cartagena, Havana, and Vera Cruz. The war began well for the British. Royal Navy vice admiral Edward Vernon, with six small ships of the line, moved against Puerto Bello (now Portobelo, Panama) in the Viceroyalty of New Granada, a major transshipment point for gold and silver from Peru and Ecuador. The English had taken Puerto Bella twice before: by Sir Francis Drake in 1596 and Sir Henry Morgan in 1668.

Vernon attacked on November 22, 1739, and soon overran Puerto Bella's defenses and captured and sacked the town. Vernon stayed in there until the next March, when he sailed to Fort San Lorenzo at the mouth of the Chagres River in Panama, taking it after a two-day naval bombardment. After sacking the customs house, Vernon destroyed the fort on March 29 and then returned to Porto Bello.

> **A Premature Tribute**
>
> Confident of final victory in the siege of Cartagena, Admiral Vernon informed London that the city was about to fall. The British government responded by ordering a medal struck commemorating the "victory," with the obverse showing Cartagena and the inscription "He has taken Cartagena," while the reverse side had a likeness of Admiral Vernon and the inscription "To the Avenger of his Country." With the British defeat, the medal was withdrawn.
>
> Spencer C. Tucker

These two easy and profitable victories caused widespread satisfaction in Britain and made Vernon something of a national hero.

The next major British operation should probably have been against Havana, Cuba. The administrative center of the Spanish New World empire, Havana also had the largest dockyard in the Americas and was a major transshipment point for precious metals. Certainly, it was the most important Spanish city in the Americas. Capture of its large harbor and dockyard were considered essential for the Royal Navy to be able to remain on station for a prolonged period. Although his instructions urged a descent on Havana first, London gave Vernon full discretion as to priority, and Vernon saw Havana as likely being a prolonged operation against strong fortifications with the impact of tropical diseases on the attackers. He decided on Cartagena de Indias as the next target.

This would be the major British military effort of the entire war. Now reinforced, Vernon now commanded a quarter of the Royal Navy: the largest fleet in the region to that point in history. Including 29 ships of the line, smaller warships, bomb ketches, fire-ships, and transports, it numbered in all 124 ships manned by some 15,400 sailors. The British land contingent, numbering some 12,000 men (including 3,600 North American colonial volunteers), was to have been commanded by Major General Lord Cathcart. Vernon greatly respected Cathcart and looked forward to working with him, but Cathcart died en route to the Caribbean and was succeeded by Brigadier General Thomas Wentworth. He and Vernon were soon at odds and certainly this had an impact on what was to come. The British effort was delayed several months for a number of reasons, and this would have considerable impact later. Setting out from Jamaica, the British ships arrived in Playa Grande Bay on March 4.

Cartagena de Indias, then in the Viceroyalty of New Granada and now in Colombia, boasted a large, excellent harbor and, as an important gold-trading center, had a considerable population of at least 10,000. Although it had been captured by Drake in 1585 and by the French in 1697, its defenses had recently been enlarged and substantially improved. Fortunately for the Spanish, admiral and governor general of Cartagena Don Blas de Lezo had charge of the defense. He could count only some 4,000–6,000 men, including Spanish regulars and 300 native archers. There were also six Spanish ships of the line. Just as the British were hindered by their being no overall commander with decisions made in councils of war, differences between Blas de Lezo and Viceroy of New Grandad Sebastián de Eslava at times hindered Spanish defensive efforts.

Cartagena is located directly on the Caribbean and faces it to westward. Rocks and surf prevented approach from that direction. Cartagena was divided into two parts: the city itself and its suburbs known as Ximani. The Bay of Playa Grande lies to the south. Its two entrances were the Boca Chica (Little Mouth) and Boca Grande (Large Mouth). Boca Chica was the only deepwater entrance for ocean-going ships, but the strait was narrow and only one ship at a time could pass through it. Defending the passage on the Tierra Bomba side of the channel was the Castle of San Luis de Bocachica, while on the other peninsula was the Baradera battery. A boom could also be raised to block the strait from Tierra Bomba to Fort San Jose across the channel. Beyond Boca Chica lay the lagoon of the outer harbor. Cartagena itself was walled and mounted some 160 cannon, while Ximani boasted another 140. The city was surrounded by a moat and its gates were protected by recently constructed bastions. Ximani also had a moat. Castle San Felipe de Barajas (identified as Fort San Lázaro) situated on the hill of San Lázaro controlled access to Cartagena by land.

Given the odds against him, Lezo planned to effect a fighting withdrawal and then a defense designed to delay the British until the arrival of the rainy season in early May, which would inhibit the attackers, force them to their ships, and weaken them with a scarcity of supplies and the spread of illness and disease.

In a week-long bombardment, Vernon's ships attacked a number of the Spanish forts. The British troops came ashore on the Isla de Tierra Bomba on March 22. They offloaded a number of ship guns and began erecting batteries, then on April 5 attacked the Castle San Luis by land and sea. Some of the British ships supported the troops ashore, while others engaged the Spanish ships of the line firing on the British in an attempt to prevent their forcing the Boca Chica channel. Finally, Lezo ordered his ships scuttled to block British entry, but one ship was taken by the British before it could sink and scuttling of the others was only partially successful. Lezo was among the Spaniards wounded in the action.

The British ships then passed through the channel and entered the harbor. The next British effort was to try to isolate Cartagena on the land side by taking the San Felipe de Barajas fortress, now fully manned by the withdrawing Spaniards with some1,000 men. If the British could take the fortress, they would be able to shell Cartagena into submission. Protected by British cannon fire from the ships, Wentworth's men came ashore on April 16. The British effort to take the fort in a night assault by some 2,000 men at 4:00 a.m. on April 20, failed. Sunrise allowed cannon at Cartagena to locate and fire on the British and a column of troops from the city threatened to cut them off. Having suffered some 600 casualties, the British withdrew.

This reversal, the inability of Vernon and Wentworth to cooperate, the arrival on schedule of the tropical heavy rains, and increasing British deaths and sickness from scurvy and disease, especially Yellow Fever, all prompted the decision on May 14 to evacuate. After destruction of the fortifications that they had taken, all British guns and equipment were re-embarked, followed by the men, only 3,569 of whom were fit for duty. The ships then sailed for Jamaica on May 20.

The siege had lasted 67 days, during which the British sustained some 9,500 dead and 7,500 wounded. Fifty British ships had been lost, damaged, or had to be abandoned for lack of crews. Less than half of the North Americans who had volunteered returned home. One of them was Lawrence Washington, George Washington's elder brother. When he returned to his Virginia plantation, he named it Mount Vernon after Admiral Vernon.

Spanish losses were considerably fewer. They amounted to some 800 dead and 1,200 wounded. Blas de Lezo, however, died in September of plague brought on by all the unburied corpses. The Spaniards also lost their six ships of the line and five of their forts and three of their batteries had also been destroyed.

The war continued, but other British naval operations against Spanish interests in the World were repelled, including assaults against St. Augustine in Florida; and Havana. The upshot of the fighting was that Spain retained its colonial empire in the Americas until the early nineteenth century.

Spencer C. Tucker

Further Reading
Clowes, William Laird. *The Royal Navy: A History from the Earliest Times to 1900.* Vol. 3. London: Chatham, 1996.

Ford, Douglas. *Admiral Vernon and the Navy: A Memoir and Vindication.* London: T. Fisher Unwin Ltd, 1907.

Fortescue, J. W. *A History of the British Army.* Vol. 2, *To the Close of the Seven Years' War.* New York: AMS Press, 1978.

Harding, Richard. *Amphibious Warfare in the 18th Century.* Woodbridge, Suffolk, UK: Boydell Press, 1991.

Laughton, J. K. "Vernon, Edward." In *Dictionary of National Biography*, edited by Sidney Lee, Vol. 58, 267–272. London: Smith, Elder & Co., 1899.

Leach, Douglas Edward. *Arms for Empire: A Military History of the British Colonies in North America, 1607–1763.* London: Macmillan, 1973.

Le Fevre, Peter. *Precursors of Nelson: British Admirals of the Eighteenth Century.* Mechanicsburg, PA: Stacpole, 2000.

Vernon, Edward. *The Vernon Papers.* London: Navy Records Society, 1958.

Siege of Fort William Henry (August 3–10, 1757)

The August 3–10, 1757, siege of Fort William Henry (New York), situated at the head of Lake George, is best remembered through James Fenimore Cooper's thrilling, albeit inaccurate, *Last of the Mohicans* and its various adaptations. The siege of Fort William Henry and the subsequent "massacre" of the Anglo-American garrison there demonstrated the limitations of both French and British power in upstate New York and the difficulties of fighting alongside allies from an alien culture. This event occurred at the height of the French and Indian War (1754–1763).

Left with a reduced garrison by John Campbell, Lord Loudoun, who was concentrating his forces for an attack on Louisbourg, and damaged by a surprise winter attack, Fort William Henry in 1757 was not in a particularly good position to resist a siege. Although the fort's strong walls could only be breached by cannon, and it was impractical to bring cannon overland, the winter attack had destroyed the nearby British boats and ships. With them removed as a threat, the French could transport artillery to the fort via Lake George.

Meanwhile, Major General Louis-Joseph, Marquis de Montcalm, had decided that Fort William Henry and the chain of British posts stretching south would be his primary targets for 1757. As such, Montcalm gathered 6,000 French regulars, Canadian militiamen, Troupes de la Marine, and almost 2,000 Native American allies drawn from as far away as Wisconsin and Iowa. Language barriers frequently hampered Montcalm's control of this multinational force, as did the fact that the natives came as allies to the French force, not auxiliaries.

At the same time, Lieutenant Colonel George Monro prepared to defend Fort William Henry with some 1,500 mixed British regulars and colonials, and a battery of 18 heavy cannon. An initial reconnaissance in force to ascertain French intentions ended in disaster when it was ambushed at Sabbath Day Point. The local commander, Major General Daniel Webb, beat a hasty retreat to Fort Edward, promising support for his soon to be besieged subordinate.

Montcalm's forces began the siege on August 3, 1757. He followed European practices, building a series of trenches that moved his batteries ever closer to the fort. British efforts to disrupt the French advance became increasingly ineffective as the fort's own cannon burst one by one under the pressure of sustained use. Monro's casualties mounted, both because of his own defective cannon and French high-angle fire into the fort. On August 7, 1757, Montcalm passed to Monro an intercepted message from Webb declining to send reinforcements. With the walls of the fort crumbling under French fire he could no longer effectively return fire himself and, with the final French breaching battery in place, Monro sought cease-fire terms two days later on August 9, 1757.

Montcalm offered terms including safe passage to Fort Edward and the retention of both personal effects and a symbolic field cannon. Fort William Henry's stores would thus become the property of France. These terms were intended to honor the British for their courageous defense, but Montcalm failed to consult his allies in issuing them. The Native Americans accompanying his expedition had done so in pursuit of personal honor, reflected in captives, scalps, and booty, rather than any love of the French cause. This failure to communicate set the stage for trouble even worse than that between Montcalm and his native allies at Fort Oswego the previous year.

It is unclear exactly how well the terms of surrender were conveyed across the language barriers to the assorted tribes. It is possible that the French traders serving as translators, no more satisfied with the terms than the natives themselves, failed to pass them on accurately or covertly encouraged the warriors to violate them. Many natives saw the terms not only as a betrayal by Montcalm but also as a conspiracy between whites.

Following the British evacuation of Fort William Henry, several Native Americans entered the fort and scalped the wounded and ill who were left behind as unable to travel. French sentries and missionaries were able to save only a few of them. The night of August 9–10, 1757, was spent in terror by many of the British, as the natives' unhappiness with Montcalm's terms became clear.

As the British column began the march to Fort Edward, some warriors demanded personal possessions as booty of war. Panicking soldiers and civilians handed over their packs, which precipitated a chaotic crisis. The majority of the natives had not been involved in the initial seizures but quickly joined in when they realized that there was booty to be had after all. Many in the British column panicked, fleeing in all directions as warriors began seizing captives as well as booty. Panic fed panic along the British column, and the heavily outnumbered French escort proved reluctant to intervene. Montcalm, hurrying to the scene, actually made matters worse as natives, seeing that Montcalm was attempting to deprive them of their captives, scalped them to retain these second-best trophies.

By historian Ian Steele's count, between 69 and 184 British died in the confusion, with the remainder becoming permanent captives in Canada and beyond. Many more were held temporarily and ransomed or exchanged. Hundreds made their way to Fort Edward where their stories, exaggerated by panic and confusion, stunned the British who then expected an immediate attack. Instead of attacking, however, Montcalm burned Fort William Henry and returned north. His forces were substantially reduced as his native allies, who had obtained their purpose in accompanying him, returned home rather than follow on south.

Montcalm was deeply distressed by the violation of his terms of surrender and thereafter minimized Native American participation in his campaigns, which substantially weakened the defenses of New France. Montcalm's allies were also weakened by smallpox contracted from their captives. The British eventually recovered from the shock of the incident, although thereafter British commanders denied surrendering French garrisons the honors of war in retaliation for the supposed betrayal at Fort William Henry.

Grant T. Weller

Further Reading

Anderson, Fred. *Crucible of War: The Seven Years' War and the Fate of the Empire in British North America, 1754–1766.* New York: Random House, 2000.

Leach, Douglas Edward. *Arms for Empire: A Military History of the British Colonies in North America, 1606–1763.* New York: Macmillan, 1973.

Steele, Ian. *Betrayals: Fort William Henry and the "Massacre."* New York: Oxford University Press, 1990.

Siege of Louisbourg (June 8–July 26, 1758)

The British siege and capture of the French fortress at Louisbourg during June–July 1758 was one of the most important battles during the French and Indian War (1754–1763), for it set the stage for subsequent British operations against Québec.

The fortified town of Louisbourg was located on the east coast of Cape Breton Island. It commanded a large harbor some three miles long and about a half-mile wide. The channel providing access to the harbor was only about a half-mile wide and was flanked by rocky shoals. Louisbourg was often called the "Gibraltar of the New World" because of this imposing Vaubanesque fortress's stone walls and

Siege of Louisbourg

The port of Louisbourg on Cape Breton Island, Nova Scotia, viewed from the headlands above the lighthouse in 1768. An important French military base at the port guarded access to the St. Lawrence River, which made it a prime English military target, leading to its siege and capture in 1758. (Library of Congress)

ample cannon, but in fact it depended heavily on naval support for its defense. Indeed, it was begun as an anchorage for the French Navy to help defend the Gulf of St. Lawrence.

This was not the first time the British had assaulted the French stronghold. In 1745 during King George's War (1744–1748), the New England militia, supported by a strong British navy squadron, had shocked London and Paris by capturing the fortress. The October 1748 Treaty of Aix-la-Chapelle ending the war returned Louisbourg to French control, however, enraging New Englanders.

When warfare began anew in 1754 between the French and English in North America, it was clear to both sides that control of Louisbourg would be vital to the outcome. In French hands, Louisbourg served as a base from which attacks could be mounted against New England and Nova Scotia. It was also a haven for French privateers attacking English fishing boats and merchant ships plying the principal North Atlantic sea lanes between North America and Britain, as well as a center for illicit trade between the French and New England. If the British were to gain control of Louisbourg, they could turn it into a powerful base from which they might close off the St. Lawrence to French resupply and establish an assembly point there for an invasion up the St. Lawrence to Québec. They would also control the Atlantic fisheries.

In 1757 British prime minister William Pitt made it clear that he intended to emphasize the North American theater of war with the ultimate goal of ending French rule there. The capture of Louisbourg would be the essential first step in moving against the heart of New France at Québec. Pitt's overall strategy called for a three-pronged attack: the first against Fort Duquesne, the second against Fort Ticonderoga and Crown Point, and the third against Louisbourg. Following the successful realization of these three objectives, offensives could be mounted against Québec and Montréal. In many respects, Louisbourg was the key to the overall British plan.

In March 1758, Pitt replaced John Campbell, Lord Loudoun, with his deputy Major General James Abercrombie as British commander in chief in North America. Abercrombie found himself the beneficiary of Loudoun's substantial training efforts and the buildup of auxiliary services.

As the English prepared to take the offensive, French forces in North America were forced on the defensive. Military commander of New France Major General Louis-Joseph de Montcalm was severely handicapped by serious shortages of men, weapons, supplies, and even food. Anticipating an English assault on Louisbourg, however, Montcalm increased the size of the French squadron there. When the British attacked, 11 French warships, five of them ships of the line, were in the harbor to add their numerous cannon to the defense of the fortress. Montcalm also added two reasonably well-equipped battalions to the defending force. In all, the defenders numbered some 6,000 men: 2,000 land troops, 1,000 marines, 2,600 seamen, and 400 militiamen.

The British effectively isolated the battlefield. They blockaded and prevented French ships in Mediterranean ports from sailing to North America. While they were unable to achieve the same result off the French Atlantic ports, of 23 French ships dispatched to Louisbourg, including 12 transports, only 7 managed to reach that place. A major French fleet arrived too late.

In March 1758, Major-General Jeffery Amherst took command of the British invasion force. Rear Admiral Charles Hardy also arrived at Halifax that same month to assume command of the British squadron already dispatched there by Pitt. As soon as weather permitted, he took up station off Louisbourg. In all, the British earmarked for the invasion 39 warships manned by 14,000 officers and men. Admiral Edward Boscawen, the designated naval commander, arrived at Halifax on May 9. The expeditionary force, numbering in all 167 ships of all kinds, sailed on the 29th.

Amherst's land force of 13,200 men consisted of 14 infantry companies, 4 ranger companies, and an artillery detachment. This force was formed into three brigades under the command of Brigadier-Generals James Wolfe, Charles Lawrence (governor of Nova Scotia), and Edward Whitmore.

On June 8, the British invasion force began coming ashore on Cape Breton Island. The landing site was Gabarus Bay about four miles to the southwest of the fortress, the same general location as in 1745.

Governor of Louisbourg Augustin de Boschenry de Drucour had done what he could to prepare for a British assault. The French had repaired and strengthened the fortress after its return to their control in 1748, and they mounted more guns and constructed extensive shore defenses manned by 2,000 men along Gabarus Bay to prevent a repeat of 1745. Drucour saw the warships, commanded by Admiral Jean-Baptiste Degaulle, in a purely defensive role, however. The ships' guns were to help protect the fortress from its water side.

En route to Louisbourg, the British fleet was dispersed by bad weather, but it rendezvoused off Gabarus Bay southwest of the French fortress on June 2. Amherst and Wolfe surveyed possible landing sites, but bad weather kept them from carrying out a landing until June 8. The British boats made for shore in three groups. Those in the center and on the right were feints. The main attack was by Wolfe's brigade on the left at the extremity of the French line. Seven ships provided covering fire for the assault. Once Wolfe was ashore, the other two brigades were to slip to the west and land behind him.

The troops came ashore in surf and under heavy fire from the shore. The landing almost failed. Both sides understood that if the British gained a foothold and began their siege, it would simply be a matter of time for, without outside reinforcement, Louisbourg must fall. The British troops fixed bayonets and, after a hard fight, drove the French defenders from the beaches. The remainder of the British troops came ashore by nightfall.

High wind ended any British communication with the troops ashore for several days. On June 11, the British were able to bring some artillery ashore. At the same time Boscawen's ships blockaded the harbor entrance. Ashore in heavy fog and under almost constant fire from the fortified town and French ships in the harbor, the British began to dig siege lines and slowly extend them closer to the fortress. As much of an impediment as was the weather, it actually served to aid the British.

Fog masked Wolfe's attack on and seizure of Lighthouse Point on June 12. Soon the British had established a battery there, overlooking the Island Battery that guarded the harbor entrance. On June 18, the French sank four of their smaller warships in the middle of the channel to block the harbor entrance, but the next day the British opened fire on the Island Battery. It was finally silenced on the 26th.

By July 1, the British took possession of the high ground overlooking the Dauphin Gate, the main entrance to the fortress. Two days later, the British placed their guns on the high ground and began to bombard the French positions and, by July 6, the town itself. The French attempted several night sorties against the British positions but with scant success. Meanwhile, the British continued to extend their trenches.

On July 9, the French attempted a night sortie with their ships but without major result. By July 16, British guns were just 200 yards from the Dauphin Gate. The French ships off the fortress were providing effective fire against the British troops ashore, but on July 21 the 74-gun *Entreprenant*, one of the two largest French ships, caught fire, possibly from a lucky British shot, and blew up. Its flames caught on fire two other ships of the line, the *Célèbre* and *Capricieux* (both 64 guns). All three ships were a total loss. On July 22, the settlement's church and other building were set ablaze by the British bombardment. With the other two ships of the line continuing to fire on British troops, Boscawen launched a boat attack against them on the foggy night of the 25th. Some 600 British seamen in 50 boats succeeded in capturing the *Prudent* (74 guns), which being aground, was burnt. The British towed the *Bienfaisant* (64 guns) off to the northeast of the harbor. Boscawen then prepared to enter the harbor with six of his ships of the line, but that action proved unnecessary.

There was little the French could do at this point but surrender. On July 26, 1758, Drucour asked for terms. The defenders had conducted themselves with honor and in accordance with the accepted European rules of warfare and should have been allowed easy terms, yet Amherst denied the French all honors. Memories of the 1757 campaign and what had occurred on the British surrender of Fort William Henry were fresh, particularly among the Massachusetts men who participated in the expedition. Those who had taken up arms against the British became prisoners of war and were transported to England. The civilian population of the fort and the French population of Cape Breton and today's Prince Edward Island, more than 8,000 men, women, and children, were subsequently deported to France.

During the siege, the British lost 195 men killed and another 363 wounded. French losses were estimated at between 400 and 800 men killed. There were 3,600 prisoners, including 1,400 wounded. In addition, the British secured 216 guns and some mortars.

The fall of Louisbourg dealt a serious blow to morale in New France. With Louisbourg in British hands, the possibility of reinforcements from metropolitan France was greatly diminished. It was also clear that the next major British thrust would be against Québec itself. Strategically as well as symbolically, the British capture of Louisbourg was a defeat from which the French would never recover. Britain also gained control over the lucrative Atlantic fisheries.

Marcia Schmidt Blaine and Spencer C. Tucker

Further Reading

Anderson, Fred. *Crucible of War: The Seven Years' War and the Fate of Empire in British North America, 1754–1766.* New York: Vintage Books, 2000.

Hawke, David. *The Colonial Experience.* Indianapolis, IN: Bobbs-Merrill Educational Publishing, 1980.

Hittsman, J. Mackay, and C. C. J. Bond. "The Assault Landing at Louisbourg, 1758." *Canadian Historical Review* 35 (December 1954): 314–330.

Peckham, Howard H. *The Colonial Wars: 1689–1762.* Chicago: University of Chicago Press, 1964.

Siege and Battle of Quebec (June 26–September 13, 1759)

The British siege of the French city of Quebec beginning on June 26, 1759, and the ensuing Battle of the Plains of Abraham (Battle of Quebec) on September 13, 1759, was certainly one of the most important military engagements in the history of North America, for it secured British predominance on the continent.

In 1756 after fighting an undeclared war against the French in North America for two years (the French and Indian War, as the American colonists called it), Britain and France formally went to war. The ensuing conflict was known as the Seven Years' War (1756–1763) in Europe. Although both countries and their allies fought on the continent, the British government decided to make the main effort in America in a bid to win colonial mastery. The British therefore sent strong naval detachments and some 25,000 troops to North America.

The weight of the British commitment was not felt until 1758. That July, the British captured the great French fortress of Louisbourg on Cape Breton Island, Nova Scotia, that guarded Atlantic access to the St. Lawrence River. The next month British officers led a largely colonial force to capture Fort Frontenac on Lake Ontario. Its fall cut French communications westward and forced the French to abandon Fort Duquesne, which the British renamed Fort Pitt. Only at the recently constructed French Fort Ticonderoga on Lake Champlain did the British meet rebuff.

British prime minister William Pitt planned to deliver the decisive blow in 1759. In September 1758, he named Jeffery Amherst, who had commanded the successful expedition against Louisbourg, as major general and commander in North America, entrusting him with the seizure of Canada. With Louisbourg in their hands, the British could cut off French resupply. The British plan to take Quebec called for Amherst and 11,000 men, half of them colonials, to capture Ticonderoga and Crown Point on Lake Champlain, then advance down the water route to Montreal. After taking the city, they would move down the St. Lawrence to Quebec. An additional 9,000 troops under Major General James Wolfe, supported by naval forces under Rear Admirals Charles Saunders and Charles Holmes, would depart Louisbourg, enter the St. Lawrence, and take Quebec.

On June 26, 1759, Wolfe's men began disembarking at Île d'Orléans and on the south bank of the St. Lawrence, some four miles east of the city. Quebec stands on the northern shore of the St. Lawrence at the point where the river widens from three-quarters of a mile to nearly two miles across. Enclosed by walls, the Upper Town is situated at the top of steep bluffs overlooking the St. Lawrence River and the much smaller St. Charles River that flows into it. There were few possible means to assault the city by river. Below the town, the St. Charles and Montmorency Rivers presented formidable obstacles. West of Quebec farmland flattened into a plateau known as the Plains of Abraham, after early settler Abraham Martin.

French general Louis Joseph, Marquis de Montcalm, commanded the French fortress at Quebec. He had 12,000 regular troops and militia assisted by some Indians to defend what appeared to be an impregnable fortress. The eastern (downstream) approach to Quebec seemed the least formidable, and Wolfe first tried it. However, Montcalm had strongly fortified the riverbank for some distance. British efforts to draw the French troops out of Quebec and the entrenchments proved unsuccessful. The British cut off the city from Montreal, lobbed shells into Quebec, and raided nearby French settlements with a view toward demoralizing the Quebecois, but all of Wolfe's efforts to gain a foothold failed. To make matters worse, Wolfe was sick with a fever, and many of his men believed him to be dying. Saunders, fearing that his ships would be trapped in the winter ice in the St. Lawrence, threatened to depart. Wolfe realized that unless he could bring Montcalm to battle by the end of September, he would have to abandon the campaign.

Wolfe sought the advice of Captain Robert Stobo, who had been held prisoner in Quebec by the French and knew the city better than anyone in the British force. Stobo informed Wolfe of a narrow footpath that angled up the steep cliffs just north of the city at Anse de Foulon. At the same time, the Royal Navy

The Death of General Wolfe, by Benjamin West (1770). The 1759 British siege and battle of Quebec effectively gave the British control of Canada, but it cost the army its commanding general, Major General James Wolfe. (Library of Congress)

discovered that it could get some vessels through the supposedly impassable narrows upstream from Quebec.

Wolfe was determined to try this approach, and he secretly got his troops up this path during the night of September 12–13. French pickets assumed that the British boats were part of a French supply convoy due from Montreal. They had not been informed that the convoy was cancelled. Colonel William Howe's light infantry gained the top and captured the French positions overlooking the landing site. Wolfe and the main body of British troops then followed. By dawn Wolfe had some 4,500 men drawn up in line of battle facing east on the Plains of Abraham.

Montcalm carried out a personal reconnaissance of the British lines and decided to attack immediately with what forces he had before Wolfe could solidify his position and construct field fortifications. By midmorning on September 13, 1759, Montcalm had assembled a mixed force of French regulars and poorly trained colonial militia numbering about 4,500 men to face an equal number of well-trained British regulars. Montcalm had no artillery because his rival, French governor-general Pierre de Rigaud de Vaudreuil de Cavagnial, Marquis de Vaudreuil, insisted on retaining it for the defense of the city.

The battle began at about 10:00 a.m. when Montcalm's force attacked the British. The French militia fired too early, and there was little cohesion in the French force. The British showed excellent fire discipline, on the other hand, standing and firing in volleys when the French reached a range of 60 yards. When the French were at 40 yards, the British fired a devastating volley and moved forward.

The French broke and fled back into Quebec. The entire battle had lasted little more than half an hour. Casualties were comparable—some 644 French to 658 for the British—but the French never recovered from the psychological shock of the defeat.

Both commanders were mortally wounded in the fighting, but Wolfe at least had the satisfaction of knowing he had been victorious. French reinforcements under Count Louis Antoine de Bougainville came up from the west too late to affect the battle. De Vaudreuil decided to abandon Quebec and join up with Bougainville. The mayor of the city, Jean Baptise Nicholas Roche de Ramezay, entered into talks with the British in the hope that he might spin out negotiations until French reinforcements arrived, but he surrendered the city on September 18 to Wolfe's successor, Brigadier General George Townshend.

The loss of Quebec broke French resistance in Canada. The British victory was sealed by the Battle of Quiberon Bay on November 20, 1759, when Admiral Sir Edward Hawke's British ships defeated the French Brest Squadron, ensuring that the French would not be able to resupply their forces in America. The French did attempt to retake Quebec in April 1760 but failed. The French then withdrew to Montreal, where they held out until that September. On September 8, 1760, de Vaudreuil signed an instrument of surrender ceding all Canada to the British.

Spencer C. Tucker

Further Reading

Anderson, Fred. *Crucible of War: The Seven Years' War and the Fate of Empire in British North America, 1754–1763.* New York: Knopf, 2000.

Hibbert, Christopher. *Wolfe at Quebec.* London: Longmans, Green, 1959.

La Pierre, Laurer L. *1759: The Battle for Canada.* Toronto: McClelland and Stewart, 1990.

Lloyd, Christopher. *The Capture of Quebec.* New York: Macmillan, 1959.

May, Robin, and Gerry Embleton. *Wolfe's Army.* London: Osprey, 1997.

Parkman, Francis. *Montcalm and Wolfe.* New York: Atheneum, 1984.

Siege of Havana (June 6–August 13, 1762)

The June 6–August 13, 1762, siege of Havana occurred during the Seven Years' War (1756–1763; known in America as the French and Indian War of 1754–1763). Located on the northern coast of the island of Cuba, Havana was an important New World city. Founded in 1511 as San Cristóbal de la Habana, it was both the principal Spanish American colonial port city and an important administrative center for most of the Spanish Empire in the Americas.

In 1519 Spanish conquistador Diego Velázquez Cuellar relocated San Cristóbal de la Habana to the north coast of Cuba on Havana Harbor. Its new location, a scant 103 miles from Key West, Florida, gave the city an even more important presence in the Caribbean and the Americas, as well as aiding Spanish control of the important Florida Straits. Soon it was the principal Spanish base for expeditions to secure control of the Americas.

> ### Early Mortars
>
> Mortars are an important weapon in siege warfare. These high-angle fire muzzle-loading weapons are designed for plunging fire to surmount obstacles such as fortress walls. Mortars utilize explosive shell. With guns and howitzers, mortars form the triad of artillery types.
>
> The first mortars were short, only two to four times the diameter of the bore. Most were of bronze, although some were cast in iron. Mortars had powder chambers at the base of the bore for their powder charge. Cast with trunnions (pivot) at the base, mortars were usually fixed to fire at a 45° angle with range determined by the amount of the powder charge.
>
> The shell was positioned so that the fuse faced the top of the bore. Placing the fuse against the powder chamber might cause its malfunctioning on firing. If the fuse was toward the muzzle, it was lit by means of linstock or portfire, just before the main charge was lit and the shell lofted into the air. Ultimately, gunners learned that windage allowed some of the charge to escape around the shell and ignite the fuse. This greatly reduced the hazard for the gunners.
>
> Eighteenth-century British Army mortars ranged from the small 4.5-inch cohorn that could be transported by two men through 5.8-, 8-, 10-, to 13-inch models for siege work.
>
> **Spencer C. Tucker**

With Spain's conquest of the Aztec and Inca empires, Havana became the entrepôt for vast quantities of gold and silver shipped to metropolitan Spain. Cuba itself boasted mines and great plantations with the production of sugar and tobacco. This wealth attracted pirates. In 1538 French pirates arrived and plundered Havana, producing a slave revolt that saw the city destroyed by fire. Rebuilt and strengthened, Havana was, however, again taken, plundered, and burnt in 1555 by French pirate Jacques de Sores. Again, the city was rebuilt and its defenses strengthened, but in 1622 and in 1638 English freebooters again took the city.

In 1762 Havana boasted extensive shipyards capable of building ships of the line. Two forts defended the entrance to Havana Harbor: On its north side on Cavannos Ridge was the powerful Castillo de los Tres Reyes del Morro (known to the English as Morro Castle). The key to Havana and first constructed in 1597, it mounted 64 heavy cannon. On the south side of the channel was the Castillo de San Salvador de la Punta. The harbor entrance itself could be blocked to shipping by means of a chain from del Morro to La Punta. The city was also protected on the land side by a wall some three miles in length.

The Seven Years' War found Spain and England on opposite sides, but before joining France against England, Spanish king Charles III appointed Juan de Prado Mayera Portocarrero y Luna as colonial governor of the island. De Prado arrived in Cuba in February 1762 and immediately set about trying to strengthen the island's defenses. In June, Spanish admiral Gutierre de Hevia arrived at Havana with seven ships of the line, bringing two Spanish infantry regiments totaling some 1,000 men. These, however, proved quite inadequate, given that yellow fever soon reduced the Spanish military presence in Cuba to only 3,850 soldiers, some 5,000 sailors and marines, and 2,800 militiamen.

For most of the Seven Years' War, Spain remained neutral, but growing fears that a British victory over France would upset the balance of colonial power, Charles in August 1761 signed the so-called Family Compact with France (both countries had Bourbon family rulers). With Spain obviously preparing to go to war, on January 4, 1762, Britain declared war first. Securing Havana and Cuba was a major part of the British war plans.

On March 5, British admiral Sir George Pocock sailed from Portsmouth, England, with 7 ships of the line and 64 transports carrying 4,365 land troops under Lieutenant General George Keppel, Earl of Albemarle, for the planned descent on Cuba. Arriving at Barbados on April 20, Pocock then proceeded to the recently captured island of Martinique, where it added 8,461 men of Major General Robert Monckton's force there as well as 8 ships of the line belonging to Rear Admiral Sir George Rodney's Leeward Islands squadron. Pocock then set sail with 15 ships of the line as well as lesser warships and transports. On May 20, off northwestern Saint-Dominique (present-day Haiti), he added a squadron under Commodore Sir James Douglas. The considerable expeditionary force now numbered 21 ships of the line, 24 smaller warships, and 168 transports and supply ships with some 17,000 sailors and 12,862 land troops.

The British arrived at their destination on June 6, whereupon 12 British warships took up station off the channel entrance to Havana Harbor to prevent any Spanish egress. The British troops came ashore northeast of the city on June 7.

The first British objective was securing formidable Morro Castle, the British believing that the capture of this strategically placed fort would necessarily bring the city's surrender. The British expected to take it by conventional siege methods, but the fort was located on high rocky ground and thus not subject to the traditional trenches and parallels of a normal siege operation.

Cuban governor de Prado and admiral de Hevia were surprised by the large size of the invasion force and adapted the only recourse open to them of attempting to delay the attackers in hopes that yellow fever and other diseases would cripple the British and that either a hurricane that would greatly cripple the British fleet or a relief force would arrive in time to prevent surrender.

The Spaniards closed the channel entrance with the chain. Three Spanish ships of the line in poor repair (one of 74 guns and two of 64 guns) were then scuttled in place behind the chain, while the sailors and marines were sent, along with many of the battery ship guns, powder, and shot, to garrison the two principal forts, which now passed under naval command. Able Spanish Navy captain Luis Vicente de Velasco e Isla assumed command of the 700-man garrison at Morro Castle. The army garrisons that had held the two forts were relocated to defend the city itself.

The British landing went smoothly and the troops easily brushed aside a militia force and reached Havana by the end of their first day ashore. On June 11, the British captured an isolated redoubt on the Cavannos heights, and on June 13, they began construction of siege works. On June 22, following the landing of siege artillery, 12 heavy guns and 38 mortars opened fire on the Morro. The British then gradually advanced their works. By June 29, some 500 British shot and shell were hitting the fort daily, with Velasco losing some 30 men a day amid the need for constant repairs.

Velasco convinced de Prado that a raid on the besiegers was absolutely necessary, and on June 29, nearly 1,000 men sortied from Havana and attacked the besiegers from the rear and began spiking their guns, but the Spaniards were driven off before they could effect serious damage. Then, on July 1, the British launched a combined land and naval bombardment of the Morro. Four British ships of the line joined the land guns, but the ship guns could not be sufficiently elevated for their shot to reach the fort, while counterbattery fire from 30 of the Morro guns inflicted 192 casualties and serious damage on the British warships and forced their withdrawal. The land shelling was effective, however, for by the end of the day only three Spanish guns were able to fire at the British land batteries.

The next day, however, a fire broke out in the British artillery position and largely destroyed the siege works. Velasco took advantage of the respite to relocate some of his guns to that part of the fortress facing the British land artillery and to effect some repairs.

As the Spaniards had hoped, yellow fever had by now incapacitated half of the British invasion force and hurricane season was fast approaching. Albemarle secured sailors to man the land batteries, with heavy 32-pounder from the lower decks of the ships of the line brought ashore to augment the artillery.

By July 17, the British had silenced all but two of Velasco's guns, and it was now impossible to carry out repairs to the fortress. By July 20, the British had advanced their siege works sufficiently to allow them to begin mining one of the Morro's bastions. Meanwhile some 600 British shot and shells were striking the Morro daily with increasing Spanish casualties.

Early on July 22, some 1,300 Spaniards sallied from Havana against the British siege works but were driven back. Two days later Albemarle called on Velasco to surrender, offering to let him write his own terms. Velasco refused. On July 27, British reinforcements from North America arrived, consisting of two British regiments and some 3,000 provincials.

Very early on July 30, the Spaniards launched a naval attack by two schooners in the harbor against the British miners. This failed but Albemarle ordered the mine detonated that same day. The debris from the blast partially filled in the great moat before the fortress and Albemarle sent in an attack force of some 700 men, with a few gaining a foothold. Leading an effort to drive them off, Velasco was shot in the ensuing hand-to-hand combat and mortally wounded. British surgeons tried to save him, but he died the next day.

With capture of the Morro Fortress on July 30, the British held ground that commanded Havana itself. British artillery was brought up and placed in the fort, and when de Prado rejected a surrender demand from Albemarle, the British opened fire on Havana on August 11. With Fort la Punta silenced that same day, de Prado had no choice but to open surrender negotiations. These were concluded on August 12, with the formal surrender the next day and the Spaniards accorded the honors of war.

With Admiral de Hevia having failed to order the burning of his ships, the British now secured some 20 percent of the entire Spanish Navy: 10 ships of the line, 3 frigates, and 9 smaller warships, along with a number of armed trading vessels. Two almost completed ships of the line were taken in the dockyards. The English also gained some £3,000,000 in specie and other valuables. British casualties totaled 2,764 killed, wounded, and missing, but disease claimed another 4,708 dead. Spanish losses were 3,800 dead from all causes, 2,000 wounded or sick, and another 5,000 taken prisoner.

The British capture of Havana and western Cuba and their taking of Manila in the Philippines dealt a major blow to Spanish prestige and revealed the fragile nature of its empire as well as confirming British naval supremacy. Ironically, Cuba did not remain in British hands long. In the Treaty of Paris that ended the war on February 10, 1763, the island returned to Spain in exchange for Florida.

Spencer C. Tucker

Further Reading

Elliot, J. H. *Imperial Spain, 1469–1716*. New York: Penguin, 2002.

Gardiner, Asia Bird. *The Havana Expedition of 1762 in the War with Spain*. London: Forgotten Books, 2016.

Karmen, Henry. *Empire: How Spain Became a World Power, 1492–1763*. New York: Harper, 2004.

Montalvo, Maria. *Havana: History and Architecture*. Havana: Monacelli Press, 2000.

Syrett, David. *The Siege and Capture of Havana, 1762*. London: Navy Records Society, 1970.

Siege of Boston (April 19, 1775–March 17, 1776)

The Patriot siege of the city of Boston, Massachusetts, was one of the most important battles of the American Revolutionary War (1775–1783). It began on April 19, 1775, when, after the clash at Lexington and Concord, colonial militiamen followed the British troops back to Boston and closed around the city from the land side. The Massachusetts Provincial Congress meeting at Watertown authorized the formation of the colony's militia regiments into what was called the "Army of Observation" and charged it with containing the 3,500 British troops in Boston under British Army commander in North America Lieutenant General Thomas Gage.

Within a month, the besieging forces had grown to 24 Massachusetts regiments, supported by contingents of militia from Connecticut, Rhode Island, and New Hampshire, totaling as many as 16,000 men. Massachusetts general Artemas Ward had initial command. The siege lines ran from Chelsea around the peninsulas of Charlestown, Boston, and Dorchester Heights, to Roxbury. Gage evacuated by water the British troops in Charlestown and ordered a defensive line at Roxbury as well as the fortification of four hills in Boston proper. An informal agreement allowed people to move in and out through Boston Neck, providing no firearms were involved. Perhaps 9,000–10,000 Patriot residents fled the city, while a number of Loyalists moved in the opposite direction with many of the men joining newly formed Loyalist military units.

Because the besiegers had no heavy artillery and the harbor was left open, Vice Admiral Samuel Graves's Royal Navy ships were able to resupply the Boston garrison from Nova Scotia and other places. Nonetheless, conditions were difficult and the British troops were soon on short rations.

In an operation that would have major implications for the siege, on May 10 hastily organized Patriot forces under colonels Ethan Allen and Benedict Arnold captured the British bastion of Fort Ticonderoga on the western shore of Lake Champlain and there secured 78 serviceable cannon, ranging from 4- to 24-pounders, 6 mortars, 3 howitzers, thousands of cannon balls, 9 tons of musket balls, and 30,000 flints, as well as a large quantity of other military supplies.

With Boston running out of fresh meat and in need of hay for the British horses, Gage ordered men to Grape Island in Boston's outer harbor to secure hay. The British were met there by some local residents and Patriot militiamen who set fire to a barn on the island, destroying most of the hay. In response to this incident, Patriot militiamen worked to clear the islands in the harbor of cattle. In the Battle of Chelsea Creek on May 27–28, Royal Marines attempted to stop the removal of cattle and the Americans resisted. The British schooner *Diana* (6 guns) grounded and was burnt, but not before the Patriot side recovered its ordnance. Congress promptly promoted Israel Putnam, who led this action, to major general.

The British position at Boston was greatly strengthened on May 25 with the arrival of reinforcements under Major Generals John Burgoyne, Henry Clinton, and William Howe. British strength was now 6,500 men. The newly arrived generals also brought orders for Gage to impose martial law throughout Massachusetts, and the generals pressed Gage to undertake offensive action. Unlike Gage, who believed the Americans would fight hard and well, many of the officers did not hold the colonists in high regard and were eager to teach them a lesson. Clinton strongly urged that the British immediately take Dorchester Heights, which commanded Boston from the south. Gage agreed, but neither he nor his successor did so.

On June 12, Gage issued a proclamation demanding an end to the rebellion and that the insurgents turn over their weapons, promising a full pardon to all save John Adams and John Hancock. The appeal was ignored.

Meanwhile, on June 14, the Second Continental Congress, meeting in Philadelphia, authorized the establishment of 10 rifle companies for the Continental Army (Army of the United Colonies). This was the first regiment and generally regarded as the beginning date for the U.S. Army. The next day, Congress appointed Virginian George Washington as general and commander in chief of the army.

Learning that British forces in Boston were preparing to launch attacks on June 18 to occupy some of the high ground that dominated Boston, on June 15 the Massachusetts Committee of Safety ordered Ward to move forces into Charlestown Peninsula. This was a rash decision, with no military justification. Because the Patriot side lacked heavy guns capable of keeping British ships at bay, any force in the peninsula could easily be cut off by British troops landed behind them at Charlestown Neck.

Ward ordered Colonel William Prescott and three regiments of some 1,600 men into the peninsula. On the night of June 16, the Americans occupied and began fortifying Bunker Hull, the highest ground and a favorable position as long as the adjacent land and narrow escape route could be held. They also occupied the lower Breed's Hill, which was closer to Charlestown, there to repel the expected British disembarkation.

Howe had command of the attacking force, which would make a frontal assault on the colonial positions. Gage rejected Clinton's sound advice that he be allowed to lead another force to be delivered by the Royal Navy behind Breed's Hill, cutting off the colonials. Gage claimed it was against established military principles to place troops between two hostile forces.

The ensuing Battle of Bunker Hill on June 17 saw the two British assaults beaten back, but the third attempt brought a British victory. It was, however, won at very heavy cost for the attackers. Out of some 2,400 men engaged, Howe's force suffered 1,054 casualties (including 82 officers), 226 of them dead. Probably only some 1,500 Americans of perhaps 3,200 on the peninsula had actually taken part in the fighting; of these, some 140 were killed, 380 were wounded, and 39 were captured. In terms of percentage of casualties to force engaged, Bunker Hill was one of the most sanguinary battles of the entire century. The battle shook Howe and may well have a major factor in his subsequent failure as commander in chief to press home attacks in battle.

On July 3, 1775, Washington arrived at Cambridge, west of Boston, and assumed command from Ward of the provincial troops there, now some 17,000 men. Washington's generals estimated that the British then numbered about 11,000–12,000 men, but their actual strength was some 6,000–7,000. Washington's first priorities were keeping the army fed and supplied and training it. He reorganized the army into three wings and ordered an extension of the fortifications surrounding Boston.

Fearing that the winter would make it difficult to hold his army together, on September 11, Washington called a council of war and presented a plan for an amphibious assault across Back Bay in flat-bottom boats capable of carrying some 50 men each. The council unanimously opposed the plan and it was dropped. But with Continental Army enlistments about to run out, there was growing pressure on Washington to attack, and on October 18 he called another council of war. All save Brigadier General Nathanael Greene opposed an attack as too risky, and Greene supported it only if could be made with 10,000 men. Washington accepted the council's decision.

Learning that he had been recalled to London, Gage departed on October 10. Howe received promotion to lieutenant general with the local rank of general and now took command of British forces in the war. Believing that effective offensive operations could not be mounted from Boston, Howe sought to relocate the army elsewhere. William Legge, Lord Dartmouth, who was secretary of state for the colonies and thus charged with running the war, concurred. In a letter of September 5, which Howe received on November 9, he urged Howe to evacuate Boston and proceed to New York City. The lack of sufficient ships to move the men and their equipment prevented this, however.

In early September, Washington had authorized the arming of a number of small vessels for intelligence gathering and to capture isolated British supply ships. On November 29, the lightly armed schooner *Lee* (6 guns) of "Washington's Navy" captured the British brigantine *Nancy*, which had become separated in a storm. The *Nancy* was found to be carrying 2,000 muskets, 31 tons of musket balls, 100,000 musket flints, 3,000 round shot, and a considerable quantity of cartridges, as well as a large bronze 13-inch mortar in what was the most important American acquisition of British arms taken at sea during the war.

Winter posed major problems for both sides. Both the Patriots and the British suffered from supply shortages, but the Patriots were much more vulnerable to the elements. Their pay was also in arrears, gunpowder was in extremely short supply, and most Continental Army enlistments would expire at the end of the year.

In November on Washington's orders, chief of the Continental Army artillery Major General Henry Knox began the demanding operation of transporting from Fort Ticonderoga via sledges pulled by oxen overland and across the frozen Hudson and Connecticut Rivers, 59 of the artillery pieces captured from the British. This operation was completed on January 24, 1776. Meanwhile, in mid-January, acting in accordance with orders from London, Howe had detached some 1,500 men under Clinton to participate in an operation against the southern colonies, which met rebuff off Charles Town (Charleston), South Carolina, in the Battle of Sullivan's Island (June 28, 1776).

Washington wanted to attack the British, and on February 16, with the water having frozen between Boston and Roxbury, he again called a council of war and suggested an attack across the ice. Counting militiamen, Washington had some 13,500 men. Again, his generals demurred.

Washington settled for another plan. Fortunately for the Americans, Howe had made no effort to take and hold Dorchester Heights, the high ground overlooking Boston from the south. Washington planned to take that terrain, which he believed would force Howe to attack, an option Washington welcomed. Washington's plan called for a surprise occupation of the heights and completion of defensive fortifications there in only one night.

Because the ground was frozen, the soldiers constructed heavy wooden breastworks that could later be strengthened with earth. Barrels filled with earth would be rolled into place and wooden abatis installed.

To conceal his plans, on the night of March 2 Washington ordered a heavy bombardment from Lechmere Point, Cobble Hill, and Roxbury. This continued for three nights. The British replied but little damage was done by either side. On the third night, March 4–5, as soon as the firing began, 2,000 American troops with 360 oxcarts of materials occupied Dorchester Heights. As the cannon fire blocked noise of their activity, 1,200 men labored on the defenses while 800 others stood watch. By the morning Patriot forces were firmly entrenched and, with cannon in place, they were in position to bombard the British at will. Boston was now untenable for the British, who were astonished at the completed works and the speed with which they had been accomplished.

Howe had been planning to evacuate what was now a smallpox-ravaged city, but Washington's move caused him to change his mind. British artillery opened fire but had little effect against the American positions at such heights, killing only four men. Howe then gave orders for an attack that night by 2,200 men, but a British council of war later that day reversed the decision.

Howe then began loading his nearly 10,000 troops and their equipment, as well as several thousand Loyalists aboard 140 ships to sail to Halifax, Nova Scotia. An informal agreement was reached whereby Washington would not harass the British with artillery fire, while Howe pledged not to destroy the city. On March 17, the winds turned favorable and the British sailed away.

Washington named Greene as military governor of Boston. The Americans recovered 69 usable cannon and other valuable stores. Boston was now under permanent American control, with the British evacuation of the city marked the end of the first stage of the war. In early April, Washington began transferring resources south to New York City, which he correctly assumed would be the next major British military objective.

Spencer C. Tucker

Further Reading

Chidsey, Donald Barr. *The Siege of Boston: An On-the-Scene Account of the Beginning of the American Revolution.* New York: Crown Publishers, 1966.

French, Allen. *The Siege of Boston.* 1911. Reprint, Spartanburg, SC: Reprint Co., 1969.

Frothingham, Richard, Jr. *History of the Siege of Boston and of the Battles of Lexington, Concord, and Bunker Hill.* 1849. Reprint, New York: Da Capo Press, 1970.

McCullough, David. *1776.* New York: Simon & Schuster, 2005.

Ward, Christopher. *The War of the Revolution.* Edited by John Richard Alden. New York: Skyhorse Publishing, 2011.

Siege of Fort Stanwix, New York (August 2–23, 1777)

The siege of the Continental Army's Fort Stanwix, New York, by the British and Allied Native Americans occurred during August 2–23, 1777, in the American Revolutionary War (1775–1783). British Army Lieutenant General John Burgoyne had returned to England early in 1777 and presented to King George III and Secretary of State for the Colonies Lord George Germain a plan to split off New England, the font of the rebellion, from the remainder of the colonies and thus snuff out the revolt. Burgoyne envisioned a three-pronged campaign. The major thrust would drive from Canada down the Lake Champlain–Hudson Valley corridor, while a secondary and diversionary effort pushed eastward from Lake Erie. The two forces were to meet at Albany and join the third prong, a British drive up the Hudson from New York City.

The plan took little account of logistics, and it depended heavily on simultaneous execution. It was further hampered by the fact that while he was approving Burgoyne's plan, Germain also approved a different plan submitted by General William Howe, commanding British forces in the war. Howe proposed to move south from New York against Philadelphia. He believed that Continental Army commander General George Washington would commit the bulk of his army to defend the capital and that the rebel army might thus be destroyed.

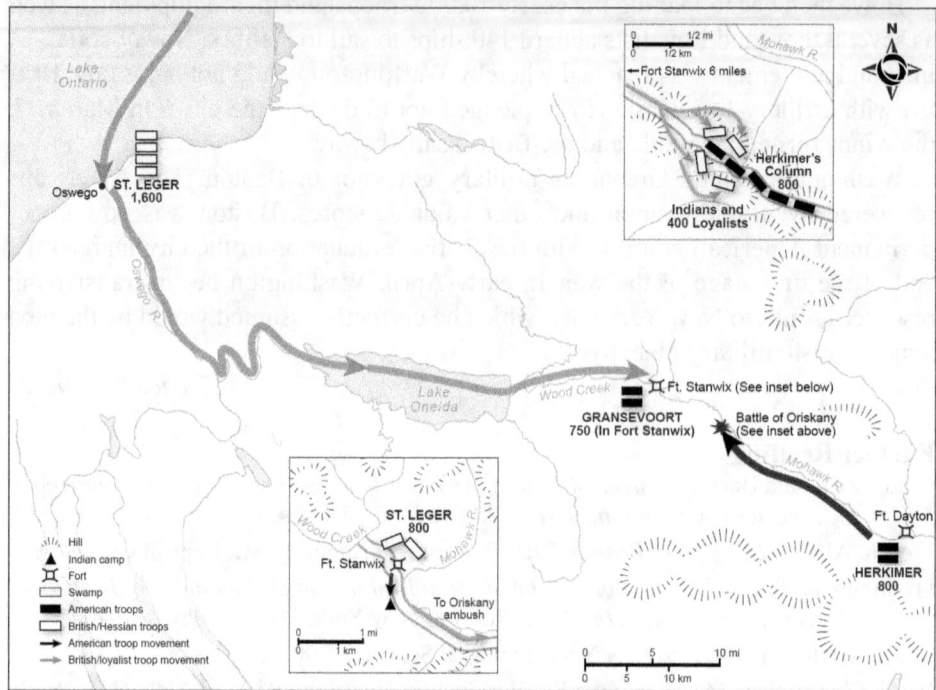

Map showing the siege of Fort Stanwix and the Battle of Oriskany during the American Revolutionary War. The failure of the British and their Indian allies to take Fort Stanwix helped bring an end to the British invasion of New York from Canada, which prevented them from splitting off New England from the rest of the colonies. (ABC-CLIO)

Germain made no effort to reconcile these two plans. Nor did he order the two commanders to cooperate, and neither Howe nor Burgoyne made any effort to coordinate with the other, although Howe did inform the British commander in Canada Major General Sir Guy Carleton of his intentions. Howe promised to position a corps in the lower Hudson River area to maintain communications through the Highlands, which might then "act in favor of the northern army." Later this force went up the Hudson to a point above Hyde Park. Although Burgoyne saw this letter, it did not affect his planning.

Burgoyne and the main British force assembled at Saint Jean, south of Montreal. Lieutenant Colonel Barrimore (Barry) St. Leger, given the temporary rank of brigadier general, was to carry out the diversionary operation to the west, advancing up the St. Lawrence River and then proceeding down the Mohawk Valley to link up with Burgoyne's main force, in the meantime drawing off American forces that might otherwise confront Burgoyne along his route of march down the Lake Champlain corridor.

On July 23, 1777, St. Leger departed Montreal with a force of some 875 British regulars and Loyalists under colonels Sir John Johnson and John Butler. Moving up the St. Lawrence to Lake Ontario, they were at Oswego, New York, on July 25. There they were joined by 800–1,000 Indians under Chief Joseph Brant. There also St. Leger was informed that the only major obstacle to his advance was Fort Stanwix, and that it was in poor repair and had only about 60 defenders. Based on this information, St. Leger decided to leave behind his heavy siege artillery.

Averaging about 10 miles a day, St. Leger's force proceeded along the Mohawk River valley toward Fort Stanwix. The fort was situated in a key location at the head of navigation of the Mohawk River on a portage between that river and Wood Creek that flows westward to Oswego. Built by the British during the French and Indian War (1754–1763), Fort Stanwix had then been abandoned. At the start of the Revolutionary War in 1775, it was in a state of considerable disrepair. In April 1777, however, Colonel Peter Ganesvoort had assumed command of the fort, renamed Fort Schuyler. He, his second in command lieutenant colonel Marinus Willett, and their 550-man 3rd New York Regiment of the Continental Line labored to repair and strengthen the fort's defenses. Although work had not been completed by St. Leger's arrival, the fort nonetheless presented a formidable obstacle for an enemy without heavy artillery. In August 1777, the fort was held by some 550 men.

On August 2, St. Leger's advance column arrived at the fort, only to see an American pack column and reinforcements entering the fort, bringing much needed supplies and increasing the size of the garrison there to 750 men. St. Leger's main body came up the next day. In an effort to intimidate the Americans, St. Leger paraded his entire force in full view of the fort. Being made aware that Native Americans constituted the majority of the British force only served to strengthen the determination of the defenders, who reasoned they could expect no quarter from the Indians were the British to be victorious. Also strengthening Gansevoort's resolve was the news that an American relief force under Brigadier General Nicholas Herkimer was on its way. Gansevoort promptly rejected a demand for surrender, and St. Leger commenced siege operations.

Unable to make a tight investment, St. Leger distributed his men in three camps forming a rough triangle, with the posts about a mile apart. Most of the regulars were in the main camp to the north of Fort Stanwix. To the south, at Lower Landing, he posted the Canadians, Loyalists, Indians, and the remainder of his regulars. Loyalists manned the third post, located west of the fort on Wood Creek. During the next few days St. Leger employed a large number of his men cutting a supply road through the forest. On August 4–5, he had jäger and Indian marksmen snipe at Fort Stanwix, without significant result.

Meanwhile, having gathered some 800 Tryon County militiamen, Herkimer set out on August 4 from Fort Dayton with 60 Oneida scouts to march to Stanwix, 30 miles distant. St. Leger learned of this, and despite the strain of his resources, detached some 250 of his troops and an equal number of Indians under Brant in the hopes of ambushing Herkimer's column. On the morning of August 6, only some six miles from his goal, Herkimer's force blundered into a perfectly staged ambush near the village of Oriskany, for which location the battle is named. Johnson, Butler, and Brant and their Loyalist and Iroquois forces overwhelmed Herkimer. Following a bloody six-hour-long fight at very close quarters, the Indians tired of the battle and broke off the attack, forcing the Loyalists to withdraw as well. The surviving New York militiamen then fell back on Fort Dayton. Still, the Patriot side sustained perhaps 200 dead, 50 wounded (Herkimer mortally), and 30 captured. The Loyalists and Native Americans together may have suffered 100–150 total casualties.

This Loyalist victory was offset by a concurrent American sortie from Fort Stanwix, which Herkimer had requested as a diversion timed for his arrival. Lieutenant Colonel Willett led 250 men with one gun to destroy one of St. Leger's three camps. Willett marched against the British post at the Lower Landing and easily swept aside the defenders, who fled into the woods. The Patriots then methodically looted the abandoned camp, returning to the fort with 21 wagon loads of supplies and Sir John Johnson's personal papers. Now short of supplies and having already sustained significant manpower losses, Native Americans allied with St. Leger lost heart and began to desert.

On August 7, St. Leger again called on Gansevoort to surrender. Trumpeting Herkimer's defeat, he also claimed incorrectly that Burgoyne had reached Albany. In a thinly veiled threat, St. Leger also suggested that if the fort had to be taken by force, he might not be able to control his Indian allies, who would slaughter not only the garrison but also settlers up and down the Mohawk Valley. Gansevoort refused, but he did agree to a three-day truce with the plan to take advantage of it to secure reinforcements, for on August 9 Willet slipped through the British lines and traveled to Fort Dayton. Burgoyne's main army was then at Fort Edward, only 29 miles distant, but Continental Army Major General Philip Schuyler, who had only 4,500 men to Burgoyne's 8,000, took the risky decision of detaching 950 men from his force of 4,500 men, sending them under Major General Benedict Arnold and Brigadier General Ebenezer Leonard to Fort Stanwix.

Reaching Fort Dayton on August 21, Arnold was joined by 100 men of the Tryon County militia. Arnold now decided on a stratagem to deceive St. Leger, sending ahead to the British camp a mentally handicapped Dutch resident of the Mohawk Valley by the name of Hon Yost (or Hon Yost Schuyler). Yost had earlier been condemned to death for involvement in a Loyalist plot, but Arnold promised to pardon him if would present an exaggerated picture of the relief column to the British. Yost did as instructed, telling the British and Indians that the relief column was "more numerous than the leaves on the trees." This false information led many of the allied Iroquois, who held the insane in superstitious awe, to desert.

On August 22, Arnold learned that St. Leger had pushed his approaches to within 150 yards of Fort Stanwix's northwest bastion and that Gansevoort's position was perilous. The next day, however, with Arnold's relief column near, St. Leger raised the siege, abandoning both stores and cannon in a precipitous withdrawal to Oswego.

In the siege of Fort Stanwix the British, Hessian, and Loyalist forces sustained 5 killed, 47 wounded or sick, and 41 captured or missing. Allied Indian losses were 32 killed, captured, or missing, and 34 wounded. American losses were 7 killed, 18 wounded, and 9 missing.

Arnold sent a column to pursue St. Leger, but it reached Oswego only to see the British sailing away. Arnold left 700 men at Fort Stanwix, then moved eastward with 1,200 men to strengthen the Patriot forces opposing the main British force under Burgoyne. St. Leger's failure to take Fort Stanwix undoubtedly contributed to Burgoyne's ultimate defeat in October 1777 in what was one of the war's pivotal battles.

Spencer C. Tucker

Further Reading
Ketchum, Richard M. *Saratoga: Turning Point of America's Revolutionary War.* New York: Henry Holt, 1997.
Nester, William R. *The Frontier War for American Independence.* Mechanicsburg, PA: Stackpole Books, 2004.
Nickerson, Hoffman. *The Turning Point of the Revolution.* 1928. Reprint, Port Washington, NY: Kennikat Press, 1967.
Pancake, John S. *1777: The Year of the Hangman.* Tuscaloosa: University of Alabama Press, 1977.
Scott, John Albert. *Fort Stanwix and Oriskany: The Romantic Story of the Repulse of St. Leger's British Invasion of 1777.* Rome, NY: Rome Sentinel Company, 1927.
Watt, Gavin K., and James F. Morrison. *Rebellion in the Mohawk Valley: The St. Leger Expedition of 1777.* Toronto: Dundurn Press, 2002.

Siege of Gibraltar (June 21, 1779–February 6, 1783)

Gibraltar is the promontory on the southern coast of Spain that commands the strait between the Atlantic Ocean and the Mediterranean Sea. Known as "the Rock," Gibraltar is a formation of limestone and shale that rises to 1,396 feet and stands across the Strait of Gibraltar from Africa, 14 miles distant. As a "choke point," Gibraltar is one of the world's most strategic places, and it has been continuously fortified since the eighth century.

During the War of the Spanish Succession (1701–1714), British and Dutch forces under Admiral Sir George Rooke captured Gibraltar from Spain on July 24, 1704. Britain was confirmed in its possession of Gibraltar by the Treaty of Utrecht in 1713, and British control has continued to the present.

Although the British navy almost immediately began construction of major naval facilities there, the Royal Navy preferred Minorca to Gibraltar because of better anchorages and closer proximity to French bases. Yet Gibraltar was of immense importance to Britain's position in the Mediterranean and to preventing a combination of France's Mediterranean and Atlantic fleets.

Spain had long sought to recover Gibraltar and made one unsuccessful effort in 1727. Britain's preoccupation with the American Revolutionary War prompted a second and major effort. Indeed, the Spanish decision to go to war hinged on a pledge from France in the Treaty of Aranjuez (April 12, 1779) to remain at war until Spain had recovered Gibraltar. On June 21, 1779, Spain declared war on Britain, a decision that came too late in the conflict to have major impact in the Revolutionary War, however.

The siege primarily consisted of bombardment by the attacking forces and counterbattery fire by the besieged. The first phase saw a blockade of Gibraltar by

> **Shrapnel**
>
> The artillery projectile known as shrapnel or spherical case shot was invented in 1784 by Lieutenant (later lieutenant general) Henry Shrapnel (1761–1842) of the British Royal Artillery. Shrapnel came up with the idea in order to extend the range of highly effective case or canister shot against enemy troops.
>
> In 1784, Shrapnel improved on the British improvisation of firing mortar shells from long guns by inventing what he called "spherical case shot." This new artillery ammunition was later known simply by its designer's name. It consisted of a thin-walled hollow round shell filled with a small bursting charge and small iron or lead shot. A time fuse set off the charge in the air, scattering the shot and pieces of the shell casing among opposing troops. The bursting charge was only a small one, allowing the scattered balls and burst casing to continue on the same trajectory as before the explosion (a greater charge would increase the velocity but scattered the balls more widely and reduced their effectiveness). Explosive shell had for some time been utilized in high-trajectory fire mortars but had not before been widely projected in horizontal fire by guns.
>
> **Spencer C. Tucker**

Spanish warships commanded by Admiral Don Antonio Barceló, while General Martín Álvarez de Sotomayor carried out a buildup of land forces. By September 1779, the Spaniards had some 7,000 men in place.

The defenders, ably commanded by the governor of Gibraltar general George Augustus Eliott, and supplied and supported by the British fleet, initially numbered some 5,400 men, including Hanoverian and Corsican troops. During the winter of 1779 with supplies running low, the British sent out a convoy of 66 supply and ordnance ships along with some 300 merchant ships, all escorted by a substantial naval force of 22 ships of the line and 14 frigates under Admiral Sir George Rodney. After capturing a Spanish convoy off Cape Finisterre (January 8, 1780) and then defeating a Spanish squadron of 11 ships of the line under Admiral Juan de Lángara in the Battle of Cape St. Vincent (January 16, 1780), Rodney's relief convoy reached Gibraltar.

In June 1780, Spanish fireships carried out an unsuccessful attack at Gibraltar. In April 1781, during the arrival of another British relief convoy of 100 store ships escorted by 29 ships of the line commanded by Vice Admiral George Darby, a heavy Spanish bombardment inflicted considerable damage on the town of Gibraltar and on the British fortifications. On November 27, 1781, just before the Spaniards were about to launch a major land assault, the British carried out a sortie at La Linea, destroying a number of the Spanish siege works and a large quantity of supplies, as well as spiking the Spanish guns. Following their capture of Minorca on February 5, 1782, Spanish and French troops under the Duc de Crillon were added to the besiegers, bringing the strength of the latter up to some 33,000 men, in addition to 30,000 sailors and marines.

The siege saw a number of military innovations. The allies constructed at Cádiz 10 large floating batteries. Designed by French military engineer Michaud d'Argon, they were essentially armored hulks. Touted as nonflammable and unsinkable, they were covered to provide protection against plunging fire from

Siege of Gibraltar

A rendering of the protracted Spanish and French siege of Gibraltar during 1779–1783 showing Spanish sailors struggling in the waters off Gibraltar as their ships founder under British fire from the fortress high above. (Library of Congress)

British mortars and were designed to be fought on one side only. The floating batteries mounted large, 36-pounder guns behind reinforced bulwarks and had a system of water pipes to keep them damp against fire.

On September 13, 1782, the Spanish and French forces launched their attack. The 10 floating batteries mounting a total of 138 guns and manned by 5,190 officers and men had been towed into position. The allies also had 18 ships of the line, 40 gunboats, and 20 bomb vessels. Awaiting the demolition of the British defenses by the floating batteries were some 35,000 land troops supported by 86 land guns.

The result was not what the allies expected, however. The British employed fewer than 100 guns to fire 8,300 rounds against the floating batteries. The key was the use of hot shot. After the powder charge was loaded in the gun, a wet wad was rammed home, followed by shot heated in an oven. Another wad was then inserted, and the cannon barrel was then depressed and fired as quickly as possible. In this fashion, the British set fire to a number of the floating batteries and heavily damaged the remainder, which were then scuttled by their crews. D'Argon blamed the loss on insufficient crew training and a lack of support from the other warships.

The British also came up with a depressing gun carriage to allow the British long guns to be fired down a slope. Another innovation during the siege was the British use of shell fired from long guns. To this point explosive shell had been restricted to mortars. With their batteries 1,700 to 2,000 yards from the

Spanish lines, the British employed 5.5-inch mortar shell with short fuses in their 24-pounder long guns, which were of the same caliber as the mortars. A trial on September 25, 1779, was successful, leading to interest in projecting shell from guns in flat trajectory and to Lieutenant Henry Shrapnel's invention of spherical case, or shrapnel, designed for use against personnel.

Despite the failure of their floating batteries, the allies continued the siege, forcing the British to send out a third relief expedition under Admiral Lord Richard Howe in September 1782. Joined by other ships en route, it ultimately numbered 186 vessels, with 34 ships of the line and 31 transports. A storm scattered a Spanish and French fleet of 46 warships anchored off Algeciras, and the convoy arrived at Gibraltar intact on October 11, 1782. This brought British strength at Gibraltar up to some 7,000 men.

The preliminary peace agreement ending the American Revolutionary War brought the siege to an effective close. Formally lifted on February 6, 1783, it had lasted 1,320 days and claimed 333 British troops killed in battle and 911 wounded, with 536 dead from illness. Spanish and French casualties together totaled some 6,000 men killed, wounded, captured, and missing.

The siege of Gibraltar of 1779–1783 remains one of the great British military feats and, on the British side, a superb example of the success of combined arms in warfare. It raised British morale at home, and the Rock of Gibraltar came to be regarded as a symbol of British determination and invincibility. Still, the cost of defending Gibraltar during the siege spread British resources and contributed to British failures elsewhere in the American Revolutionary War.

Spencer C. Tucker

Further Reading

Chartrand, René, and Patrice Courcelle. *Gibraltar 1779–1783: The Great Siege.* Oxford, UK: Osprey, 2006.

Drinkwater, John. *A History of the Late Siege of Gibraltar, 1779–1783: With a Description and Account of That Garrison from the Earliest Times.* London: John Murray, 1905.

Falkner, James. *Fire over the Rock: The Great Siege of Gibraltar 779–1783.* Barnsley, South Yorkshire, UK: Pen & Sword Military, 2009.

McGuffie, Tom Henderson. *The Siege of Gibraltar: 1779–1783.* Philadelphia: Dufour Editions, 1965.

Rodger, N. A. M. *The Command of the Ocean: A Naval History of Britain, 1649–1815.* New York: W. W. Norton, 2005.

Russell, Jack. *Gibraltar Besieged: 1779–1783.* London: Heinemann, 1965.

Siege of Charles Town (Charleston), South Carolina (March 29–May 12, 1780)

The British siege of the city of Charles Town (present-day Charleston), South Carolina, during March 29–May 12, 1788, occurred during the American Revolutionary War (1775–1783). A major American seaport city, Charles Town had attracted British attention early in the conflict. In June 1776, British forces under

Major General Henry Clinton had tried to take the city, but British naval forces were driven off in the Battle of Sullivan's Island (June 28, 1776). Three years later in May 1779, Major General Augustine Prevost mounted a raid on Charles Town in an effort to draw off American forces under Major General Benjamin Lincoln, Continental Army commander in the South, from an attack on Augusta, Georgia, but Prevost had been forced to withdraw.

This time Clinton, now a lieutenant general and commander of British forces in North America, was determined to succeed. Georgia was already in British hands, and indeed in October 1779, the British had beaten back a joint American and French effort to retake Savannah. Securing Charles Town would give the British a secure base for the reconquest of the two Carolinas before moving northward against Virginia. Clinton anticipated taking areas, then training and arming Loyalist militias who would then hold them for the Crown.

On October 11, 1779, Clinton ordered the abandonment of Newport, Rhode Island. Its 3,000-man British garrison departed on October 15. Aware of the threat to Charles Town and its vulnerability, on November 20, a small American naval squadron was ordered there to help protect against a British seaborne assault. Commanded by Commodore Abraham Whipple, it consisted of the frigates *Boston* (24 guns), *Providence* (28 guns), and the *Queen of France* (28 guns), along with the sloop *Ranger* (18 guns).

On December 26, leaving German lieutenant general Baron Wilhelm von Knyphausen in command in the North, Clinton sailed from New York with 8,500 men in 90 transports, convoyed by 5 ships of the line and 9 frigates. Vice Admiral Mariot Arbuthnot had command of the naval operation in what was the largest British expeditionary force of the war after only that mounted by General William Howe against Philadelphia in 1777. The British ships reassembled off Tybee Island, at the mouth of the Savannah River for a brief rest and refit, then sailed northward for Charles Town on February 10, 1780.

The next day, February 11, British troops came ashore on Johns Island, 30 miles south of the city. Counting British forces already in the area, Clinton now commanded some 14,500 men and enjoyed significant naval support from Arbuthnot's squadron. South Carolina governor John Rutledge employed 600 slaves to dig earthworks to protect the city. Among these defensive works was one named "the Citadel," later the site of South Carolina's military college of the same name.

On March 29, Clinton crossed the Ashley River with 7,000 men and commenced the siege of Charles Town. Lincoln agreed to an appeal from the city leaders that he defend the city, and virtually the entire American army in South would soon be bottled up there. The besiegers made good progress, meanwhile, and by April 1, they had advanced their trenches to within 800 yards of the American defenses. On April 6, however, Brigadier General William Woodford managed to slip past the besiegers and reinforce Charles Town with 750 Virginia Continental Army troops.

On April 8, Admiral Arbuthnot managed to run a number of his ships past the heavy guns of American Fort Moultrie located on Sullivan's Island and guarding the mouth of Charles Town Harbor. These were the fourth-rate *Renown* (50 guns); fifth-rates *Roebuck* (44 guns) and *Romulus* (44 guns); the frigates *Richmond* (32

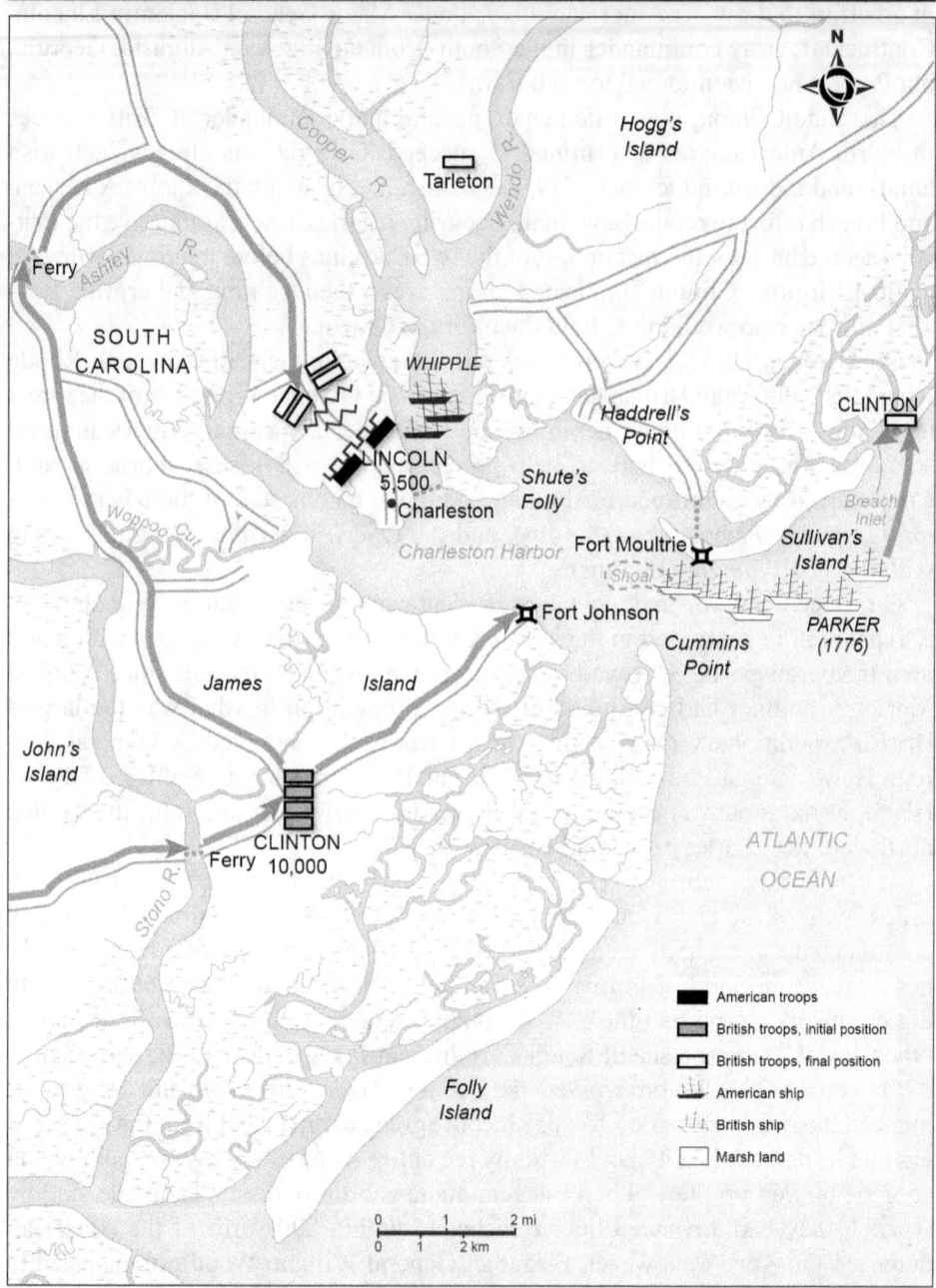

The British victory in the siege of the city of Charles Town (present-day Charleston, South Carolina) was the most costly Patriot defeat in the American Revolutionary War. (ABC-CLIO)

guns), *Blonde* (32 guns), *Virginia* (28 guns), and the *Raleigh* (32 guns); and the armed ship *Sandwich* (24 guns) and several smaller ships. The operation claimed 27 British casualties and the *Arteus*, an ordnance ship that grounded and was burned. There were no American casualties in the fort, commanded by Brevet Brigadier General Charles C. Pinckney.

Having thus effected a major breach in the American defenses, the British ships anchored off Fort Johnson. Lincoln, meanwhile, rejected an escape from Charles Town by crossing Biggin Bridge over the Cooper River.

With the British forces ashore having now completed their first series of parallel trenches, Clinton called on Lincoln to surrender but the American general refused. On April 13, British siege guns and the ships in the harbor commenced what would be a month-long bombardment.

A viable escape route for the Americans remained open across the Cooper River to Moncks Corner, 30 miles distant. On April 12, to guard the upper reaches of the Cooper River, Lincoln dispatched Brigadier General Isaac Huger and his cavalry of some 500 men to Biggin Bridge near Moncks Corner to guard a large quantity of supplies intended for American forces at Charles Town. Clinton responded to this move by sending Lieutenant Colonel Banastre Tarleton and his British Legion and Major Patrick Ferguson's Loyalist troops, altogether some 1,400 men, to attack Huger and take possession of Moncks Corner and the nearby bridge over Biggin Creek, where Huger was stationed. On April 13, they were joined by Lieutenant Colonel James Webster and the 33rd and 64th Infantry regiments. The British plan called for Tarleton and Ferguson to proceed ahead quickly to Moncks Corner and take Huger's position by surprise at night. En route, the British captured a messenger carrying a letter from Huger to Lincoln, describing the deployment of his men.

Arriving at Moncks Corner around 3:00 a.m. on April 14, the British caught the Americans completely by surprise. Not only had there been no patrols, but Huger had positioned his cavalry in front of his infantry. With swamps on either side of the causeway preventing a flanking attack, Tarleton led an immediate cavalry charge against the Americans. In the ensuing Battle of Biggin Bridge (or Biggin Church), the British easily dispersed the Patriots defending Biggin Bridge. The Americans suffered 14 dead, 13 wounded, and 67 captured; British losses were only 3 wounded. Although most of the Americans were able to escape, including Huger and cavalry commander Lieutenant Colonel William Washington, the British captured 42 wagon loads of supplies as well as 200 cavalry mounts. The latter were of significant value to the British, who had lost many of their horses during the voyage to the South. The British victory at Moncks Corner cut off Lincoln's access to the interior of South Carolina and hastened the surrender of Charles Town.

On April 18, British colonel Francis, Lord Rawdon arrived at Charles Town with reinforcements. British strength there was now some 10,000 men. A day later, British forces were within 250 yards of Charles Town Neck. Lincoln, convinced that the situation was hopeless, convened a council of war. The officers were in favor of evacuation, but South Carolina lieutenant governor Christopher Gadsden was strongly opposed, and the matter was deferred until the next day. At that meeting, Gadsden brought with him the rest of the members of the governor's council and all expressed themselves opposed to a withdrawal from the city. One even said that if the army attempted to do so, the townspeople would burn their boats and assist the British. The members of the council carried the day.

On April 21, with the British siege lines having been advanced to only 200 yards from those of the Americans, Lincoln took matters into his own hands and proposed to Clinton a surrender with the honors of war. This would have allowed the American soldiers to withdraw from the city unmolested, with their weapons and baggage, and the American warships to proceed to sea. Clinton rejected this, and the fighting continued.

On May 6, Lieutenant Colonel Tarleton and 150 troopers of his British Legion surprised and routed some 350 Patriot militiamen under colonels Abraham Buford, William Washington, and Anthony White at Lenud's Ferry, near present-day Jamestown, South Carolina. The Americans suffered 40 killed and wounded and 65 taken prisoner. The British also captured 18 of their soldiers who had been taken prisoner at Awendaw Creek by the Americans the day before.

On May 7, Lieutenant Colonel William Scott surrendered Fort Moultrie. Captain Charles Hudson of the British frigate *Richmond* had threatened to storm the fort with 500 Royal Marines. Most of Moultrie's garrison had been evacuated earlier, but the British still took 217 prisoners and captured 41 guns and 4 large mortars as well as considerable quantities of artillery ammunition and equipment.

On May 11, with their artillery now advanced close to Charles Town, the British opened fire directly into the city itself. The city leaders then called on Lincoln to capitulate, and he did so the next day, May 12. The siege claimed 89 Americans killed and 138 wounded. British losses were 76 killed and 189 wounded. At Charles Town, the British captured 5,466 officers and men (including 7 generals), some 400 cannon, and 6,000 muskets. They also secured the Continental Navy frigates *Boston* and *Providence*, and the sloop *Ranger*. The *Queen of France* had been scuttled to prevent its capture. Clinton paroled the militiamen, who were thus allowed to return home, but the Continental Army soldiers passed into British captivity.

The British capture of Charles Town was the largest single defeat for American arms of the entire war and the greatest defeat for an American army before the fall of Bataan in the Philippines in 1942. Believing that the campaign in the South was now pretty much won, Clinton left behind his second-in-command Lieutenant General Charles, Lord Cornwallis, and 8,500 men to continue mopping up operations and on June 8 returned with the remainder of the British troops to New York, where he arrived on June 17. On May 18, meanwhile, Cornwallis set out with 2,500 men to pacify the remainder of South Carolina.

Spencer C. Tucker

Further Reading

Borick, Carl P. *A Gallant Defense: The Siege of Charleston, 1780.* Columbia: University of South Carolina Press, 2003.

Chartrand, Rene. *The French Army in the American War of Independence.* London: Osprey, 1992.

Kaufmann, J. E. *Fortress America.* Cambridge, MA: Da Capo Press, 2004.

Mattern, David B. *Benjamin Lincoln and the American Revolution.* Columbia: University of South Carolina Press, 1998.

Siege of Pensacola, West Florida (March 9–May 10, 1781)

Determined to complete the conquest of British West Florida, Spanish governor of Louisiana Bernardo de Gálvez assembled an expeditionary force in Cuba. On March 9, he arrived with a naval squadron off Pensacola, Florida, having sailed from Havana, Cuba, on February 18 with the third-rate ship of the line *San Ramón* (74 guns), the frigates *Santa Clara* (36 guns) and *Santa Cecila* (36 guns), and the *Caimán* (20 guns). These escorted the storeship *San Pío* and 28 transports carrying more than 1,500 ground troops taken from Cuban garrisons. Gálvez had sent dispatch boats to Mobile and New Orleans for reinforcements. Colonel John Campbell commanded the British garrison of 1,600 men at Pensacola behind strong defenses.

On arrival, Gálvez immediately began landing troops on Santa Rosa Island, which he took on the morning of March 10, the English defenders there having withdrawn. The Spaniards came under fire from the British sloops *Mentor* (16 guns) and *Port Royal* (14 guns) before the latter were driven off by longer-range Spanish 24-pounder guns brought ashore on March 11. Shortly thereafter, the Spaniards attempted to get their ships across the bar, but the *San Ramón* drew too much water and the effort was temporarily abandoned. After a week of asking the Spanish commodore José Calvo de Irazábal to make another attempt, on March 18 Gálvez proceeded in his private brig *Gálveztown*, the sloop *Valenzuela*, and two armed launches, successfully passing British Fort Red Cliffs. This goaded Calvo de Irazábal into action and all other Spanish warships, except the flagship, made it over the bar and past the British fort that afternoon.

On the morning of March 19, 905 Spanish reinforcements arrived at Pensacola by land from Mobile, followed on March 20 by an additional 1,348 others sailing from New Orleans in 14 ships. These brought total Spanish strength at Pensacola up to some 3,500 men. Gálvez then began transporting men from Santa Rosa Island to the mainland. Campbell had already abandoned Pensacola and taken up position at the British stronghold of Fort George. Meanwhile, Indians allied with the British harassed the Spaniards as they moved closer to this remaining British fortification.

Gálvez began a close siege of the British position on April 19 when Admiral José Solano y Bote arrived with a sizable fleet of 11 ships of the line, 2 frigates, and 2 brigantines. These were accompanied by a French squadron of 4 ships of the line, 2 brigantines, and 1 cutter commanded by Commodore François Aymar, Baron de Monteil. These ships carried 1,600 Spanish and 725 French troops. Now commanding more than 7,400 men, Gálvez had a crushing ground force advantage.

The Spaniards and French steadily advanced siege lines toward British Fort George and by May 1 they had in place six 24-pounders capable of shelling the British positions. A British sortie killed 18 Spanish soldiers, wounded 16, and captured others, and also spiked several Spanish fieldpieces, but the allied force continued to advance their siege lines ever closer. On May 8, a Spanish shell detonated the magazine in the Queen's Redoubt of Fort George, killing 76 British defenders and wounding another two dozen. Spanish light infantry then immediately rushed forward and occupied the redoubt. They quickly install cannon there capable of firing at point-blank range into the remaining British positions. This situation left Campbell and British governor Peter Chester no option but to request terms.

The formal British surrender occurred on May 10. The British suffered 105 dead, 102 wounded, and 1,113 taken prisoner. The Spaniards and their French allies also captured the two British sloops, along with 193 guns and field pieces, and 2,100 muskets. The entire campaign had cost the Spaniards 74 dead and 198 wounded. The Spaniards transported their British prisoners to Havana, from where they were repatriated to New York by July 12. Colonel Arturo O'Neill was appointed the Spanish governor of Pensacola and West Florida. West Florida remained in Spanish hands until 1819.

Spencer C. Tucker

Further Reading

Gayarré, Charles. *History of Louisiana*. Vol. 3, *The Spanish Domination*. New York: Widdleton, 1867.

Haarmann, Albert. "The Spanish Conquest of British West Florida, 1779–1781." *Florida Historical Quarterly* 39, no. 2 (October 1960): 107–134.

Nester, William R. *The Frontier War for American Independence*. Mechanicsburg, PA: Stackpole Books, 2004.

Siege of Yorktown (September 28–October 19, 1781)

The siege of Yorktown, during September 28–October 19, 1781, was the last major engagement of the American Revolutionary War and arguably the most important.

In May 1781, French commodore Louis-Jacques Barras de Saint-Laurent had arrived with a small squadron at Newport, Rhode Island, bringing news that Admiral François-Joseph-Paul, Comte de Grasse-Tilly, was on his way to the West Indies from France with a powerful fleet and that de Grasse would bring the fleet north during the hurricane season.

In the meantime, Washington dispatched 1,200 men under Continental Army Major General Marie Joseph du Motier, Marquis de Lafayette, to trap British forces under the turncoat Brigadier General Benedict Arnold raiding along the James River in eastern Virginia. British Lieutenant General Charles, Lord Cornwallis, came up from the south and arrived in Virginia at this time and assumed command of all British forces there, now about 7,000 men and representing a quarter of British armed strength in North America.

On August 4, with the allies having called off their offensive against New York, General Clinton sent new orders to Cornwallis, allowing him to keep all his troops in Virginia. Having tried and failed to bag the far smaller Continental Army forces under Lafayette, Cornwallis retired with 7,000 men to the small tobacco port of

Yorktown at the mouth of the York River on Chesapeake Bay, where he could be in communication by water with his superior and commander of British troops in North America Lieutenant General Sir Henry Clinton in New York. Lafayette, with 4,500 men, kept watch from West Point on the York River, informing Washington of developments.

On August 5, de Grasse, having taken on 3,300 French troops and a small siege train supplied by Santo Domingo governor Comte de Lillancourt, sailed from Cap François for North America with 28 ships of the line. British rear admiral Samuel Hood pursued with 14 ships of the line.

On August 14, Washington, who had wanted to attack the British in New York, learned that de Grasse would not be coming to New York but instead would sail to the Chesapeake Bay, arriving there later the same month and remaining until mid-October. Washington and Rochambeau (who had opposed an offensive in New York) immediately saw the possibilities. If de Grasse could hold the bay while Washington came down from the land side, they might bag Cornwallis at Yorktown.

Washington ordered Lafayette to contain Cornwallis, and on August 21 he sent 2,000 American and 4,000 French soldiers in forced marches southward, leaving only 2,000 men under Major General William Heath to watch British forces at New York under Clinton. Not until early September did Clinton realize what had happened. Although Clinton promised Cornwallis a diversion, he in fact did little to help his subordinate, with whom he did not get along. On August 24, meanwhile, Barras sailed from Newport with 8 ships of the line and 18 transports carrying 1,000 ground troops, bound for the Chesapeake.

Having arrived at their assembly point of Williamsburg, Virginia, on September 14, Washington and Rochambeau met with de Grasse-Tilly to coordinate strategy, and on September 28 the combined French and Continental Army forces marched the 12 miles from Williamsburg to Yorktown, which is situated at the mouth of the York River on Chesapeake Bay, to commence the siege of the British forces there. Washington now had at his disposal some 17,600 men, including 3,000 American militiamen who played no role in the battle and 7,800 French troops under de Rochambeau. Washington also had both French field and siege artillery, as well as the services of highly trained French military engineers, including Continental Army chief engineer Brigadier General (and French Army lieutenant colonel) Louis Lebègue de Presle Duportail, who now directed a siege of Yorktown with European-style zigzag trenches and parallels dug toward the British lines.

Once a busy tobacco export port, Yorktown was a collection of about 60 buildings situated on a bluff about 30 feet above the water. It was hardly an ideal defensive position, but Cornwallis had anticipated British naval control of the bay.

That situation had dramatically changed with the arrival off the Virginia Capes on August 30 of de Grasse-Tilly's French fleet of 28 ships of the line and 3,100 ground troops under Maréchal de camp Claude-Anne de Rouvroy, Marquis de Montblerú et Marquis de Saint-Simon. De Grasse then detached transports and smaller ships to carry the other allied forces and supplies down the bay from Head of Elk (Elkton, Maryland), Baltimore, and Annapolis.

On September 5, de Grasse-Tilly was informed of the approach of a British fleet of 19 ships of the line under Rear Admiral Thomas Graves, and he hastily put to sea short-handed but with 24 ships of the line to do battle. Graves had been in pursuit of Barras and his ships but, sailing faster, had gotten to his presumed destination ahead of him. The ensuing Second Battle of the Chesapeake that day was inconclusive and, following several more days of maneuvering and the arrival of the eight additional French ships of the line and transports with siege guns and more troops under Barras, Graves departed with his ships for New York to gather more ships. This Second Battle of the Chesapeake ranks as one of the most strategically important naval battles in history, as Cornwallis was now left entirely to his own resources.

Cornwallis did what he could to prepare for the inevitable American and French onslaught, aided by the labor of some 2,000 African Americans who had fled their American owners and who were now employed in digging redoubts. In all, Cornwallis had no more than 9,000 men, including British Army and German troops, and some 1,000 Royal Navy personnel, but he dispatched about 700 men under Colonels Thomas Dundas and Banastre Tarleton and about 700 men across the York to hold Gloucester Point.

The allied siege commenced on September 28. It would be carried out along classic European lines that eschewed attacks by infantry and allowed heavy artillery to do the work. The next night, Cornwallis abandoned his outer works, which could have been held for some time, giving him the opportunity to strengthen the inner works. The French and Americans then occupied these three redoubts given to them and added a fourth. On September 30, the allies completed the outer ring of their siege lines. On October 1, they opened fire on the British positions with the siege guns brought by Barras. On October 6, the allies began construction of the first parallel, only 600 yards from the British positions. This was undertaken by about 1,500 fatigued men guarded by 2,800 men under arms. Then on October 9 the Americans and French began a sustained bombardment that grew to include some 100 artillery pieces, 52 of them heavy siege guns. On October 10, allied artillery fire resulted in the burning of the Royal Navy fifth-rate frigate *Sharon* (44 guns) and sinking of several transports in the York River.

On October 11, the allies commenced construction of a second siege line, only 400 yards from the British line. Then on the night of October 14 in a surprise attack, they stormed and captured two key British redoubts in fierce hand-to-hand combat, with the French forces commanded by Lieutenant Colonel Guillaume de Deux-Ponts (Wilhelm von Zweibrücken) taking redoubt No. 9 and the Americans under Lieutenant Colonel Alexander Hamilton seizing redoubt No. 10. This success enabled the allies to complete their second siege line and to establish new firing positions that compromised the British defensive line, sealing the fate of the defenders.

In an effort to salvage something of his military reputation, on October 15 Cornwallis launched a desperate British counterattack by 350 men under Lieutenant Colonel Robert Abercrombie in an effort to spike the guns in the new

Painting by John Trumbull depicting the British surrender of Yorktown to besieging Continental Army and French forces on October 19, 1781. This decisive victory brought down the British government and led to the peace negotiations that ended the American Revolutionary War. (National Archives)

batteries. The British took two redoubts and spiked seven guns, but they were soon driven back with 8 killed and 12 taken prisoner and the guns were all back in action several hours later. Too late, on the night of October 16 Cornwallis attempted to escape across the York River to Gloucester Point, which Washington had largely neglected. The British plan was thwarted by a severe storm, however.

Now running low on food and with his men demoralized, on the morning of October 17, four years to the day after the British surrender at Saratoga, a British drummer mounted a parapet and beat a "parley." Cornwallis sought parole for his men, but Washington insisted that the British surrender as prisoners of war, and Cornwallis reluctantly agreed. The formal surrender took place on October 19. In it the British were granted "the honors of war" marching out to lay down their arms and then returned to Yorktown. A total of 8,077 men, including 840 seamen, 80 camp followers, and 7,157 soldiers surrendered.

During the siege the British lost 156 killed and 326 wounded. It was a cheap victory for Washington. The allies suffered 75 killed and 199 wounded, with two-thirds of the casualties among the French.

Clinton's relief force did not arrive in the Chesapeake until October 24. It then returned to New York. The consequences of the capture of an entire British Army at Yorktown were momentous. It brought down Frederick, Lord North's government in London and led the new British government to negotiate an end to the war.

Spencer C. Tucker

Further Reading

Davis, Burke. *The Campaign That Won America: The Story of Yorktown.* New York: Dial Press, 1970.

Greene, Jerome A. *The Guns of Independence: The Siege of Yorktown, 1781.* New York: Savas Beatie, 2005.

Larrabee, Harold A. *Decision at the Chesapeake.* New York: Clarkson N. Potter, 1964.

Lumpkin, Henry. *From Savannah to Yorktown: The American Revolution in the South.* Columbia: University of South Carolina Press, 1981.

Morrissey, Brenden. *Yorktown, 1781: The World Turned Upside Down.* London: Osprey, 1997.

Wickwire, Franklin, and Mary Wickwire. *Cornwallis: The American Adventure.* Boston: Houghton Mifflin, 1970.

Siege of Toulon (September 18–December 19, 1793)

The French revolutionary government's September 18–December 19 siege of the Mediterranean port city of Toulon, which had declared for the counterrevolution and welcomed in the English and Spanish, was a major engagement of the War of the First Coalition (1792–1797) during the French Revolution (1789–1799). Fighting had begun the year before between France on the one side and Austria and Prussia on the other. The revolutionaries tried and executed King Louis XVI in January 1793, and Britain entered the fray against France in April.

The French Navy was not in the best condition at the start of hostilities. Revolutionary activities during the previous three and a half years had all but wrecked both the army and the navy. In the navy, virtually all senior professional officers were nobles, and most of these had either fled France or had been purged. Merchant captains were pressed into service as substitutes, but much more than with the land forces, enthusiasm was no substitute for the long years of training required to operate warships at sea, let alone to be successful with them in combat.

French ship crews in 1792 were both mutinous and poorly trained. Naval yards and shore facilities, having been starved of resources, were in poor repair. While the French possessed some 76 ships of the line at the start of hostilities, fewer than half could be manned and put to sea. The British Royal Navy could send to sea 125 ships of the line, although seamen were in short supply. Spain added another 56 ships of the line, with indifferently trained crews. The Dutch contributed 49 ships of the line, but these were somewhat lighter than most ships of the line in other navies.

Admiral Lord Richard Howe commanded the British Atlantic fleet, while Vice Admiral Lord Alexander Hood commanded in the Mediterranean. In the summer of 1793, Hood had 21 ships of the line, including the 100-rates *Victory* and *Britannia.* Opposing him at Toulon, French rear admiral Jean Honoré, Comte de Trogoff de Kerlessy, had 58 warships, nearly half the French Navy. Seventeen of these were ships of the line ready for sea, including the giant 120-gun *Commerce de Marseille.* Trogoff had another four ships of the line being refitted and nine being repaired.

In July, Toulon overthrew its revolutionary Jacobin government and declared for the monarchy. When Paris dispatched troops to Toulon, the city's counterrevolutionary leaders invited Hood to defend them. Accompanied by a Spanish squadron of 17 ships of the line under Admiral Don Juan de Lángara, Hood arrived off Toulon in mid-August. Many of the French crews were willing to fight, but a great many simply deserted. On August 27, Hood's ships sailed into the port. Hood provided not only naval artillery to help defend the port against the revolutionary forces but also 2,000 British seamen, 8,000 Neapolitan troops, and 8,000 Spanish soldiers, almost doubling the number of defenders of the city and port. The British also disarmed the French ships and put 5,000 captured French seamen on board four disarmed and unserviceable 74-gun ships of the line to sail under passport to French Atlantic ports.

Young French Army captain Napoleon Bonaparte directs artillery fire during the successful recapture by French government forces of the Mediterranean port city of Toulon from French Royalists and British and Spanish forces in December 1793. (Library of Congress)

On September 18, French Republican forces under General Jean François Carteaux arrived at Toulon to bolster republic forces already there and invested the port from the land side. Among them was young artillery captain Napoleon Bonaparte. Although assigned to the French Army of Italy, he had learned of the wounding and departure of Carteaux's artillery commander Elzéar Auguste Cousin de Dommartin. Bonaparte made straight for influential Jacobin Antoine-Christophe Saliceti, who also hailed from Corsica and was an old friend of the Bonaparte family, and begged him to secure the artillery command. Saliceti then convinced Republican commissioners with the army Paul Barras and Augustin Robespierre, and Carteaux grudgingly accepted the young captain, as he had no one else, breveting him major.

Bonaparte tried to convince Carteaux that a large part of the army should be concentrated to take Fort Eguillette, situated on high ground between the outer and inner harbors. Bonaparte pointed out that artillery positioned there could fire directly down on the allied warships and force them to depart. Carteaux had about 35,000 men, the defenders close to the same, and he feared that while he was concentrating his resources for such an attack the defenders, who enjoyed shorter, interior lines, could strike elsewhere and perhaps even envelop his army. Carteaux was well aware that unsuccessful French Revolutionary army generals were likely to wind up on the guillotine, and he was therefore quite content to continue careful, slow siege operations until victory was secured. Bonaparte was supremely confident of his military abilities and despised Carteaux, who lacked formal military training and had been a court painter before the Revolution. In a major breach of command authority, Bonaparte bypassed Carteaux and wrote directly to Lazare Carnot, the member of the Committee of Public Safety in Paris directing the armies of the French Republic. Bonaparte not only presented his own plan but recommended that Carteaux be removed from command.

Carnot approved Bonaparte's plan. He had already approved a new commander, General Jacques Dugommier, a professional army officer, who on arrival agreed with Bonaparte. The attack on Fort Eguillette and its covering fort, Mulgrave, began on December 14. The two forts were taken on December 17, with Bonaparte having received a slight bayonet wound in the leg.

Bonaparte had soon emplaced his artillery and began shelling the allied ships. On the night of December 18–19, the British and Spanish ships departed, taking with them the allied land force and a number of French royalists.

Captain Sir Sidney Smith meanwhile volunteered to burn the dockyard and those French ships that could not be gotten off. His improvised effort was only partially successful. Although his men were able to fire some smaller storehouses, the large magazine escaped destruction. In all, 19 French ships (11 of them ships of the line), including those under construction, were destroyed. The Spanish took off 3 small French warships, and the British secured 15 French warships, including 3 ships of the line.

Few of the ships captured were of value. The *Commerce de Marseille*, which became the largest ship of the Royal Navy, was too weak structurally for fleet service and became first a storeship and then a prison hulk. The French recovered largely intact at least 16 warships, including 13 ships of the line. Later these formed the nucleus of the fleet that carried then general Napoleon's expedition to Egypt.

Within days, Carnot had promoted the 24-year-old Bonaparte to brigadier general, signaling the beginning of his meteoric rise. The ending of the siege also marked the end of Spanish participation in the naval war on the British side. Following the Toulon fiasco, the French could rely only on their Atlantic fleet, and it was in poor repair.

Spencer C. Tucker

Further Reading
Connelly, Owen. *Blundering to Glory: Napoleon's Military Campaigns*. Rev. ed. Wilmington, DE: Scholarly Resources, 1999.

Crook, Malcolm. *Toulon in War and Revolution: From the Ancient Regime to the Restoration, 1750–1820*. Manchester, UK: Manchester University Press, 1991.

Gardiner, Robert, ed. *Fleet Battle and Blockade: The French Revolutionary War, 1793–1797*. London: Chatham, 1996.

Siege of Acre (March 17–May 20, 1799)

In 1798 a French army under Napoleon Bonaparte, sailing from Toulon, invaded Egypt. The leaders of the Directory then ruling France hoped to secure control of that Ottoman territory and remove British influence in the region. Egypt was important to the British trade system, and removal of British influence there would deal both an economic and psychological blow to France's arch-enemy. In addition, France claimed it would liberate Egypt from the often-oppressive rule of the Mamluks and return control to the Ottoman Empire, a French ally. There was also an expectation that once these had been accomplished, Bonaparte would proceed overland to threaten British rule in India.

Bonaparte's subordinates for the expedition included Generals Alexandre Berthier, Jean Lannes, Joachim Murat, Louis Charles Desaix, and Jean-Baptist Kléber. These generals led an army of between 35,000 and 40,000 soldiers, almost 200 cannon, and more than 1,000 horses, ferried on the 2,000-mile trip to Egypt by 335 ships. On May 19, 1798, Bonaparte's forces departed Toulon. Three weeks later, they landed at Malta, an island critical to control of the Mediterranean Sea routes.

In a week at Malta, Bonaparte deposed the ruling Knights of St. John, instituted numerous reforms, and improved the island's defenses. He also confiscated the treasury. The French then set sail for Egypt.

In July, Bonaparte's forces landed near Alexandria and quickly took that city. Bonaparte then marched with the main force across the desert, then reached the Nile. After defeating the Mamluk forces of Murad Bey near Shubra Khit (July 13), Bonaparte proceeded toward Cairo. On July 21, near the famous Pyramids of Giza in the Battle of the Pyramids, the French were victorious over the Mamluks.

Although the Mamluk army had been defeated, the campaign suffered a major blow with the discovery that Admiral Horatio Lord Nelson's warships had destroyed the French fleet near Alexandria in what the British called the Battle of the Nile, on August 2. Furthermore, Sultan Selim III, refused to accept French claims of protecting Ottoman interests in Egypt. Indeed, he declared war on France and mobilized two armies for expedition to Egypt. Then, on October 21 and 22,

The Rosetta Stone

One positive by-product of Napoleonic imperialism in Egypt was the discovery of the Rosetta Stone, a carved black granodiorite stele, found in July 1799 by a French soldier near the Rosetta mouth of the Nile. It is inscribed with three versions of a decree issued at Memphis, Egypt in 196 BCE on behalf of King Ptolemy V. The top and middle texts are in ancient Egyptian using hieroglyphic script and Demotic script, respectively, while the bottom is in ancient Greek. As the decree is the same (with some minor differences) in all three versions, the Rosetta Stone proved to be the key to deciphering Egyptian hieroglyphs and unlocking the secrets of ancient Egyptian civilization. Upon the capitulation of the French in Egypt in 1801, the stone came into British possession and was transported to London. On public display since 1802, it is the most visited object in the British Museum.

Spencer C. Tucker

many citizens of Cairo rose up in opposition to the French occupation. The revolt was put down, but it was clear that the French position was rather precarious.

Nevertheless, French operations in the Upper Egypt met some success as Desaix pursued the Mamluks of Murad Bey. On October 7, 1798, the French defeated a Mamluk force in a savage battle at al-Lahun but were unable to completely remove Murad Bey's influence in the region. Always elusive, Murad Bey now refused to be brought to battle, leading the French on a chase through Upper Egypt. On January 20, 1799, however, Murad Bey finally engaged Desaix's army in open battle at Samhud but suffered another defeat and retreated as far as Aswan. By the summer, the French extended their authority to the Red Sea port of al-Qusair.

Meantime, facing the prospect of an Ottoman invasion of Egypt, Bonaparte chose to attack first, turning his attention to the Ottoman army approaching through the Holy Land. Bonaparte expected to meet and defeat the Ottomans, stir up rebellion in Syria against Ottoman rule and perhaps move against Istanbul (Constantinople). Any attempt to move overland against British rule in India seemed unlikely, given the size of his force.

Bonaparte's expeditionary force was hastily organized, poorly equipped, and inadequately supplied. Now at the head of some 13,000 men, dubbed the Army of Syria, Bonaparte invaded Palestine, capturing El Arish. Proceeding northward along the coast, the French reached Jaffa on March 3. The French assaulted and took the city on March 7, in heavy fighting that was costly to both sides. The French slaughtered 2,000 men in the garrison rather than allowing them to surrender, but to Bonaparte's anger 3,000 Ottoman soldiers at the Citadel were allowed to surrender. With no means to feed, guard, or transport these, and using the excuse that a number were found to be men who had been taken prisoner earlier and released on a pledge that they would not again fight the French, Bonaparte ordered them all executed. This and the subjecting of Jaffe's civilian population to looting and rape were grist for the mill of Bonaparte's critics thereafter.

Moving up the coast, on March 17, Bonaparte arrived at, and laid siege to, the fortified Mediterranean port city of Acre (Acco). Bonaparte expressed the conviction that Acre would surrender within two weeks, and he would then be able to march on to Jerusalem. Acre's commander Jezzar Pasha refused to surrender, however.

With Acre defiant, there was little the French infantry and field artillery could do on their own against Acre's thick stone walls and some 250 guns inside the fortress, many of them with European-trained gunners. Jezzar was also ably assisted by French émigré colonel Antoine le Picard de Phélippeaux, who had been a classmate of Napoleon at the École Militaire.

Bonaparte also made a major mistake in deciding to send his siege artillery (44-, 24-, and 16-pounder guns and heavy mortars) by sea, as British Captain Sydney Smith's squadron intercepted and captured the flotilla transporting these and then offloaded them at Acre to assist in its defense, along with supplies and gunners. Smith also anchored his ships of the line *Tigre* and *Theseus* broadside to the shore and added their heavy guns to those of the fortress, while the gunboats captured from the French were used to shell the coastal road and also help repel the French infantry assaults. Bonaparte would later remark of Smith, "That man has caused me to lose my fortune; except for him I would be Emperor of the Universe."

Bonaparte has been much criticized for his error in sending his heavy guns by sea but also for failing to provide adequate provisions and sufficient medical care for his men.

Repeated French infantry assaults failed, with increasing casualties. While the siege continued, Bonaparte's forces did manage to win important victories over Ottoman and Mamluk forces attempting to relieve Acre in battle near Nazareth and at Mount Tabor on April 16, although these also cost Bonaparte several hundred men. Meanwhile, bubonic plague felled many more.

During the more than two-month siege, both sides attempted to secure the support of Shihab leader Bashir, who controlled most of what is present-day Lebanon. The French suffered the most from his decision to remain neutral. Had he sided with them, it might have turned the balance.

By early May, some replacement French siege guns had arrived, and these effected sufficient damage for the infantry to make a breach in Acre's walls. The assaulting French troops soon discovered, however, that the defenders had built a second wall just behind the first. News of this and the knowledge that Smith was preparing to ferry an Ottoman army to Egypt, caused Bonaparte to break off the siege on May 20 and order a return to Egypt. Before departing, he issued orders, which were disobeyed, that the worst-off of his men with the plague were to be given lethal doses of drugs on the assumption that they would be massacred if left behind. Of his original force of 13,000, 2,500 had died (half of them from disease); another 2,500 were wounded, and only half of these would reach Egypt.

When the second Ottoman army arrived by sea at Aboukir near Alexandria, Bonaparte was ready, and his victory there on July 25, 1799, removed the Ottoman threat for the foreseeable future. Shortly after the battle, in a meeting aboard Smith's flagship regarding an exchange of prisoners, Smith passed along to the French a number of French newspapers, from which Bonaparte learned of the political crisis then occurring in France itself. Seeing opportunity, and without having received orders to do so, Bonaparte departed Egypt for France in a fast frigate on August 23. Arriving in France, he took a leading role in the coup d'état of 18 Brumaire (November 9, 1799) that brought him to power and led to establishment of the French Empire.

Although the French Army of Egypt won additional victories over the British and Ottomans, and crushed rebellions in Cairo, it was finally forced to surrender in September 1801. By the terms of Franco-British agreement, the British fleet evacuated the surviving troops back to France. Bonaparte had arrived in Egypt with some 34,000 land troops and some 16,000 sailors. Of this number only about 23,000 (3,000 of them sick or wounded) returned.

Spencer C. Tucker

Further Reading

Chandler, David G. *The Campaigns of Napoleon.* New York: Macmillan, 1966.
Herold, J. Christopher. *Bonaparte in Egypt.* New York: Harper & Row, 1962.

Markham, J. David. *Napoleon's Road to Glory: Triumphs, Defeats & Immortality.* London: Brassey's, 2003.

Schur, Nathan. *Napoleon in the Holy Land.* London: Greenhill, 1999.

Strathern, Paul. *Napoleon in Egypt.* New York: Bantam, 2007.

Sieges of Zaragoza (June 15–August 17, 1808; December 20, 1808–February 20, 1809)

The two sieges of Zaragoza (Saragossa), Spain, during June 15–August 17, 1808, and December 20, 1808–February 20, 1809, occurred during the Peninsular War of 1808–1814, which was one of the Napoleonic Wars.

Following the conclusion of peace between France and Russia at Tilsit in July 1807, Emperor Napoleon of France turned his attention to Great Britain. The naval Battle of Trafalgar (October 21, 1805) had established Britain as mistress of the seas. To get at the British thereafter, Napoleon resorted to a war against British trade, denying British goods entry into all parts of Europe. This Continental System as it came to be called alienated many Europeans and forced Napoleon to overextend his forces. To prevent British goods from entering the Iberian Peninsula, for instance, in 1807 Napoleon sent French troops into Portugal. The next year he sent them into Spain, where he had forced King Ferdinand VII to abdicate. Napoleon installed his brother Joseph on the Spanish throne, but riots broke out in Madrid on May 2, 1808, and spread throughout the country. Napoleon had not anticipated the depth of the Spanish nationalist reaction.

One of the principal centers of resistance was the city of Zaragoza (Saragossa). The chief urban center of Aragon, Zaragoza is about 200 miles northeast of Madrid on the Ebro River. In 1808 it had a population of about 60,000 people. General Don José Rebolledo Palafox y Melzi had charge of the city's defense. He had only 300 royal dragoons, and only a third of these had horses, but Palafox recruited volunteers, called up retired and half-pay officers, and organized the city defenses as best he could, to include establishment of a munitions factory. Although he had artillery, few of his men were trained in its use.

The first fighting for Zaragoza took place on June 8 at Tudela, where a French force of 5,000 infantry, 1,000 cavalry, and two artillery batteries under the command of General François Joseph Lefèbvre-Desnouettes clashed with some 6,000 Spanish levies and armed peasants who tried to bar the way to Zaragoza. The French soon scattered them. A second and last effort to block the French approach occurred shortly thereafter at Alagon, where Palafox led 650 men and four guns against the French. He was wounded, and his force was defeated.

On June 15, 1808, Lefèbvre and his troops arrived at Zaragoza and commenced military operations against the city. Situated on a plain, Zaragoza was protected by the Ebro to the north. Its buildings were sturdy and tightly packed—ideal for defensive purposes—and the city was surrounded by a 12-foot-high stone wall. Palafox commanded about 10,000 men.

Lefèbvre assumed that a determined attack would soon carry the city. He directed his artillery against the west walls, while his infantry and some cavalry

> **Origin of the Term "Guerrilla"**
>
> The term "guerrilla" arose as a consequence of the Peninsular War. The word is Spanish and the diminutive of "Guerra" ("war") and means "little war." The term was used in English as early as 1809. "Guerrilla warfare" is usually employed in reference to the widespread operation of irregular forces as opposed to those of a professional state army.
>
> **Spencer C. Tucker**

attacked the Santa Engracia Gate to the south. Several French attacks encountered ferocious Spanish resistance, the attackers sustaining 700 casualties. Lefèbvre then decided to await reinforcements. Learning that a force of 4,000 Spaniards was en route to the city, Lefèbvre feigned an attack on Zaragoza but slipped away with most of his men, surprising and destroying the Spanish relief column.

On June 29, an additional French division with siege guns arrived at Zaragoza under General Jean Antoine Verdier, who took overall command of operations. Verdier ordered his men to drive 300 Spanish defenders from Mount Torrero, a dominating hill south of the city where the French then placed their siege guns. From that position at midnight on June 30, 46 French guns opened fire on Zaragoza. Following a 12-hour bombardment, Verdier ordered his infantry forward.

Desperate fighting ensued, during which Augustina Saragossa, a heroine of the siege, made her appearance. Immortalized by British poet Lord Byron, who was her lover, Saragossa carried food to a gun crew and then took the place of one of its members, reportedly firing the gun herself and shouting that she would not leave the position while she was still alive. At the same time a young boy seized a banner from a wounded standard-bearer and waved it. These actions helped rally the defenders, who were able to drive out those French troops who had gotten inside the city. The attackers sustained 500 casualties.

Verdier now decided to conduct a conventional siege. With only 13,000 men, however, he was unable to seal off access to the city and the Spanish continued to receive both supplies and reinforcements. Gradually the French pushed their lines forward and continued their bombardment. On August 4, the French made another breach in the walls. That afternoon 3,000 French troops attacked, entered the city, and took about half of it. The fighting was desperate, with no quarter given by either side. Verdier demanded that Palafox surrender, but the latter replied, "*Guerra a chillo*" ("War to the knife"). Desperate fighting raged over the next days, with priests and monks fighting alongside the people.

On the morning of August 14, Verdier withdrew his troops from the part of the city they had captured; on August 17 he broke off the siege entirely. Verdier had learned that on July 19, 1808, a French army of 20,000 men commanded by General Pierre Dupont was surrounded at Baylen by some 32,000 Spanish troops and levies and was forced to surrender, the first capitulation of a Napoleonic army anywhere in Europe. The news of Baylen, his inability to seal off the city, and

The Defence of Saragossa by Scottish painter David Wilkie (1828). The painting depicts Augustina Saragossa, a heroine of the first of two French sieges of this Spanish city and lover of British poet Lord Byron, who joined a Spanish gun crew against the attackers. (Photos.com)

word that additional Spanish reinforcements were en route to Zaragoza all caused Verdier to end the siege operations.

Following the French disaster of Baylen, Napoleon took personal command in Spain, and on December 20, 1808, the French returned to Zaragoza and again placed it under siege. This time the Spanish were ready. Palafox had managed to substantially improve the city defenses, which were now manned by 34,000 regular Spanish troops supported by 10,000 armed peasants. He also had 160 artillery pieces. Marshal Bon Adrien de Moncey led the French, reinforced by troops under Marshal Edouard Mortier. Moncey commanded 38,000 infantry, 3,000 sappers and gunners, 3,500 cavalry, and 144 guns.

Again concentrating on Mount Torrero, the French captured it on December 20, driving its 6,000 defenders into the city and capturing seven Spanish guns. Moncey called on Palafox to surrender, but the latter replied, "Spanish blood covers us with honor and you with shame." French siege operations began in earnest on December 23.

On January 2, General Jean-Androche Junot arrived at Zaragoza to replace Moncey and with orders to detach Mortier and 10,000 men to keep upon the road to Madrid. The French defeated a series of small Spanish sorties directed at spiking the French guns, which now were concentrated against the southeast walls of the city at close range. By January 26, the French had made several breaches in the walls, and the next day infantry assaults penetrated the Spanish defenses.

Learning that 20,000 Aragonese were marching to relieve Zaragoza, Napoleon sent reinforcements to the city and entrusted command of operations to Marshal Jean Lannes, who ordered Mortier to move against the Spanish relief column, which the French surprised and scattered at Nuestra Señora de Magallón.

Inside Zaragoza, bitter house-to-house fighting raged and continued without letup for the next three weeks. With much of the city reduced to rubble and his main equipment factory destroyed by a mine, Palafox announced that he would surrender, which occurred on February 20, 1809. Zaragoza was by then a smoking ruin, with about a third of the city destroyed. The siege had claimed 54,000 Spanish lives, and only 8,000 of the Spanish garrison were still alive. Some 10,000 French had perished, 4,000 killed in action and 6,000 dead of disease.

Although the French triumphed at Zaragoza, the city's defenders had again distinguished themselves. Zaragoza's defiance became a symbol of defiance and a standard for other Spanish cities resisting the invader. Napoleon was never able to solve the problem of Spanish nationalism. The "Spanish Ulcer," as Napoleon styled his effort to control Spain, continued to sap French manpower and encourage resistance elsewhere.

Spencer C. Tucker

Further Reading

Gates, David. *The Spanish Ulcer: A History of the Peninsular War.* New York: W. W. Norton, 1986.

Humble, Richard. *Napoleon's Peninsular Marshals: A Reassessment.* New York: Taplinger, 1974.

Rudorff, Raymond. *War to the Death: The Siege of Saragossa, 1808–1809.* London: Hamish Hamilton, 1974.

Siege of Cádiz (February 5, 1810–August 24, 1812)

The French siege of the Spanish port city of Cádiz was the longest and arguably most important of the many sieges during the 1808–1814 Peninsular War, itself part of the Napoleonic Wars of 1800–1815. The siege of Cádiz began on February 5, 1810, and lasted until August 24, 1812.

There was almost no siege of the city. French Marshal Nicolas Jean-de-Dieu Soult invaded Andalusia in January 1810 from the north. Cádiz was then largely without a garrison, and had Soult detached even a small force he might have easily taken the city. But the French preoccupation with securing Seville, then the seat of government of the Spanish Junta and the actions of Spanish general José María de la Cueva, 14th Duke of Alburquerque saved Cádiz. The first French troops, Soult's I Corps under Marshal Claude Victor-Perrin, were not dispatched there until February 2, the day after Seville fell, but they were two days late. Alburquerque's 12,000-man Army of Estremadura, ordered to the defense of Seville, had been unable to reach there in time and, without orders to do so, Alburquerque marched his men to Cádiz instead, arriving there on February 3.

French strength during the siege varied widely from as much as 60,000–70,000 men to as few as 20,000. British general Arthur Wellesley Viscount Wellington, who commanded British and Portuguese forces in the Iberian Peninsula, reinforced the initial Spanish garrison of 12,000 men by dispatching there some 2,000 Portuguese and perhaps 5,000 British troops, while additional Spanish troops brought total allied strength up to some 26,000 men.

On his arrival at Cádiz on February 5, Marshal Victor called on the city to surrender. Military governor of Cádiz General Francisco Javier Venegas refused the French demand. Victor then called for siege artillery and reported that it would take time to construct a flotilla of small craft with which to mount an assault. Napoleon's brother Joseph, now installed as king of Spain, was pessimistic. Following an inspection trip there, he wrote to Napoleon and requested that the French Mediterranean fleet be sent. Unwilling to risk a confrontation with the Royal Navy, Napoleon refused.

Located on a spit of land on the Atlantic coast of southern Spain, Cádiz is today recognized by many as the oldest continuously inhabited city in western Europe with ruins dating back some 3,100 years to Phoenician times. In 1810 it was home to the principal Spanish naval base, and it came to enjoy special significance as the new seat of the free Spanish government.

Cádiz was well situated to resist a siege. The city was at the end of a four-mile long north-south peninsula paralleling the mainland and was located at the northern portion of the triangular Isla de Leon that was a natural breakwater for the inner and outer harbors of Cádiz. A saltwater channel, the Rio Santi Petri separated the Isla de Leon from the mainland and ran from the southeastern corner of the inner harbor to the sea. Salt marshes prevented the French from easy access to the channel, which was also protected by Spanish gunboats. Access to the island had been by a bridge at Zuazo, but the Spaniards destroyed this so the only approach was by the channel, but the French never attempted to cross this by boat. Spanish fortifications included the naval arsenal of La Carraca at the north end and Punta de Santri Petri Castle at the southern end.

Had the French been able to gain the Isla de Leon, they would have had to advance four miles along the narrow peninsula linking the island to Cadiz. At its mid-point the peninsula was only some 200 yards wide and here the Spaniards had a continuous line of fortifications known as the Cortadura. Even if the French had gained the Isla de Leon, they would have faced heavy shelling from British warships offshore. Had they managed to get past the Cortadura and reach Cádiz itself, the city was protected by additional fortifications on a front of only 400 yards, with deep water to the sides.

The only possible weak point in the Spanish defenses from the land side was the Trocadero Peninsula that separated the inner and outer harbors. It faced the wide point in the Isla de Leon leading to Cadiz. The Spaniards had fortified both sides of the entrance to the inner harbor, with the forts of San José, San Luis, and Matagorda on the Trocadero and Puntales Castle on the peninsula. Matagorda is some 3,000 yards from the southern tip of the city but only 1,200 yards from Puntales. The heaviest French artillery then had an effective range of some 2,500 yards, and even the massive mortars introduced by the French later in the siege (one of which was later presented as a gift to the Duke of Wellington) only managed to fire a single shell into Cádiz. Before the French arrived, the Spaniards destroyed the three Trocadero forts. The French did take and rebuild them, making it possible for them to shell Puntales and also impede the movement of ships in and out of the inner harbor.

Victor's first effort to get at Cádiz came in an unsuccessful attempt to cross the salt marsh next to the Rio de Santi Petri. Following this failure, the French established their main base some two miles inland at Chiclana, then attempted and failed to take the naval arsenal of La Caracca.

Victor's next objective was the offshore fort of the Matagorda north of Cádiz, which he hoped to secure as a base for an attack on the Pentales. This had been destroyed by the Spanish, but on February 22, British Army engineers and infantry reoccupied and rebuilt it. The French then bombarded the Matagorda for two months, killing 64 members of its 140-man strong garrison. On April 22, the survivors were withdrawn. The last man to leave, a British major, was to have touched off a slow match to explode a mine that would destroy the fort, but he was killed before he could accomplish this.

Although the French now occupied the Matagorda, they were still too distant from the Puntales to effect much damage there. The two sides exchanged long-range fire with British and Spanish ships able to move in and out of the inner harbor at night.

During the struggle for the Matagorda, the area was buffeted by a hurricane during March 6–9. The winds forced one Portuguese and three Spanish ships of the line onto the French controlled shore. Some 600 French prisoners held on prison hulk were able to overpower their guards and escape. A second attempt ended badly for most of the prisoners when the ship drifted onto a mud bank within artillery range of the Spanish guns.

By May 1810, the Cádiz garrison had grown to 26,000 men. Although the French had built impressive earthworks and had some 300 pieces of ordnance, without major naval support there was no chance of them seizing the city. Indeed, Victor now found himself in the position of protecting southern Andalusia from the strong Spanish and British forces in the Cádiz.

That threat became reality in 1811. Early that year Soult invaded Estremadura and took some of Victor's men with him. Indeed, the defenders of Cádiz now outnumbered the besiegers by perhaps 26,000 to 19,000. The allies hoped to take advantage of this by landing forces south of the French lines, advancing them northward and forcing Victor to pull part of his army out of the lines, giving the remaining Cádiz forces the opportunity to attack the French siege lines and perhaps cause them to end the siege entirely.

The expedition began well. Some 9,500 Spaniards under General Manuel La Peña and 4,900 British and Portuguese troops under General Sir Thomas Graham landed at Algeciras on February 23 and began their moving north. The commander of the Cádiz breakout force, General José Pascual de Zayas y Chacón, however, moved too soon, allowing Victor to drive him back into Cádiz and then turn to deal with the allied expeditionary force. Still, as the allies approached his lines, Victor could only field some 10,000 men. The Battle of Barrosa on March 5 lasted only two hours but was a bloody affair with some 2,000 French dead, and British casualties only slightly fewer. While Graham's forces drove Victor's from the field, the inept La Peña remained immobile some two miles distant. Had he joined the battle, Victor would likely have been forced to abandon the siege. A disgusted Graham refused to serve under La Peña and returned to the Isla de Leon, followed the next day by La Peña. The siege continued.

Wellington's victory over Marshal Auguste Marmont's French forces near Salamanca on July 22, 1812, finally brought an end to the siege. Fearing that their men at Cádiz would be trapped, the French raised the siege. During August 23–24, under cover of a heavy artillery bombardment, the French destroyed the heavy guns and anything they could not carry off and departed.

The successful Spanish and British defense of Cádiz prevented the French from completing their conquest of Andalusia and pinned down a substantial part of Soult's French Army of Andalusia. Cádiz also served as the principal British and Spanish base for allied amphibious operations along the southern Spanish coasts, as the large garrison there could easily detach thousands of men for raiding operations against French coastal garrisons as well as carry out the resupply of isolated Spanish forces. Also during the siege, the government at Cádiz, the Cádiz Cortes, drew up a new constitution that limited the monarch's powers and became a model for liberal constitutional documents, although it was subsequently revoked by restored King Ferdinand VII.

Spencer C. Tucker

Further Reading

Clowes, William Laird. *The Royal Navy: A History from the Earliest Times to 1900.* Vol. 5. 1900. Reprint, London: Chatham, 1996.

Esdaile, Charles. *The Peninsular War: A New History.* New York: Palgrave Macmillan, 2003.

Gates, David. *The Spanish Ulcer: A History of the Peninsular War.* New York: W. W. Norton, 1986.

Glover, Michael. *The Peninsular War, 1807–1814: A Concise Military History.* London: Penguin, 2001.

Humble, Richard. *Napoleon's Peninsular Marshals.* New York: Taplinger, 1974.

Third Siege of Missolonghi (April 15, 1825–April 23, 1826)

There were three sieges of Missolonghi during the Greek War of Independence (1821–1830), with the third siege of April 15, 1825–April 23, 1826, being the most important.

Although Greece had been part of the Ottoman Empire since the mid-fifteenth century, loose Ottoman rule there had allowed the Greeks to retain their national identity, and although Orthodox Christians enjoyed certain political rights and a number held important positions, the Greeks were regarded as inferior subjects. The Greek Orthodox Church served as a rallying point and helped keep Greek identity alive. Sympathy in western Europe for the Greeks, which became known as Philhellenism, resulted in large measure from the role played by the ancient Greeks and their myriad contributions to Western civilization in the arts and letters and to the concept of democracy (itself a Greek word).

The period of the French Revolution and Napoleonic (1789–1815) was highly influential. It saw the beginning of modern European nationalism and the concept that peoples of the same language and ethnicity should be able to live together in their own nation-state. Greek intellectuals, many of them living abroad and educated in western Europe, took up the cause of an independent Greece and promoted it in their writings.

The long Greek War of Independence (also known as the Greek Revolution and the Greek Uprising) began when an insurrection in Wallachia (in present-day Romania) in February 1821 against the Ottoman Empire triggered a revolt in the Peloponnese (Morea) in southern Greece against Ottoman rule. The Ottomans easily put down the revolt, but on March 17 Maniots in the Peloponnese rose against the Ottomans, and by the end of the month the entire Peloponnese was in open rebellion. From there it spread northward.

Turks were in the minority in Greece, but there were a number of scattered Ottoman military garrisons there, and the revolt saw widespread atrocities by both sides. Greeks led by Theodoros Kolokotronis laid siege to the Ottoman garrison at Tripolitsa, then the largest city of southern Greece. The attackers took that city on October 5, 1821, and during the next several days the Greeks massacred there some 10,000 Turks, including women and children, many of whom were tortured to death. Savage Ottoman reprisals followed, and all Greece then rose against Ottoman rule. On January 13, 1822, at Epidauros, Greek nationalists proclaimed Greek independence.

In March, following atrocities committed against Turks on Chios, the Ottoman sent a large force to the island and massacred or starved to death some 42,000 Greeks and enslaved another 50,000.

In July, two Ottoman armies invaded and soon overran all Greece north of the Gulf of Corinth. The new Greek government took refuge in the Greek islands. Ottoman forces under Reşid Mehmed Pasha were, however, halted before the strategically located Greek fort of Missolonghi (Messolonghi) in western Greece that guarded the entrance to the Gulf of Corinth. The Missolonghi fortress was situated on a long spit of land surrounded on three sides by a lagoon with islands, three of which controlled access to the lagoon. The Ottomans arrived at Missolonghi on October 25 but made the mistake of entering into negotiations. The defenders led by Alexandros Mavrokordatos numbered only some 2,000 men, while the Ottoman commanders Omer Vrioni and Reşid Mehmed Pasha had 10,000–12,000. The defenders dragged out the surrender negotiations, and on November 8 more than 1,500 Greeks reinforcements arrived by sea to reinforce the garrison.

Too late, the Ottomans realized their mistake and resumed siege operations. After a month of bombardment and futile assaults, the Ottomans hoped to catch the Greeks by surprise on the night of Christmas Eve. Forewarned, the Greeks beat back the attack, and the Ottomans then withdrew. Missolonghi withstood a second lesser Ottoman siege during September 20–November 30, 1822.

The Greeks failed to take advantage of their military success, however, dissipating their energies in leadership struggles that flared into civil war in 1824.

With the Ottoman military intervention in Greece going badly, Sultan Mahmud II appealed for assistance to his powerful vassal, Muhammad Ali of

Egypt, who then dispatched a considerable fleet and land force to Greece under his son Ibrahim Ali. The Egyptian expeditionary force landed in Greece on February 24, 1825, and soon subdued virtually all of it. As result of this intervention, the Porte formally ceded Crete to Egypt, the forces of which conquered that Greek island during 1822–1824.

In the spring of 1825, the Ottoman force moved south and on April 15 opened a third siege of Missolonghi. This time Reşid Pasha had some 20,000 men: 8,000 professional soldiers, another 8,000 Albanian irregulars, and some 4,000 enslaved Greek laborers. Reşid was determined to be successful this time, having been warned by Sultan Mahmud II, "Either Missolonghi falls or your head."

The 5,000 defenders were mostly Greeks with a smattering of philhellenes and were led by a three-man committee, with the dominant figure being Nótis Bótsaris. The fortress had been strengthened by the addition of 17 triangular-shaped bastions projecting from the main fort that allowed more effective defensive fire and mounted 45 cannon and 4 mortars. Each was named for a perceived defender of liberty, such as the American Benjamin Franklin and the British philhellene Lord Byron (who died in Missolonghi in 1824).

Offered honorable terms, the defenders were of no mind to negotiate, and Reşid quickly put the Greek slaves to work constructing entrenchments and presenting the defenders with the difficult choice of having to fire on their own countrymen. Zigzag communication trenches resulted in new lines of parallel trenches that ultimately brought the besiegers to within 100 yards or so of the walls. Although the attackers' artillery was able to effect breaches in the walls, the assaults that followed were fiercely met and halted, with all the inhabitants of Missolonghi then working at night to repair the walls.

In August, Reşid put the Greek slaves to work building a large raised earthen area that enabled the attackers to fire down into Missolonghi. This led to the capture the Franklin bastion, but the defenders dug a large ditch behind the bastion that prevented further Ottoman-Egyptian inroads. Construction of a second mound was halted by the Greeks digging a mine and detonating an explosive charge. In nighttime raids, the Greeks also carried off much of the soil from the first mine and used it to help rebuild the walls before they destroyed what remained with another mine. A more ambitious mining operation in September killed a large number of Ottoman soldiers.

Reşid's hopes that he could starve the defenders into surrender came to naught. The Greeks were able to hold out because Greek admiral Andreas Miaoulis was able to resupply the fortress by water. In October, heavy rains turned the besiegers' positions into quagmires. Now confident they could withstand the siege, many of the wives and children whom Miaoulis had earlier evacuated to the island of Kalanos now returned to Missolonghi.

This confidence was misplaced, for Mohammad Ali now sent a fleet of 135 vessels with 10,000 additional troops to assist his son Ibrahim Pasha already in Greece. In January 1826, laying waste to the Peloponnese as he proceeded, Ibrahim and 15,000 Egyptian troops arrived at Missolonghi. Having brought with them additional artillery and an ample supply of ammunition, on February 24 they commenced a fierce bombardment of some 8,500 cannon shot and mortar shells that during a three-day span destroyed much of Missolonghi.

With the failure of three different assaults on the fortress, Ibrahim turned to cutting off the fortress from resupply by outfitting a flotilla of shallow-draft gunboats to secure the islands that controlled access to the lagoon. Vastly outnumbered and outgunned, the defenders of Vasiladhi surrendered in one day of fighting on March 9, while the Egyptians took both Dolmas and Poros islands on March 12. Anatolikon soon fell also. With these islands under Egyptian control, Missolonghi was effectively cut off from resupply.

Ibrahim then demanded that Missolonghi surrender with the inhabitants converting to Islam or being sold into slavery. The Greeks refused. On April 6, Reşid led 2,000 men in taking the important fortified island of Klisova but the effort soon became bogged down in mud flats, making the attackers easy prey for Greek snipers with Reşid among those wounded. That same morning an Egyptian force of 3,000 suffered the same fate, with their leader Hussein Bey killed. Reşid then called off the assault, with the Greeks securing some 2,500 enemy small arms.

Despite the failure of this operation, the situation in Missolonghi was now desperate, as starvation was taking a heavy toll. On the night of April 22, 7,000 of the defenders attempted a breakout, known as the "Exodus of its Guards" or "the Sortie." Made aware of the plan by deserters, the Ottomans and Egyptians were ready and a planned diversion by other Greeks failed to materialize. Only some 1,000 Greeks managed to reach the forests of Mount Zygos and most of these later perished there.

On the morning of April 23, the Ottomans entered Missolonghi. Many of the Greeks left alive there committed suicide rather than surrender; the rest were killed or sold into slavery. The Ottomans reportedly displayed some 3,000 severed heads on the city walls. The siege claimed the lives of more than 8,000 Greeks; the number of Ottoman and Egyptian casualties is unknown.

The siege and its effects helped build philhellenism in western Europe, and the bravery and suffering of Missolonghi was commemorated in its being awarded by the Greek government with the title of Hiera Polis (the Sacred City), unique among Greek cities. The siege was also the inspiration for great art in Eugène Delacroix's 1827 painting "Greece Expiring on the Ruins of Missolonghi."

The war continued, with Reşid Pasha turning his attention to Athens, which surrendered on the first Ottoman assault on August 25, 1826. The attackers then initiated a close blockade and bombardment of the Acropolis, which surrendered only after another protracted siege of more than a year, on May 24, 1827.

With Ottoman and Egyptian forces now controlling virtually all Greece, major foreign powers at last intervened. Britain, France, and Russia sent naval squadrons to Greece and, following unsatisfactory responses to their demands on the Egyptian and Ottoman governments, on October 20 their combined 26 warships entered Navarino Bay and there destroyed some 66 Egyptian and Ottoman warships. This battle led directly to an Egyptian withdrawal from the war and to Greek independence.

Spencer C. Tucker

Further Reading

Brewer, David. *The Greek War of Independence: The Struggle for Freedom from Ottoman Oppression and the Birth of the Modern Greek Nation.* Woodstock, NY: Overlook Press, 2001.

Clogg, Richard. *A Concise History of Greece.* 2nd ed. Cambridge, UK: Cambridge University Press, 2002.

Dakin, Douglas. *The Greek Struggle for Independence, 1821–1833.* Berkeley: University of California Press, 1973.

Woodhouse, C. W. *The Greek War of Independence: Its Historical Setting.* London: Hutchinson's University Library, 1952.

Siege of Puebla (September 14–October 12, 1847)

The siege of the U.S.-held stronghold of Puebla, Mexico (September 14–October 12, 1847) occurred during the United States' war with Mexico (1846–1848).

Puebla had first been occupied by U.S. forces under Brigadier General William J. Worth in May 1847. Although U.S. Major General Winfield Scott had taken the Mexican capital of Mexico City following a week-long series of battles during September 8–15, 1847, the war was by no means over. Nothing was more critical to Scott's force in Mexico City than U.S. control of the National Road between Mexico City and the port of Veracruz on the Gulf of Mexico. A series of U.S. garrisons were stationed along the road to protect this vital line of communication and supply from the U.S.-held port city. The most crucial of these was probably that in the city of Puebla, at roughly the halfway point on this route. There Scott had placed in command Colonel Thomas Childs, a reliable regular army officer and veteran of both the Seminole Wars in Florida as well as fighting in Mexico. The Americans held three strategic positions within the city: the citadel of San José, Fort Loretto, and a walled convent. Childs commanded a garrison of slightly more than 400 men. In case of attack, Scott and Childs planned to press into service additional convalescing U.S. soldiers, as indeed occurred.

Upon withdrawing his troops from Mexico City, Mexican general Antonio López de Santa Anna resigned the presidency. Pressured by empowered political enemies and a frustrated populace, Santa Anna planned one last military gamble to restore his national reputation and perhaps win the war. While part of his command under General José Joaquín de Herrera would pull back to the town of Querétaro to regroup, the other portion, led by Brigadier General Joaquín Rea, would launch a surprise attack on Puebla.

Rea's forces had begun harassing the Americans at Puebla shortly after Scott had departed for Mexican City. The Mexicans attacked supply trains, and they destroyed the aqueduct bringing water into the city. On August 25, the Mexican forces captured most of the garrison's livestock, threatening its food supply. Rea's force greatly outnumbered the Americans in Puebla: some 4,000 men to only 500, counting invalids.

On September 16, Rea demanded that the Americans surrender unconditionally, which Childs immediately refused. Rea then launched two separate attacks

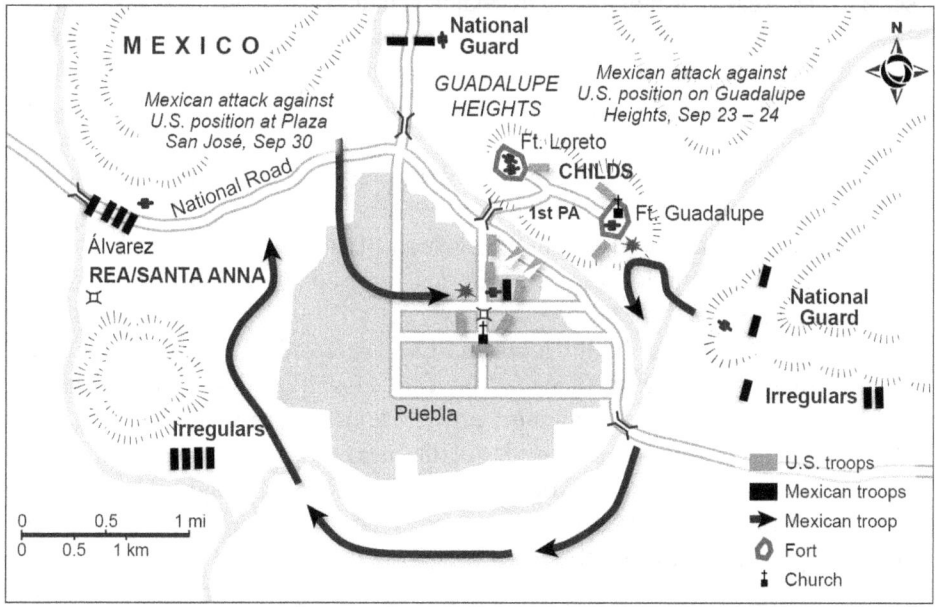

Disposition of forces during the siege of Pueblo in Mexico (September 14–October 12, 1847), in which Mexican forces attempted to dislodge the Americans from this important base on the National Road from Veracruz to Mexico City. (ABC-CLIO)

by his dragoons in an effort to take the San José citadel, both of which were repulsed by devastating American artillery fire. Santa Anna arrived on September 22 and launched yet another Mexican assault on the city, which the defenders also repulsed. In spite of the failed attack, the Mexican commander again called for the city's garrison to surrender. Again, Childs refused. A frustrated Santa Anna renewed the attack on September 27. This continued for the next five days with little success, however. Rea kept the Americans inside their fortifications during the next several days but did not provoke further conflict.

Knowing that Scott could not send reinforcements from his position in Mexico City to Childs because of rain-soaked roads, Santa Anna then shifted his effort to east of the city, where fresh American troops were mustering at Veracruz and would soon be moving westward. On September 30, Santa Anna moved the majority of his forces from Puebla to intercept these impending American reinforcements. Meanwhile, noticing the depletion of forces in the Mexican lines, Childs carried out several small raids on Mexican strong points to weaken the siege, in the course of which the Americans inflicted some casualties.

Santa Anna, meanwhile, planned to ambush and destroy the American relief column en route from Veracruz. Major General Joseph Lane departed Veracruz with 1,700 men but added reinforcements from various garrisons along the way, notably at Perote, increasing his force to nearly 3,000 men.

Santa Anna engaged Lane's column on October 9, just outside the town of Huamantla, northeast of Puebla along the northern branch of the National Road. In hard fighting, Santa Anna's forces were driven from the field in disorder following a series of U.S. cavalry charges led by Major Samuel H. Walker, who was however mortally wounded. When Lane learned of the death of the popular Walker, he let loose his poorly disciplined volunteers on the town. They proceeded to pillage and destroy—the only instance in the war in which a sizable U.S. force sacked a Mexican city.

The next morning, October 10, Lane's troops pressed on to Puebla. They arrived there two days later and engaged the remainder of Rea's besiegers outside of the city. Following a brief, hard-fought engagement, Lane drove the Mexican troops from the field, reaching the besieged American garrison that afternoon and lifting the 28-day-long siege.

American forces under both Childs and Lane suffered 22 killed, 52 wounded, and one missing during the siege. Mexican casualties during the siege are unknown. The disorganized remnants of the Mexican Army continued to resist in the Puebla area with guerilla raids for the next several weeks, which forced Lane to launch several punitive raids in guerilla-friendly villages. However, the American victory at Puebla signaled the end of conventional organized Mexican military opposition in the conflict.

Bradford A. Wineman

Further Reading

Carney, Stephen A. *The Occupation of Mexico, May 1846–July 1848*. Washington, DC: U.S. Army Center of Military History, 2006.

Levinson, Irving. *Wars within Wars: Mexican Guerillas, Domestic Elites, and the United States of America, 1846–1848*. Fort Worth: Texas Christian University Press, 2005.

Winders, Richard Bruce. "Puebla's Forgotten Heroes." *Military History of the West* 24 (Spring 1994): 1–23.

Siege of Venice (August 1848–August 27, 1849)

The siege of Venice, during August 1848–August 27, 1849, was part of the nineteenth-century movement to unify Italy known as the "Risorgimento" (resurgence). When the wars of the French Revolution and Napoleonic Era began in 1792, Italy was little more than a geographical expression—a patchwork of 15 small states, each in rivalry with, if not openly hostile to, the others. Not since the days of the Roman Empire had the Italian peninsula been united politically.

The wars of the period 1792–1815 had profound impact. Under Napoleon Bonaparte, the French had conquered much of Italy, and Napoleon introduced a uniform system of laws and administration. He also reduced the number of states to three. Parts of northwestern and east central Italy were incorporated into France, and there was the Kingdom of Italy in the northeast and the Kingdom of Naples in the south. Yet the Congress of Vienna of 1814–1815, called to redraw

> **Balloon Incendiaries**
>
> The use of balloon incendiaries against Venice was suggested by Austrian navy lieutenant Franz von Uchatius. He proposed that balloons carrying explosives be launched from the blockading Austrian ships to drift over Venice, then explode in midair from timed fuses, causing fires and panic below. The balloons were apparently quite large and each carried 33 pounds of explosives set off with a half-hour fuse.
>
> The first effort, on July 9, 1849, failed. The balloons took to the skies as planned, but when the wind shifted, they actually threatened the Austrian ships. The Venetians watched the proceedings and reportedly applauded the effects. The second effort, on August 22, caused only minimal damage to Venice, with some of the balloons again drifting back toward the Austrians before exploding. Venice, however, surrendered five days later.
>
> **Spencer C. Tucker**

the map of Europe after the defeat of Napoleon, resurrected the old Italy of many different monarchal states.

In northern Italy, the Austrian Empire dominated. Lombardy (with its capital of Milan) and Venetia (capital of Venice) passed under its rule as the Kingdom of Lombardy–Venetia. Venetia included the city of Venice, Istria, and Dalmatia. Although Vienna had held out the prospect of home rule, this soon disappeared when it was clear that the people of Lombardy and Venetia wanted independence. Although Austria rule was not harsh, it was exploitive. By 1848 a broad coalition of intellectuals, manufacturers, bankers, and agrarian leaders had come together demanding change.

Attempts in the early 1830s to shake off foreign rule had been crushed, but the dreams of a unitary state remained and in late 1847 unrest broke out throughout Italy, ushering in the revolutionary wave that swept much of Europe in 1848. Grand Duke Leopold of Tuscany and King Charles Albert, ruler of the Kingdom of Sardinia (most often known at the time and since as Piedmont-Sardinia or Sardinia-Piedmont for its two component territories) were both forced to grant constitutions. In January 1848, the reactionary ruler of Sicily, King Ferdinand II, was also forced to grant a constitution.

On March 18, revolt broke out in Milan. In the so-called Five Days of Milan, Austrian field marshal Joseph Radetzky von Radetz was forced to withdraw his troops from the city. They retreated to the stronghold at the foot of the Alps, known as the Quadrilateral, comprising the cities of Mantua, Verona, Peschiera, and Legnago.

With the unrest and seeming success of revolutionaries in various parts of Italy, on March 22, King Charles Albert of Piedmont-Sardinia declared war on Austria in what he believed would be a war of national liberation won by Italians alone. Indeed, he boasted "Italia fera da se" (Italy will do it by itself). Thousands of volunteers from other parts of Italy, including troops from the Papal States, joined the Army of Piedmont-Sardinia.

Also, on March 22, fortified by what had happened in Milan, revolutionaries in Venice seized control of the arsenal, the great naval yard and munitions depot, and proceeded to organize both a civic guard and then a provisional government. This embraced all Venetia save Verona, which was the key to the so-called Quadrilateral of fortresses and under firm Austrian control.

Austrian forces evacuated Venice on March 26, and Venice declared independence as the Republic of San Marco under the leadership of Daniele Manin. The Venetian Assembly then voted to join the rest of northern Italy and merge their new republic with Piedmont-Sardinia in a new Kingdom of Alta Italia (Upper Italy).

In mid-June, however, Radetzky assumed the offensive and defeated Charles Albert's poorly trained and ineffectively led troops in the Battle of Custoza near Verona during June 24–25. Soon Radetzky reestablished Austrian control in Lombardy and in most of Venetia, save Venice. The Austrians then concluded an armistice with Sardinia-Piedmont in order to concentrate on the revolution that had broken out in Hungary.

Revolt also occurred in Rome and Pope Pius IX fled the city. In February 1849, a constituent assembly declared Rome a republic. The effects of this were great, especially in northern Italy, where Charles Albert, under considerable pressure from radicals in Piedmont, renounced the armistice and again took up arms against Austria. Radetzky then invaded Piedmont and defeated again Charles Albert's army in the Battle of Novara (March 22–23). Charles Albert was forced to abdicate in favor of his son, Victor Emmanuel II. His victory allowed Radetzky to send part of his forces north to assist against the Hungarians. Then on July 3, French troops, having been sent to Italy by Emperor Napoleon III to assuage French Catholics, marched into Rome and ended its republic after a two-month siege.

Meanwhile, Venice kept the Republican cause alive in northern Italy. Although the city had come under Austrian blockade by land the previous August, the Republic of San Marco remained intact. Radetzky's victory at Novara, however, changed all that. On March 26, 1849, soon after news was received of the battle, the Venice Assembly, which had been elected on the basis of universal suffrage and secret ballot, met at the Doge's Palace. Manin presented an honest appraisal of the situation. There was hope that the situation in Hungary would inhibit the Austrians or that France or Britain might intervene, but these possibilities seemed remote. He then asked the Assembly members whether they wanted to continue to resist. They replied unanimously in the affirmative and passed a resolution calling on resistance "at all costs" and investing Manin with "unlimited powers." This sentiment met strong public support from Venetians of all classes.

The area of the republic was now limited to the lagoon some 90 miles in circumference with its several hundred small islands and population of 200,000 people in all with the 125,000 in Venice itself and 50,000 at Chioggia at the other end of the lagoon. The lagoon contained some 60 forts manned by 18,000 men. The most important of these were Fort Brondolo at Chioggia guarding the southern approaches and Malghera on the mainland end of the railroad bridge to Venice.

On May 4, the Austrians had begun a bombardment of Malghera. In just a few hours, they fired some 7,000 shot and shell. Radetzky fully expected the inexperienced Venetians to surrender. That was not the case, and indeed by the end of the bombardment more Austrian than Venetian guns had been put out of action.

The next day, Radetzky called on the Republic of San Marco to surrender. He offered only a general pardon and permission for those wishing to emigrate. There were no concessions to the Venetians regarding their government, and the general feeling was that this would simply be a return to the status quo ante bellum. The Venetians were determined to continue resistance in the hope that eventually foreign intervention and diplomacy would work in their favor.

The siege of Fort Malghera then continued. After three weeks, the Austrians had expended some 60,000 shot and shell, killing 400 of its 2,400 defenders. Venetian sorties from the fortress had cut dikes and flooded the plain but the shelling continued, and, although working waist-deep in water, the Austrians built new artillery emplacements closer to the fort and on May 24 opened fire from these. On May 25 alone, they fired some 15,000 rounds. By now, the fortress walls were crumbling.

With the Austrians massing men for an infantry assault on May 27, Manin ordered Malghera abandoned on the night of May 26–27. Slow matches kept the Venetian guns firing over a three-hour span, masking the withdrawal across the exposed railroad 2.5-mile long bridge. The Venetians turned one of the five repair stations on the bridge into a fort with seven guns and two mortars and blew up the part of the bridge between it and the mainland.

This placed the Austrians in a difficult position, as their artillery normally had not the range to reach the city 2.5 miles distant. The real danger to the Venetians would be securing adequate food for the population. For a month the Austrians bombarded the station, now named Fort St. Antonio, and a battery on the small island of San Secondo. Damage inflicted by the Austrian guns in daytime was repaired by the defenders at night.

The Austrians tried an attack on Fort Brondolo at Chioggia, but it proved even stronger than Malghera, and they soon gave up. They then tried sending balloons with bombs on fuses all sent aloft from a frigate in prevailing winds, but these proved a failure. Food shortages had brought a riot in June and by July the population was subsisting principally on bread. On July 10, bottles drifting in the lagoon brought news of the fall of Rome and the defeat of Hungarian forces by the Austrians and Russians.

On the night of July 29, with Austrian guns mounted at 45-degree angles and firing from makeshift carriages, hot shot and shells began falling on the western two-thirds of Venice itself. During the next three weeks, the Austrians fired some 25,000 shells. The Venetians could not respond as their homemade powder was too weak. Damage was slight in the shelling, but it did force a majority of the city population to relocate. Sanitary conditions now rapidly deteriorated and cholera broke out.

The only hope for the Venetians was breaking the Austrian naval blockade. Ironically, the Venetian navy, once the pride of the city, was now its weakest link. At the beginning of the revolt, most of the officers and sailors had been tricked by the Austrians into remaining at their posts at Pola and Trieste. Others at Venice were dispersed among the lagoon fortresses, and until the Battle of Navaro, building up the navy had not been a priority as the Piedmont-Sardinian fleet was blockading the Austrians at Trieste. But even after Novara, Manin was slow to recognize the threat. When the Piedmont-Sardinian ships were withdrawn from the Adriatic, the Austrians were able to attack Venice from the sea. Twice in August, Manin ordered what ships were available to engage the Austrians, but each time the admiral in command returned without having battled the far more powerful Austrians.

On August 24, 1849, with food and ammunition now both exhausted and having received authorization to do so, Manin negotiated the city's capitulation to go into effect on August 27. The Austrians granted amnesty for all save Manin and 39 others who were nonetheless allowed to go into exile. Manin departed Venice with his family on August 28 in a French ship; his wife died of cholera within a few hours of sailing, and Manin died almost destitute in exile at Marseille, France, in 1857 having abandoned republicanism in favor of the unification of Italy under the Piedmont-Sardinia monarchy.

The Risorgimento continued, however. In 1859 Austrian stumbled into a war with France and Piedmont-Sardinia. Austria was then forced to cede Lombardy to Piedmont-Sardinia, which with other territories added in northern Italy became the Kingdom of Italy in 1861. An Italian alliance with Prussia in the Austro-Prussian War (1866), at last brought the kingdom Venetia. Rome followed in 1871.

Spencer C. Tucker

Further Reading

Bassani, Ugo. *Venezia nel 1849*. Milan: Ceschini, 1938.

Beales, Derek Edward Dawson. *The Risorgimento and the Unification of Italy*. New York: Barnes and Noble, 1971.

Davis, John A., ed. *Italy in the Nineteenth Century, 1796–1900*. Oxford, UK: Oxford University Press, 2000.

Holt, Edgar. *The Making of Italy 1815–1870*. New York: Atheneum, 1971.

Keates, Jonathan. *The Siege of Venice*. London: Pimlico, 2006.

Martin, George. *The Red Shirt & the Cross of Savoy: The Story of Italy's Risorgimento (1748–1871)*. New York: Dodd, Mead, 1979.

Pascolato, Alessandro. *Manin e Venezia nel 1848–49*. Milan: Alfieri & Lacroix, 1916.

Siege of Sevastopol (October 17, 1854–September 9, 1855)

The siege of the great Russian naval base of Sevastopol (Sebastopol) on the Crimean Peninsula was the primary allied military objective and military event of the Crimean War (1853–1856). Beginning on September 13, 1854, French, British, and Ottoman troops landed on the Crimean Peninsula and then moved south just north of Sevastopol. In their advance south, the allies won battles on the Alma River on September 20, at Balaclava on October 25, and at Inkerman on November 5.

Although the Russians were defeated in all three battles, they did purchase time for military engineer Colonel Francis E. I. Todleben to improve Sevastopol's defenses. Because the Russians had blocked the mouth of the harbor with sunken

Commencement of the Siege of Sebastopol, by Thomas Packer (1884). The siege of this important Russian naval base by the Allies was the central event of the Crimean War of 1853–1856. (Photos.com)

ships, the allied fleets were unable to approach the port from the south. The allies might still have taken Sevastopol by land assault in mid-October, but British commander Fitzroy James Henry Somerset, Lord Raglan, rejected such an approach in favor of a siege.

The allies opened their first bombardment of Sevastopol from the northern (land) side on October 17. Because they lacked sufficient numbers of heavy guns, the initial shelling accomplished little. The allies settled in for the winter after the Battle of Inkerman.

Unprepared for a long campaign and winter conditions, the British forces were particularly hard hit, lacking even tents. The British lost large numbers of men to the cold and disease. Cholera was a major killer. The French were somewhat better prepared than the British, although cholera also claimed French commander Marshal Armand-Jacques Leroy de Saint-Arnaud. General François Certain Canrobert succeeded him. The Russians also suffered, sustaining numerous casualties, although Todleben actually improved the defenses in the midst of the allied shelling. Reports of the horrible conditions by British war correspondents (notably William Howard Russell of the *London Times*) led to the fall of the British government under Prime Minister George H. Gordon, Lord Aberdeen. One of the important changes that came out of this was improved medical facilities, including the sending out of nurses under Florence Nightingale.

In January 1856, the Kingdom of Sardinia (Sardinia-Piedmont) entered the war. Its government dispatched 10,000 men under General Alfonso Ferrero di La Marmora. Additional allied forces also arrived; ultimately the allies deployed more than 160,000 men and 500 heavy guns to operations against Sevastopol. In early

1855, the allies also improved the logistical net connecting the siege lines to their coastal bases. In an effort to disrupt this work, on February 17 new Russian commander Prince Mikhail Gorchakov mounted an attack on the allies at Eupatoria (Yevpatoriya), but the Ottomans met and drove this back.

The allies steadily pushed their siege lines closer to Sevastopol. On April 8, the allies opened a furious 10-day bombardment that destroyed a large section of the Russian defenses and killed some 6,000 Russian soldiers positioned to resist an assault. Angered by squabbling between the field commanders and their home governments, French commander General Canrobert resigned. General Aimable Jean Jacques Pélissier replaced him.

On May 24, the allies captured Kerch and cleared the Sea of Azov, cutting Russian communications from Sevastopol to the northeast. On June 7, the allies mounted a major assault on Sevastopol, taking part of the Russian outer defenses at a cost of 6,900 allied and 8,500 Russians casualties. The allies resumed their assault on the two Russian strong points of the Malakoff and the Redan during June 17–18. The attack was poorly coordinated, and both the French assault on the Malakoff and that of the British on the Redan failed. The attackers lost 4,000 men, and the defenders lost 5,400 men. Raglan died 10 days later and was succeeded by General Sir James Simpson.

The allies now subjected Sevastopol to constant shelling. Russian casualties amounted to some 350 a day, slowly draining the defenders' strength. With time running out, the Russians mounted one last effort to sever the allied lines to Sevastopol. On August 16, Gorchakov sent two corps against 32,000 French and Sardinian troops. The Battle of the Takir Ridge, fought on high ground above the Chernaya River, ended in a Russian defeat. The battle claimed 8,200 Russian (3,200 dead) and 1,700 allied casualties.

Following an intense four-day bombardment, on September 8 the French carried out perhaps the only well-planned and effectively executed assault of the war against the Malakoff. No signal was given; the attack was launched at midnight by the synchronization of watches alone. In fierce hand-to-hand combat, the French secured the Malakoff by nightfall. The Russians turned back a British assault on the Redan, but the French now directed their fire on the Redan, producing a Russian withdrawal from it with heavy losses. Gorchakov began blowing up the remaining Russian fortifications that night and evacuated Sevastopol on September 9. The final assault on the Russian fortress had claimed more than 10,000 allied casualties. Russian losses were perhaps 13,000.

Although fighting also took place in the Balkans and on the Black Sea, the siege of Sevastopol was the central event of the Crimean War. With Sweden threatening intervention and Austria presenting Russia with an ultimatum, on February 1 the Russians agreed to preliminary peace conditions. Each side lost about a quarter million men to battle and disease.

The Congress of Paris occurred during February 25–March 30, 1856. Although French emperor Napoleon III had hoped that the conferees would discuss all pressing European matters, including Italy and Poland, Britain sided with Austria in pushing a return to the status quo ante bellum. Their interest was solely in checking Russian expansionism and propping up the Ottoman Empire.

Under the terms of the Treaty of Paris therefore, the great powers upheld the territorial integrity of the Ottoman Empire. Russia was forced to cede the mouth of the Danube River and a strip of Bessarabia and also agreed to return Kars, taken during the war. Moldavia and Wallachia were placed under joint custody of the major powers. Elections in the principalities occurred in 1862, and in 1878 they achieved their independence as the Kingdom of Romania. Russia had to agree to the neutralization of the Black Sea. In the Declaration of Paris, the major powers also adopted new rules of international law regarding naval warfare. These made privateering illegal, stipulated that neutral flags protected enemy goods except for contraband, provided that neutral goods other than contraband were protected from capture, and stipulated that a blockade must be effective in order to be binding under international law.

Spencer C. Tucker

Further Reading

Barker, A. J. *The War against Russia, 1854–1856.* New York: Holt, Rinehart and Winston, 1970.

Edgerton, Robert B. *Death of Glory: The Legacy of the Crimean War.* Boulder, CO: Westview, 1999.

Siege of Saigon (March 1860–February 1861)

The 11-month siege of Saigon (today Ho Chi Minh City) in Vietnam during March 1860–February 1861 by Vietnamese against the French and Spanish occurred during the long French effort to secure control of Indochina.

The French established their first regular trading post in Vietnam in 1680. Christian missionaries were soon active there and Christianity spread. The Vietnamese emperors saw in this a direct threat to their rule, but their attempts to root out Christianity provided an excuse for French military intervention. After the French Revolution and Napoleon (1879–1815), France experienced a considerable religious resurgence and persecution of Vietnamese Catholics during the reign of Emperor Minh Mang (1820–1841) aroused a French popular outcry.

Of course, missionary fervor was not the only factor behind French intervention in Vietnam. The French sought to challenge the British for the vast China trade and hoped to be able to penetrate the Chinese interior by means of the Mekong River into Tibet and the Red River into Yunnan.

Alleged mistreatment of Catholic missionaries, however, was the excuse for French intervention. Already on April 15, 1847, an armed clash occurred between French warships and Vietnamese ships at Tourane (now Da Nang). Then, during Napoleon III's Second Empire (1852–1870), Paris adopted a more militant policy toward furthering its interests in Asia with defense of the Catholic Church abroad one of the pillars of Napoleon III's regime. In 1856 when the French protested the executions of Catholics in Vietnam and the Vietnamese court refused any explanations, a French warship bombarded Tourane.

In mid-July 1857, Napoleon III decided to undertake major military operations in Asia. Charles Admiral Rigault de Genouilly received command of

French naval forces in Chinese waters, cooperating with the British against China in the Second Opium War (1856–1860). The success of operations in China in 1858 then freed the French squadron for employment in Indochina waters. Both Spain and France sought redress from Vietnam for the execution of missionaries, and Emperor Napoleon III hoped to secure a port there along the lines of Hong Kong.

It was no accident that the French chose to penetrate southern Vietnam first; it was the newest part of the country and its people were not as wedded to Vietnamese institutions. Indeed, the French conquest of Vietnam would prove more difficult the farther it moved north.

In January 1858, orders issued in Paris the previous November finally reached Rigault de Genouilly. Paris instructed him that while operations in Indochina were to be only an appendix and entirely subordinate to those in China, he was to halt religious persecution and assure toleration of Catholics there. Paris thought this could best be achieved by occupying Tourane, mistakenly considered the key to the entire kingdom. Future Indochina operations were to be entirely at Rigault de Genouilly's discretion.

On August 31, 1858, Rigault de Genouilly's squadron of 14 warships carrying 3,000 men (including 1,000 troops from the Spanish possession of the Philippines) anchored off Tourane. The admiral believed that decisive military action would bring fruitful negotiations with the Vietnamese, and on September 1 he landed his men. The invaders stormed Tourane's forts after only perfunctory Vietnamese resistance, taking them and the port. This auction inaugurated the first phase of the French conquest of Indochina.

Within a few months, Vietnamese resistance, heat, disease, and a lack of supplies forced the French from Tourane. Leaving a small French garrison and several warships at Tourane, Rigault de Genouilly shifted his attention southward to the fishing village of Saigon. He selected it because of its proximity, its promise as a deepwater port, and the fact that it was next to Ta-ngon (today Cholon and part of Saigon), center of the southern rice trade, so vital to all Vietnam.

On February 2, Rigault de Genouilly proceeded southward with his ships. After stopping at Cam Ranh Bay to meet four supply ships, the French and Spanish arrived at Cape Saint-Jacques on February 10 and began bombarding the Vietnamese forts, soon silencing their return fire. A landing force of French and Spanish troops then went ashore and took possession of the forts.

The allied force then moved up the Saigon River, proceeding cautiously and reducing Vietnamese river forts as they proceeded. On February 15, they came upon two forts defending Saigon from the south that had been built earlier by French engineers in the service of Emperor Gia Long (r. 1804–1820). Early on February 16, the French ships opened fire on the forts, which returned fire. Infantry then went ashore, and within a few hours the forts had been taken. The next day, February 17, the French assaulted the Saigon Citadel and captured it, beating back a Vietnamese counterattack. With the fortress covering some 2.5 acres and too large to be held by the troops available, Rigault de Genouilly decided to blow it up, which was accomplished by 35 explosive charges on March 8.

Rigault de Genouilly then returned to Tourane after leaving behind a small force under naval commander Bernard Jauréguiberry. It included a company of French marine infantry, a company of Filipino infantry under Spanish command, and 400 sailors to man the artillery. Left behind as well were a corvette, two gunboats, and a transport. The defenders then repaired one of the southern forts taken earlier as their principal base.

In April 1859, Jauréguiberry led an attack on Vietnamese fortifications west of Saigon. Although successful, the allied cost of 14 dead and 31 wounded led Jauréguiberry to suspend further such efforts.

Saigon was now on its own. Confronted by the major manpower demands of the war involving France and the Kingdom of Sardinia (Piedmont-Sardinia) against Austria (April–July 1859), Paris would not be sending out reinforcements. French government officials also criticized Rigault de Genouilly for his actions at Saigon, and he then asked to be relieved of his command; Admiral Théogène François Page replaced him in November 1859. Paris instructed Page not to seek territorial concessions but to sign a treaty that would guarantee religious liberties and French consuls in the major Vietnamese ports.

Before Page could carry out his instructions, he was ordered to China with his squadron as fighting had again broken out there. The French force ashore in southern Vietnam was too small to accomplish anything save to try to hold on to what it had already taken. The Vietnamese court hoped that European events would cause the French to depart. Meanwhile, both Da Nang and Saigon both came under siege. Although the small French force at Da Nang soon evacuated it by ship that at Saigon remained in place.

Some 12,000 Vietnamese now besieged at Saigon a small allied garrison under French Navy commander Ariès of some 800 men (600 marine infantry and 200 Spanish troops). In addition to Saigon, Ariès had also to defend Cholon.

By March 1860, the allied garrison was completely cut off from outside contact. They did have three corvettes, and they armed a number of smaller craft for river patrols. They also managed to recruit some Annamese and Chinese as auxiliaries, raising their total strength to some 1,000 men.

At Saigon, the allied force came under increasing pressure from the Vietnamese to the west of Saigon and Cholon, who steadily dug trenches closer to the defenders and mounted occasional costly attacks. Disease also took a toll on the defenders. The French, however, consolidated their control of Cholon by taking and fortifying four pagodas there. These roughly paralleled the Vietnamese lines to the west and formed the heart of the French defense.

With the French and British victorious in China in September 1860, the French were again free to concentrate their Asian resources in Indochina. In early 1861, Admiral Léonard-Victor-Joseph Charner received orders to relieve the Saigon garrison and complete the conquest of Cochinchina. In mid-February, Charner departed Chinese waters with a powerful fleet of some 70 ships, including two steam frigates, lifting 3,000 troops under General Élie de Vassoigne. These were joined off Saigon by a small Spanish force of some 270 men.

The Vietnamese had had a year to prepare for the French relief effort and Nguyen Tri Phuong, governor of Gia Dinh Military District that included

Saigon, now had at his disposal some 20,000–30,000 men. Extending westward from Saigon and Cholon was the Ky Hoa plain of shallow ravines and gullies, which the French would have to cross to take the principal Vietnamese works in the village of Ky Hoa. The Vietnamese defenses were some seven miles in length, and extending outward from these was a maze of redoubts and outposts. What the Vietnamese lacked was modern weaponry. Their flintlock muskets, iron cannon, and a few war elephants were no match for modern French rifles and artillery.

The French attacked in force on February 25, 1861. Charner's plan was risky as he knew nothing about his enemy's defenses, but early that day he moved in force against what was known as the Redoubt at the southern end of the Vietnamese line, with the plan to proceed northward to prevent the Vietnamese from reinforcing and take their principal fortifications from the rear. Fighting was fierce, especially for the Mandarin Fort, but the allies were victorious. In the Battle of Ky Hoa, the French and Spaniards sustained 225 casualties, 12 of them dead; the Vietnamese suffered at least 300 dead as well as many prisoners. The siege was at an end, and France would remain in Vietnam.

Emperor Tu Duc (r. 1847–1883), deprived of rice from the French-controlled South and facing a rebellion in the North under the leadership of a remote Le dynasty descendant, was obliged in 1862 to sign a treaty with France that provided for a 20 million-franc indemnity, three treaty ports in Annam and Tonkin (central and northern Vietnam, respectively), and French possession of the eastern provinces of Cochinchina, including Saigon. Despite ongoing guerrilla opposition, France continued to expand its holdings in Indochina by fits and starts, often with little or no initiative on the part of Paris. By 1867 the French had conquered all of Cochinchina, but they had also learned that the Mekong was not navigable to the interior of China.

The Franco-German War of 1870–1871 put a temporary halt to French imperialism in Asia, but soon the process began anew, propelled by the French desire to recoup overseas the power and prestige they had lost in Europe. In the 1870s, the French turned their attention to northern Vietnam, where Tu Duc's hold was weak, and by 1884 they had created French Indochina, comprising Cochinchina, Annam, and Tonkin, along with Laos and Cambodia. Cochinchina was the only outright colony, with Annam and Tonkin protectorates, along with the kingdoms of Laos and Cambodia. In reality, all Indochina was subject to French rule, however.

Spencer C. Tucker

Further Reading

Chapuis, Oscar. *The Last Emperors of Vietnam: From Tu Duc to Bao Dai*. Westport, CT: Greenwood, 2000.

Osborne, Milton E. *The French Presence in Cochinchina and Cambodia: Rule and Response (1859–1905)*. Bangkok: White Lotus, 1997.

Thomazi, Auguste. *Histoire militaire de l'Indochine française des débuts à nos jours (Juillet 1930)*. 2nd ed. Hanoi: Imprimerie de l'Extreme Oriente, 1931.

Thomazi, Auguste. *La Conquête de l'Indochine*. Paris: Payot, 1934.

Tucker, Spencer C. *Vietnam*. Lexington: University Press of Kentucky, 1999.

Siege of Fort Sumter (December 26, 1860–April 14, 1861)

By 1860 the United States was bitterly divided by slavery and sectionalism. On November 6, 1860, Republican Party candidate Abraham Lincoln was elected president of the United States with a plurality of the vote and largely because the Democratic Party split on the issue of slavery. The Republican platform called for no more slavery in the territories but promised no interference with slavery in the states. Nonetheless, many southern leaders refused to accept a "Black Republican President," and on December 24, 1860, the state of South Carolina voted to secede from the Union.

State conventions in Alabama, Georgia, Florida, Mississippi, Louisiana, and Texas followed South Carolina's lead. On February 8, 1861, representatives from the seven seceded states met at Montgomery, Alabama, and there formed the Confederate States of America. The next day the Confederate Congress elected Jefferson Davis president.

U.S. president James Buchanan, who would hold office until Lincoln's inauguration in March 1861, was afraid of using force and alienating the border states, chiefly Virginia, and he took no action. In his March 4, 1861, inauguration address, Lincoln renewed his promise to respect slavery where it existed and to enforce the fugitive slave laws, but he also said that he would not countenance secession.

The Confederates had now taken control of all Federal forts and navy yards in the seceded states except Fort Pickens off Pensacola, Florida, and Fort Sumter in Charleston harbor, South Carolina. Lincoln reluctantly concluded, against the advice of a majority of his cabinet, that he had to send relief expeditions to these two installations even though this would probably bring the secession of Virginia.

On November 15, 1860, Major Robert Anderson, a southerner who owned slaves and was thus thought able to communicate with the secessionists, had been appointed to command the small U.S. Army garrison at Fort Moultrie in Charleston. On December 11, Anderson received word that Secretary of War John B. Floyd, a Virginian and secessionist sympathizer, had denied his request for reinforcements. The next day in Washington, President Buchanan, seeking to avoid a confrontation with South Carolina authorities, also declined to send reinforcements, which decision led Secretary of State Lewis Cass to resign.

With Fort Moultrie vulnerable to land attack, on the night of December 26 Anderson relocated his men to the more easily defensible Fort Sumter in Charleston Harbor. This Third System masonry fort, as yet incomplete, was located on an artificial island of 70,000 tons of granite deposited on a sand bar at the mouth of Charleston harbor and controlled access to it. Anderson's action enraged South Carolina authorities.

South Carolina forces then occupied both Fort Moultrie and Castle Pinckney ringing Charleston harbor, in effect the first act of military aggression by South Carolina against the United States. South Carolina authorities also seized the U.S. Revenue Service Cutter *William Aiken* and all remaining Federal properties in Charleston, save Fort Sumter.

In a stiffening of resolve, President Buchanan finally agreed that something must be done to resupply and reinforce Anderson's garrison. The War Department chartered the sidewheeler steamer *Star of the West*, which sailed from New York City on January 5, 1861, with supplies and 200 reinforcements. Efforts to keep this operation secret failed when the Northern press published news of the ship's sailing and its intended mission. This information was duly telegraphed to Charleston.

Early on January 9, when the *Star of the West* arrived off Charleston harbor and attempted to reach Fort Sumter, cadets of the Military College of South Carolina (The Citadel), who were manning batteries at Fort Moultrie and Morris Island, opened fire on the ship, which than ran up a large, 20×40-foot American flag. This failed to deter the gunners, who proceeded to hull the ship twice. These were in effect the first hostile shots of the long and bloody American Civil War (1861–1865), although Buchanan refused to consider it an act of war as no blood had been shed.

His ship moderately damaged, the captain of the *Star of the West* returned to New York. On January 11, Anderson rejected demands by South Carolina governor Francis W. Pickens that he surrender Fort Sumter to state authorities. He again refused similar demands on January 15 and 18.

The situation was at stalemate, but on March 3, Confederate president Davis appointed Brigadier General Pierre G. T. Beauregard to command Confederate forces at Charleston and ordered him to begin planning for the reduction of Fort Sumter by force.

On March 4, Lincoln succeeded Buchanan as president of the United States. Lincoln also held off regarding a decision on Sumter, hoping for a cooling of Southern passions and the avoidance of war but, after nearly a month in office and with Sumter running out of supplies, Lincoln was forced to do something.

Lincoln discussed with his cabinet a relief expedition for Sumter. Secretary of State William Seward argued against it in the belief that it would probably lead to war and cause Virginia to secede; he proposed evacuating Sumter and holding on to Pickens. General-in-Chief Lieutenant General Winfield Scott favored evacuation of both forts in the belief that this would ensure the loyalty of the eight slave-holding states still in the Union. When Lincoln polled his cabinet on the matter, only Postmaster General Montgomery Blair and Interior Secretary Caleb B. Smith favored an expedition to Sumter. The other five members were opposed.

Lincoln was torn, but he believed he had to take action. Northern opinion was hardening against the South, and the press was demanding that something be done to reinforce Sumter. Former U.S. Navy officer Gustavus V. Fox, brother-in-law of Blair and introduced by him to the president, assured Lincoln that the navy could run boats filled with supplies and men to Sumter under the cover of darkness and protected by that fort's guns and those of nearby ships. Fox seems to have reinforced Lincoln's own view that both Anderson and Scott were unduly pessimistic.

Ignoring the simpler course of evacuating Sumter and holding on to Pickens, on March 30 Lincoln ordered Secretary of the Navy Gideon Welles to prepare a relief expedition for Sumter based on Fox's plan. The expedition was to be ready by April 6, with Lincoln to make the final decision at that point. The key warship in the planned relief of Sumter was the powerful side-wheeler steam frigate *Powhatan* of 16 guns.

A Currier & Ives lithograph depicting the bombardment of Fort Sumter by South Carolina forces on April 12–13, 1861. The siege and subsequent surrender of this important fortress in Charleston Harbor marked the beginning of the American Civil War and saw a wave of patriotic fervor sweep the North. (Library of Congress)

On April 6 also, Lincoln directed State Department clerk Robert S. Chew to proceed to Charleston and there inform South Carolina governor Francis W. Pickens that Lincoln had ordered the resupply of Anderson's garrison. Chew was instructed to inform Pickens that this would be "of provisions only" and that if no armed attempt was made to thwart this effort no additional men, arms, or ammunition would be introduced without prior notification or a Confederate attack. On April 7, Beauregard ordered all intercourse ended between Federal troops holding Fort Sumter and Charleston.

The Sumter expedition with Fox in charge that sailed on April 10 consisted of two warships—the screw sloop *Pawnee* (8 guns) and side-wheeler Revenue Service *Harriet Lane* (4 guns)—escorting the unarmed troop and supply ship unarmed *Baltic* carrying 200 reinforcements and supplies. On Seward's suggestion, Lincoln secretly diverted the *Powhatan* to relieve Fort Pickens without informing Secretary of the Navy Gideon Welles. Its absence probably did not affect the outcome at Sumter, however.

Being informed of developments by Chew, Governor Pickens promptly informed Confederate president Jefferson Davis in Montgomery, Alabama, and Davis ordered Brigadier General Pierre G. T. Beauregard at Charleston to demand the surrender of Fort Sumter. If refused, Beauregard was to reduce it. Beauregard made this demand on April 11. Following an unsatisfactory reply from the U.S. commander, Major Robert Anderson, Beauregard ordered fire opened before the Union relief expedition could arrive.

Firing against Sumter commenced on April 12, 1861, at 4:30 a.m. Beauregard and some 500 men shelled the fort with 30 heavy guns and 18 mortars. Anderson had only 85 men and 43 civilian engineers. Fort Sumter had 43 guns but, to conserve ammunition, Anderson ordered return fire restricted to 6 guns only. About 7:00 a.m., Captain Abner Doubleday, Anderson's second in command fired the first shot in defense of the fort. The firing continued all day, the Federals firing slowly to conserve ammunition. That night Fort Sumter ceased fire, but the Confederates still lobbed an occasional shell at the fort. Although the Union relief expedition had arrived off Charleston harbor, rough weather precluded any attempt to launch boats to resupply Sumter and Fox was reluctant to expose his ships to enemy fire.

Heavy Confederate shelling recommenced on April 13, while Union return fire was limited to one gun every 10 minutes. With the Confederate batteries holding the Federal ships at bay and Sumter nearly out of food and fires having broken out in the fort, after 34 hours of bombardment Anderson arranged a truce on the afternoon of April 13 and formally surrendered on April 14.

As part of the terms of capitulation, Sumter's garrison was permitted to run the American flag back up the flagpole and fire a 100-gun salute to it. Firing commence at 2:00 p.m., but on the 50th shot, powder sparks ignited stacked shells, which exploded, killing one Union soldier outright (Private Daniel Hough) and wounding two others, one (Private Edward Galloway) mortally. They were the only casualties in the engagement that began the bloodiest war in U.S. history. Anderson and his garrison were subsequently evacuated by the Union ships off Charleston and returned to the north.

The shelling of Sumter galvanized opinion on both sides. It ended any sympathy in the North for the Confederate cause. With the South having fired on the U.S. flag, a patriotic fervor swept the North. Whether Lincoln had intended to maneuver the South into this is unclear, but on April 15, Lincoln declared the existence of an "insurrection" and called for 75,000 volunteers to serve three months. America was now at war with itself.

Spencer C. Tucker

Further Reading

Detzer, David R. *Allegiance: Fort Sumter, Charleston and the Beginning of the Civil War.* New York: Harcourt, 2001.

Niven, John. *Gideon Welles, Lincoln's Secretary of the Navy.* New York: Oxford University Press, 1973.

Porter, David Dixon. *Incidents and Anecdotes of the Civil War.* New York: D. Appleton and Co., 1985.

Tucker, Spencer C. *Blue and Gray Navies: The Civil War Afloat.* Annapolis, MD: Naval Institute Press, 2006.

Sieges of Vicksburg (May 18–July 4, 1863) and Port Hudson, Louisiana (May 21–July 9, 1863)

The siege of the city of Vicksburg on the Mississippi River was one of the most important battles of the American Civil War (1861–1865). Control of the Mississippi was vital for the Union. By controlling the river, the Union could cut off the Trans-Mississippi West comprising Texas, Arkansas, Missouri, Indian Territory,

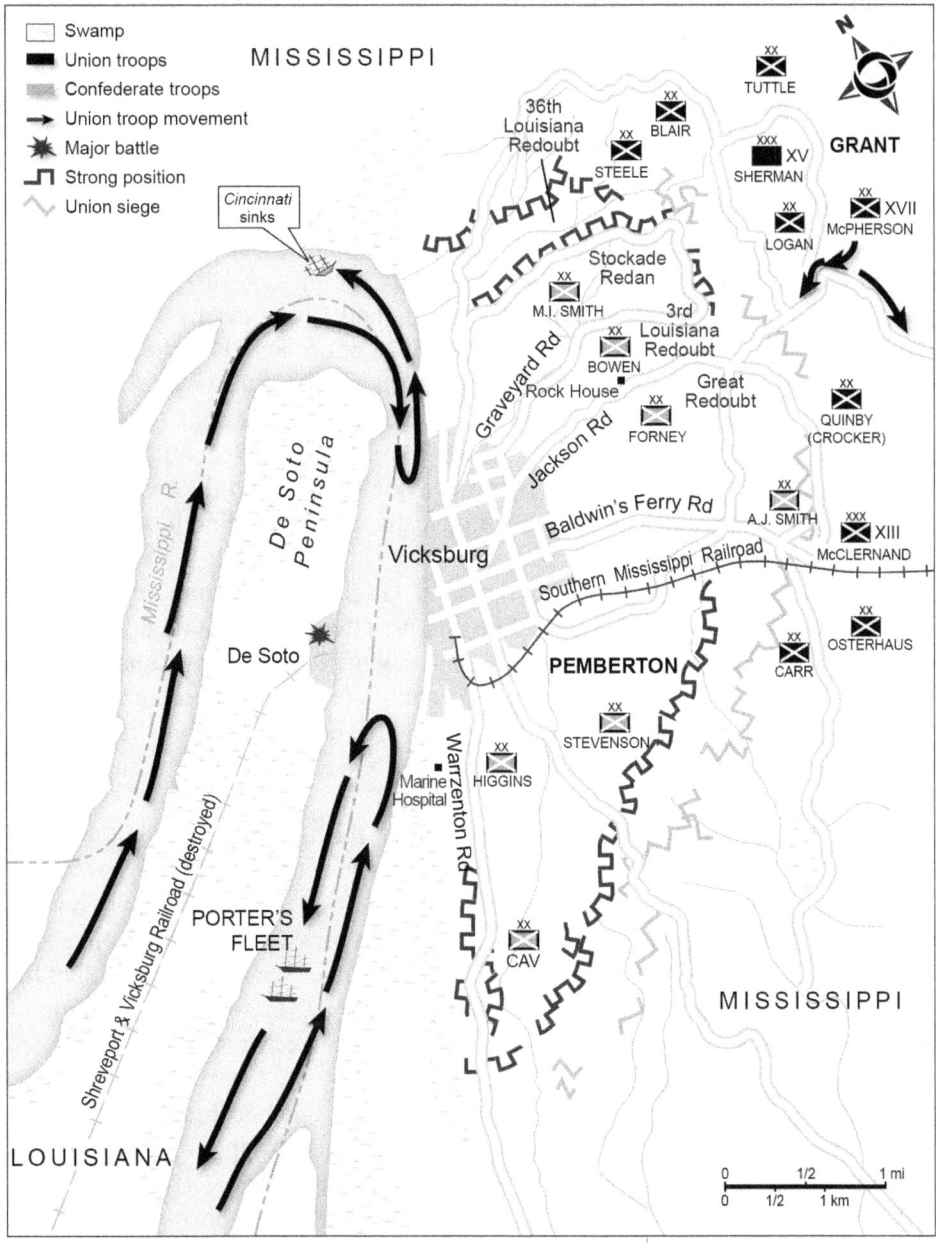

The disposition of forces during the siege of Vicksburg (May 18–July 4, 1863) during the American Civil War. Securing Vicksburg was necessary in order for the Union to control the Mississippi River and cut the Confederacy in two. (ABC-CLIO)

and parts of Arizona and Louisiana from the rest of the Confederacy. Victory at Vicksburg and Port Hudson to the south would not only give the Union control of the river but also help bind the Midwest to the Union cause by securing the movement of its goods southward on the Mississippi to the Gulf of Mexico. The Union assault against Confederate positions on the mighty river began in early 1862. While Flag Officer Andrew Hull Foote's Western Flotilla moved down the Mississippi and tested its northern defenses, Flag Officer David G. Farragut's West Coast Gulf Blockading Squadron would attempt to take New Orleans and move up river from the south.

The northern Union flotilla worked in combination with U.S. Army forces ashore to capture a series of Confederate strongholds: Island No. 10 on April 8, Fort Pillow on June 4, and Memphis on June 6. On April 24, Farragut's ships ran past the Confederate forts at the river's mouth, and Union troops occupied New Orleans on May 1. The Union now controlled the entire length of the Mississippi except the fortified town of Vicksburg, located in a bend of the river.

Confederate lieutenant general John C. Pemberton commanded the city's defenses. Attempts at naval assault failed in May and June 1862, and in late summer and autumn the Confederates reinforced Vicksburg from the east and added a bastion downstream at Port Hudson, Louisiana, giving the South control of the intervening length of river.

In October 1862, Major General Ulysses S. Grant took command of the Army of the Tennessee. Operating from Memphis, he attempted but failed to take the city in the First Vicksburg Overland Campaign, which lasted through late December 1862. Vicksburg was strongly fortified and protected by the natural defenses of its high bluffs facing the river and swamps to the north. The city was most vulnerable from the south and east, but these were remote from Grant's supply base at Memphis to the north.

In January 1863, Grant encamped his Army of the Tennessee on the Louisiana side of the river, above Vicksburg, and began a series of unsuccessful efforts to get around the city, assisted by Rear Admiral David Dixon Porter's flotilla via various creeks and bayous. Then on March 29, 1863, Grant crossed the Mississippi above Vicksburg and marched down the Louisiana side of the river to a point south of the city where Porter's ships, which ran past the Vicksburg batteries on the night of April 16–17, ferried him across the river on April 30. In effect Grant now planned to attack Vicksburg from the rear.

Defying instructions from Washington, Grant abandoned his base at Grand Gulf and marched northeast with 20,000 men, carrying supplies in wagons and partially living off the land. Grant believed that any delay would give the Confederates time to reinforce and fortify. He therefore employed a daring cavalry raid to keep Pemberton confused as to his movements. Grant quickly took Jackson, Mississippi, held by only 6,000 Confederates. The Union troops destroyed everything of military value. Abandoned by Grant, the town was soon reinforced by the Confederates but was no longer available as a logistical center for Vicksburg to the west.

Confederate Theater commander General Joseph E. Johnston ordered Pemberton to advance from Vicksburg and cut Grant's tenuous supply line. Grant learned of this plan through a spy and countered Pemberton's move. The two armies collided at Champion's Hill on May 16. Grant commanded 32,000 men, and Pemberton had 25,000 men. Although the battle was hard fought, Grant was victorious. Union casualties amounted to some 2,500 men, while the Confederates sustained 4,000 losses. Pemberton was forced back into the Vicksburg perimeter. Johnston had warned Pemberton not to get shut up in Vicksburg and to abandon the city if necessary, but Pemberton thought he knew better.

Outnumbered at the outset of the campaign, Grant had marched 200 miles in less than three weeks, had won five battles, and ended by shutting up the opposing army in a fortress. Grant made two futile and poorly planned assaults against Vicksburg on May 19 and 22 that failed in their intent. He then settled in for a prolonged siege.

Union siege guns and guns on the Union ships in the river kept the city and the Confederate lines under constant bombardment. At night Union soldiers advanced their trenches ever closer to the Confederate lines. The strain on the inhabitants of Vicksburg was immense. Food was in short supply, and starvation soon set in; people subsisted on whatever they could find. To escape the bombardment, they dug caves in the hard clay hillsides.

Two days' march to the east at Jackson, Johnston hovered with some 31,000 men raised specifically to lift the siege. Grant, reinforced, countered with a heavily manned line of eastward-facing defenses. Johnston, despite the urging of Confederate authorities, never attempted to test these or to relieve the garrison.

After six weeks of the Union siege, at 10:00 a.m. on July 4 Pemberton surrendered Vicksburg and 29,495 men. Union casualties of the Vicksburg campaign from October 1862 to July 1863 amounted to around 9,000 men. Confederate casualties were 10,000, not counting prisoners.

Simultaneous with the siege of Vicksburg, Union forces laid siege of Port Hudson, Louisiana, during May 21–July 9, 1863. Some 25 miles above Baton Rouge, Louisiana, Port Hudson was situated on high bluffs overlooking a sharp, 150-degree bend of the river and surrounded by bayous. In May, Major General Franklin Gardner commanded some 7,500 defenders manning defensive works that included some 15 heavy guns controlling the river approaches and an equal number on the land side.

Following an abortive effort in March 1863 that saw the destruction of the U.S. Navy sidewheeler frigate *Mississippi* during Rear Admiral David G. Farragut's passage of Port Hudson unsupported by Union troops under Major General Nathaniel P. Banks, Union forces tried again in May. As a preliminary to a ground assault by Banks's 30,000-man Army of the Gulf, U.S. Navy ships in the river shelled Port Hudson during May 8–10. Banks then closed off Port Hudson from the land side on May 21.

Banks planned a ground attack supported by the large guns aboard the Union ships in the river, but the inept Union general mounted a series of uncoordinated attacks that also failed to make full use of his available manpower. The Union assault opened at dawn on May 27 with an attack on the Confederate left, above Port Hudson. It included two regiments of African American troops from

Louisiana in the first employment of such troops by the Union side in the war. The attack failed. About 2:15, the Union left attacked. It, and a still later advance by the Union center, were rebuffed. The attackers sustained nearly 2,000 casualties to only 250–275 for the defenders.

Claiming insufficient resources, Banks then settled for a siege, during the course of which he received some 10,000 reinforcements. Banks was determined to try again. On the morning of June 13, Union troops and ships in the river opened a furious bombardment of the Confederate works, firing shells at the rate of about one per second. After an hour, the firing ceased, and Banks sent a note to Gardner demanding his surrender. Although his men were low on ammunition and short of supplies, Gardner refused. Banks ordered the shelling resumed and planned an assault for the next day in the form of a probe of the Confederate right with the main attack on the center.

Early the next morning, a Union division assaulted the large fort in the Confederate center known as the Priest Cap. Although some of the Union troops breached the Confederate lines, they lacked sufficient strength to exploit the situation. Repeated follow-on attacks also failed, with the Union suffering as many as 1,805 casualties. With his subordinate commanders objecting to a continuation, Banks agreed to a halt.

Meanwhile, the Union side employed zigzag trenches to snake closer to the Confederate positions. They also tried mining the Confederate lines, but the defenders sank a countermine and used explosives to collapse the Union shaft. The distances were sufficiently short for both sides to employ hand grenades.

Banks planned a third attack for July 7, but bad weather caused it to be postponed. News was then received of the fall of Vicksburg to the Union on July 4. This event rendered Port Hudson untenable, and Gardner opened negotiations on July 8 and formally surrendered the next day. The siege had lasted 48 days. Although some Confederates escaped through Union lines on the night of July 8–9, about 6,400 surrendered. The Confederates had suffered 146 killed and 447 wounded. Operations at Port Hudson claimed Union losses of more than 708 dead, 3,336 wounded, and 319 missing. Another 4,000 to 5,000 were incapacitated by heatstroke or sickness. Throughout the siege, Union ships and mortar boats had provided effective gunfire support.

Coming at the same time as the great Union victory at Gettysburg, the captures of Vicksburg and Port Hudson lifted Northern morale and depressed that of the South. The entire Mississippi was now under Union control and the Confederacy was split north to south. A week later, a steamer from St. Louis arrived at New Orleans with a cargo of Midwestern products. As President Abraham Lincoln summed up, "The Father of Waters again goes unvexed to the sea."

Spencer C. Tucker

Further Reading
Arnold, James R. *Grant Wins the War: Decision at Vicksburg.* New York: Wiley, 1997.
Ballard, Michael B. *Pemberton: A Biography.* Jackson: University Press of Mississippi, 1991.
Bearss, Edwin C. *The Vicksburg Campaign.* 3 vols. Dayton, OH: Morningside, 1995.

Hewitt, Lawrence L. *Port Hudson: Confederate Bastion on the Mississippi.* Baton Rouge: Louisiana State University Press, 1994.

Milligan, John D. *Gunboats down the Mississippi.* New York: Arno Press, 1980.

Tucker, Spencer C. *Blue and Gray Navies: The Civil War Afloat.* Annapolis, MD: Naval Institute Press, 2006.

Winschel, Terrence J., ed. *Triumph and Defeat: The Vicksburg Campaign.* Campbell, CA: Savas, 1998.

Winschel, Terrence J. *Vicksburg: Fall of the Confederate Gibraltar.* Abilene, TX: McWhiney Foundation Press, 1999.

Siege of Petersburg (June 15, 1864–April 2, 1865)

The nearly 10-month-long Petersburg campaign (June 15, 1864–April 2, 1865) during the 1861–1865 American Civil War saw the longest siege in American military history. It was not a siege in the strict definition of the term in which supply lines were completely cut; nor was the campaign strictly limited to Petersburg, for the Union goal was to capture the Confederate capital of Richmond and fighting occurred over a wide area. The campaign might best be called the longest sustained operation of the war. It also saw the largest concentration of African American troops during the conflict.

In March 1864, U.S. president Abraham Lincoln appointed Major General Ulysses S. Grant as general-in-chief of the Union armies with the revived rank of lieutenant general. While Major General George Gordon Meade continued in charge of the Army of the Potomac, Grant went with him in the field. Grant planned to use his superior numbers to methodically hammer away at and defeat Confederate general Robert E. Lee's Army of Northern Virginia.

Grant planned a multifaceted and simultaneous offensive. In the Western Theater, Major General William T. Sherman would move across Georgia to Savannah, while Major General Nathaniel P. Banks would try to take Mobile. In what became known as the Overland Campaign, Meade's Army of the Potomac, now more than 100,000 men, would drive south from Culpepper, Virginia, to capture Richmond, assisted by Major General Benjamin Butler's 36,000-man Army of the James moving up the south bank of the James to cut Lee off from the Lower South. Other Union forces would move against Virginia's Shenandoah Valley from the west and north to seize the railheads of Staunton and Lynchburg. To oppose Meade and Grant, Lee had 60,000 men, supported by General P. G. T. Beauregard and 30,000 men in the Richmond-Petersburg area.

The Overland Campaign began on May 4 and led to a series of sanguinary battles, commencing with the Battle of the Wilderness (May 5–7) and extending through Cold Harbor (June 1–3), during which Grant repeatedly tried, and failed, to turn Lee's flank. Extremely costly, through June 12 the fighting claimed nearly 60,000 Union casualties—a figure equal to Lee's total strength—against Confederate losses of only 25,000–30,000, but Lee's army never quite recovered from the punishment it received.

In the Bermuda Hundred Campaign of May 5–11, meanwhile, the inept Butler fumbled away a chance to take Richmond, then held by relatively few Confederate

> **The "Dictator"**
>
> The Union 13-inch iron mortar was a formidable weapon. Weighing 17,250 pounds, it rested in a 4,500-pound bed. With a 20-pound charge of powder and at an elevation of 41°, the mortar could hurl a 204-pound shell loaded with 7 pounds of powder nearly 3 miles. At maximum range, the shell took 30 seconds in flight.
>
> Such mortars were employed by the Union navy in mortar boats, especially against Confederate fortifications on the Mississippi River to include Vicksburg. But the most famous 13-inch mortar of the war was undoubtedly the Union "Dictator." Cast by Fort Pitt Foundry in Pittsburgh, Pennsylvania, in 1862 and mounted on a railroad flatcar that had been strengthened to withstand the shock of firing, it took part in the siege of Petersburg in the summer and fall of 1864.
>
> The mortar was run up the tracks from City Point on the City Point and Petersburg Railroad with a side track being constructed especially for the mortar to take it to behind the Union line. The track was curved to allow the gunners to change the direction of fire. Manned by Company G of the 1st Connecticut Heavy Artillery, it was credited with causing Confederate gunners to end attempts at enfilade fire along the right side of the Union line.
>
> **Spencer C. Tucker**

troops under Beauregard. But Beauregard managed to bottle up Butler in the Bermuda Hundred peninsula. On June 9, Butler, aware that Lee had shifted resources north to meet Grant at Cold Harbor, tried again. In what is known as the First Battle of Petersburg, a Union force of 4,500 men met defeat at the hands of 2,500 Confederates east of the city.

Grant was determined to keep the offensive going, and he decided to shift his forces south of the James to concentrate on Petersburg. Located 20 miles south of Richmond, this city of 18,000 people was the key rail supply point for the Confederate capital. If Grant could take Petersburg, it would force the evacuation of Richmond.

On the night of June 12–13, the Army of the Potomac secretly decamped from Cold Harbor and, screened by cavalry, crossed the James on a pontoon bridge more than 2,100 feet in length. In the Second Battle of Petersburg, on June 15 Grant attacked Petersburg with two corps of some 15,000 men under Major Generals William T. Smith and Winfield S. Hancock in what is known as the Second Battle of Petersburg (June 15–18). Beauregard then held the city with only about 5,400 Confederates. Smith failed to press the assault, while Hancock, without definite orders, failed to lend Smith adequate support. During the next three days, Beauregard gambled boldly, stripping his forces containing Butler at Bermuda Hundred to reinforce against Grant and turn back the successive Union attacks. By June 16, Beauregard, now with some 14,000 men, faced 50,000 Federals. Lee, finally aware of Grant's relocation, answered Beauregard's pleas for reinforcements. By June 18, some 67,000 Union troops faced 20,000 Confederates.

With stalemate, both sides dug in. Field fortifications ultimately became elaborate siege lines presaging those of World War I that extended some 30 miles from the eastern outskirts of Richmond and Petersburg to the south and then southwest of Petersburg itself.

Soldiers on both sides endured periodic enemy shelling that included on the Union side fire from mammoth 13-inch siege mortars. Both sides labored to improve their defensive works, all the while contending with alternating heat and cold, rain, thick mud, and choking dust. Letters from home describing the desperate conditions now facing many Southern families, coupled with the difficult conditions in the trenches, led to growing Confederate desertions. Suffering was particularly intense in the winter of 1864–1865 with scores of Confederates crossing the lines nightly to surrender.

The residents of Petersburg suffered along with the troops. The city was ill prepared for a long siege, and conditions worsened, as it was within range of Union guns. During the siege, more than 500 residential and commercial buildings were destroyed or damaged and food was often in short supply.

The key for the Confederates was continued control of the roads and three railroads from the south and the west that supplied Richmond and Petersburg. Well aware of this, Grant attempted to extend his lines westward and secure control of the rail lines.

In the Battle of Jerusalem Plank Road during June 21–23, Union forces pushed west. The inconclusive fighting saw the Confederates retain control of the Weldon Railroad. At the same time, a Union cavalry raid during June 22–30 destroyed Confederate track, bridges, and rail stations to the south and southwest but had no lasting effect. Within several weeks, the lines were back in operation, with the raid having cost 1,445 Union casualties, about a quarter of the force involved.

In the First Battle of Deep Bottom (July 27–29), Grant sought to draw Lee's men elsewhere in preparation for what became known as the Battle of the Crater. He ordered Hancock to fix the Confederates at Chaffin's Bluff, while Major General Philip H. Sheridan led two cavalry divisions across the James southeast of Richmond in an effort to take the capital or at the least ride around the city from the east and north and cut the Virginia Central Railroad from the Shenandoah Valley.

On July 30, Union forces detonated a huge mine placed in a tunnel dug under one of the major Confederate forts by Pennsylvania miners in the Union Army. Inept planning for the attack following the blast, a late change in plans, and poor Union leadership coupled with effective Confederate reaction turned what became known as the Battle of the Crater into a Union fiasco with nearly 3,800 Union casualties compared to only 1,500 for the Confederates.

In the Second Battle of Deep Bottom (August 13–20), Grant attempted another thrust against Richmond, led by Hancock. Grant then sent Major General Gouverneur K. Warren's V Corps to attack the Weldon Railroad. The Federals ended up on the defensive in the Battle at Globe Tavern (August 18–21), although they were able to tear up a considerable quantity of track. Grant then sent Hancock's corps against the Weldon Railroad and, although the Confederates won a clear victory in the ensuing Second Battle of Reams Station (August 29), they lost an important portion of the Weldon line, forcing them to send supplies into Petersburg partly by

The Globe Tavern, near Petersburg, Virginia, in mid-August 1864. During the siege of Petersburg, Union forces under Major General Gouverneur K. Warren gathered here for their offensive against the Confederate supply line of the Weldon Railroad. (Library of Congress)

wagon. The South Side Railway from Petersburg west to Lynchburg was now the only rail line supplying Lee's army.

Most of the subsequent fighting occurred to the west as Grant endeavored to secure the South Side Railroad and also Boydton Plank Road. On September 16, in the Hampton-Rosser Cattle Raid (Beefsteak Raid), the Confederates sent 4,000 men to near City Point, securing nearly 2,500 beef cattle.

In the Battle of Chaffin's Farm (New Market Heights) of September 29–30, Butler's Army of the James crossed the James to attack the Richmond defenses north of the river. The Federals enjoyed initial success, but the Confederates contained the attack and erected a new line of works.

Grant knew that to meet Butler's attack, Lee would necessarily have weakened his line elsewhere, and he sought to extend his left flank and cut the Confederate lines of communication southwest of Petersburg. The ensuing Battle of Peebles' Farm (September 30–October 2) extended the Union left flank.

Lee, worried about the heightened Federal threat to Richmond from the east, attacked the Federal right flank on Darbytown Road on October 7. The Confederates routed the Union cavalry here but were halted at the main Union line on New Market Road. On October 13, Union forces assaulted the Confederates north of Darbytown Road but were repulsed. Butler attacked the Confederates again during October 27–28 only to be repulsed in the Battle of Fair Oaks and Darbytown Road.

Taking advantage of his superior numbers and at the same time as Butler's attack, Grant sent more than 30,000 men under Hancock west against the Boydton

Plank Road. In the major Battle of Boydton Plank Road (October 27–28), the Confederates drove back the attackers and continued to control this key supply route throughout the winter.

In early February 1865, Union troops again advanced against the Boydton Plank Road. In the Battle of Hatcher's Run (February 5–7), Lee sustained heavy casualties but pushed the Federals back from this important supply line. The Federals, however, had extended their left flank.

The last major battle of the siege of Petersburg was the Confederate attack against Union Fort Stedman on March 25, 1865. Well aware of growing Federal strength (Grant now had some 125,000 men and Lee only 50,000), Lee also knew that Sheridan would soon be joining Grant from the Shenandoah Valley with an additional 50,000 men. To disrupt an anticipated major Federal attack (which Grant had planned for March 29), Lee planned a major strike against Stedman.

Launched with half of Lee's infantry, the attack was initially successful with the Confederates occupying the fort. The Federals soon counterattacked, however, restoring the line. This was Lee's last attempt to breach the Union defenses and regain the initiative.

On April 1, Sheridan with three Union cavalry divisions crushed the Confederates in the Battle of Five Forks, a major road intersection 10 miles west-southwest of Petersburg and 5 miles west of where Lee's lines ended. The next day, Grant mounted a massive assault on the thinly held Confederate lines, which now collapsed. Only a valiant stand at Fort Gregg saved the retreating Confederates from total defeat, but the Federals were in Petersburg by nightfall. The fighting at Petersburg had claimed some 70,000 casualties: 42,000 Union and 28,000 Confederates.

Lee now evacuated Richmond and headed west, hoping to link up with General Joseph E. Johnston in North Carolina. Grant pursued, and cut off by Union cavalry, Lee surrendered his remaining troops to Grant at Appomattox Courthouse on April 9, 1865.

Spencer C. Tucker

Further Reading
Greene, A. Wilson. *The Final Battles of the Petersburg Campaign: Breaking the Backbone of the Rebellion.* Knoxville: University of Tennessee Press, 2008.
Horn, John. *The Petersburg Campaign: June 1864–April 1865.* Conshohocken, PA: Combined Books, 1993.
Sommers, Richard J. *Richmond Redeemed: The Siege at Petersburg.* Garden City, NY: Doubleday, 1981.
Trudeau, Noah Andre. *The Last Citadel: Petersburg, Virginia, June 1864–April 1865.* Baton Rouge: Louisiana State University Press, 1991.

Siege of Metz (August 19–October 27, 1870)

The German 54-day siege of the French fortress of Metz (August 19–October 27, 1870) was a decisive event in the Franco-Prussian War (1870–1871), itself the most important geopolitical event of the second half of the nineteenth century.

> **Marshal François Achille Bazaine**
>
> Tried by a military court in 1873 on a charge of treason, Marshal Bazaine claimed there was no legitimate authority to obey. The judge answered that there was always France. Convicted, he was sentenced to death, although this was commuted to 20 years' seclusion on Îsle Sainte-Marguerite off Cannes in the Mediterranean. There during the night of August 10, 1874, Bazaine escaped from the island using ropes to climb down 300-foot cliffs to a sailboat from Cannes supplied by his wife. They then sailed to Italy and finally settled in Spain.
>
> Spencer C. Tucker

In 1866 Prussian minister-president Otto von Bismarck had secured Russian and French neutrality and taken Prussia into war with Austria. Prussia's rapid victory in that war settled the long-standing issue of which of these two states would dominate the Germanies. Yet Bismarck had made an enemy of France for he failed to deliver his promise to French emperor Napoleon III of remaining neutral in return for territorial compensation along the Rhine. Bismarck knew that he could not realize his dream of fully unifying Germany under Prussian leadership without first defeating France. Convinced that Prussia would win such a war, Bismarck isolated France diplomatically and then successfully goaded the French government, which was buoyed by popular widespread support, into declaring war on Prussia on July 19, 1870. Bismarck had previously concluded defensive treaties with the south German states of Baden, Bavaria, and Wittenberg, so the conflict was in reality the Franco-German War.

By the end of July, Prussian Army chief of staff General Helmuth von Moltke had positioned three armies of some 386,000 men in the Rhineland along the French frontier: General Karl F. Von Steinmetz's First Army of 66,000 men; Prince Friedrich Karl's Second Army of 175,000 men; and Crown Prince Friedrich Wilhelm's Third Army of 145,000 men. Moltke held another 95,000 troops in reserve until it was certain that Austria would not intervene. Prussian king Wilhelm I had nominal command, but Moltke exercised actual command authority. The Prussians were fully prepared for the war and their military intelligence and maps of France were both excellent.

The situation in France was quite different. The French Army's mobilization was not even complete by the time the war began, and there was rampant disorder. The French Army deployed some 224,000 men in eight army corps. While the army had élan, its recent military experience was in North Africa rather than in Europe. Although in all respects save heavy artillery, their weaponry was equal to or superior to that of the Prussians, the French military was sadly deficient in logistical arrangements and military intelligence. There was no general staff in the Prussian sense of the term, and the senior French military leadership proved inept and unimaginative.

At the end of July, Napoleon III ordered a general advance into Germany. The emperor was not well but nonetheless chose to personally accompany the army in the field. French forces were grouped into two armies: the Army of Lorraine (five corps) under Marshal François Achille Bazaine and the Army of Alsace (three corps) under Marshal Patrice MacMahon, Duc de Magenta.

Moltke attacked to the south, driving French forces there back toward Strasbourg and forcing MacMahon to evacuate Alsace. A second Prussian thrust to the north also enjoyed success, and Napoleon III ordered Metz abandoned. The emperor's defeatism now rapidly spread through the army. On August 12, Napoleon yielded field command to Bazaine, who commanded a reorganized Army of the Rhine. Napoleon departed for Châlons to raise a new army.

On August 16, the Prussian Second Army collided with Bazaine's withdrawing Army of the Rhine on the Verdun-Metz Road. A piecemeal engagement ended in a large-scale battle. The French lost some 13,761 men to 15,780 for the Germans. Both sides claimed success, yet it was a clear strategic victory for the Prussians because Bazaine then gave up his withdrawal effort and retired back on the fortress of Metz, assuming a defensive position about six miles in length facing west between the Moselle and Orne Rivers. The bulk of the German armies, totaling some 200,000 men, moved into the area between Metz and Paris.

Moltke now assumed personal command of the Second and First armies facing Bazaine's Army of the Rhine and attacked, hoping to destroy the French. The Battle of Gravelotte-St. Privat occurred on August 18 between the villages of St. Privat la Montaigne and Gravelotte. It pitted more than 188,000 Prussians with 732 guns against 112,000 French with 520 guns. At St. Privat, the elite Prussian Guard of the Second Army attacked Marshal François Certain Canrobert's VI Corps. Bazaine ignored Canrobert's pleas for reinforcement. In the battle, the Germans lost 8,000 men, with Canrobert's corps of 23,000 men holding against some 100,000 attacking Prussians. Only the arrival of a Saxon Corps to the north threatening to cut off his force obliged Canrobert to withdraw back toward Metz.

On the French right, meanwhile, two Prussian corps battled their way east of Gravelotte only to become trapped in a ravine. Their attempt to disengage led to a panicked withdrawal. A French counterattack was checked only by effective Prussian artillery fire and Moltke's personal intervention with reinforcements.

Although the French withdrew, there was little sense of victory among the Germans as they had lost 20,163 men, against only 12,273 for the French. The tragedy of St. Privat-Gravelotte for the French is that, had Bazaine made a concerted effort, he would most likely have achieved a victory and broken free. As it was, on August 19 the French were back at Metz, where the Prussians promptly sealed them in. The separation of their two field armies proved a disaster for France.

From August 19, Metz was under siege. However, Metz simply did not have facilities for an army of 140,000 men and its 12,000 wounded. Yet in the course of the next two weeks, Bazaine made only two efforts to break out. The first on August 26 was a rather timid affair. The second, on August 31, was more ambitious; it involved some 90,000 men in eight infantry divisions, several cavalry brigades, and 162 guns against at most three German divisions. It was almost as if Bazaine wanted the breakouts to fail as he ordered withdrawals as soon as Prussian resistance stiffened. Many Frenchmen would ascribe this to treachery or intrigue, but Bazaine's adjutant colonel Napoleon Boyer attributed it simply to an innate pessimism. The French garrison then settled into inactivity, which was a great relief to Moltke, who was able to improve his lines around the fortress.

The Germans, who eventually numbered nearly 200,000 men, however, lacked accommodations and a large number of them soon fell sick. They brought up artillery and commenced shelling Metz, but the fortress was too strong for this to be decisive.

Napoleon III, meanwhile, refused to adopt the one plan that might have saved France—a delaying action back on the city of Paris while additional forces were being gathered. Fearful of the political effects of a retreat, the emperor accompanied the 120,000-man French Army of Châlons commanded by Marshal Patrice MacMahon in an attempt to relieve Bazaine at Metz. The French departed Châlons on August 21, heading northeast toward the Belgian border then planning to trike southward and link up with Metz.

Realizing the opportunity to trap MacMahon, Moltke took some troops from the force besieging Metz and turned the bulk of his forces against MacMahon with the plan of encircling him. On August 30, the French and Germans collided at Beaumont and MacMahon then withdrew toward the fortress city of Sedan, pursued by the Prussian Third Army and Crown Prince Albert of Saxony's Army of the Meuse.

In the ensuing Battle of Sedan (September 1–3), 250,000 Prussians and Bavarians with some 500 artillery pieces shelled some 85,000 French packed into an area of only two square miles. MacMahon was wounded early in the battle and thus escaped onus for the result. With French casualties steadily mounting in what was obviously a lost cause, Napoleon III insisted on surrender, the emperor being among the 83,000 French soldiers taken prisoner. The Prussians also secured substantial stocks of weapons and supplies, including 419 artillery pieces.

The Germans then advanced on Paris, where news of the defeat at Sedan had led to the overthrown of Napoleon and the proclamation of the Third French Republic. On September 19, troops of the Army of the Meuse reached the outskirts of the capital and four days later the city was completely surrounded.

The government in Paris had reason to hope as new forces were being organized south of Loire, and the Germans were now stretched thin. Bazaine and his Army of the Rhine, although shut up at Metz, were nonetheless tying down more than their number of Germans. In addition, the siege of Paris required 250,000 German troops, and other forces were necessary to protect the lines of communication back to Germany, now under harassment from irregular French forces (*francs-tireurs*).

French hopes were dashed, however, for on October 27 Bazaine surrendered his army of 140,000 men. Bazaine rejected a Prussian offer of the honors of war, and on October 28 ordered his regiments to leave their flags and eagles at the arsenal to be surrendered to the Germans. In another of his inexplicable decisions, he refused to order the destruction of his army's arms. The Prussians thus gained some 600 French artillery pieces in working order. On October 29, Prussian flags were raised over Metz, and the French soldiers passed into captivity. Most important, however, Bazaine's surrender released the Prussian First and Second armies for operations against the French forces along the Loire.

The surrender of Metz was inevitable, but Bazaine can rightly be blamed for the failure to follow through on plans in August to break out and for his failure to recognize the value to the national defense of an army in being. By careful planning, Bazaine might have held out at least until mid-November. Bazaine was not a traitor, but he was certain incompetent.

Mistakenly believing that Paris could no long hold out, in November and December the new French armies in the south were committed before they were really ready and suffered defeats. On January 28, 1871, the government in Paris agreed to an armistice.

Spencer C. Tucker

Further Reading
Howard, Michael. *The Franco-Prussian War: The German Invasion of France, 1870–1871.* New York: Routledge, 2001.
Moltke, Helmuth. *The Franco-German War of 1870–71.* Translated by Archibald Forbes. New York: Harper, 1892.
Quintin, Barry. *The Franco-Prussian War, 1870–1871.* Vol. 1, *Helmuth von Moltke and the Overthrow of the Second Empire.* Solihull, UK: Helion, 2010.
Quintin, Barry. *The Franco-Prussian War, 1870–1871.* Vol. 2, *After Sedan: Helmuth von Moltke the Defeat of the Government of National Defence.* Solihull, UK: Helion, 2010.
Wawro, Geoffrey. *The Franco-Prussian War: The German Conquest of France in 1870–1871.* New York: Cambridge University Press, 2005.
Wetzel, David. *Duel of Giants: Bismarck, Napoleon III, and the Origins of the Franco-Prussian War.* Madison: University of Wisconsin Press, 2003.

Siege of Paris (September 19, 1870–January 28, 1871)

The siege of Paris was the culminating act of the Franco-Prussian War (1870–1871). (See the siege of Metz for information on the causes of the war and the early fighting.) On September 2, 1870, the French Army of Châlons surrendered to the Prussians and Bavarians at Sedan. The Germans took prisoner 83,000 men and 419 guns. Among those captured was French emperor Napoleon III, who, following several months in Germany, went into unlamented exile in England.

The emperor, but not the empire, survived the disaster of Sedan. When news of the defeat reached Paris, there was an immediate explosion of popular outrage. On September 4, crowds converged on the Corps Legislatif, and a new republican government, the third in French history, was proclaimed. Full of the myth of the Battle of Valmy in 1792, many Frenchmen believed, even as the German armies advanced unopposed on Paris, that a great national effort might yet bring victory. Dynamic young Léon Gambetta, the chief figure in the new government, took the posts of minister of war and minister of the interior and set about organizing the national defense. On September 6, Foreign Minister Jules Favre announced that the government would not yield an inch of French soil.

On September 19, troops of the Prussian Third Army and the Army of the Meuse reached the outskirts of Paris. Several forts guarded the city, which was

French illustration of fighting during the siege of Paris by the Germans during September 19, 1870–January 28, 1871, in the Franco-Prussian War. (Photos.com)

also ringed by a bastioned enceinte, but little had been done to prepare for a prolonged siege. General Jules Trochu, military governor of Paris and now also president of the new Third Republic, manned the forts defending the city with 120,000 men (including veterans, reservists, and 20,000 marine infantry), 80,000 *gardes mobiles* (untrained recruits under 30), and 300,000 *gardes nationales* (untrained recruits between the ages of 30 and 50).

The Prussians set up their headquarters at the château of Versailles outside the city. Prussian Army chief of staff Count Helmuth von Moltke had no intention of trying to take Paris by storm. He ringed the city with two belts of German troops, cut off food supplies into Paris, and waited for hunger to do its work. By September 23, Paris was completely surrounded. Eventually the only way out was by balloon.

On October 7, in order to organize other forces for the relief of Paris, Gambetta made the hazardous trip out. The winds blew him and a friend almost to Belgium before they descended and were able to make their way on foot to southeastern France. Trochu made three attempts to break the siege in November, December, and January. All were unsuccessful, although the strongest attempt on November 29–30 by 140,000 men and 400 guns destroyed a Bavarian corps and almost broke free before it was turned back.

Gambetta had reason to hope, for French marshal François Achille Bazaine and his 140,000-man Army of the Rhine, although shut up by the Germans at Metz, were nonetheless tying down more than that number of the enemy. The siege of Paris required another 250,000 German troops, and additional forces were necessary to maintain lines of communication back to Germany, which were now under harassment from irregular French forces (*francs-tireurs*).

Gambetta's hopes were dashed, however, when Bazaine surrendered the Army of the Rhine at Metz on October 27. Bazaine had refused to order the destruction of his arms. The Prussians thus gained 600 French guns in working order. More important, this released the Prussian First Army and Second Army for operations elsewhere.

Whatever chance Gambetta had of liberating Paris now depended on securing time to train new provincial French armies from the south. Mistakenly believing that Paris could not hold out long, Gambetta in November and December committed these forces to battle before they were fully ready. Heavy fighting occurred at Orléans during December 2–4. Gambetta's Army of the Loire was soon cut in two, and he was forced to withdraw to the southwest to Bordeaux.

Paris was now alone in its hunger, cold, and disease. As is usually the case in such circumstances, the wealthy fared far better than the poor. A black market was soon flourishing, and all manner of animals, including those from the zoo as well as common dogs, cats, and even rats, were sold for gold. Plague reached alarming proportions. On January 5, at Bismarck's insistence, the Prussians began shelling the city in the assumption that this would demoralize the civilian population and force a capitulation. It did not. Several hundred Parisians died, however, before the Prussians, who came under considerable international pressure, broke it off. The siege ended only after shortages of food, medicine, and fuel had worked their effect.

On January 26, 1871, the government in the city opened negotiations. Two days later, over Gambetta's objections and with an estimated eight days of food remaining for the city, French foreign minister Favre agreed to an armistice. All Parisian forts were given up, and the city was required to pay a tribute of 200 million francs. There would be a three-week armistice all over France except at Belfort, which—in a glorious chapter of French arms—still held out. The armistice was to allow the country to decide whether the war would continue.

On February 8, with the Germans occupying much of France, Frenchmen went to the polls to decide the issue of war or peace. Except for Republican Paris and the northeast, the country voted overwhelmingly for monarchist candidates and for peace. French politician Adolphe Thiers, one of the few members of the Corps Legislatif who had refused to vote for the war, now was charged with negotiating its end. He tried to get Bismarck to accept overseas territorial compensation, including Indochina, but to no avail. Bismarck blamed the French for prolonging the war and for the harsh peace he imposed.

The preliminary peace signed at Versailles was confirmed in the Treaty of Frankfurt on May 10. The Prussians took Alsace (except Belfort) and much of Lorraine and were allowed a triumphal parade through Paris. France agreed to an indemnity of 5 billion francs, more than twice the actual cost of the war, and German troops would occupy northeastern France until it was paid off.

The effects of the war and the peace treaty that ended it were momentous. A France of 36 million people now faced a united Germany of 41 million people, for on January 18, 1871, Bismarck proclaimed at Versailles the establishment of the German Empire. German unification was thus at last achieved but on Bismarck's terms and under a constitutional arrangement that left Prussia dominant and the bulk of the powers in the hands of the king of Prussia, now also emperor of the Germans.

The harsh Treaty of Frankfurt dealt France by German chancellor Otto von Bismarck following the siege of Paris may have been a great mistake. Alsace had been French since 1648, and Lorraine had been French since 1766. Both were now thoroughly French. The indemnity fueled Germany's industrial expansion after the war, but if Bismarck had hoped that the payments would allow Germany to meddle further in French affairs, he was mistaken. In an outpouring of nationalist sentiment, Frenchmen oversubscribed bond issues and paid the indemnity off well ahead of schedule. Most important, the Prussian diktat made cooperation between Germany and France next to impossible, for Frenchmen were determined to recover the two lost provinces and to secure revenge. Bismarck later boasted that he had been responsible for three wars. This is undoubtedly correct, but it is also true that the treaty he imposed on France sowed the seeds that sprouted World War I, which in turn gave rise to World War II.

Spencer C. Tucker

Further Reading
Horne, Alistair. *The Fall of Paris: The Siege and the Commune, 1870–1871.* New York: Doubleday, 1965.
Howard, Michael. *The Franco-Prussian War.* New York: Routledge, 2001.
Wawro, Geoffrey. *The Franco-Prussian War: The German Conquest of France in 1870–1871.* New York: Cambridge University Press, 2003.

Siege of Pleven (July 19–December 10, 1877)

In the early 1870s, Ottoman power was in decline, but the empire still controlled most of the Balkan Peninsula. In the south, Greece was independent, while to the north, Romania, Serbia, and Montenegro enjoyed the status of autonomous principalities. In 1875 and 1876, uprisings occurred in Herzegovina, Bosnia, and Macedonia. Then in mid-1876, the Bulgarians also rose, only to be slaughtered by the Ottomans. Serbia and Montenegro then declared war on the Ottoman Empire. Russia, defeated in the Crimean War of 1854–1856 by a coalition that included the Ottomans, sought to recoup its prestige in the Balkans and secure a warm-water port on the Mediterranean. As a result, concerns mounted that fighting in the Balkans might lead to a general European war.

While the major European powers discussed intervention, the Ottomans, led by Ghāzī Osmān Pasha, were winning the war. By the autumn of 1876, it was clear that they would soon capture Belgrade, the capital of Serbia. That October Russia demanded an armistice, which the Ottomans accepted. A conference at Istanbul (Constantinople) in December soon disbanded without tangible result, and in March 1877 Serbia made peace with the Ottoman Empire. Sentiment in Russia was then so strong for intervention that despite warnings of bankruptcy from his minister of finance, Czar Alexander II declared war on the Ottomans in April 1877, beginning the Russo-Turkish War of 1877–1878.

Because the Ottomans controlled the Black Sea with ironclad warships, a Russian land invasion proved necessary. In the last week of April 1877, two Russian armies invaded: one in Caucasia, advancing on Kars, Ardahan, and Erzurum, and the other in the Balkans. Romania was essential to a Russian drive down the eastern part of the Balkan Peninsula, and following agreement between Prince Charles of Romania and Alexander II, Russian troops crossed the Prut (Pruth) River into Moldavia. The Ottomans responded by shelling Romanian forts at the mouth of the Danube, whereupon on May 21 Romania declared both war on the Ottoman Empire and its independence. Serbia reentered the war in December. Bulgarian irregular forces fought with Russia, and Montenegro remained at war, as it had been since June 1876. Romanian support was vital to the Russian effort in terms of both geographical position and manpower in the ensuing campaign.

Russian forces under nominal command of Grand Duke Nicholas, brother of the czar, crossed the Danube River on June 26 and took Svistov (Stistova) and Nikopol (Nicopolis) on the river before advancing to Pleven (Plevna, Plevne), about 25 miles south of Nikopol. The Bulgarians acclaimed the Russians as liberators. Russian general Nikolai P. de Krüdener, who had actual command, established his headquarters at Tirnovo and sent forces across the Balkan Mountains into Thrace, then back toward Shipka Pass through the mountains to defeat the Ottomans. Russian troops, assisted by Bulgarian partisans, also raided in the Maritza Valley, seemingly threatening Adrianople.

The military situation changed when Sultan Abdul Aziz appointed two competent generals: Mehemed Ali, named Ottoman commander in Europe, and Ghāzī Osmān Pasha. Mehemed Ali defeated the Russians in the south, driving them back to the Balkan Mountains with heavy losses. To the north, the main Russian armies encountered a formidable obstacle in Ottoman forces sent to the Danube under Osmān Pasha. Soon he had entrenched his men at Pleven. Ottoman engineers created a formidable fortress of earthworks with redoubts, trenches, and gun emplacements in the rocky valley there. The 10-mile Ottoman defensive perimeter was lightly held, with reserves in a secure central location from which they could rush to any threatened point.

Superior numbers led the Russians to underestimate their adversary. Failing to adequately reconnoiter the Ottoman positions, on July 19, 1877, the Russians assaulted the strongest portion of the line and, to their surprise, were repulsed with 3,000 casualties. The battle demonstrated the superiority of machine weapons in the defense, as the Ottomans were equipped with modern breech-loading rifles imported from the United States. They also had light mobile artillery. On July 30, Russian forces again attacked and again were repulsed.

During the course of the next six weeks, Osmān Pasha worked to improve his defenses, while the Russians demanded that Prince Charles of Romania furnish additional manpower. Charles agreed on the condition that he receive command of the joint Romanian-Russian force. Confident of victory, the allies then planned an attack from three sides with 110,000 infantry and 10,000 cavalry. On September 6, 150 Russian guns began a preparatory bombardment. The Ottoman earthworks suffered little damage, and there were relatively few personnel casualties. Wet weather also worked to the advantage of the defenders.

The infantry attack began on schedule on September 11. With Alexander II in attendance, at 1:00 p.m. the artillery fire ceased, and the infantry began their assault. The attackers took a number of Ottoman redoubts, and for several days it appeared that the allies would be victorious. But on the third day, the Ottomans successfully counterattacked. The allies suffered 21,000 casualties for their efforts.

Russian war minister Dimitri Aleksevich Miliutin now recalled brilliant engineer General Franz Eduard Ivanovich Todleben, who had directed the defense of Sevastopol during the Crimean War. Todleben advised that Pleven be encircled and its garrison starved into submission. Osmān Pasha, having twice defeated a force double his own in size, would have preferred a withdrawal while it was still possible, but the battle had captured the attention of Europe and created a positive image of Ottomans as heroic and tenacious fighters. Sultan Abdul Hamid therefore ordered him to hold out and promised to send a relief force.

The Russians committed 120,000 men and 5,000 guns to the siege. They also placed Todleben in charge of siege operations. Other Russian forces under General Ossip Gourko ravaged the countryside, preventing Ottoman supply columns from reaching Pleven from the south. The Russians also easily defeated and turned back the sultan's poorly trained relief force.

Winter closed in, and the Ottoman defenders at Pleven, short of ammunition, were soon reduced to starvation. Osmān Pasha knew that his only hope was a surprise breakout.

On the night of December 9–10, the Ottomans threw bridges across the Vid River to the west and then advanced on the Russian outposts. The Ottomans carried the first Russian trenches, and the fighting was hand to hand. At this point, Osmān Pasha was wounded and his horse shot from beneath him.

Rumors of Osmān Pasha's death led to panic among the Ottoman troops, who broke and fled. Osmān Pasha surrendered Pleven and its 43,338 defenders on December 10. Although the Russians treated Osmān Pasha well, thousands of Ottoman prisoners perished in the snows during their trek to captivity, and Bulgarians butchered many seriously wounded Ottoman prisoners left behind in military hospitals. Some 34,000 allied troops perished in the siege. With the Russians threatening Istanbul itself, in February 1878 the Ottomans sued for peace.

Russia imposed harsh terms in the Treaty of San Stefano on March 3, 1878, leaving the Ottoman Empire only a small strip of territory on the European side of the straits. Romania, Serbia, and Montenegro were enlarged, but the major territorial change was the creation of a new large autonomous Bulgaria, including most of Macedonia from the Aegean Sea to Albania. This would make Bulgaria the largest of the Balkan states, although the assumption was that it would be dominated by Russia. The Battle of Pleven is therefore regarded by Bulgarians as marking the birth of their nation. The treaty did not last, however. Britain and Austria-Hungary threatened war if the treaty was not revised, and Russia agreed to an international conference that met in Berlin in June and July 1878.

Under the terms of the Treaty of Berlin, Bulgaria was divided into three parts. Bulgaria proper (the northern section) became an autonomous principality subject to tribute to the sultan; eastern Rumelia, the southeastern part, received a measure of autonomy; and the rest of Bulgaria was restored to the sultan. Romania, Serbia, and Montenegro all became independent, and Greece received Thessaly. Russia received from Romania the small strip of Bessarabia lost in 1856 and territory around Batum, Ardahan, and Kars that it had conquered in the Caucasus, while Romania had to be content with part of the Dobrudja. Austria-Hungary secured the right to occupy and administer, though not annex, Bosnia and Herzegovina.

The region continued to smolder, however. During 1912–1913, there were two Balkan wars, both of which threatened to become wider conflicts. Then in June 1914, the assassination of Austrian archduke Franz Ferdinand led to a third Balkan war that this time became World War I. The military lesson of the siege of Pleven—that modern machine weapons gave superiority to the defense—was soon to be relearned.

Spencer C. Tucker

Further Reading

Herbert, Frederick William von. *The Defense of Plevna, 1877.* Ankara, Turkey: Ministry of Culture, 1990.

Kinross, Lord [John Patrick]. *The Ottoman Centuries: The Rise and Fall of the Turkish Empire.* New York: William Morrow, 1977.

Sumner, B. H. *Russia and the Balkans, 1870–1880.* Oxford, UK: Oxford University Press, 1937.

Siege of Khartoum (March 13, 1884–January 26, 1885)

The siege of Khartoum, during March 13, 1884–January 26, 1885, was a consequence of British rule in Egypt. A strong nationalist movement had developed there against foreigners, and specifically the French and British. The British had become intensely interested in controlling Egypt following the opening in 1869 of the Suez Canal that connected the Red Sea with the Mediterranean. The canal greatly cut the distance ships had to travel between the British Isles and India by some 4,300 miles as they no longer had to travel around Africa. In 1875 the British had taken advantage of the Khedive Ismail's spendthrift ways to purchase his shares in the canal.

The increasing control of Egyptian finances by the British and the French and the vast sums spent by Ismail in an effort to modernize his country led to the deposition of Ismail in 1879 in favor of his son Twefik. Then, under the slogan of "Egypt for the Egyptians," Minister of War Arabi Pasha seized power. The French and British governments agreed on a joint military intervention, but before this could occur a change of government occurred in France and that country withdrew from the plan. The British then proceeded alone in 1882. After the Royal Navy bombarded Alexandria, British troops under General Sir Garnet Wolseley came ashore, defeated Arabi's forces in the Battle of Tel-el-Kebir (September 13), and took control of Egypt. London simply announced that British forces would be withdrawn "as soon as the state of the country, and the organization of the proper means for the maintenance of the Khedive's authority, will admit of it."

Despite this, British troops remained in Egypt with the real ruler being the British consul-general and high commissioner. (The last British troops would not leave Egypt until 1956!)

The British now found themselves drawn into the Sudan, a vast open region lying to the south of Egypt that embraced the Upper Nile, and which had intermittently through history been controlled by Egypt. Egyptian efforts to establish firm control of the Sudan had been stymied in part by their efforts to stamp out the slave trade there and by heavy taxes, but corruption and mismanagement also were important factors.

In July 1881, a prophet arose in the Sudan in the charismatic Sheik Mahomed of Dongola, who proclaimed himself the Mahdi ("Messiah"). Soon he attracted a considerable and devoted following as thousands of Sudanese called Dervishes rallied to him. In January 1883, following a six months' siege, the Dervishes captured the regional capital city of El Obeid and massacred its defenders, securing there a considerable supply of weapons and money.

The Egyptian government had hoped that forces in the Sudan could deal with the situation, but with the Dervish capture of Kordofan, the richest Sudanese province, it was obliged to act. With the British authorities ambivalent, the puppet Egyptian government finally ordered Egyptian forces to crush the uprising. Former Indian Army colonel William Hicks, now in Egyptian Army service, had command. He set out up the Nile for Khartoum with some 8,000 men (7,000 infantry, 1,000 cavalry) and several thousand camp followers. On September 9, 1883, they departed for El Obeid. Five thousand camels transported supplies, machine guns and Krupp-manufactured mountain guns, and a million rounds of ammunition. On November 5, Hicks's force, misled by possibly treacherous guides and out of water, was ambushed and annihilated by 50,000 Dervish warriors at Kashgil, some 30 miles south of El Obeid. Reportedly Hicks was the last officer to die. His head was cut off and taken to the Mahdi.

The defeat of Hicks's force brought full-blown revolt in the Sudan against Egyptian rule; almost the entire Sudan now came under their control, and they now had a considerable supply of modern weapons. On February 4, 1884, the Dervishes defeated another Egyptian Army force at El Teb.

Fearful that Lower Egypt might soon also fall to the rebels, the Egyptian government called for assistance. British prime minister William Gladstone, an anti-imperialist "Little Englander," was opposed and decided that all Europeans and Egyptians should be evacuated from the Sudan. To accomplish this task, he sent out British Army major general Charles George Gordon.

Gordon had gotten the nickname of "Chinese" Gordon because of his command of the Chinese imperial army that put down the Taiping Rebellion (1850–1864). He had also served as governor of the Sudan for the Egyptians and had taken a special interest in ending the slave trade there. Deeply religious but eccentric and with a decided martyr fixation, he was certainly not the person to lead an evacuation. Efforts by Egyptian consul-general Evelyn Baring, 1st Earl of Cromer, who had a good understanding of Gordon, to block the appointment failed, however.

Reaching Cairo and agreeing with those who saw what had happened in the Sudan as the prelude to a struggle for control of Egypt itself, Gordon simply ignored his orders and convinced the Egyptian government that he could pacify the Sudan and again become its governor. He then traveled up the Nile by boat to Khartoum, where he arrived on February 18, 1884. He, however, dallied there and allowed his forces to become besieged in the capital city on March 13, 1884.

The situation at Khartoum did not appear difficult, and Gordon was confident. The city population of 34,000 included 8,000 soldiers. Gordon also had 12 artillery pieces and 9 armed paddle steamers with which to defend the river. The Khartoum arsenal held 2 million rounds of ammunition and was capable of producing 40,000 rounds a week. Gordon estimated his food supply would last six months.

Khartoum's defenses were weakest in the south, where it was open to the desert. Gordon caused a semi-circular trench some 15-feet wide to be dug there. This barrier extended from the White Nile to the Blue Nile. The southern approaches were also sowed with primitive land mines and broken glass (the Sudanese traditionally went barefoot).

Although some 30,000 Mahdists now laid siege to Khartoum, most of their forces were dispersed elsewhere in the Sudan, and no serious efforts were made to assault the British positions. The British still controlled the Nile and messages got in and out. There is every indication that Gordon could have left Khartoum at any point up until September, when the city would be out of food, and the Nile would flood, inundating the British defenses south of the city.

Gladstone was furious with what had transpired. Although the British daily press demanded that Gordon be rescued, the prime minister took his time, not announcing a relief force with General Garnet Wolseley in command until August 8, and then only after a cabinet member's threat to resign over this would have brought down the government. Wolseley's orders, drafted in Cairo, read as follows: "The primary object of the expedition up the valley of the Nile is to bring away General Gordon and Colonel Stewart [Col. J. H. D. Stewart, Gordon's second in command] from Khartoum. When that objective has been secure, no further offensive operations of any kind are to be undertaken."

Wolseley favored an all-river route up the Nile, but the river was full of cataracts and, save in flood, would only be navigable by small craft. Wolseley had served in Canada, and his preparations included construction of special whale boats and the recruitment of Canadian voyageurs to man them. By January 1885, the physical barriers had been surmounted and an advance force fought and pushed their way through dervishes at Abu Klea on January 17 and the next day at Abu Kru.

By mid-January, the situation in Khartoum was desperate, however. Hundreds of people were dead or dying and lay unburied. The Nile was now falling and this left a stretch of muddy open ground on the defenses facing the White Nile. Taking advantage of this, just before dawn on January 26 some 50,000 Dervishes burst into Khartoum by this route. Hearing gunfire, Gordon changed into a white dress uniform, armed himself with a revolver and sword and stood at the head of the stairs to the governor's palace with one hand on the hilt of the sword. Although the Mahdi had given orders that he be taken alive (he planned to force Gordon's conversion to Islam), a short time later Gordon was speared to death. Later his head was cut off and presented to the Mahdi. Gordon never intended to try to escape.

A steamer was available less than 300 yards from his residence, and its captain quickly got up steam that morning, but Gordon made no effort to flee there.

With the fall of Khartoum, the Dervishes went on a rampage, massacring some 4,000 inhabitants and selling others into slavery. Almost all the troops defending the city were also slain. Reportedly, casualties among the Mahdists were heavy.

After the fall of Khartoum, those British remaining evacuated the Sudan. Gladstone's failure to take prompt measures raised a storm of anger in Britain and was a major factor in his resignation as prime minister in June 1885. The Mahdi died that same month. Finally, in 1897, the British returned to the Sudan in force. General Horatio Kitchener, soon to be Lord Kitchener of Khartoum, led a well-prepared and supplied force of British, Egyptian, and Sudanese soldiers south and avenged Khartoum by routing the Dervishes in the Battle of Omdurman (October 2, 1898). For some 48 British, Egyptian, and Sudanese soldiers killed and 382 wounded, the Dervishes suffered an estimated 10,000 dead, as many more wounded, and 5,000 taken prisoner.

Spencer C. Tucker

Further Reading
Asher, Michael. *Khartoum: The Ultimate Imperial Adventure.* London: Penguin, 2005.
Farwell, Byron. *Prisoners of the Mahdi.* London: Longmans, Green, 1967.
Farwell, Bryon. *Queen Victoria's Little Wars.* New York: Harper & Row, 1972.
Neillands, Robin. *The Dervish War.* London: John Murray, 1976.
Royle, Charles. *The Egyptian Campaigns, 1882 to 1885.* London: Hurst and Blackett, 1900.
Von Slatin, Rudolph. *Fire and Sword in the Soudan.* London: Edward Arnold, 1896.

Siege of Tuyen Quang (November 24, 1884–March 3, 1885)

The siege of Tuyen Quang occurred between the French and Chinese armies in Tonkin (northern Vietnam) during the Sino-French War (1884–1885). The battle ranks as one of the most important in French Foreign Legion annals.

French territorial gains in Tonkin greatly alarmed Chinese leaders. Vietnam was, after all, still China's tributary state, and the Chinese were concerned about the increasing French presence along their southwestern frontier. When Vietnamese emperor Tu Duc (r. 1847–1883) in Hue appealed to Chinese emperor Guangxu (r. 1875–1908) to intervene, the Chinese proceeded to contest French control of Vietnam. This led to the Black Flag or Tonkin Wars of 1882–1885, which then morphed into the Sino-French War of August 1884–April 1885.

Following the great 1864 Taiping Rebellion in China, many Chinese armed bands had sought refuge in Tonkin. The French called them "pirates," which they certainly were. They were known as the White, Yellow, and Black Flags for the colors flown by each section and officer, but only the Black Flags submitted to the authority of the Hue court. In 1865 Liu Yongfu, self-proclaimed leader of the Black Flags, established a base at the strategically located town of Son Tay on the

Red River. Although illiterate, Liu Yongfu was a capable leader and enjoyed support from the Chinese across the border in Guangxi and Yunnan.

When some 1,500 Chinese regular troops reinforced the 3,000 Black Flags at Sơn Tay the French grew concerned about their own small garrisons in Hanoi and the port of Haiphong and sent out 3,000 reinforcements to Indochina and forced the court to sign a treaty establishing a French protectorate over Vietnam. In December 1883, 600 French troops, including a Foreign Legion battalion, attacked and took Sơn Tay. In May 1884, the Chinese agreed to withdraw entirely from Tonkin.

The fighting should have ended at this point, but in June 1884 the French sent troops to occupy Lang Sơn, the closest major Tonkinese town to the Chinese frontier. At Bac Le, 30 miles from Lang Son, Chinese troops ambushed and repulsed the French, who lost 22 dead and 60 wounded.

This brought on the short-lived Sino-French War of August 1884–April 1885, with the French dividing their resources between Tonkin and China. Their major military effort was in Tonkin, however, where they had some 9,000 men. By the summer of 1885, this force had grown to 40,000. Under aggressive Generals Louis-Alexandre Brière de l'Isle and François de Négrier, the French spent most of the spring and summer of 1884 securing the Red River Delta. In relatively easy fighting, they managed to push deep into the northwest highlands.

The Black Flags and Chinese regulars were far more numerous and for the most part much better armed, with a variety of repeating rifles, whereas the French carried only the single-shot 1874 model Gras rifle. Both the Black Flags and Chinese excelled at building defensive works. The Chinese allies preferred to fight defensively. They had artillery but they seldom used it, and they were very poor marksmen, preferring not to fire their rifles from the shoulder in aimed fire. In the end, the Black Flag/Chinese predilection for taking the defense gave the initiative to the French.

Led by aggressive officers, the French used light artillery and dynamite to blast holes in their enemies' bamboo palisades and, although often heavily outnumbered, they employed bayonet charges to rout the defenders. Both sides gave little quarter. The Chinese dug up French corpses to cut off the heads and place them on lances or flag poles. This practice led the French to slaughter their prisoners.

In early autumn 1884, Chinese regulars from Yunnan reinforced Liu Yongfu, who had positioned much of his Black Flags force around the town of Tuyen Quang on the Clear River northwest of Hanoi. That November Lieutenant Colonel Duchesne led a force of legionnaires and marines supported by gunboats up the river to Tuyen Quang. Although forced to fight through a Chinese position, the French made it there safely. The column then departed on November 23, leaving behind a garrison of 13 officers and 619 men commanded by Major Marc Edmond Dominé.

The Black Flags and Chinese closed around Tuyen Quang the next day, November 24, 1884. Duchesne had, meanwhile, pushed the Chinese from Bac Ninh to Bac Le. In January 1885, French reinforcements, including two battalions of legionnaires, arrived in Tonkin, and on February 3, 1885, General Brière de l'Isle struck north with 9,000 men to clear the road to Lang Son. On February 12, a desperate fight at Bac Viay, the last defensive position before Lang Son, cost the French 200 casualties, but the next day the French tri-color flew over Lang Son, taken without a fight. On February 23, the French marched out of Lang Son to force the Chinese from Dong Dang, 10 miles to the north on the Chinese border. Again, the French prevailed. General Brière de l'Isle then left General de Négrier in command at Lang Son, and on February 16 he proceeded southward to relieve the siege of Tuyen Quang.

Militarily Tuen Quang was of dubious importance, but what happened there could have serious consequences. No doubt General Tang Jingsong and Liu Yongfu, who commanded in all some 12,000 Chinese regulars and Black Flags saw it as an opportunity to inflict a great psychological defeat on the French.

Virtually indefensible, the town of Tuyen Quang was dominated by wooded hills, and its square citadel on the banks of the Clear River was barely 300 yards on a side. Nearly two-thirds of Major Dominé's 632 officers and men were legionnaires, with the remainder tirailleurs tonkinois (Tonkin riflemen).

On January 16, 1885, the Chinese began digging siege lines around Tuyen Quang. These were completed four days later. On the night of January 26–27, the Chinese and Black Flags launched a massive assault but were beaten back, losing perhaps 100 men. The attackers then opted for more conventional siege tactics of snaking trenches toward the French lines. During the day they built fascines—bundles of sticks used to shore up parapets—and sniped at the French positions. At night they advanced their saps forward while firing at the French.

On February 3, a Vietnamese managed to escape from Tuyen Quang to inform the French authorities at Hanoi of the situation. Five days later, the Chinese at Tuyen Quang employed artillery for the first time; soon they were also using heavy mortars. On February 12, the Chinese blew a large mine beneath the French lines and attempted to exploit the breech but were beaten back. A French sortie the next day destroyed some of the Chinese advance works, but on February 22 the Chinese again detonated a series of mines under the French lines and the next day launched another futile assault. On the 25th, the process was repeated: a mine explosion followed by an infantry assault.

By March 1, the French had only 180 working rifles to defend a perimeter of 1,200 yards. That day the French heard distant gun shots and assumed it to be a relief force, but they were too exhausted to break out. On March 2, the Chinese fire increased, causing the members of its garrison to fear it would be overwhelmed before their relief could occur. But on March 3, the French awoke to find the Chinese gone. The reason was soon apparent with the arrival of General Brière de l'Isle's relief column. At Hoa Mac, it had defeated a Chinese force in what turned out to be the bloodiest battle for the French in Tonkin since their 1883 invasion.

The siege of Tuyen Quang claimed 50 dead and 224 wounded on the French side, while the Chinese sustained some 1,000 dead and 2,000 wounded.

A series of French reversals followed. On March 29, seemingly on the brink of defeat a month earlier, the Chinese who apparently believed the French were planning to invade Quangxi, struck in force and retook Lang Son. Already the Tonkin campaign of 1884–1885 was one of the more controversial episodes in the history of the French Third Republic, and Premier Jules Ferry's political opponents used the defeat at Lang Son to drive him from office. Georges Clemenceau, later premier himself during a most difficult military test for France in World War I, accused Ferry of "treason" for bogging France down in Vietnam. France was not to quit Indochina until 1954, however.

Spencer C. Tucker

Further Reading

Blanchard, Jean-Vincent. *At the Edge of the World: The Heroic Century of the French Foreign Legion.* New York: Bloomsbury Press, 2017.

Dupuis, Jean. *Le Tonkin de 1872 à 1886: Histoire et politique.* Paris: Augustin Challamel, 1910.

Ferry, J. F. C. *Le Tonkin et la mère patrie: Témoignages et documents.* Paris: Victor-Havard, 1890.

McAleavy. *Black Flags in Vietnam.* London: Allen & Unwin, 1968.

Nguyen, Khac Vien. *Vietnam, a Long History.* Hanoi: The Gioi Publishers, 1999.

Porch, Douglas. *The French Foreign Legion: A Complete History of the Legendary Fighting Force.* New York: Macmillan, 1991.

Siege of Santiago de Cuba (July 1–17, 1898)

On April 25, 1898, the United States declared war on Spain. The chief cause of the war was the situation in Cuba. Its close proximity to Florida made this Spanish possession of great interest to the United States, which sought to pressure Spain into granting Cuba its independence. There was widespread sympathy in the United States for the plight of the Cuban people in their frequent rebellions against Spain. This sentiment was largely the result of exaggerated accounts in the sensationalist American "Yellow Press" that played up atrocities committed by the Spanish authorities and downplayed those by the rebels. A number of Americans hoped to annex Cuba; certainly American businessmen saw the island as a great financial opportunity.

President William McKinley was largely driven into requesting a declaration of war from Congress owing to the press of public opinion. The war's stated purpose was to free Cuba from oppression. Indeed, the Teller Amendment, which was attached to the joint resolution of Congress authorizing the war, declared that the United States supported Cuban independence and that the United States had no long-term claims of sovereignty or jurisdiction over the island.

This was no war of waiting and hopes deferred. Although the U.S. Army was small, poorly trained, and utterly unready for the war, the navy was not. The Atlantic Squadron undertook a blockade of Cuba, and on May 1, only a week after the declaration of war and having steamed to the Philippines from China, Commodore George Dewey's U.S. Asiatic Squadron destroyed Spanish rear admiral Patricio Montojo y Pasarón's squadron in the Battle of Manila Bay.

Then on May 19, Spanish rear admiral Pascual Cervera y Topete's Cádiz Squadron slipped into Santiago de Cuba harbor. This caused a shift in U.S. strategy from a descent on Havana to taking Santiago. Destruction of Cervera's squadron,

Washington believed, would help bring an end to the war. By June 1, U.S. Navy rear admiral William T. Sampson's far more powerful North Atlantic Squadron had taken up station off Santiago Harbor.

Three weeks later, between June 22 and 26, the 17,000 members of the U.S. Army's V Corps arrived from Florida. Commanded by Major General William Shafter, they came ashore at Daiquirí and Siboney on the southeastern coast of Cuba near Santiago. Although there was a clash with Spanish troops at Las Guásimas on June 24, this presented little obstacle to the American advance.

Shafter's orders were to capture Santiago and thus assist the navy in destroying Cervera's squadron. Shafter could either march from Daiquirí to seize the fort at El Morro that guarded the entrance to Santiago Harbor, or he could move inland from Siboney directly to San Juan Heights, which overlooked the port. The advance was to be supported by General Calixto García y Iñiguez's Cuban revolutionary forces.

Sampson wanted the objective to be El Morro. Taking it would allow the navy to clear the mines laid in the harbor's entrance. Shafter thought that the navy ought to simply enter the harbor and attack the Spanish fleet. Shafter was also concerned about reports that the Spaniards had established a strong defensive position at El Morro. Shafter elected to move inland on Santiago.

Shafter planned a two-pronged attack, with Brigadier General Jacob F. Kent's 1st Division and Major General Joseph Wheeler's dismounted cavalry division attacking San Juan Heights on the left and Brigadier General Henry W. Lawton's 2nd Division attacking El Caney on the right. After Wheeler repulsed the Spaniards at Las Guásimas on June 24, Shafter prepared for a coordinated attack on July 1. Lawton's forces were to attack El Caney and then move south to support Kent's assault on San Juan Heights. Although stiff Spanish resistance at El Caney resulted in an all-day battle there, Kent succeeded in taking San Juan Heights in an engagement in which Lieutenant Colonel Theodore Roosevelt's Rough Riders figured prominently, making Roosevelt a national hero. With the victory at El Caney and the capture of San Juan Heights on July 1, what had been the campaign of Santiago now became the siege of Santiago.

The Spaniards meanwhile had shifted a limited number of resources to Santiago. On June 22, some 3,700 Spanish soldiers, commanded by Colonel Federico Escario García, had departed Manzanillo for Santiago, 160 miles distant. Cuban guerrillas constantly harassed the force. Although the Spanish column finally reached Santiago on the night of July 2, the men did little more than add to the strain on the city's food supply, which by now had reached a critical level with the city effectively cut off from supplies or reinforcements.

Shafter, however, believed Santiago was still much too strong to be taken by storm and that Spanish reinforcements were on their way to the city. In a communiqué to Washington, he requested authorization to withdraw to a more secure position. Washington rejected this request and ordered Shafter to hold the heights.

Shafter would no doubt have been less concerned had he known of the desperate situation inside Santiago, where the wounded Spanish commander

Lieutenant General Arsenio Linares had been replaced by Major General José Toral y Vázquez and the city's population of 50,000 were reduced to a starvation diet.

Although Santiago's garrison totaled 10,429 men at the end of June, this figure included unreliable militia and volunteers. Morale was also low, with pay for the regulars 11 months in arrears. At the same time, however, Shafter's V Corps was suffering an alarming increase in those sick from fevers brought on by the onset of the tropical disease season.

On July 3, the picture at Santiago was dramatically altered when Cervera attempted to break out of Santiago Harbor with his squadron, which was promptly destroyed by the U.S. blockaders. With the defeat of the Spanish squadron, the military value of Santiago suddenly became questionable. Accordingly, on July 3, Shafter advised General Toral to surrender or the city would be shelled. Toral declined, but negotiations nevertheless continued. Toral then proposed surrendering the city provided that the garrison was allowed to retain its arms and march unopposed to Holguín. Shafter was disposed to accept this, but President William McKinley insisted on unconditional surrender.

On July 10 and 11, the two sides engaged in a final battle, with the Spaniards sustaining 50 casualties compared to 4 for the Americans. Two days later, on July 13, Shafter and U.S. Army commanding general Lieutenant General Nelson A. Miles (who had just arrived) met again with Toral, offering to ship all Spanish troops back to Spain at U.S. expense if Toral agreed to surrender unconditionally. Recognizing that he had little choice, Toral agreed but needed the approval of Lieutenant General Ramón Blanco y Erenas, Spanish captain-general and governor-general of Cuba in Havana. Blanco eventually agreed, and on July 17, Toral surrendered the city of Santiago together with Guantánamo and a number of smaller posts that fell under the authority of the Santiago commander.

The U.S. Army campaign in Cuba was hardly a military masterpiece. Shafter, who personally suffered from malarial fever and gout during the campaign, was often out of touch with the situation and pessimistic. The Spaniards enjoyed superiority in small arms with their Mauser rifles firing smokeless powder cartridges, and American artillery support was negligible at best. In addition, Shafter had made no effort to utilize naval gunfire support or the Spanish guerrilla forces, who he perceived to be little more than laborers.

U.S. land forces also enjoyed success in Puerto Rico and, in combination with Filipino insurgents, in August captured the city of Manila. In the December 10, 1898, Treaty of Paris, Spain agreed to grant independence to Cuba and ceded Guam and Puerto Rico to the United States. Spain also agreed to sell the Philippines to the United States for $10 million.

Spencer C. Tucker

Further Reading

Cosmas, Graham A. *An Army for Empire: The United States Army in the Spanish-American War*. College Station: Texas A&M University Press, 1994.

Leech, Margaret. *In the Days of McKinley*. New York: Harper and Brothers, 1959.

Samuels, Peggy, and Harold Samuels. *Teddy Roosevelt at San Juan: The Making of a President*. College Station: Texas A&M University Press, 1997.

Trask, David F. *The War with Spain in 1898*. Lincoln: University of Nebraska Press, 1996.

Walker, Dale L. *The Boys of '98: Theodore Roosevelt and the Rough Riders*. New York: Forge, 1999.

Siege and First Battle of Manila (May 1–August 14, 1898)

The siege of Manila of May 1–August 14, 1898, occurred during the Spanish American War (April 21–August 13, 1898). The battle, which pitted troops of the U.S. Army VIII Corps against Spanish forces, was waged after the Protocol of Peace of August 12 had been signed in Cuba, which ostensibly ended hostilities. At the time, the cable linking Manila with Hong Kong had been cut, so field commanders in the Philippines were unaware of the truce agreement.

Manila, the capital and most important city of the Philippines, is located on the east side of Manila Bay on the island of Luzon. As the capital city, Manila was the center of Spanish power in the archipelago and understandably the focal point of Filipino nationalists' efforts to overthrow Spanish rule. Following his overwhelming defeat of the Spanish naval squadron in the Battle of Manila Bay on May 1, 1898, U.S. Navy commodore George Dewey realized that Manila could and should be seized. Dewey did take the Spanish naval station at Cavite, but with no available landing force to undertake such a mission, he simply blockaded Manila to await the army's arrival.

The U.S. Army's Philippine Expeditionary Force (VIII Corps) reached the Philippines in three contingents, departing from San Francisco as ship availability permitted. The first contingent of 2,500 men, under Brigadier General Thomas Anderson, arrived at the end of June, followed in mid-July by 3,500 additional men under Brigadier General Francis V. Greene. The final contingent, numbering some 4,800 troops and commanded by Brigadier General Arthur MacArthur, reached the islands at the end of July, as did commander of VIII Corps Major General Wesley Merritt.

At the end of July, the Spanish still controlled Manila and much of its environs. The city proper was split by the Pasig River, south of which stood the old walled city of Fort Santiago. The Spanish defensive line, known as the Zapote Line, was located 1.5 miles to the south from where a large blockhouse, Number 14, on the Pasay Road extended west to a stone structure known as Fort San Antonio de Abad, located near the shore of Manila Bay. A line of entrenchments connected these two strong points.

Opposing the Spanish positions were some 10,000 Filipino nationalist troops under the overall command of General Emilio Aguinaldo y Famy, who had formally proclaimed the Republic of the Philippines on June 12. Through the early summer, the nationalists had managed to isolate Manila from its source of supplies, in effect leaving it a city under siege. In Manila, food was scarce and mainly consisted of a little horseflesh and some water buffalo. At night the nationalists and the Spanish defenders maintained lively fire between the two lines but undertook no serious offensive movements.

Spanish admiral Patricio Montojo's sunken flagship, *Reina Christina*. The ship was destroyed at Manila Bay by Admiral George Dewey's forces on May 1, 1898. (Department of Defense)

During the course of the U.S. buildup, Greene's troops constructed a series of entrenchments and moved into some of the works created by the nationalists, who abandoned these positions only reluctantly when Greene persuaded them to do so. The arrangement was irregular, however. In places the nationalist forces actually occupied trench works in between the Americans and the Spaniards.

During the two weeks preceding the attack on Manila, heavy rains of the monsoon season had drenched the area. The period was also characterized by frequent exchanges of artillery and rifle fire between the Americans and the Spanish, with Greene's units sustaining a number of casualties. In addition, relations between the Americans and Aguinaldo's men, at first cordial, began to deteriorate, as the latter had grown increasingly suspicious of U.S. intentions in the islands.

During the latter part of July, Dewey, now a rear admiral, became convinced that the Spanish would surrender Manila through negotiations. Thus, he met first with Captain-General Basilio Augustín y Dávila and later with his successor, Fermín Jáudenes y Alvarez, to explore possible arrangements. Nevertheless, Greene urged naval gunfire on Spanish positions to relieve the pressure on his command. His troops had dug a line of trenches south of Fort Abad and were taking casualties from Spanish fire every day. General Merritt supported Greene in this request. Dewey, however, was reluctant to open fire from his warships, fearing that doing so would destroy any chance of securing the city by negotiation, an arrangement that he still believed to be entirely possible. Dewey suggested that perhaps the troops could be withdrawn from the trenches until a general attack became necessary. The admiral, however, did agree to support Greene should this prove absolutely necessary. In that eventuality, Greene was to burn a blue light on the beach, and the ships would open fire. Dewey hoped that it would not be necessary.

Merritt had arrived in the Philippines under orders from President William McKinley not to involve the nationalists in taking Manila because to do so would mean including them as partners in future treaty negotiations with Spain. Fermin Jáudenes y Alvarez, who had recently replaced Basilio Augustín as Spanish commander in Manila, had taken over with orders to hold the city. Inasmuch as peace negotiations were about to get under way, Spain's bargaining position would be weakened by a surrender of the city.

On August 9, 1898, Merritt and Dewey sent an ultimatum to Jáudenes demanding that he surrender Manila. They warned that if he did not, U.S. forces would attack. Jáudenes responded by convening a meeting of his subordinate commanders, putting the issue to a vote. Seven voted in favor of immediate negotiations for a surrender, while seven were opposed. Jáudenes broke the tie, with a decision to continue the present delaying tactics. He informed the Americans that he had no authority to surrender and asked to be able to communicate with Madrid through Hong Kong. On August 10, Dewey and Merritt rejected the suggestion.

In the meantime, Dewey pursued separate negotiations with Jáudenes, working through Belgian consul in Manila Edouard André. Jáudenes then agreed to consider surrendering Manila to U.S. forces but insisted that it would have to appear that a genuine effort had been made to defend the city in order to salvage Spanish honor. Perhaps most important, the Filipino nationalists could not be allowed to enter the city, as Jáudenes feared that they would show no mercy to the Spanish defenders. He also did not want to make it appear as if Spain were surrendering to the Filipinos. Thus, Spain and the United States each had its reasons for wanting to keep Aguinaldo's men from entering Manila.

Finally, the two sides agreed that the Spanish would offer a token defense of their outer works but not of the walled city itself. However, neither of the U.S. commanders who were to lead the attack, Generals Greene and MacArthur, had been made aware of the pact because General Merritt feared that if they had known of the arrangements, their respective attacks would have lacked authenticity.

Following expiration of the 48-hour truce, Merritt's forces prepared to move. The axis of their attack would be south to north in two essentially parallel columns. Greene's brigade would advance along the northern flank nearest Manila Bay, while MacArthur's brigade was to move along the southern flank. By prearrangement, Dewey's flagship, the *Olympia*, would fire a few token rounds at the heavy stone walls of Fort San Antonio de Abad before raising the international signal flag calling for Spain's surrender.

On the morning of August 13 amid a heavy rain, reveille was sounded. Following the naval bombardment, directed against Fort San Antonio de Abad as agreed, the American artillery opened fire, and the assault moved forward, with the troops advancing under what had turned into a drenching deluge. The Spanish resistance turned out to be heavier than Merritt had expected although not sufficient to thwart the advance. The Spanish defenders gradually fell back, and Greene moved into the city unopposed to accept the Spanish surrender.

On the right flank MacArthur found the going much tougher, exacerbated by Filipino nationalists determined to be involved in the capture of the city. As MacArthur's troops moved north along the Singalong Road, Spanish infantry positioned in a blockhouse inflicted numerous casualties on a regiment of Minnesotans. MacArthur's biggest challenge, however, was in keeping the nationalists from entering the city. As his troops moved closer to Manila, their ranks became increasingly intermingled with those of the Filipinos, and MacArthur was compelled to have his commanders hold the nationalists back from the city.

By the end of the day, U.S. troops had occupied all of Manila proper, but outside the city, Aguinaldo's troops, angry at being denied entrance, were in an ugly mood. Fortunately, for the Americans, the heavy tropical storm served to help defuse the hostile mob. On August 14, a joint group of American and Spanish officers agreed to a formal capitulation agreement supplementing a preliminary agreement signed by Merritt and Jáudenes the day before.

The capture of Manila yielded some 13,000 Spanish prisoners. In addition, the United States garnered 22,000 stands of small arms, 10 million rounds of ammunition, and 70 pieces of artillery. Because Manila had been seized after the Protocol of Peace had been signed, Spanish negotiators in Paris during the autumn of 1898 argued that the U.S. capture of Manila was not valid, a point that the U.S. peace commissioners countered successfully. With Germany anxious to acquire the Philippines, the McKinley administration decided to take possession of the islands, paying Spain $10 million for them. This decision gave the United States an excellent base in Southeast Asia but brought on the Philippine-American War of 1899–1902 and set up a future confrontation with Japan.

Jerry Keenan

Further Reading
Cosmas, Graham A. *An Army for Empire: The United States Army in the Spanish-American War*. College Station: Texas A&M University Press, 1994.
Linn, Brian McAllister. *The Philippine War, 1899–1902*. Lawrence: University Press of Kansas, 2000.
Musicant, Ivan. *Empire by Default: The Spanish-American War and the Dawn of the American Century*. New York: Henry Holt, 1998.
Wolff, Leon. *Little Brown Brother: America's Forgotten Bid for Empire Which Cost 250,000 Lives*. New York: Kraus Reprint, 1970.

Siege of Mafeking (October 13, 1899–May 17, 1900)

The siege of Mafeking occurred at the beginning of the Boer War or South African War (1899–1902) and lasted from October 13, 1899, to May 17, 1900. The war took its name from the Dutch word for farmer. The causes of the war were essentially the large number of foreigners (Uitlanders) living in the Boer Republic of the Transvaal and the aspirations of certain leading British imperialists who

A large Boer artillery piece in the siege of Mafeking in 1900 during the Boer War. (The Illustrated London News Picture Library)

wanted to bring the Boer republics of the Transvaal and Orange Free State under British rule and exploit their resources, especially the gold mines.

The British had taken the original Dutch colony at the Cape of Good Hope in 1796 during the Wars of the French Revolution. When the British abolished slavery, some 10,000 Boers left the Cape Colony in 1835–1837 and in the so-called Great Trek moved northward and established the two republics of the Transvaal and the Orange Free State. These were recognized as independent republics in the 1850s, but the British continually harassed the Boers, and there had been some fighting in which the Boers were victorious in the Battle of Majuba Hill in 1881. Gradually, the British largely closed off the Boers from access to the sea.

The discovery of major gold deposits in the Transvaal in 1886 brought a great influx of foreign workers (known to the Boers as Uitlanders), most of them of British nationality. Cecil Rhodes, who became prime minister of the Cape Colony in 1890, and other British imperialists demanded the Uitlanders be allowed citizenship and the right to vote (seen as a step toward annexation). Transvaal president Paul Kruger refused, not willing to see the Boers subsumed by the growing numbers of British.

The Jameson Raid of December 29, 1895–January 2, 1896, arranged by Rhodes and British administrator in Rhodesia Leander Starr Jameson without London's knowledge, saw an armed column invade the Transvaal with the plan to support an Uitlander uprising in Johannesburg. While the operation was a fiasco and Rhodes was forced to resign, the raid convinced Kruger that the British were intent on seizing the Transvaal. In March 1896, the Transvaal and the Orange Free State concluded an alliance.

In 1897 Sir Alfred Milner became high commissioner for British South Africa. Determined to bring all of southern Africa under British rule, he strongly supported Uitlander rights and actively sought war. Talks with Kruger in May and June 1899 failed to resolve differences regarding the residency requirement to enable the Uitlanders to vote.

Despite the division of British politicians on the subject, Kruger was entirely convinced that the British were intent on annexing the Transvaal and was determined to strike first, while the British then had only small forces in South Africa. He sent an ultimatum that the British would certainly reject, giving them 48 hours to reply. The ultimatum did, however, unite politicians in London regarding the Boers.

The Transvaal and Orange Free State declared war on October 12, 1899. The Boers decided that the best defense was to take advantage of their numerical advantage and go on the offense. Boer forces were well equipped with magazine Mauser rifles that employed smokeless powder cartridges, and Krupp and Creusot artillery hastily secured from abroad. They also benefited from excellent intelligence about their adversary and from superior mobility and adroit use of cover and concealment. Their haphazard organization mitigated against sustained offensive operations, however.

The Boers quickly sent against the British an invasion force of 34,000 men, while 20,000 others kept an eye on the native Kaffirs (blacks) and Uitlanders at home. The British then had only 25,000 men in all of southern Africa, but they were not unduly concerned for they did not hold the Boers in high reward militarily. It also took the British four months to assembly an expeditionary force for South Africa.

The Boers were well led and were organized into commandos of mounted riflemen. The British were handicapped by their relative lack of mobility and the fact that most of their forces were in forward positions in Natal in anticipation of their own plans to invade the Transvaal. The Boer war plan was to cut off and surround the British in these positions and force their surrender. This was a double-edged sword, however. While an excellent short-term measure of tying down British resources, as well as potential relief forces, and thus protecting Boer territory from invasion, it also tied down Boer resources and likely prevented a full-scale invasion of Cape Colony.

The Boers went on a short-lived rampage. On October 14, Orange Free State Boer forces under Commandant Cornelius Wessels laid siege to the diamond-mining town of Kimberley in the Cape Colony, where Lieutenant Colonel Robert George Kekewich had command. Then on November 2, Lieutenant General Sir George White allowed himself and most of the British forces in Natal to be besieged at Ladysmith by Transvaal forces under Boer general Petrus Jacobus Joubert.

The British base of Mafeking in northwestern Cape Colony was the first to be besieged, however. Boer general Piet A. Cronjé commanded the Transvaal forces charged with taking that town, where British colonel Robert S. S. Baden-Powell held command. The same day as the Boer declaration of war, October 12, Cronjé's men cut both the Mafeking railroad and telegraph line and the next day brought Mafeking under siege.

Baden Powell had raised two regiments of mounted riflemen in Rhodesia, and in mid-September 1899 he had begun to build defenses at Mafeking, which was located in a precarious position in northwestern Cape Colony close to Boer-controlled areas. Eventually, the town boasted both trenches and gun emplacements along its six-mile perimeter. Anticipating offensive operations with his mobile mounted force, however, Baden-Powell was caught with much of this outside Mafeking when Cronjé arrived with some 8,000 men.

As a local administrative center, Mafeking had considerable stocks of food. During the siege, the defenders numbered some 2,000 men, including local volunteers. Baden-Powell also armed some 300 blacks with rifles. Known as the "Black Watch," they were placed on the town's perimeter. Baden-Powell also established a Cadet Corps of boys aged 12 to 15, said to be the inspiration for the Boy Scouts, which he subsequently founded.

Cronjé concluded that Mafeking was too strongly held to be taken by storm and so settled in for a siege. Later Cronjé was succeeded in command by Boer general J. P. Snyman. The number of Boers taking part in the siege fluctuated wildly (in November 4,000 of them were ordered elsewhere), and Baden-Powell certainly had the capacity of breaking out, at least until his men's horses had to be killed for food. Despite repeated orders to that effect, he remained on the defensive. His sole attack on the besiegers came in the form of sending an armored train with sharpshooters on the Mafeking railway right to the main the Boer camp and then back again. This was made possible by the failure of the Boers to remove the rails. Baden-Powell made adroit use of deception, as in laying in plain sight of Boer spies in the town fake land mines on its approaches.

The siege was notable for frequent cease-fires on Sundays. These were marked by church services and even sports competitions that included cricket matches between teams from the two sides.

Historians Pat Hopkins and Heather Dugmore charge that Baden-Powell reserved scarce rations for whites, causing many African residents of Mafeking to starve to death. In fact, during the war neither the British nor the Boers cared at all about the Africans. It was indeed a "White Man's War" as both the British and Boers were fond of saying, but the blacks paid a terrible price and in the end were the war's chief losers.

Two of the Boer sieges were ended early: Kimberley on February 15 and Ladysmith on February 28, 1900. Mafeking was the last. Finally, British commander Field Marshal Frederick Sleigh, Viscount Roberts, detached a flying column of some 2,000 cavalry and mounted infantry under Major General Bryan T. Mahon and ordered them to Mafeking.

Aware of the approach of the British relief column, the Boers made a final effort to assault Mafeking. Early on May 12, 1900, and guided by a British deserter, 240 Boers succeeded in capturing a police barracks on the outskirts of Mafeking, killing one and taking 29 British prisoners. The Boer commander used a telephone there connected to the British headquarters to boast of the deed to Baden-Powell. The British reacted quickly, however, and with Snyman not supporting the attack, the Boers were defeated. The ensuing firefights cost the British side 12 dead and 8 wounded (most of the casualties being Africans). Boer losses were 60 dead and wounded and an additional 108 taken prisoner.

Five days later, on May 17, the siege was finally lifted. It had claimed 812 British casualties, while the Boers sustained some 2,000. The siege had been widely covered by the British press, and celebrations in British cities on news of the raising of the 217-day siege produced the word "mafficking," meaning wild rejoicing.

The British soon captured the Boer capitals of Johannesburg (Transvaal) and Pretoria (Orange Free State) on May 31 and June 5, 1900, respectively. Britain then annexed both Boer republics. In a major failure, however, Roberts allowed a large Boer force to escape from Pretoria, believing that once their capital had been taken the Boers would give up. Instead, the Boers went over to guerrilla warfare. Some 20,000 Boers remained in the fight, attacking isolated British units and raiding into Cape Colony. By January 1901, the British had 200,000 men (including 140,000 regulars) in southern Africa, but fighting continued. Ultimately, the British committed some 450,000 men against a Boer force that never exceeded 88,000.

New British commander General Herbert Kitchener introduced concentration camps where Boer civilian families were relocated, with much suffering, to prevent them from supporting those still in the fight, while British forces destroyed the Boer farms. This policy produced some 28,000 civilian deaths, mostly from disease, twice the number of military personnel killed in the war.

The suffering of the Boer families, improved British intelligence, and new pacification tactics to include block houses and barbed wire, and the use of black scouts finally brought an end to the war in 1902 in the Treaty of Vereeniging in May 1902, by which the British agreed to share political power with the Boers. In 1910 Cape Colony became the Union of South Africa.

Hailed as a hero, Baden-Powell returned to Britain in 1903 and was promoted to major general, then the youngest in the British Army.

Spencer C. Tucker

Further Reading

Gardner, Brian. *Mafeking: A Victorian Legend*. London: Cassell, 1966.

Hopkins, Pat, and Heather Dugmore. *The Boy: Baden-Powell and the Siege of Mafeking*. London: New Holland Books, 1999.

Willan, Brian. "The Siege of Mafeking." In *The South African War: The Anglo-Boer War, 1899–1902*, edited by Peter Warwick and S. B. Spies, 150–155. Harlow, Essex, UK: Longman, 1980.

Yorke, Edmund. *Battle Story Mafeking 1900*. Stroud, Gloucestershire, UK: The History Press, 2014.

Young, Filson. *The Relief of Mafeking: How It Was Accomplished by Mahon's Flying Column, with an Account of Some Earlier Episodes in the Boer War of 1899–1900*. Salt Lake City, UT: Project Gutenberg, 2007.

Siege of Peking (Beijing) (June 20–August 14, 1900)

In the nineteenth century, China suffered a series of catastrophic defeats at the hands of the Western powers and Japan. During the so-called Opium War of 1840–1842, the British defeated Chinese imperial forces. Britain had initiated the war when Chinese authorities sought to halt imports of opium from India. China was forced to cede Hong Kong to Britain and to open treaty ports in Guangzhou (then Canton) in Kwangtung Province, Xiamen (Hsian-men) in Fujian (Fukien) Province, Fuzhou (Foochow) in Fujian Province, Ningbo (Ningpo) in Zhejiang (Chekiang) Province, and Shanghai in Jiangsu (Kiangsu) Province. Other countries, including the United States, demanded and received similar commercial concessions.

The Chinese soon found themselves second-class citizens in their own land. Foreigners enjoyed special privileges, including the right of extraterritoriality whereby Europeans accused of crimes against Chinese could be tried in European courts. Chinese culture was also under attack from foreign Christian missionaries.

These circumstances gave rise to Chinese nationalist societies, which the imperial government of Empress Cixi (Tz'u-hsi) encouraged. Among them was the Society of Harmonious Fists, dubbed the "Boxers" by Westerners because of its martial arts exercises. This movement, which formed in Shandong and southern Chihli (now Hebei Province), soon spread to the capital, encouraged by the antiforeign Manzhu (Manchu) clique at court.

With the Boxers came increasing violence against foreigners in China, and members of the foreign diplomatic corps in Peking (now Beijing) demanded that the imperial government take action. The empress promised to act but nevertheless allowed the Boxers to carry out antiforeign demonstrations in Peking. Alarmed, the diplomats then requested that crewmen be sent to Beijing from their national naval vessels stationed at Dagu (Taku). These detachments arrived in the Chinese capital at the end of May and in early June 1900, although a larger allied contingent from Tianjin was forced to turn back. Troops of the Chinese Imperial Army under General Rong Lu (Jung-lu) also arrived at Beijing.

On June 19, Cixi demanded that the foreign legations relocate to Tianjin. The diplomatic corps requested additional time and adequate military escort. The next day, however, German minister Baron von Kettler was killed in Beijing by Boxers, and the foreign legations found themselves under siege. That same day the Chinese government declared war on the foreign governments for the Western seizure of the Dagu forts on June 17.

All the legations were located in the same area of Beijing, within the so-called Tatar City section. The ministers of Austria-Hungary, Belgium, France, Germany, Great Britain, the Netherlands, Spain, and the United States met and decided to abandon the legations belonging to Belgian and Netherlands, which were deemed too difficult to defend, and to withdraw into a quadrilateral formed by the remainder. All the women and children were collected at the large British legation, which was less exposed to attack. Defenders occupied portions of the Great Wall, which ran nearby, to observe Chinese troop movements.

Another gathering point for foreigners, isolated from the legations, was Beidang (Pei-Tang), the residence and cathedral of the Catholic archbishop of Beijing. It was defended by French sailors and some Italians. A number of European men living in Beijing as well as some Chinese assisted in the defense at Beidang and the legations. The defenders dug trenches and constructed barricades. They included only 364 foreign troops: 72 Russians, 61 British marines, 51 Italians,

50 U.S. sailors, 45 French, 31 Italians, 30 Austrians, and 24 Japanese. They had only small arms, one machine gun, and several small artillery pieces.

On the afternoon of June 20, with the deadline for the diplomats' departure past, a force that ultimately reached some 18,000 regular Chinese troops surrounded the legation quadrilateral. These regular forces opened fire on the legations, in effect making common cause with the Boxers, who were led by Dong Fuxiang (Tuan Fu-hsiang). The Chinese attacks, most of which were carried out by the Boxers, were only half-hearted, however. Then in mid-July a truce was arranged, and the empress sent in several wagons of food to the besieged, who were by then fast running out of provisions.

On August 9, the regular Chinese forces departed, leaving the siege to the Boxers, a sign that an allied relief column from Tianjin (taken by the allies in July) was on the way. Dong's troops tried to stop the foreign force from reaching Beijing during the night of August 11–12 but were rebuffed. The relieving troops were in two columns: 7,000 Japanese in the first column and 10,000 British, French, German, Italian, Russian, and U.S. troops (the first time since the American Revolutionary War that American troops had participated in an allied operation) in the second column. Russian artillery battered down the heavy gate of the Chinese City sector of Beijing and entered on the night of August 13–14. Early on the morning of August 14, the British made contact with the legations. On August 15, the imperial court fled to Sian (Xi'an) in Shaanxi (Shensi) Province, where in December it accepted allied demands.

Elsewhere, Chinese killed at least 231 foreigners, mostly missionaries, in Shanxi (Shansi). Russians at Blagoveshchensk drove thousands of Chinese to their deaths in the Amur River in response to Chinese artillery fire from across that waterway. The Russians also seized southern Manchuria. German troops, who had arrived late at Beijing but were encouraged by Kaiser Wilhelm II to take reprisals, mounted three dozen punitive missions.

Repercussions for China were severe. Under the terms of the Boxer Protocol of September 1901, the imperial government was forced to apologize, punish 96 officials, allow a larger legation quarter, raze all forts, and make payment from customs collections to the foreign governments of more than 450 million taels with interest (in gold, some $740 million). Chinese leaders now realized the absolute necessity of carrying out reforms in education, the economy, and the military.

Spencer C. Tucker

Further Reading

Bodin, Lynn E. *The Boxer Rebellion.* London: Osprey, 1996.

Elleman, Bruce A. *Modern Chinese Warfare, 1785–1989.* New York: Routledge, 2001.

Esherick, Joseph W. *Origins of the Boxer Rebellion.* Berkeley: University of California Press, 1987.

Fleming, Peter. *The Siege at Peking: The Boxer Rebellion.* New York: Dorsey, 1990.

Gernet, Jacques. *A History of Chinese Civilization.* New York: Cambridge University Press, 1994.

Martin, Christopher. *The Boxer Rebellion.* London: Abelard-Schuman, 1968.

O'Connor, Richard. *The Boxer Rebellion.* London: Robert Hale, 1974.

Siege of Port Arthur (February 8, 1904–January 2, 1905)

Port Arthur (present-day Lüshunkou, China) was the site of both an important naval battle and a siege during the Russo-Japanese War (1904–1905). Japan was victorious in its 1894–1895 war with China, and in the Treaty of Shimonoseki the Japanese forced the Chinese to cede the island of Taiwan (Formosa) and the Liaodong (Liaotung) Peninsula in southern Manchuria, pay a heavy indemnity, and recognize Korea as an independent kingdom, in effect under Japanese control.

The Russian government strongly opposed Japan's acquisition of territory on the Asiatic mainland. Japan's acquisition of Korea gave it control over both sides of the Tsushima Strait, the southern outlet of the Sea of Japan, upon which the Russian Pacific port of Vladivostok was located. Moreover, Japanese control of Port Arthur and the Liaodong Peninsula would prevent Russia from obtaining a warm-water port in that region.

Assisted by France and Germany, Russia forced Japan to renounce its claim to the Liaodung Peninsula. Russia then concluded a treaty of friendship with China and secured the right to build the Chinese Eastern Railway across Manchuria to Vladivostok, a much more direct route than the circuitous Trans-Siberian Railway. In 1898 Russia also secured a 25-year lease on about 500 square miles of territory—including part of the land surrendered by Japan in 1895—at the end of the Liaodong Peninsula and the right to construct a branch rail line to connect it with the Chinese Eastern Railway at Harbin. The Japanese were furious at this development.

The Russians subsequently improved the harbor of Dalny (Dairen) for commercial use and began construction on a powerful fortress and a naval base at Port Arthur as well. Russia now had a warm-water outlet for its Trans-Siberian Railway. It also appeared that Manchuria would invariably come under Russian control.

In January 1902, Japan secured an alliance with Britain. The terms of the alliance provided for the "independence" of China and Korea but recognized Japan's special interests in the latter. The terms also provided that if either power became involved in war with a third power, the other would remain neutral. If another power or powers should join the war, however, the allied power was committed to joining the conflict. Japan then attempted to reach an agreement with Russia in 1903. St. Petersburg delayed making a definite reply, however, and Tokyo broke off diplomatic relations. The Japanese believed with considerable justification that Russia was seeking to postpone a war until it was ready. Czar Nicholas II and his advisers were certain that Japan would never dare to initiate hostilities, but the Japanese decided not to wait.

For Japan, the necessary prerequisite to a land war in Manchuria was control of the seas. Aside from a few warships at Chemulpo (Inchon), Korea, the Russians had at Vladivostok 4 first-class cruisers and 17 torpedo boats. Their most powerful ships—7 battleships and 4 cruisers—were at Port Arthur. The Japanese cut the telegraph cable between Port Arthur and Korea early on February 7, 1904. Thus, the Russians did not know of the earlier Japanese attack on Chemulpo without declaration of war.

Wrecked Russian warships in Port Arthur in December 1904 as a consequence of the Japanese siege of that important Russian base during the 1904–1905 Russo-Japanese War. (Library of Congress)

At 11:50 p.m. local time on February 8, Japanese Combined Fleet commander Admiral Tomgom Heihachirom launched an attack against Port Arthur, sending in his destroyers in a surprise torpedo attack. The Russian squadron had just returned to Port Arthur after a period at sea and was outside the harbor. The Russian battleships *Retvizan* and *Tsarevitch* and the cruiser *Pallada* were all hit and badly damaged. The *Pallada* grounded near the harbor; both battleships attempted to make it to the dockyards but grounded in the channel.

Near noon the next day Tomgom brought up six battleships, five armored cruisers, and four protected cruisers to shell the Russian ships, shore batteries, and town from long range. The Russian ships, now anchored next to the forts, and the shore batteries replied. Only one Russian ship, the cruiser *Novik,* ventured out and fired a torpedo in the direction of the Japanese ships. Most of the Japanese vessels were hit by Russian shells, and Tōgō reluctantly ordered his ships to withdraw after about an hour.

Four Russian ships were damaged in the exchange, but all eventually returned to duty, as did the three ships badly damaged in the torpedo attack. The Japanese had suffered considerable damage to four battleships and a cruiser, among others. The Japanese sustained 132 casualties and the Russians sustained 150 casualties. There were no pangs of conscience in Tokyo over the surprise attack, and only on February 10 did Japan formally declare war on Russia.

Frustrated at their inability to destroy the Russian naval forces at Port Arthur in their initial attack and to safeguard the lines of communication to Korea, the Japanese adopted attrition tactics at Port Arthur. On March 8, however, Russian vice admiral S. Ossipovitch Makarov took command there and initiated a series of sorties to harass the Japanese cruisers while avoiding contact with Tōgō's battleships. Both sides also laid mines, but Makarov was killed and the battleship *Petropavlovsk* was lost when he ran it over a known Japanese minefield. In all, the Russians lost one battleship and the Japanese lost two battleships to mines off Port Arthur.

The Japanese brought Port Arthur under siege from the land as well. Lieutenant General Baron Anatoli M. Stoessel commanded the Russian Port Arthur garrison of 40,000 men and more than 500 guns. During May 5–19, 1904, the Japanese Second Army, commanded by General Oku Yasukata, landed at Pitzuwu, 40 miles northeast of Port Arthur. The Japanese moved south but were halted at the Port Arthur outpost of Nanshan Hill. This key terrain feature guarded the entrance of the Liaodong Gulf and was held by 3,000 Russians.

On May 25, however, the Japanese flanked the Russian left by wading through the surf and in heavy fighting forced the garrison to withdraw. Japanese casualties were 4,500 of 30,000 men engaged, while the Russians lost 1,500 men. The capture of Nanshan Hill uncovered the port of Dairen, which became a Japanese base. Port Arthur was now cut off from the land side.

Japanese general Nogi Maresuke (who had captured Port Arthur from the Chinese in 1894) now concentrated his Third Army at Dalny. While the Second Army moved north to counter a Russian offensive, the Third Army took over the investment of Port Arthur. Three defensive lines, some of them incomplete, protected Port Arthur from the north. Stoessel, however, had insufficient food stocks for a protracted siege.

The Japanese steadily built their strength to more than 80,000 men and some 474 guns. On June 23, with his damaged ships repaired, Admiral Vilgelm Vitgeft, Makarov's successor, sortied. Tōgō, with only four battleships and a reduced cruiser force, prepared to meet the Russians, but Vitgeft returned to Port Arthur. His second attempt resulted in the August 10 Japanese victory in the Battle of the Yellow Sea in which Vitgeft was killed. Only one Russian cruiser was sunk in the battle; most of the ships made it back to Port Arthur.

The land fighting continued. On August 7–8, the Japanese attacked the hills constituting the Russian outer defenses and were victorious in hard fighting. Three weeks later, during August 19–24, the Japanese struck again. Much of the fighting was at night, with Russian searchlights and flares illuminating the attackers and machine guns exacting a frightful toll. The Japanese lost 15,000 men. Russian losses were only 3,000 men.

Nogi now called for heavy siege guns and resorted to systematic siege operations, sapping closer to the Russian positions. His third assault of September 15–30 was partially successful but failed to take its chief objective of 203 Meter Hill, the key point in the Russian defenses. In October 1904, the Japanese began shelling Port Arthur with 500-pound projectiles from 19 10.9-inch (28-centimeter) howitzers. During October 30–November 1, the Japanese mounted their fourth assault, concentrating on 203 Meter Hill, but they were again defeated with heavy losses. A fifth attack on November 26 was also repulsed at a cost of 12,000 Japanese casualties.

Finally, after an assault during November 27–December 5 that claimed 11,000 Japanese, the attackers at last took 203 Meter Hill. It overlooked the harbor only 4,000 yards away, and its fall sealed the fate of the Russian fleet. The day after taking 203 Meter Hill, the Japanese opened fire on the Russian ships in the harbor. Japanese land assaults continued against the remaining Russian forts as well; the last fell on January 1, 1905. Stoessel surrendered his 10,000 starving men the next day.

The Japanese captured considerable stocks of arms and foodstuffs, a shocking testimony to Stoessel's mismanagement. Japanese losses in the siege were 59,000 killed, wounded, or missing and another 34,000 sick. The Russians suffered 31,000 casualties.

The Russian defeat at Port Arthur and in the battles at Mukden and Tsushima led to the Treaty of Portsmouth that transferred Port Arthur to Japan.

Spencer C. Tucker

Further Reading
Connaughton, Richard Michael. *The War of the Rising Sun and the Tumbling Bear: A Military History of the Russo-Japanese War, 1904–1905.* London: Routledge, 1991.

Walder, David. *The Short Victorious War: The Russo-Japanese Conflict, 1904–5.* New York: Harper & Row, 1973.

Warner, Denis, and Peggy Warner. *The Tide at Sunrise: A History of the Russo-Japanese War, 1904–1905.* New York: Charterhouse, 1974.

Westwood, J. N. *A New Look at the Russo-Japanese War, 1904–1905.* Boulder, CO: NetLibrary, 1999.

Siege of Liège (August 5–16, 1914)

The Belgian city of Liège is located on the Meuse River and is the gateway to Belgium for any force invading from Germany. The city dominates the narrow gap between the so-called Limburg Appendix to the north and the Ardennes Forest to the south, guarding access to the rich Brabant Plain. The Meuse itself is also a formidable barrier; it is some 200 yards wide at Liège, with steep banks and boggy lowlands.

At the beginning of the twentieth century, German Army chief of staff Generaloberst Alfred von Schlieffen recognized that if a general European war occurred, Germany would have to fight both France and Russia. Because France had the more powerful military, Schlieffen planned to concentrate the bulk of German military resources against that country to defeat it quickly and then turn against the Russian Army, which would be slower to mobilize. In Schlieffen's view, the best way to defeat France quickly was a broad-front invasion from Belgium, and the key was the reduction of Liège.

In the crisis that followed the assassination of Austrian archduke Franz Ferdinand in Sarajevo by Serbian terrorists on June 28, 1914, Russia mobilized its military in support of Serbia in the hope of bluffing down Austria-Hungary. This

> **"Big Bertha"**
>
> The 420 mm German siege howitzer, known as "Big Bertha" was officially designated the 42 cm Mörser [mortar] L/14. The gun's nickname came from Bertha Krupp von Bohlen und Halbach, daughter of its manufacturer Alfred Krupp. Although designated a mortar, it was actually a howitzer. It fired a 420 mm round weighing 1,719 pounds with a high degree of accuracy out to a range of 10,253 yards. Its specially designed projectile had a hardened conical nose with the fuse at the base of the round, which made it especially effective for penetrating reinforced ferroconcrete fortifications.
>
> Weighing 93,720 pounds in action, the Big Bertha had to be moved in five separate pieces and assembled on site using a crane carried by one of the prime mover tractors. At just more than 19 feet, its relatively short barrel was only 14 times as long as the diameter of the bore. Only two Big Berthas were manufactured and fielded. Together they comprised a unit called Kurz Marin Kanone Batterie Nr. 3, manned by 200 gunners and 80 mechanics and drivers. Big Bertha's relatively short range made it increasingly vulnerable to Allied counter battery fire as the war progressed, and by 1917 the Germans withdrew these guns from service.
>
> **David T. Zabecki**

triggered the German war plan and that country's declarations of war against Russia on August 1 and France on August 3. Consequently, Liège became the first major German military objective in the war.

The city of Liège was ringed by 12 forts, 6 large and 6 smaller forts, located on high ground and divided equally between each bank of the river. The forts were four to five miles from the center of Liège and two to three miles from each other. Built in the 1880s at the insistence of King Leopold II and under the supervision of military architect Henri Brialmont, the forts (and those built at the same time at Namur) were sufficiently strong to resist shells from any weapon of the time. They had extensive underground chambers and were capped with massive concrete crowns. They were also surrounded by wide and deep dry moats defended by earthen breastworks.

The dozen forts contained a total of 400 artillery pieces, the largest being 210-millimeter (mm) howitzers. These large guns were mounted in rotating, disappearing cupola turrets. Between the forts, Belgian general Gérard Mathieu Leman's 3rd Infantry Division manned field fortifications. Three regiments garrisoned the forts themselves, the largest of which each held 400 men. In all, the Belgians had some 25,000 troops at Liège. They hoped to hold the Germans as long as possible in the area before and between the forts and then withdraw toward other forces forming on the Gette River, 30 miles to the west.

The Germans planned to knock out the forts and capture Liège within three days. Chief of the German General Staff generaloberst Helmuth von Moltke ("Moltke the Younger") hoped to defeat France in only 39 days, so he could tolerate no delay here. The Germans hoped to accomplish this while their First Army and Second Army were still completing their concentration. These two armies would then pass on either side of Liège on their way to France. For the reduction of Liège, the Germans allocated 60,000 German troops from Generaloberst Karl von

Bülow's Second Army, consisting of the 2nd and 4th Infantry divisions (a total of six infantry brigades) and the 9th Cavalry Division. General der Infanterie Otto von Emmich commanded this attacking force, designated the Army of the Meuse. Generalmajor Erich Ludendorff, the staff officer who had developed the German plan, accompanied the attackers as liaison between Emmich and Bülow.

The Germans advanced cautiously. Although the Belgians blew up the main bridges over the Meuse, the attackers crossed north of the city at Visé, arriving in the wooded hills near the forts on August 4. They encountered unexpectedly strong Belgian resistance. During the night of August 5, Emmich's troops attacked but sustained heavy losses for little or no progress. That same night, German Army zeppelin *LZ.6* dropped converted artillery shells rigged as bombs on Liège. It was the first strategic bombing raid in history, but it was also ineffective.

Gradually the weight of German numbers and superior firepower told, and the Belgian 3rd Division began to withdraw. Some of the defenders fell back on the resisting forts; most retired to the riverbanks and the city itself. Crossing the Meuse at Visé and Lixhe to the north of Liège, the Germans moved between Forts Barchon and Pontisse, surrounding them.

After two days of fierce fighting, on August 6 Liège itself came under fire, and conditions for civilians in the city became increasingly difficult. At 7:30 a.m. on the 6th, Leman ordered his 3rd Division to withdraw on the Gette. The last troops departed the nearly surrounded city the next day. At 6:00 a.m. on August 7, the German 14th Brigade entered Liège with the help of a Belgian traitor. The Germans soon reached the Belgian headquarters, but Leman had escaped to Fort Loncin. Although Liège itself had surrendered, the forts kept up constant artillery fire on the roads that would have to be taken by the Second Army. The Germans therefore could not continue their advance without first taking the forts.

On August 8 after four bloody and frustrating days of infantry assaults against the forts, German heavy artillery, brought up expressly for that purpose, opened up. Fort Brachon came under fire from heavy 305 mm (12-inch) Skoda siege howitzers and surrendered at 4:30 p.m. that same day. The Germans then moved the heavy howitzers into position to fire on Fort d'Evegnée. They opened fire on it the evening of August 10, and the fort surrendered the next morning. From August 12 even heavier, although less mobile, guns became available in German 420 mm (16.5-inch) Krupp "Big Bertha" howitzers. Fort Pontisse was the first victim of their 1,700-pound shells. One after another, the forts were destroyed by the German heavy weapons.

Conditions inside the forts were appalling: ventilation was soon inadequate, shells destroyed plumbing and released sewer gases, water was scarce, and concussions from the huge explosions took a heavy toll on the defenders. Three-quarters of the garrison at Pontisse died before the wounded officer left in command surrendered it on August 13. That same day Embourg and Chaudfontaine fell. At the latter fort, hundreds of defenders died when a German shell struck its magazine.

The remaining forts fell one after the other. Leman commanded at Fort Loncin until August 15, when its magazine exploded, wounding all the defenders. The Germans carried Leman unconscious from the debris. The two remaining forts of Hollogne and Flemalle surrendered on August 16. On August 17, the Second Army implemented the next stage of the German war plan.

The siege of Liège marked the rise of Ludendorff. He had taken a leading role in the siege and secured the surrender of the city. By 1916 Ludendorff was the first quartermaster general of the German Army, its de facto chief of staff with a major say over military operations. The fall of Liège also convinced many observers that forts could not withstand concerted attack. This led French Army commander General Joseph J. C. Joffre to remove artillery from the Verdun fortress complex and send it elsewhere, with unfortunate consequences for the French in February 1916. Finally, Belgian resistance at Liège and throughout the country may have delayed the German timetable by only a few days, but this was crucial given the tight time requirements of the Schlieffen Plan. Widespread German atrocities in Belgium also provided the Allied side with both an example and a cause.

Spencer C. Tucker

Further Reading
Gliddon, Gerald. *1914*. Stroud, Gloustershire, UK: Sutton, 1997.
Hilditch, A. Neville. *The Stand of Liège*. London: Oxford University Press, 1915.
Tuchman, Barbara W. *The Guns of August*. New York: Macmillan, 1962.

Siege of Qingdao (August 23, 1914–November 7, 1914)

The only major World War I land battle to occur in East Asia, the siege of Qingdao (Tsingtao), pitted Japan against Germany. The siege also marked the first time that a unit of the British Army fought under non-European command.

Between 1897 and 1913, Germans built from scratch a European-style fortress city on the tip of China's Shandong (Shantung) Peninsula. Located halfway between Tianjin (Tientsin) in Hobei (Hopeh) Province and Shanghai in Jiangsu (Kiangsu) Province, Qingdao commanded the entrance to Kaiochow Bay, the principal German Navy base in the Pacific.

Qingdao had extensive port facilities, including one of the largest dry docks in the world. The city was defended by a ring of small sea forts around the lower end of the peninsula, anchored by a major fort on the bay side and another on the Yellow Sea side. The main forts mounted 210 mm and 240 mm guns in revolving turrets.

Remembering all too well the Russian experience at Port Arthur (called Lushang by the Chinese) during the 1904–1905 Russo-Japanese War, the Germans also constructed land defenses to thwart any ground attack from China. Qingdao's main defenses were set into two ranges of low hills that spanned the peninsula above the city. Four miles from the city, the inner defensive line was based on powerful Fort Bismarck in the center, supported by a fort at either end of the line. Fort Bismarck was armed with 280 mm howitzers and 210 mm guns in reinforced concrete casemates, while the two flank forts had 105 mm and 120 mm guns in open batteries. Interspersed between the forts, the Germans placed some 90 guns, ranging in size from 37 mm to 90 mm.

The far weaker outer line was 8 miles above the city, where the peninsula was 12 miles wide. Unfortunately for the Germans, the Qingdao garrison was never large enough to man both defensive lines adequately. The key terrain on the outer line, 1,200-foot-high Prince Heinrich Hill on the southern flank, was never sufficiently fortified. Between the two lines of forts, the German intermediate defensive zone in the flat, marshy Haipo (Hai P'o) River Valley contained five reinforced concrete redoubts, each with a garrison of about 200 troops.

Japan had signed an alliance with Great Britain in 1902, and the leaders in Tokyo saw in World War I an opportunity to eject Germany from East Asia. On August 15, 1914, using the justification of the Japanese-British alliance, Japan issued an ultimatum to the Germans in Qingdao. They had until August 23 to evacuate and abandon the colony without compensation.

Qingdao's governor, German Navy captain Alfred Meyer-Waldeck, rejected the ultimatum and prepared for a siege as the Germans began to evacuate nonessential civilians. Even before the Japanese ultimatum, on August 4 the German cruiser squadron under the command of Vice Admiral Maximilian von Spee departed Qingdao for the safety of open waters. Spee did not wish to repeat the mistake the Russians had made 10 years earlier in allowing their ships to be bottled up at Port Arthur.

Even after calling in German reservists from all over Asia, Meyer-Waldeck had only about 4,600 troops. His sole remaining naval units were the obsolete Austrian cruiser *Kaiserin Elizabeth*, the torpedo boat *S-90*, and five small gunboats. His air force consisted of one observation balloon and one Rumpler Taube monoplane, piloted by German Navy lieutenant Gunther Plüschow.

Believing themselves obligated to support the Japanese operation, the British sent the old predreadnought *Triumph* and a token land force consisting of the 2nd Battalion, South Wales Borders from Tianjin, and a half battalion of the 36th Sikhs. British ground troops were under the command of Brigadier General Nathaniel Barnardiston, who was outraged at being the first British commander to serve in the field under a non-European commander.

On September 2, the Japanese ground force, commanded by Lieutenant General Kamio Mitsuom, began coming ashore at Longkou (Lungkow) Bay, some 100 miles north of Qingdao. By the time the Japanese were ready to mount their main attack, they had more than 50,000 troops ashore, with another 10,000 in reserve offshore. The 24th Heavy Artillery Brigade alone had in excess of 100 guns and howitzers larger than 120 mm. The German defenders were outnumbered at least 13 to 1.

On September 28, the Japanese attacked and captured Prince Heinrich Hill, and the rest of the outer defensive line fell within hours. Continuing the fight from the intermediate defensive zone, the German artillery put up a stiff and effective resistance. On October 7, though, the sole German observation balloon broke loose of its mooring and drifted to sea. From that point on, the German artillery was firing blind.

It took the Japanese most of October to move their heavy artillery forward for the attack on the intermediate defensive zone. Most of the interim fighting took place at sea, with the German coastal batteries exchanging fire with the Japanese fleet in addition to the small handful of German fighting ships carrying out hit-and-run raids. On October 17, the torpedo boat *S-90* managed to sink the minelayer *Takashio*, with the loss of 250 Japanese sailors.

On October 31, Japanese heavy artillery commenced firing on Qingdao itself. Japanese ground forces simultaneously began attacking the intermediate defensive zone using classic siege techniques. By November 1, Meyer-Waldeck knew that the end was near, and he ordered the systematic destruction of anything in Qingdao that might be useful to the Japanese.

By November 5, Japanese artillery fire had neutralized almost all the German minefields and wire entanglements, and the German artillery was almost out of ammunition. Early on November 6 under orders from Meyer-Waldeck, Lieutenant Plüschow loaded Qingdao's war diaries and other secret papers into his monoplane and headed for neutral Chinese territory. Plüschow eventually made it back to Germany.

The last German position surrendered at 9:30 a.m. on November 7. The operation had cost the Japanese 1,445 killed and 4,200 wounded. The British lost 14 killed and 61 wounded. Despite the massive pounding they had taken from both sea- and land-based heavy artillery, the Germans suffered only 200 killed and 500 wounded.

As a consequence of their victory here, at the 1919 Paris Peace Conference the Japanese were able to secure the former German cession of the Shandong peninsula, a decision bitterly opposed by China. The siege is also significant as one of history's last large-scale actions involving coastal artillery. It also was one of the first major battles in which air, land, and sea power all combined to play key and mutually supporting roles. Despite its relatively high casualty rate, the Japanese military demonstrated a mastery of joint operations far beyond the capability of most armies of 1914.

David T. Zabecki

Further Reading

Burdick, Charles B. *The Japanese Siege of Tsingtao*. Hamden, CT: Archon, 1976.

Edgerton, Robert B. *Warriors of the Rising Sun: A History of the Japanese Military*. New York: W. W. Norton, 1997.

Hoyt, Edwin P. *The Fall of Tsingtao*. London: A. Barker, 1975.

Jones, Jefferson. *The Fall of Tsingtau: With a Study of Japan's Ambitions in China*. Boston: Houghton Mifflin, 1915.

Siege of Przemyśl (September 16, 1914–March 22, 1915)

Przemyśl was the longest siege of World War I and a major defeat for Austria-Hungary. This powerful Austro-Hungarian fortress in Galicia controlled the San River and a natural passage through the Carpathian Mountains, Przemyśl had been a fortress town since the eighth century. The Habsburgs converted it to a ring fortress beginning in 1887, and Archduke Franz Ferdinand was a special patron of Przemyśl. Covering over nine square miles and consisting of some 30 smaller forts, bastions, and gates, it was the third-largest fortification in

Europe and, at the beginning of World War I, housed the Austrian Army General Headquarters.

The jewel in the Austro-Hungarian defensive crown, as well as the gateway to Hungary and the key to Galicia, Przemyśl was twice besieged during World War I. It held a garrison of 120,000 men and, supposedly, supplies adequate to withstand a three-year siege. The railway line to Budapest was in any case direct, double-tracked, and capable of carrying heavy fast trains that would enable rapid reinforcement. Chief of the Austro-Hungarian General Staff General of Infantry Franz Conrad von Hštzendorf placed so much faith in Przemyśl that he slept on a field bed in the Zasani Barracks there during the opening days of the war.

Although the Austrian high command intended that Przemyśl would function as a supply depot and rearguard support, the fortress became the launching point for the initial attacks of August 1914. Plagued by uncertainty, the General Staff initially sent several divisions south against Belgrade, only to recall them two days later for use in the northward thrust against Russia.

Imperial railroad officials, already overwhelmed by the logistics of mobilization, routed the troop train only to Przemyśl, mistakenly thinking that the track beyond was incapable of bearing the traffic. The Habsburg troops therefore detrained at the fortress and were marching to the planned attack zones nearly 75 miles forward when they encountered the Russians. When Russian forces pushed the Habsburg armies back in mid-September, the fortress was thus isolated and then was besieged by Russian general Selivanov's Eleventh Army beginning on September 16. The Russians, however, could not take Przemyśl.

Reinforced by Germany's newly created Ninth Army, Conrad set out to rescue Przemyśl in early October. The attack caught the Russian forces as they were repositioning, allowing the Austro-Hungarians to lift the siege of the fortress on October 17, 1914. This success was fleeting, however, as the numerically superior Russians quickly regrouped and drove the Austro-Hungarian forces back across the San, and the Eleventh Army once again invested Przemyśl at the end of the month. The multinational garrison now found itself nearly 50 miles behind enemy lines, with its stores significantly reduced from having provisioned its would-be rescuers and with winter fast approaching.

Not until January 1915 could Conrad even muster the forces to mount a second relief operation. Employing two and a half German infantry divisions and one of cavalry in combination with an equal-sized Austro-Hungarian force, Conrad struck at the center of the Russian line on January 23. The attack rolled forward until bad weather struck. The roads, which had briefly thawed, froze again as a cold front swept over the front lines. Entire bivouacked units froze to death while the offensive stalled. Only after a month of fighting did Conrad's troops take the Carpathian passes that had been the first day's objective.

A second Central Powers offensive launched in mid-February met a similar fate. All told, these two actions cost Conrad 800,000 casualties. Faced with this situation, the defenders of Przemyśl elected to surrender on March 22, 1915, although eyewitnesses reported more than a year's worth of supplies remaining. The Russians took 117,000 prisoners. The Austro-Hungarian forces did explode much of the useful war matériel prior to the surrender, however.

Austro-Hungarian propaganda of the day trumpeted the heroic defense of the bastion. In truth, little fighting took place during the siege. The Russians did not possess sufficient heavy artillery to shell the fortress and could not maneuver what guns they had through the heavy ice and mud. The garrison made only token attempts to break the siege and, according to contemporary reports, appeared indifferent to its capture. Victory at Przemyśl was more a matter of Habsburg ineptitude and internecine rivalry among the troops than anything the Russians did. Observers styled the fall of Przemyśl as a "Second Metz" (in reference to the siege of that French fortress during the Franco-Prussian War of 1870–1871), noting that the Russians now held a splendid base for an advance into Hungary.

On May 2, 1915, however, before the Russians could take advantage of their prize, Conrad launched yet another offensive to retake the fortress. This attack, spearheaded by German troops, carried through to Przemyśl on June 4, and the outnumbered Russians quickly withdrew. They had in any case rendered the fortress largely useless by stripping it of most defensive matériel, including entrenching tools and wire. Much of this had been sold to the local populace.

In November 1918, the fortress became a bone of contention between Ukrainian and Polish partisans. Seven days after the Ukrainian coup d'état of November 3–4, General Wladyslaw Sikorski led the new Polish Army to victory at Przemyśl. His campaign ensured that L'viv (L'vov) and Galicia would become part of the new Polish state.

Timothy C. Dowling

Further Reading

Herwig, Holger H. *The First World War: Germany and Austria-Hungary, 1914–1918.* New York: St. Martin's, 1997.

Materniak, Ireneusz. *Przemyśl, 1914–15.* Warsaw: Altair, 1994.

Sondhaus, Lawrence. *Franz Conrad von Hštzendorf: Architect of the Apocalypse.* Boston: Humanities Press, 2000.

Stone, Norman. *The Eastern Front, 1914–1917.* New York: Scribner, 1975.

Siege of Kut (December 7, 1915–April 29, 1916)

The World War I Ottoman siege of Kut (Al Kumt, Kut-Al-Amara, Kut El Amara) in Mesopotamia ended in a major British military defeat. The great plain of Mesopotamia that comprises present-day Iraq is drained by the Tigris and Euphrates Rivers, which in 1914 provided the region's chief avenues of communication. Military operations in the region were difficult especially in summer, when water had to be transported for both men and horses and temperatures could reach 120°F for as long as 10 hours a day. Sunstroke, heatstroke, diarrhea, malaria, typhoid, yellow fever, and cholera all took their toll on both sides. The area was important to Britain, however, as its new capital ships were dependent on oil from the refinery at Abadan Island, at the head of the Persian Gulf. Baghdad, the largest city of the region, lay 415 miles upriver.

The First Aerial Resupply

In what is believed to be history's first aerial resupply mission, in April 1916 Royal Aircraft Factory B.E.2 and Farman MF.11 Shorthorn aircraft of the Royal Flying Corps' No. 30 Squadron began dropping food and ammunition to the besieged troops at Kut. The squadron reportedly flew 140 sorties to Kut with some 19,000 pounds of cargo. The drops consisted of two 50-pound bags, one slung under each side of the fuselage, and another 25-pound bag attached to the undercarriage. Aircraft flight speed was, however, much reduced owing to the prevailing headwinds and the cargo being carried. The supply aircraft also had to be accompanied by fighters when German aircraft attempted to intercept the operation.

The operation was less than a success. According to a British soldier at Kut, "as often as not their parcels go into the Tigris or into the Turkish trenches!"

Spencer C. Tucker

Prior to the Ottoman Empire's entry into the war, the British sent a reinforced brigade to the mouth of the Shatt al-Arab waterway to protect Abadan. After Britain declared war on the Ottomans and increased its strength to a division, in late November 1914 Indian Army forces moved upriver and took both Basra and Qurna. This also protected the Abadan refinery, which lay 50 miles south.

During the first half of 1915, additional British reinforcements arrived, largely from the Indian Army and commanded from Basra by Indian Army general Sir John E. Nixon. London favored a defensive strategy to protect the oil fields, but before Nixon had left India, the commander of the Indian Army General Sir Beauchamp-Duff counseled an advance on Baghdad up the Tigris.

In May 1915, Nixon ordered Major General Charles V. F. Townshend to carry out a reconnaissance in force. At the head of an Indian division and a cavalry brigade and assisted by a small naval flotilla, on May 31 Townshend routed the Ottomans at Qurna. This easy victory gave the British a false impression of Ottoman military ability.

Townshend's amphibious force continued its advance and on June 3 took Amara (Al Amamrah). Nixon now secured grudging approval from London to continue on to Kut, more than 100 miles farther upriver. Kut fell to the British during September 26–28, but the long march, weather, and low water in the Tigris prevented Townshend from pursuing the Ottomans, the bulk of whom escaped to the north.

Despite the fact that the British river supply line was now twice as long as that of the Ottomans (200 miles to Basra versus only 100 to Baghdad), London authorized Nixon to move against Baghdad if he was satisfied that he possessed sufficient strength for the task. London promised to supply two divisions from France but only to assist with occupation duties. Nixon was not worried; he depreciated Ottoman ability and overestimated the capabilities of his own forces.

Townshend, however, opposed an advance on Baghdad without reinforcements and so informed Nixon, explaining the problems posed by the weather, lack of water, and supply shortages. Townshend required more than 200 tons of supplies a day but, partly from pillage, was receiving only 150 tons. Undeterred, Nixon ordered the offensive to proceed, and in late November Townshend dutifully began to move on Baghdad, supplied by riverboats and improvised camel and donkey transport.

The Ottomans benefited from reinforcements, and during November 22–26, 1915, in the Battle of Ctesiphon, fought on the outskirts of Baghdad, they halted his advance. Townshend lost half the number of men as did Ottoman commander General Nur-al-Din (4,600 to 9,500), but unlike Townshend, Nur-al-Din continued to receive additional manpower. The Ottomans then forced the British to fall back.

On December 3, following an epic retreat, Townshend's exhausted troops arrived back at Kut. Townshend wired Nixon that he had one month's full rations for his British troops, two months' worth for the Indians, and plenty of ammunition. Nixon responded that he would make every effort to relieve Townshend and hoped to accomplish this within two months. Nixon ordered Townshend to send ahead his cavalry and as many vessels as possible. Townshend, however, informed Nixon that within two months he would be surrounded by six Ottoman divisions. Townshend believed that it would be best if he retreated to Ali Gharbi, but Nixon ordered him to stay where he was; at Kut he would be tying down superior numbers of Ottoman troops.

By December 7, the Ottomans had closed the ring around Kut, and the siege had begun. In January 1916, Nixon gave up his command, ostensibly for health reasons, and was succeeded by Lieutenant General Sir Percy Lake. That same month, the two Indian divisions arrived from France. Under Major General Fenton J. Aylmer, they tried to reach Kut but were halted by the Ottomans. The steamer *Julnar* tried to run the blockade but was taken by the Ottomans when it became trapped in wire stretched across the river by the besiegers. British aircraft also dropped bags of food to the besieged garrison.

In March, Aylmer's successor, Major General George F. Gorringe, attempted a surprise attack on the south bank of the Tigris. The Ottoman Sixth Army, now led

Damage to the interior of the bazaar at Kut in Mesopotamia (present-day Iraq) during the successful Ottoman Army siege of British forces there from December 7, 1915, to April 29, 1916, in what proved to be a major setback for the British Empire's plans in the Middle East. (National Archives)

by German Field Marshal Colmar von der Goltz, repulsed it. The relieving forces suffered some 23,000 casualties while trying to rescue the 13,000 trapped men. At the same time, the Russians mounted a half-hearted relief operation of their own from northwestern Persia, but it soon bogged down.

In Kut, food was in short supply. Townshend made an effort to ransom the garrison, offering the Ottomans £1 million and all the artillery in Kut in exchange for paroling the garrison. The Ottomans, however, insisted on unconditional surrender. After destroying as much equipment as possible, Townshend surrendered on April 29. The Ottomans took more than 2,700 British and 6,500 Indian troops prisoner. Although Townshend was treated well, nearly 5,000 of his men died of mistreatment and starvation before the end of the war. Their successful siege of Kut greatly raised both Ottoman morale and their prestige in the Middle East. A shocked British government now took over direction of the Mesopotamian front, to include reorganizing and greatly strengthening forces there.

Spencer C. Tucker

Further Reading

Barker, A. J. *The Bastard War: The Mesopotamian Campaign of 1914–1918.* New York: Dial, 1967.

Barker, A. J. *Townshend of Kut: A Biography of Major-General Sir Charles Townshend K.C.B., D.S.O.* London: Cassell, 1967.

Braddon, Russell. *The Siege.* New York: Viking, 1970.

Erickson, Edward J. *Ordered to Die: A History of the Ottoman Army in the First World War.* Westport, CT: Greenwood, 2001.

Millar, Ronald William. *Death of an Army: The Siege of Kut, 1915–1916.* Boston: Houghton Mifflin, 1970.

Moberly, F. J. *The Campaign in Mesopotamia, 1914–1918.* 3 vols. Nashville, TN: Battery Press, 1997–1998.

Townshend, Sir Charles V. F. *My Campaign in Mesopotamia.* London: Thornton Butterworth, 1920.

Siege of the Alcázar at Toledo (July 21–September 27, 1936)

On July 17, 1936, with leaders of the Popular Front government of Spain learning of their plans, rightist plotters in the army were forced prematurely to begin their effort to seize power in what became the Spanish Civil War (1936–1939). An important battle early in the conflict was the siege of the Alcázar in Toledo during July 21–September 27, 1936.

The reformist Popular Front had won the recent national elections and was determined to bring Spain into alignment with the rest of western Europe. Those opposing the Republicans sought to preserve the character and traditions of ancestral Spain. As historian Herbert Matthews has put it, the central question of the Spanish Civil War was "whether the Catholic, traditional, agrarian, and centralized rule of the past centuries should continue, or whether the great issues that the

French Revolution had resolved for France and much of the Western world should be accepted. These included democratic government, capitalism, civil freedoms, separation of church and state, and land reform."

The Spanish Civil War was both hard-fought and sanguinary. Both sides were equally ruthless, and there were millions of casualties. Whatever the outcome, the war would have been over earlier had it not been for the intervention of other countries, principally Germany and Italy lining up with the Fascists and the Soviet Union supporting the Republicans.

The Nationalists, or Fascists as they were also known, had some two-thirds of the army and 90 percent of the officers. They also had the support of the Catholic Church, die-hard monarchists, and the conservative old-line families who possessed the bulk of the country's wealth. They also had the Spanish Foreign Legion and the many powerful armies of the paramilitary groups, the Carlists and the Falange.

The government side was known as the Republicans or Loyalists. Led by Spanish president Manuel Azaña Diaz, the Republicans had the navy and most of the air force. It also had strong support from the peasants and workers in the most industrialized part of Spain, the Madrid-Valencia-Barcelona triangle. The loyalties of the middle class were fairly evenly divided.

Nationalist leader General José Sanjurjo y Sacanell was killed in a plane crash on July 20, and leadership devolved to General Francisco Franco, who would emerge as the *Caudillo* (Leader) and the most durable of twentieth-century dictators. Opinions differ as to which side would have won the civil war had it been left to the Spaniards themselves, but certainly the conflict would have been over much more quickly. Foreign military intervention greatly prolonged the suffering and dramatically augmented the death toll.

German and Italian aid came early. German chancellor Adolf Hitler loaned the Nationalist side transport aircraft and fighter escorts, with German crews, to ferry 20,000 of Franco's troops from Morocco to Spain, for Republican control of the navy blocked access by water. Getting these troops to Spain was critical if the Nationalists were to be successful. Italy also sent aircraft and the most men, but German assistance, especially the Kondor Legion that enabled the Fascists to win control of the skies, was critical to the outcome. Soviet aid, while it bought influence and eventually subverted the Republic, was late and never in sufficient quantities to overcome that supplied to the Fascists by Germany and Italy. Unfortunately, the Western democracies remained aloof. Fearful of a general war, British leaders insisted on nonintervention and forced France to act accordingly. It was therefore almost a miracle that the Republicans were able to hold on as long as they did.

At the end of July 1936, however, the Spanish capital city of Madrid remained Republican, thwarting Nationalist plans for a quick coup. Most other major cities also remained loyal. Battles raged everywhere, with atrocities committed by both sides.

The rebels hoped to take Madrid early on, believing that its capture would bring the war to a speedy conclusion. Franco and his Army of Africa now moved north from Seville, where they had been ferried by the Germans. But the Republicans had secured control of the city of Toledo about 45 miles south-southwest of Madrid. However, Nationalists there had barricaded themselves in the large Alcázar (fortress) and were refusing to surrender.

Toledo and the Alcázar were important symbolically to Spaniards. The city had been the capital of the Visigothic Kingdom, and the Spanish monarchs had lived in the Alcázar, built in 1520 on high ground and looming over the city, until it had been abandoned by King Philip II and turned into the Spanish Military Academy. The Alcázar was a formidable fortress structure with 10-foot walls. In 1936 it and the military academy were commanded by Nationalist supporter Colonel José Moscardó Ituarte.

On July 18, Moscardó had ordered the Guardia Civil of the province to Toledo and on July 19 and 20 had rejected efforts by the Republican government in Madrid to secure munitions from the city's arms factory. The government then sent some 8,000 militiamen men south, with seven field artillery pieces and a few small tankettes. They would be aided during the siege by the Republican air force. Unfortunately, the attackers lacked the modern heavy artillery necessary to breach the fortress walls.

On July 21, the Republican force arrived and moved against the arms factory, where 200 Guardia Civil were then located. The latter used the time during surrender negotiations to load trucks with ammunition and remove it to the Alcázar before destroying what they could and withdrawing to the Alcázar.

By July 22, the Republicans controlled most of Toledo and commenced shelling the Alcázar in hopes of inducing its surrender. Throughout the siege, the Nationalist side adopted a passive stance, returning fire only when threatened by attack.

There were now some 1,500 people inside the Alcázar. Moscardó probably commanded 150 officers and noncommissioned officers assigned to the Academy, 650 members of the Guardia Civil, and 7 cadets (the others being on vacation). There were also more than 500 military dependents. In addition, the colonel had taken about 100 civilian hostages, including the provincial governor and his family. The defenders possessed only rifles and a few machine guns and grenades but were now well supplied with ammunition.

On July 23, in what is touted as the most celebrated single incident of the entire war, Republican militia leader in Toledo Candido Cabello talked by telephone with Moscardó inside the Alcázar and informed him that unless he surrendered the fortress within 10 minutes, he would shoot Moscardó's 17-year-old son Luis. Cabello put the boy on the phone, and the colonel told his son that he should commend his soul to God and prepare for a hero's death and shout "Viva Christ the King" and "Viva Spain." "That I can do," Luis replied. The elder Moscardó then informed Cabello that he would never surrender. Later asked for his report of the day, Moscardó replied, "Sin novedad" (Nothing new). The Republicans indeed executed young Moscardó, claiming this occurred on August 23 in reprisal for a Nationalist air raid.

The Republicans first concentrated their fire on the northern side of the fortress, but shelling here failed to achieve the desired results, and from August 14 for five weeks they attacked the House of the Military Government located close to the fortress, mounting 11 separate efforts, all of which were turned back. Had the Republicans been able to take this structure, they would have been able to mass a large number of men only 40 yards from the Alcázar.

On September 9, Moscardó again rejected a demand from an emissary, Spanish Army major Vicente Rojo Lluch, that he surrender. Two days later on Moscardó's request, the Republicans allowed a priest of leftist views into the fortress to baptize two newly born infants. The priest also granted the defenders absolution. That evening Rojo again met with Moscardó and requested the release of the women and children. All the women rejected this, saying that if necessary, they would themselves take up arms in defense of the fortress.

On September 18, the attackers exploded a large mine that they had been preparing for a month. The blast collapsed the tower on the Alcázar's southeast corner and opened a breach in the wall. In the next few hours, the Republicans launched four separate attacks on the breech, employing their tankettes. These met determined resistance and failed.

With most of the outlying structures having been destroyed, on the night of September 21 the defenders abandoned these and concentrated the defense on what remained on the Alcázar itself. Unaware of this, the attackers were slow to occupy the abandoned structures, but in a surprise attack at 5:00 a.m. on September 23 the Republicans gained access to the Alcázar's courtyard. However, the defenders rallied and drove them back. Later that morning, another attack led by a tankette was also defeated. Still, the situation appeared dire, but relief was on the way.

General José Enrique Varela Iglesius had been headed for Madrid when Franco decided on September 21 to divert his forces to Toledo. Franco realized this decision might well cost him Madrid, but he believed that relieving the Toledo garrison was more important from a propaganda standpoint. On September 23, Varela set out, and three days later his men cut the road between Toledo and Madrid some four miles north of Toledo.

On the morning of September 27, before the Nationalists could arrive, the Republicans exploded another mine on the northeast side of the fortress, but their attack here was defeated. At dusk the same day, the Nationalist relief force arrived and entered the Alcázar, which was then in flames. The Moroccan troops massacred all Republicans in Toledo they could find, including the wounded, doctors, and nurses, in San Juan Hospital.

Republican casualties in the siege are unknown, but the Nationalists side claimed 65 dead, 438 wounded, and 22 missing.

The siege of Toledo was important in the course of the war. Although a great propaganda victory for the Nationalists, it did secure additional time for the Republicans to solidify their control of the capital and improve its defenses. Four Nationalists columns under General Emilio Mola y Vidal attacked the capital on November 8 but were repulsed. The city held out, its defenders vowing "No pasaran" (they shall not pass). Madrid's fall on March 28, 1939, marked the end of the long conflict. The Alcázar was rebuilt after the war and today houses the Museum of the Army.

Spencer C. Tucker

Further Reading

Beevor, Antony. *The Battle for Spain: The Spanish Civil War, 1936–1939.* London: Weidenfeld & Nicolson, 2006.

Eby, Cecil D. *The Siege of the Alcazar.* New York: Random House, 1965.

Matthews, Herbert L. *Half of Spain Died: A Reappraisal of the Spanish Civil War.* New York: Charles Scribner's Sons, 1973.

Moss, Geoffrey MacNeill. *The Siege of the Alcázar: A History of the Siege of the Toledo Alcázar, 1936.* New York: Knopf, 1937.

Preston, Paul. *The Spanish Civil War: Reaction, Revolution, and Revenge.* New York: W. W. Norton, 2006.

Thomas, Hugh. *The Spanish Civil War.* Rev. ed. New York: Harper and Brothers, 2001.

Whealey, Robert H. *Hitler and Spain: The Nazi Role in the Spanish Civil War 1936–1939.* Lexington: University Press of Kentucky, 1989.

Siege of Madrid (November 6, 1936–March 31, 1939)

There were other sieges during the Spanish Civil War of 1936–1939, but two dominated: that of the Alcázar in Toledo (July 21–September 27, 1936) and that of Madrid (November 6, 1936–March 31, 1939). The two were related, for the former probably made possible the latter. On July 18, 1936, rightist plotters in the army initiated an effort to seize power. Manuel Azaña Díaz, the elected president of the Spanish Republic, led the Republican or Loyalist side. The Nationalists, also known as the Fascists, were led by General José Sanjurjo y Sacanell, but he died in a plane crash on July 20 while on his way from Lisbon to Burgos and leadership devolved to General Franco, who would emerge as the *Caudillo* (Leader) and the most durable of twentieth-century dictators. General Emilio Mola y Vidal, 1st Duke of Mola, commanded Nationalist forces in northern Spain.

Germany and Italy both furnished aid to the Nationalist side, with the German Kondor Legion probably the key factor in the ultimate Nationalist victory. Although the Popular Front government of Spain was the legitimately elected democratic government, the Western democracies remained aloof. Fearful that the civil war might grow into a world war, Britain followed a policy of nonintervention and insisted that France do likewise. Mexico provided limited aid, but the Soviet Union was the only major nation supporting the Republican side, with that aid paid for by the extensive Spanish gold reserves. Soviet assistance bought it growing political influence and the ultimate communist subversion of the Republic. Given the disparity in foreign assistance to the two sides, it was almost a miracle that the Republicans were able to hold on as long as they did.

At the end of July 1936, Madrid with a population of some 1.2 million, remained Republican, thwarting plans for a quick Nationalist coup. Barcelona also stayed loyal, as did most other major cities. Battles raged everywhere. No quarter was given, with both sides guilty of atrocities. In Republican-held Madrid, self-appointed "chekas" (for the Russian secret police) set about trying real and suspected rebels. Thousands, including many wealthy Spaniards, were summarily executed following drumhead trials. Often this was done simply to seize their money, and some 20,000 Nationalist supporters took refuge in the foreign

> **Origin of the Term "Fifth Column"**
>
> With the Nationalist forces closing on Madrid, General Mola famously remarked to an English journalist that, while four columns were about the attack that city, a "fifth column" of right-wing sympathizers would rise up inside Madrid to assist them. While this did not occur, it was the nonetheless the origin of this term, which denotes subversive activity.
>
> Spencer C. Tucker

embassies in the city. President Azaña and other leaders were appalled by the violence but powerless to stop it. Fascist atrocities during the war were, however, far worse and were a matter of stated policy, a major difference.

The rebels hoped to take Madrid early on, believing that its capture would bring the war to a speedy conclusion. As Mola prepared to move against the city from the north, Franco set his forces, now grown to some 30,000 men, in motion northward from Seville. Superior Nationalist training told and by September 21 part of the force was at Maqueda. Franco then ordered it diverted to the southwest to relieve the siege by some 8,000 Republicans a small Nationalist force in the Alcázar of Toledo, which had begun on July 21. Franco reasoned that the ensuing propaganda would be worth the delay in proceeding against Madrid. Varela's troops arrived at Toledo late on September 27, just as the Alcáza was about to fall, and raised the siege. The delay in the advance on Madrid, however, was vital for its defenders in their efforts to bring in supplies and improve the city's defenses.

Franco now moved against Madrid from the west, while Mola's men proceeded southward toward the capital from Burgos and Valladolid. Both of Mola's columns broke through mountain passes north of Madrid by July 25. The Republicans contested their advance in major fighting, but superior Nationalist training and weaponry told. Nonetheless, the Republicans had purchased additional time for Madrid.

Spanish premier José Giral y Pereira ordered some 60,000 rifles distributed to trade unionists to defend the Republic but few of these were in working condition. Nonetheless, in heavy fighting in Madrid on July 20 Loyalists in the city defeated the Spanish Army garrison of some 2,500 men there that had declared for the Nationalists. Having failed to secure French military assistance, however, Giral resigned on September 4, and Azaña named Socialist Party leader Francisco Largo Caballero, leader of the Spanish Socialist Workers' Party (Partido Socialista Obrero Español, PSOE) as his successor, but with the cost of bringing communists into the government.

In October, Soviet military aid began arriving in Spain, along with Soviet military advisors headed by General Vladimir Gorev. He worked with Spanish general José Miaja Menant, who had remained loyal to the Republic and was its minister of defense. Subsequently, Miaja became commander of the Junta de Defensa de Madrid (Madrid Defense Council). Assisted by Vicente Rojo Lluch as his chief-of-staff and aided by the Soviet advisors, Miaja oversaw the organization and training of the Republican forces in the capital. Very important at this juncture was the arrival at Madrid from Hungary of the first of the International Brigades, units formed of volunteers from other countries that fought on both sides in the war but with most supporting the Republic. On October 29 Nationalist aircraft began bombing Madrid. By November 4, the Nationalist columns from the south and west were all within striking range of Madrid. On their approach, the Republican government fled to Valencia.

The siege of Madrid officially began on November 6. The two southern Nationalist columns attacked the Madrid suburb of Carabanchel on November 8 but were repulsed by the defenders. The Hungarians played a key role in this and in halting another Nationalist attack from the west against the University City sector. Renewed Nationalist attacks gave them control of much of the University City on November 15, however. German aircraft of the newly arrived Kondor Legion bombed Republican positions, and the Nationalists also had light Italian and German tanks. The rallying cry of Republican Madrid was "No pasaran" (they shall not pass).

The Nationalists made a final assault on November 19, but their advance was checked. Having failed to take the city by assault, Franco ordered it to be destroyed by bombing and German bombers pounded the city during November 19–23, killing some 2,000 people in one of the first bombings of a civilian center in warfare. The fighting died down at the end of November, however. Nonetheless, this so-called Battle of Madrid claimed some 5,000 casualties on each side.

On December 13, the Nationalists opened a campaign in the northwest to sever the land connection between Madrid and Corunna. Casualties were heavy on both sides, but by January 15 the Nationalists were successful. They then attempted to cut the road connection with Valencia, but the Republicans prevented this. With fighting elsewhere in Spain, there was a relative lull at Madrid for the next four months.

The Nationalists enjoyed victories elsewhere. Among notable events were the German and Italian bombing of the Basque city of Guernica (April 26, 1937), the Nationalist investment and capture of Bilbao (March 31–June 19, 1937), and the captures of Santandar (August 25) and Gijon (October 21) that completed Nationalist control of northwestern Spain. A week later, the Republican government relocated from Valencia to Barcelona. On December 15, the Republicans opened a large offensive around Teruel in Aragon. Although they captured Teruel on December 19, the poorly equipped and supplied Loyalists were soon brought to a halt. The Nationalists recaptured Teruel on February 22, 1938.

In 1938 the Nationalists tightened their siege of Madrid, with civilians there suffering increasingly from a lack of food, warm clothing, and fuel. Heavy fighting occurred at Madrid in July 1938 when General Mola sought to recover ground lost earlier and drove a wedge into the Republican lines. The Republicans recovered the lost ground, but at high cost. The fighting claimed some 25,000 Republican casualties to only 10,000 for the Nationalists.

On July 25, 1938, the Republicans staked all on a great counteroffensive from Catalonia along the Ebro River, committing 100,000 men of their 400,000-man army in an effort to reestablish communication with Castile and draw the Nationalists away from Valencia. It went well initially, but largely because of

Nationalist (German) air power and artillery it ground to a halt. Nonetheless, it took the Nationalists until November 16 to push the Republican troops back across the Ebro. The failure of their offensive marked the beginning of the end for the Republican cause.

On January 26, 1939, the Nationalists captured Barcelona. They then overran all Catalonia and some 200,000 Loyalist troops fled across the border into France, where they were disarmed and interned. On February 27, the British and French governments recognized the Nationalist government without conditions.

By then conditions in Madrid were dire, with 400 people a week dying simply of starvation. The workers who died in these last months remembered the call of Dolores Ibarruri, known as "La Pasionaria" and heroine of the Revolution: "Better to die on your feet than to live on your knees." A communist, La Pasionaria nonetheless got out on a plane to the Soviet Union. The Republicans went into battle singing, "Death the bride."

With the Republican side suffering repeated defeats, it was clear that Madrid would soon fall as well, and on February 28, 1939, Colonel Segismundo Casado López led a revolt of Republican forces against then prime minister Juan Negrín, claiming the latter was planning a Communist takeover. Casado had the support of Julián Besteiro, leader of the right wing of the Spanish Socialist Workers' Party, and disillusioned anarchist leaders. They established an anti-Negrín Consejo Nacional de Defensa (National Defense Council) that would seek negotiations with Franco.

General Miaja joined the rebels on March 6, ordering communists in Madrid arrested, and Negrín fled to France. Colonel Luis Barceló, commander of the 1st Corps of the Army of the Center, opposed the coup and tried to regain control of the capital. Fierce fighting ensued during several days. Anarchist forces led by Cipriano Mera managed to defeat the 1st Corps and Barceló was captured and executed.

Casado's efforts to negotiate failed, with Franco insisting on unconditional surrender. The Nationalists entered Madrid virtually unopposed on March 28, 1939. The war ended on March 31.

The victors now took their revenge. Those suspected of being Loyalists or having aided the Republican side were ferreted out and shot. The human toll of the Spanish Civil War has never been accurately determined, but the best estimates are about 600,000 Spaniards killed on both sides, with as many as 200,000 perishing after the war at Nationalist hands. Half a million more Spaniards fled the country and lived as refugees in wretched camps opened by the French on the other side of the Pyrenees.

The Spanish economy was in ruins. Agricultural and industrial output was far below those of 1935. Much of Spain's infrastructure was gone. Half a million buildings had been destroyed or damaged. The transportation system was hit hard, with bridges and railroads in need of replacement or repair. Some 60 percent of the rolling stock had been lost and 40 percent of the country's merchant fleet had been sunk or damaged.

Franco immediately established a dictatorship. An edict gave him sole authority to take emergency measures without consulting his council of ministers and his one-man rule continued. The Catholic Church was restored to its full pre-Republican prominence. Land taken under the Second Republic was returned to the original owners. Strikes were banned and rigid censorship was introduced. The government demanded complete loyalty. Swift punishment was the lot for those who refused to comply. Some 200 special prisons held anywhere from 367,000 to 500,000 political prisoners.

Franco's Spain may not have been the equal of Nazi Germany or the Soviet Union, but it was nevertheless a stifling dictatorship and the deep wounds of the Spanish Civil War were long in healing. An entire generation of Spaniards grew up in a nation unaccustomed to words such as democracy, freedom, liberty, justice, and compassion.

The Western world lost a great deal in Spain. Now it would be difficult if not impossible to work up international enthusiasm or commitment for a just cause. A succession of Western concessions to the dictators followed in the war's wake. But perhaps the most dramatic effect of the Spanish Civil War on the international level was to bring the two fascist partners in aggression, German and Italy, together in what came to be known as the Rome-Berlin Axis. Certainly, the Spanish Civil War was an important link in the chain of events that led to World War II.

Spencer C. Tucker

Further Reading

Alpert, Michael. *The Republican Army in the Spanish Civil War, 1936–1939*. New York: Cambridge University Press, 2013.

Beevor, Antony. *The Battle for Spain: The Spanish Civil War, 1936–1939*. London: Weidenfeld & Nicolson, 2006.

Graham, Helen. *The Spanish Republic at War, 1936–1939*. New York: Cambridge University Press, 2002.

Matthews, Herbert L. *Half of Spain Died: A Reappraisal of the Spanish Civil War*. New York: Charles Scribner's Sons, 1973.

Payne, Stanley G. *The Spanish Civil War, the Soviet Union, and Communism*. New Haven, CT: Yale University Press, 2004.

Thomas, Hugh. *The Spanish Civil War*. Rev. ed. New York: Harper and Brothers, 2001.

Siege of Dunkirk (Dunkerque) (May 26–June 4, 1940)

The World War II siege of Dunkirk during May 26–June 4, 1940, ending in the escape of the British Expeditionary Force (BEF) and a number of French soldiers from France was one of the most important battles of World War II as well as one of the largest military extractions in history.

On September 1, 1939, German armies invaded Poland. Two days later Britain and France declared war on Germany, officially beginning World War II (1939–1945). Poland, invaded from the east by the Soviet Union on September 17, was overwhelmed in less than a month. In April 1940, German forces invaded Denmark and Norway.

The German invasion of France and the Low Countries, unleashed on May 10, 1940, caught the Allies by surprise. British and French forces advanced into Belgium to come to the aid of that country, but the BEF was soon in danger of being cut off by the surprise powerful German armored thrust through the Ardennes Forest. This dire situation resulted in large part because the Belgian government decided to surrender, despite pledges to its allies that it would not do so unilaterally. In a critical decision, with the battle for France in effect lost, BEF commander General John Vereker, 6th Viscount Gort, rejected French demands for a push against the principal German invasion force to its south, and took the unilateral decision in defiance of orders to withdraw northward instead in order to save his army. Already on May 19, contingency planning was begun in Britain under the supervision of Vice Admiral Bertram Ramsay, naval commander of Dover, for the possible evacuation of British forces from France. That the BEF was able to consolidate along the coast of northeastern France was in large part because German chancellor Adolf Hitler ordered a halt in the advance of his tanks for nearly three days. Hitler's stop order was critical, for it allowed the BEF to escape and Britain to continue in the war.

Commander of the Luftwaffe Reichsmarshall Hermann Göring had requested of Hitler that the destruction of the British ground forces be left to the Luftwaffe and its dive-bombers. Göring even requested that the German panzers be pulled back several miles to leave the area clear for the aircraft. The Luftwaffe had not received much credit for its brilliant efforts in Poland in September 1939 and the Western offensive, and Göring believed that it could destroy the BEF alone in France. Hitler concurred in part because he wanted time for the German infantry to catch up with the fast-moving tanks in order that they could operate in tandem. As it turned out, the dive-bombing was largely ineffective; the German bombs burrowed deep into the soft sand before exploding.

In late May 1940, some 250,000 men of the BEF were pinned against the English Channel in the vicinity of the French port of Dunkirk (Dunkerque), facing annihilation or capture. At best, officials in London hoped to rescue 40,000 men over a two-day period. In Operation DYNAMO, however, the British sent across the Channel virtually everything that could float, including civilian craft, to assist in the evacuation.

Royal Air Force (RAF) fighters were not available in sufficient numbers to provide adequate air cover, and the vessels involved took a horrible pounding from the Luftwaffe. Flying from bases in southern England, the RAF pilots did what they could and probably made the evacuation possible. British destroyers rescued the most men, but they were also the chief targets for Luftwaffe attacks. By the fourth day of the evacuation, 10 destroyers had been sunk or put out of action.

Such losses induced the Admiralty to make the difficult decision to remove all modern destroyers from the operation. The same reasoning limited the number of fighter aircraft available. Head of Fighter Command Air Marshal Hugh Dowding refused to sacrifice valuable aircraft in a battle already lost. He believed that the planes would be desperately needed for the defense of Britain, certain to be the next target. In so doing, he greatly angered Prime Minister Winston Churchill, but his decision was the correct one.

The Dunkerque evacuation was assisted by bad weather and fires from burning equipment on the beaches that inhibited Luftwaffe operations. From May 26 through June 4, the Royal Navy—assisted by a large number of civilian craft and some vessels from other nations—evacuated a total of 364,628 men from the vicinity of Dunkirk; 224,686 were members of the BEF. Before the evacuation was over the BEF had lost in France more than 68,000 men killed, captured, or

Soldiers of the British Expeditionary Force (BEF) awaiting evacuation by ship on the beaches of Dunkirk, France, in 1940. Although the soldiers were forced to abandon all their heavy equipment and stores, their escape allowed Britain to continue the struggle against Germany. (Photos.com)

wounded, including at least 2,000 during DYNAMO itself. RAF Fighter Command lost 106 aircraft and 80 pilots, and Bomber Command lost an additional 76 aircraft. Of 693 British vessels in the operation, 226 were sunk, including 6 destroyers; 19 other destroyers were put out of action. Other nations lost 17 of 168 vessels taking part. The BEF was also forced to abandon in France virtually all its equipment but escaped largely intact as far as personnel were concerned.

In Britain the evacuation swept away the phoniness of the war, but the British also falsely believed that they had been betrayed. Many were oblivious to the fact that in May 1918 there had been 10 times the number of British divisions in France than in May 1940, that the British evacuation had left the French in the lurch, or that the French First Army had held the Germans from the beaches and allowed them to get away. The French troops contested every bit of ground, and ultimately between 30,000 and 40,000 of the First Army's 50,000 men were forced to surrender.

Britain now appeared to be in grave peril. The bulk of the 12 BEF divisions that had been in Europe returned to Britain, joining 15 other divisions (6 formed only in May), still only partially trained. In early June, there was only one properly equipped and trained division to defend the British Isles. BEF equipment abandoned in France included 120,000 vehicles, 600 tanks, 1,000 field guns, 500 antiaircraft guns, 850 antitank guns, 8,000 Bren guns, 90,000 rifles, and 500,000 tons of stores and ammunition. The army had in Britain only about 500 artillery pieces and a like number of tanks, half of them light models. There was one battalion of 50 infantry tanks, with the remaining tanks scattered at training schools. The fleet was kept far to the north, away from the Luftwaffe. In speaking to the British people, Churchill did not call the evacuation a victory, but he assured them that Britain would fight on.

In sharp contrast to the British military position, the German Army numbered 114 divisions and 2,000 tanks. If its forces could have landed in Britain in the weeks after the Dunkirk Evacuation, there would have been few means of stopping them. But Hitler and his military chiefs were caught off guard by the speed of the French defeat and had no plans for a follow-up invasion of Britain. Not until late July did the Germans begin planning for a descent on England, code-named SEALION (SEELÖWE), but the necessary precondition to that was German command of the air and that was never achieved.

Spencer C. Tucker

Further Reading
Divine, David. *The Nine Days of Dunkirk*. New York: W. W. Norton, 1959.
Gelb, Norman. *Dunkirk: The Complete Story of the First Step in the Defeat of Hitler*. New York: William Morrow, 1989.
Harman, Nicholas. *Dunkirk: The Patriotic Myth*. New York: Simon & Schuster, 1980.
Lord, Walter. *The Miracle of Dunkirk*. New York: Viking, 1982.
Sebag-Montefiore, Hugh. *Dunkirk: Fight to the Last Man*. New York: Viking, 2006.

Siege of Malta (June 11, 1940–November 20, 1942)

The World War II siege of the British island of Malta occurred during June 11, 1940–November 20, 1942, and pitted German and Italian aircraft and ships against British aircraft and ships. Located in the central Mediterranean, Malta is only some 60 miles from Sicily. The archipelago of 122 square miles had a 1939 population of 270,000 people, and its siege by the Axis was a critical aspect of the struggle to control the Mediterranean.

Just as Malta had been a key location for forces traveling to the Near East in support of the Crusades and during the French Revolution and Napoleonic Wars, so it proved a vital link in the defeat of Axis forces in North Africa. A British possession since 1814, Malta had the only British port and shipyard facilities between Gibraltar and Alexandria, Egypt. However, because it was 1,000 miles from the nearest British base, it was both difficult to defend and to resupply. Indeed, when the war began there were few defenses on the island as the British had judged this impossible. British naval assets in the Mediterranean came to be centered to the east on Alexandria, Egypt, to protect the Suez Canal and to the west on Gibraltar. Malta boasted only the monitor *Terror* and a few submarines. The governors of Malta, also its military commanders, during the siege were Lieutenant General William Dobbie (April 1940–May 1942) and General John Vereker, 6th Viscount Gort (May 1942–September 1944).

The German victory in France in the spring of 1940 brought Italy into the war on the German side. With the forthcoming disarmament of the French fleet, Italy would hold a clear naval and air advantage over the British in the Mediterranean. When Italy declared war on the Allies on June 10, 1940, it immediately

> **Rommel's Assessment of the Importance of Malta**
>
> Field Marshal Erwin Rommel recognized that unless the Axis managed to secured Malta the Axis would lose control of North Africa. Rommel believed that instead of invading Crete (the high casualties of which led Hitler to effectively end the German airborne forces) the Germans should have invaded and taken Malta, which he believed would have brought control of the Mediterranean. Rommel even volunteered to lead such an operation and believed that, had the requisite forces been provided, it would have been successful.
>
> **Spencer C. Tucker**

commenced air attacks on Malta. The first strike on June 11 involved 55 bombers escorted by 21 fighter aircraft dropping 142 bombs on Malta's three airfields. The British then had only six operational Sea Gladiator biplanes to meet them. Only three Sea Gladiators (named "Faith," "Hope," and "Charity") were able to take to the air, their pilots never having had fighter experience. One was lost, but several Italian aircraft were also downed.

Both sides recognized the importance of Malta to operations in the Mediterranean Theater. In 1938 Italian dictator Benito Mussolini had developed Plan DG10/42, in which a seaborne force of 40,000 men supported by the entire Italian navy and 500 aircraft would take possession of the island. Such a plan stood a good chance of success through 1940 and would have given the Italians air and naval supremacy in the central Mediterranean, cutting off Gibraltar from Alexandria. Mussolini's reluctance to act was, however, strengthened in the surprise successful British air attack on the Italian naval base of Taranto on November 11. The Italians, followed later by the Germans, chose the indirect approach of air attack.

The British now recognized Malta's importance as a strategically vital air and naval base for the interdiction of Axis supply lines between Italy and Libya. In October 1941, British ships and planes operating from Malta sank two-thirds of the Axis supplies sent by sea to Libya.

The Germans now increased the pressure on Malta by sending Fliegerkorps X to Sicily to neutralize Malta in order that Axis supplies and men might reach North Africa. Beginning in January 1941, Fliegerkorps X struck both the island and the British supply convoys in what became a furious, two-year aerial campaign. Malta became one of the most intensely bombed targets of the entire war, with the German Luftwaffe and the Italian Regia Aeronautica together flying some 3,000 raids against the island.

Sustaining Malta became a major Allied priority. British prime minister Winston Churchill feared the island would be "pounded to bits," but he was determined to save it and ran major naval risks to do so. British fighters were deployed to Malta, first Hurricanes and then Spitfires, although the British planes were vastly outnumbered by the attackers. From August 1940 until January 1943, the British pushed 13 convoys through to Malta, all of which sustained significant losses from Axis naval and air attacks. Critical to Malta's survival was the resupply of fighter aircraft, sent to the island via aircraft carrier. The situation became so desperate and British naval forces were stretched so thin that the United States, which had entered the war in December 1941, employed the fleet carrier *Wasp* to fly in Spitfire aircraft during April and May 1942. This was at a time when the U.S. Pacific Fleet desperately needed every available carrier in the Pacific to stem Japanese advances there.

Despite Allied efforts, the situation in Malta remained precarious for much of 1942. With no natural resources of its own, Malta had to import virtually all of its fuel, food, and war supplies. By April 1942, the people on the island were on starvation rations and antiaircraft ammunition was in desperately short supply. Resupply was extremely hazardous. Between August 1940 and August 1942, 31 of 82 ships sent to Malta were sunk by the Axis. By June 1942, other than the arrival of the Spitfires, it had been nine months since a resupply convoy had gotten through.

The largest effort to resupply Malta came in Operation PEDESTAL (August 3–15, 1942), when the British sent 4 aircraft carriers, 2 battleships, 7 cruisers, and 24 destroyers to escort a convoy of 14 merchantmen to the island. After numerous air and U-boat attacks, the convoy limped into Malta's harbor on August 12 with just 5 merchant ships, 3 of them damaged. In the operation the Royal Navy sustained losses of 1 aircraft carrier, 2 cruisers, and 1 destroyer, while another carrier and 2 cruisers were damaged. Operation PEDESTAL was, however, deemed a success in that the supplies were sufficient to allow operations from Malta to continue.

In the spring of 1942, Axis leaders had discussed a plan, dubbed Operation HERKULES, that would have included a sea invasion, supported by German and Italian paratroopers, to seize the island, but the Italians' lack of preparation, the high paratrooper casualties in the German capture of Crete, the desire to move German air units to the Eastern Front, and German colonel general Erwin Rommel's recent success in Libya all led German chancellor Adolf Hitler to cancel it.

The tide of battle in North Africa turned in November 1942 with the British victory in the Second Battle of El Alamein (October 23–November 11) and the British and American landings in Vichy French Morocco and Algeria in Operation TORCH (November 11). Axis air attacks on Malta were then significantly reduced as their resources were diverted to the struggle for Tunis. Some date the siege as ending on November 20, but Axis air attacks against Malta continued and a more logical ending date is May 1943 with the Allied victory in the Battler of Tunis (May 3–13) that cleared Axis forces from North Africa altogether.

In December 1942, air and sea forces operating from Malta took the offensive, and by May 1943, they had sunk 230 Axis ships in just 164 days, the highest Allied sinking rate of the war. Certainly, the Allied victory in the siege of Malta was critical to the eventual Allied success in North Africa.

More than 1,500 Maltese were killed in the Axis attacks, and some 30,000 structures on the island had been destroyed or damaged. In recognition of the stoutness of the Maltese and to improve their morale during the bleakest of times, Britain's king George VI bestowed on the entire population of Malta the George Cross for valor.

C. J. Horn and Spencer C. Tucker

Further Reading

Bradford, Ernle. *Siege: Malta, 1940–1943*. New York: William Morrow, 1986.

Cull, Brian, Nicola Malizia, and Frederick R. Galea. *Spitfires over Sicily: The Crucial Role of the Malta Spitfires in the Battle of Sicily, January–August 1943*. London: Grub Street, 2000.

Gilbert, Martin. *Road to Victory: Winston S. Churchill, 1941–1945*. London: Minerva, 1989.

Hammond, R. J. "The British Anti-shipping Campaign in the Mediterranean 1940–1944: Comparing Methods of Attack." PhD dissertation, University of Exeter, England, 2011.

Rogers, Anthony. *Battle over Malta: Aircraft Losses and Crash Sites, 1940–42*. Stroud, Gloucestershire, UK: Sutton, 2000.

Smith, Peter C., and Edwin Walker. *The Battles of the Malta Striking Forces*. Shepperton, Surrey, UK: Ian Allan, 1974.

Vella, Philip. *Malta: Blitzed but Not Beaten*. Valletta, Malta: Progress Press, 1989.

Siege of Tobruk (April 10–December 5, 1941)

The siege of by the Germans and Italians of British Commonwealth forces at the port city of Trobruk in Cyrenaica, Libya (April 10–December 5, 1941), was a major battle of the North African Theater during World War II. On June 10, 1940, with the German defeat of France imminent, Italy declared war on both France and Great Britain. The fighting then spread to North Africa with Italian dictator Benito Mussolini seeking to take advantage of the defeat of France and the weakness of Britain. The stakes were high: control of the Mediterranean, the Suez Canal, and access to Middle East oil. In August, Italian forces invaded and captured British Somaliland. Then on September 13, 1940, Italian field marshal Rudolfo Graziani invaded Egypt from Libya with five divisions, a tank brigade, and 300 aircraft.

This began a critical campaign for the British. If the Italians reached Suez, they could control the canal and cut Britain's imperial lifeline to Asia. The Axis powers would also perhaps be able to secure the oil assets of the Persian Gulf. At the height of the Battle of Britain, British prime minister Winston Churchill had to divert vitally needed military resources to the Near East.

With the Italians advance proceeding slowly, however, the British were able to reinforce and halt the offensive. Their own counteroffensive was delayed by the need to dispatch forces from North Africa to Greece, but on December 9, Major General Richard N. O'Connor hurled his Western Desert Force against the Italians. Although it had only a quarter the manpower of the Italians, the Western Desert Force rolled up one Italian strong point after another.

On January 6, in the First Battle of Tobruk, the 7th Armored Division ("The Desert Rats") cut off the Italian garrison there, assaulted it from the south, and on January 22 forced it to surrender. At a cost of some 500 casualties, the British took 25,000 prisoners. They also captured 208 guns, 23 medium tanks, and 200 trucks. Although the Italians had been able to damage some of its facilities before surrendering, the British were soon able to get the port back into working order. Most of the city, including two water-distillation plants, was undamaged.

A British soldier stands guard at the harbor in Tobruk, Libya, in 1942. British Commonwealth forces held out against the Germans and Italians in their siege of this important Mediterranean port during April 10–December 5, 1941. Tobruk finally fell to the Axis in June 1942 but was retaken later that same year. The long Allied defense of Tobruk had saved Egypt from invasion and possibly the entire Middle East from Axis control. (Library of Congress)

The Desert Rats then drove due west across Cyrenaica cutting off remaining Italian troops, while the main British forces proceeded along the coastal road. On February 5, at Beda Fomm on the Gulf of Sirte, the remaining Italian forces surrendered. In two months, Western Desert Force had advanced 500 miles, destroyed 9 Italian divisions, and taken more than 130,000 Italian and Libyan prisoners, along with 380 tanks and 845 guns. British losses were 500 killed and 1,373 wounded, and 55 missing.

The Western Desert Force could have driven on to Tripoli and cleared the Axis out of Africa completely, but British Middle East commander Lieutenant General Sir Archibald Wavell was forced to halt O'Connor in order to shift assets to Greece. This reduced O'Connor's force to only 2d Armored Division, part of an infantry division, and a motorized brigade. Then in January 1941 the first German reinforcements arrived in North Africa in the form of air assets: X Air Corps of 500 planes from Norway to Sicily. Its bombers soon neutralized Benghazi as a British base.

In March, Adolf Hitler sent General of Panzer Troops Erwin Rommel and his Afrika Korps to Tripolitania. Rommel soon opened an offensive against O'Connor's weakened force. Striking with 21st Panzer Division and two Italian divisions (one armored and one motorized), he drove back the British at El Aghella on March 24, 1941. He then sent Afrika Korps in a reprise of O'Connor's advance, only in reverse. The Italian forces followed the coastal road to Derna, while 21st Panzer sliced across the desert of Cyrenaica for the port of Tobruk. O'Connor's 2d Armored Division, endeavoring to delay the Axis drive, was split. One brigade, short of fuel, was cut off at Derna and forced to surrender on April 6. The remainder of the division was captured the next day. Then, on April 17, O'Connor was captured by a German patrol while on reconnaissance.

Wavell was determined to hold Tobruk in order to deny it to the Axis as a supply port close to the Egyptian border (Benghazi lay 560 miles west of the Egyptian frontier) but also to serve as a threat to the flank of the Afrika Korps. Wavell reinforced Tobruk by sea, and on April 9 the 9th Australian Division commanded by Major General Leslie Morshead arrived there, along with some tanks. Morshead now commanded all Allied forces in Cyrenaica, which meant in effect only Tobruk. Morshead had 14,236 Australians and just under 8,000 British troops.

The siege of Tobruk begun on the night of April 10–11, 1941, when Rommel launched a determined attack on the port only to have his forces thrown back after three days of fierce combat. He then encircled Tobruk from the land and besieged it. Morshead did what he could to rebuild and improve the earlier Italian defenses. Tobruk's semi-circular defensive perimeter ran in for some 30 miles. Morshead established a series of small posts supported by minefields designed to slow down any Axis breakthrough and provide flanking fire, while he brought up a mobile reaction force. This defensive scheme worked to perfection when, after a one-day respite, Rommel tried again on April 14. This cost the attackers 17 tanks, 150 men dead, and 250 prisoners taken.

Morshead also made a number of sorties from Tobruk against Axis outposts, netting a large number of prisoners. The defenders had a large supply of weaponry (much of it Italian) and adequate food stocks, while Rommel's supply situation was difficult, especially given the fact that the Allies, thanks to radio intercepts (Top Secret Ultra), were extracting a steady toll of Italian shipping crossing the Mediterranean. The Germans were also now stretched thin logistically, thanks to the demands of their June 1941 invasion of the Soviet Union. Meanwhile Allied naval units and aircraft provided critical support to the Tobruk garrison. Rommel attacked again on April 29. The defenders were ready for it and turned it back with point-blank artillery fire and tanks.

Under heavy pressure from Churchill, Wavell prematurely launched two efforts to relieve Tobruk. The first, Operation BREVITY on May 15–16 with three battalions and 56 tanks, was followed by Operation BATTLEAXE (June 13–15), an attack by two divisions (one armored and one infantry). Both failed. On July 1, Churchill replaced Wavell with General Sir Claude Auchinleck as British Middle East commander. In effect, Wavell became the scapegoat for Churchill's own decision to expand the already stretched-thin theater to include Greece and Crete.

During July–October, both sides built up their strength in preparation of renewing the offensive. The Western Desert Force, now renamed Eighth Army with General Alan Cunningham in command, was built up to seven divisions and 700 tanks, supported by 1,000 aircraft all in preparation for Operation CRUSADER, yet another effort to relieve Tobruk. Rommel also reorganized the Italian-German Panzerarmee Afrika of 10 divisions: 15th and 21st Panzer and the under-strength

90th and 164 Light Infantry Divisions, and six weak Italian divisions, along with 260 German and 154 Italian tanks, supported by 120 German and 200 Italian aircraft. He also brought up siege artillery. All this was in preparation for his planned seizure of Tobruk to be followed by a quick drive into Egypt.

The Allies struck first, on November 17. Operation CRUSADER saw a steady advance along the coast road by infantry and heavy tanks, while inland Cunningham pushed westward with his armor units. A portion of the Italian Ariete Division repulsed the British 22nd Armour Brigade at Bir el Gobi on November 18, but it was not until two days later that Rommel began to react to the Allied attack.

As Rommel shifted armored forces to attack the Allied mobile units, the British 70th Division in Tobruk assaulted the largely Italian infantry units holding the siege lines. Rommel hoped to force the Allies back and then drive into Egypt, but his advance failed to disrupt the Allies or to capture their supply dumps.

Believing Cunningham was moving too slowly, Auchinleck replaced him with Lieutenant General Neil Ritchie. Meanwhile, the elite 2nd New Zealand Division continued its advance to link up with the 70th Division at Tobruk.

Thanks to Ultra, Allied naval units played a key role. The destruction of the *Duisburg* convoy on the night of November 8–9 had temporarily halted all Axis convoys to Libya just as Rommel's ammunition and armor were being exhausted, leaving him no option but to withdraw. Axis forces began to pull back near Gazala, 25 miles west of Tobruk, and the Allies linked up with Tobruk on December 5. At the end of December under British pressure, Rommel withdrew to his original position at El Agheila.

Undaunted, Rommel launched a second offensive in January 1942. Striking on a narrow front, he drove the widely dispersed British forces back beyond Benghazi, where Auchinleck dug in. Having outrun their supply lines, Axis forces then halted. During the next four months both sides rested and resupplied. Eighth Army, built up to 125,000 men with 740 tanks and 700 aircraft, now confronted an Axis force of 113,000 men, with 570 tanks and 500 aircraft. Eighth Army established a heavily mined and fortified line extending from Gazala on the coast 40 miles south to Bir Hacheim, held by the Free French. Auchinleck concentrated his armor behind the French to protect Eighth Army's open left flank. Rommel struck on May 28, concentrating his resources to the south. The Italians failed to take Bir Hacheim, but Rommel's panzers swept south of the British, then turned north inside their line. But the British held and Rommel's tanks were running out of fuel. On May 31, however, Italian infantry managed to open a supply route to Rommel. This forced the French to evacuate Bir Hacheim, and on June 13 Ritchie ordered a general retirement.

During the next two weeks, the British withdrew in disorder back into Egypt. Tobruk finally fell on June 21 to a well-planned air and ground attack. Their capture of Tobruk netted the Germans 33,000 prisoners.

Auchinleck then took personal command of Eighth Army and briefly held Rommel at Mersa Matruh, before falling back on Alam Halfa ridge between El Alamein on the Mediterranean and the Qattara Depression 40 miles south. Following several German probing attacks in early July, the two lines stabilized only 70 miles from Alexandria. Rommel's offensive had cost the British 75,000 casualties and the Axis only 40,000, but his forces were now stretched thin and his logistical situation had worsened, thanks to a British naval and air buildup in the theater.

The British built up their forces and in late October launched a major offensive in the Battle of El Alamein (October 23–November 11). This forced the Axis forces to withdraw westward on Tunis, where the culminating battle occurred during November 17, 1943–May 13, 1943, clearing the Axis forces from North Africa.

The 242-day Allied defense of Tobruk had saved Egypt from invasion and possibly the entire Middle East from Axis control. Had that happened, Axis forces could have proceeded northward against the Soviet Union or even moved east to threaten India overland.

Spencer C. Tucker

Further Reading
Barnett, Correlli. *The Desert Generals*. New York: Viking, 1961.
Carver, Michael. *Tobruk*. London: B. T. Batesford, 1964.
Greene, Jack, and Alessandro Massignani. *Rommel's North Africa Campaign*. Conshohocken, PA: Combined Publishing, 1994.
Harrison, Frank. *Tobruk: The Great Siege Reassessed*. London: Arms and Armour Press, 1996.
Heckstall-Smith, Anthony. *Tobruk: The Story of a Siege*. London: Anthony Blond, 1959.
Pitt, Barrie. *Crucible of War: Western Desert, 1941*. New York: Paragon, 1989.

Siege of Leningrad (July 10, 1941–January 27, 1944)

The siege of the city of Leningrad in the Soviet Union by the Germans in World War II (1939–1945) was the longest since biblical times and the costliest ever in terms of lives lost. The siege lasted from July 10, 1941, to January 27, 1944. Czar Peter the Great had founded the city, originally named St. Petersburg, on the Baltic at the beginning of the eighteenth century as Russia's window to the West. Renamed Petrograd during World War I (1914–1918), it became Leningrad following the 1924 death of Bolshevik leader Vladimir Lenin. Today it is St. Petersburg in the Russian Federation. In 1941 the city was a vibrant urban center of 3.2 million people. By March 1943 it had been reduced to a militarized fortress of only 700,000 inhabitants.

Germany invaded the Soviet Union on June 22, 1941. The capture of Leningrad— in German leader Adolf Hitler's words the "hotbed of Communism"—was one of the strategic goals of the campaign. Hitler assigned the task to Field Marshal Wilhelm R. von Leeb's Army Group North. Leeb was confident, believing that his troops would be supported by the Finns striking from the north. The Finns had reentered the war to regain the territory lost to the Soviets in the Winter War of 1939–1940. Indeed, Finnish forces soon were driving south both east and west of Lake Ladoga toward the Svir River and Leningrad.

On July 8, the German Fourth Panzer Army reached the old fortress of Schlüsselburg (now Shlisselburg), east of Leningrad, which guarded the point where the

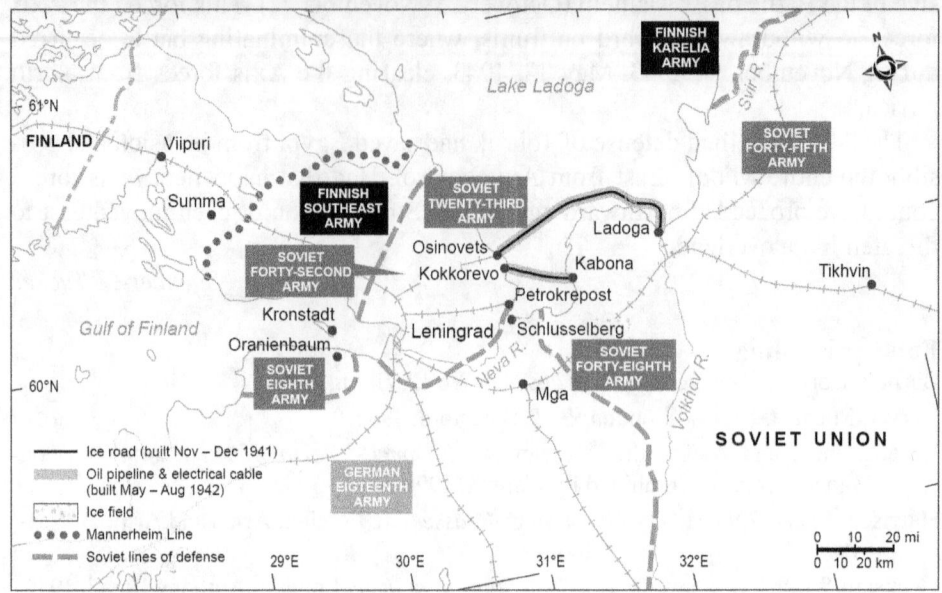

The disposition of forces during the great German siege of the Soviet city of Leningrad (today St. Petersburg) during World War II. The longest and most costly in terms of casualties since biblical times, this unsuccessful German operation claimed the lives of perhaps one million Russian civilians from starvation. (ABC-CLIO)

Neva River flows out of nearby Lake Ladoga. Taking Schlüsselburg would cut off Leningrad from the Soviet interior. The siege of the city, actually a blockade, officially began on July 10. Leeb's hopes for a quick victory were dashed, however, when the Finns merely reoccupied their former territory.

After gaining these lines in late September, the Finns did advance a slight distance into Soviet territory to about 26 miles from Leningrad, but only to shorten their front lines on the Karelian Isthmus. They steadfastly refused to take part in operations against Leningrad. This was a major factor in Leningrad's survival. Leeb's operations against the city were also severely handicapped when he lost much of his Fourth Panzer Army, which Hitler diverted to the drive on Moscow.

Hitler ordered Leningrad obliterated through artillery fire, air attack, and blockade; he specifically prohibited accepting surrender, were it offered. He intended not to take the city by storm but rather to starve it into submission. He was, he declared, "indifferent" to the plight of the civilians.

Leningraders were in difficult straits. Authorities in the city had done little to prepare for a blockade. Although Leningrad was believed to be a major German military objective, efforts to evacuate part of the population suffered from bureaucratic delays. Andrei Zhdanov, the Communist Party boss in Leningrad and second in the party hierarchy only to Joseph Stalin, and Marshal Kliment

E. Voroshilov, appointed by Stalin to defend the city, were reluctant to order any measures that might be branded as defeatist. Only on July 11, 1941, therefore, had the Leningrad Party Committee ordered the civilian population to participate in the construction of tank traps and other defensive positions in front of the city. Between July and August nearly half the city population aged 16 to 55 was engaged in this effort, which proceeded under constant German artillery and air attacks. The city government also ordered the establishment of civilian combat units, men and women alike, but they were poorly trained and had virtually no weapons.

In normal circumstances, Leningrad was dependent on outside sources for its food, fuel, and raw materials for its factories. Now it had to find food for some 2.5 million civilians as well as the forces of the Leningrad Front and the Red Banner Fleet in the Baltic. In mid-October, Hitler ordered Leeb to make a wide sweep of some 150 miles around Lake Ladoga to link up with the Finns on the Svir River. On November 8 the Germans took the vital rail center of Tikhvin, about halfway to the Svir. Soviet leader Stalin then shifted major reinforcements north, and in mid-December Hitler authorized a withdrawal. Soviet troops reoccupied Tikhvin on December 18.

Rations inside the city had been cut to a starvation level of 900 calories per day. The soldiers and sailors received priority in the allocation of food, and rationing authorities held the power of life and death. Rations were cut again and again, beyond the starvation level. People tried to survive any way they could, including by eating stray animals and glue from wallpaper. Hunger even led to instances of cannibalism. The hardships were not evenly shared, and communist officials ate relatively well throughout the siege.

Lake Ladoga was the only means of accessing the rest of the Soviet Union. In winter trucks were able to travel across the ice, and in summer some boats got through. This route was insufficient to overcome the fuel shortage, though. The temperature dropped to 30 degrees below zero, but there was still no heat, no light, and no public transportation. Surprisingly, a number of factories continued to function, producing weapons, munitions, and even some tanks. The Russians rebuilt the rail line from Tikhvin, but the Germans bombed and shelled it as well as the Lake Ladoga route.

In January 1942 Stalin ordered General Kirill A. Meretskov's Volkhov Front (army group) to strike the German lines from Lake Ladoga to Lake Ilmen. After punching a narrow gap in the German lines, however, the Soviet offensive faltered. When Stalin refused to allow a withdrawal, in June the Germans cut off the Soviet forces and restored their lines. Between January and July 1942 Soviet authorities managed to evacuate 850,000 people from Leningrad, including a large number of children.

Hitler's plans for the summer 1942 campaign called for the destruction of Leningrad and the occupation of the area between Lake Ladoga and the Baltic in order to free up the Finns for operations against Murmansk. In August, Meretskov carried out another attack against the eastern part of the German lines. Field Marshal Erich von Manstein, dispatched to Leningrad, replied with a counterattack in September. The Soviets nevertheless managed to lay both pipelines and electric cables under Lake Ladoga. The Germans responded with small E-boats, and the Italians operated some midget submarines in the lake.

In January 1943, Meretskov's forces and Red Army troops in Leningrad, which the Russians had managed to reinforce and were now commanded by General Leonid A. Govorov, struck the Germans from the north and east in Operation SPARK. The offensive was successful, with the two Russian armies meeting at Schlüsselburg on January 19, breaking the siege, and opening a 10-mile corridor. On February 7, a Russian train reached Leningrad through the corridor and across the Neva on track over the ice. Although this line came under constant German attack and had to be repaired daily, it operated continuously thereafter.

On January 14, 1944, Govorov and Meretskov, with a superiority of two to one in men and four to one in tanks and aircraft, again struck the German positions. Hitler refused to authorize a withdrawal, and the Soviets drove the Germans back in bitter fighting. On January 27, 1944, with the Leningrad-to-Moscow railroad line reopened, Stalin declared the so-called 900-day blockade at an end.

During the German siege, perhaps 1 million people in Leningrad—40 percent of the prewar population—died of hunger, with the majority perishing in the winter of 1941–1942. The entire city was within range of German artillery fire throughout the siege, and the bombing and shelling claimed many of the city's buildings and architectural and art treasures, including works from the Hermitage Museum. The travail of Leningrad became the chief subject of Soviet war literature. Like the bombings of Dresden and Hiroshima, the siege of Leningrad became a national and international symbol of the horrors of war.

Spencer C. Tucker

Further Reading

Fadeyev, Aleksandr. *Leningrad in the Days of the Blockade.* Westport, CT: Greenwood, 1971.

Gure, Leon. *The Siege of Leningrad.* Stanford, CA: Stanford University Press, 1962.

Inber, Vera. *Leningrad Diary.* New York: St. Martin's, 1971.

Meretskov, K. A. *Serving the People.* Moscow: Progress Publishers, 1971.

Salisbury, Harrison E. *The 900 Days: The Siege of Leningrad.* New York: Harper & Row, 1969.

Skrjabina, Elena. *Siege and Survival: The Odyssey of a Leningrader.* Carbondale: Southern Illinois University Press, 1971.

Siege of Sevastopol (October 30, 1941–July 4, 1942)

The World War II siege of Sevastopol, also known as the Battle of Sevastopol and Defense of Sevastopol, was fought during October 30, 1941–July 4, 1942, and was one of the great battles on the Eastern Front. Sevastopol is located on the southwestern tip of the Crimean Peninsula. In 1941 it was one of the world's most powerful fortresses and home to the Soviet Black Sea Fleet. Its location made any approach to the city difficult, and it was strongly defended by large concrete bunkers, minefields, and a dozen naval gun batteries containing 42 heavy guns ranging from 152 mm to 304 mm in caliber.

Securing Sevastopol was a major German military objective. By taking the entire Crimean Peninsula with Sevastopol, Adolf Hitler sought to deny the Red Air Force the ability to strike the Ploesti oil fields, which were vital to the German war effort. He also hoped that destruction of the Soviet Black Sea Fleet might bring neutral Turkey into the war against the Soviet Union. Hitler was determined to have Sevastopol, but Soviet leader Josef Stalin was just as determined to hold it. In Soviet hands, it could threaten any further German advance into the southern Soviet Union.

Sevastopol came under air attack in the first hours of the German invasion of the USSR on June 22, 1941. From late September to mid-November, General of Infantry Erich von Manstein's Eleventh Army overran the entire Crimean Peninsula save for Sevastopol. Meanwhile, during the last two weeks of October, the Soviets reinforced the base, sending to Sevastopol by sea from Odessa the remains of Major General I. Y. Petrov's Independent Maritime Army, some 32,000 men. Petrov, who took command of all ground forces at Sevastopol, immediately set his men to work building three defensive lines, the most northerly of which was 10 miles from the fortress. Vice Admiral F. S. Oktyabrsky had overall command of Sevastopol and used his cruisers and destroyers to bring in supplies from Novorossisk, which they could reach overnight. In all, Oktyabrsky commanded about 102,000 men. Manstein had the smallest German Army on the Eastern Front—seven divisions comprising about 100,000 troops—but with more guns and many more aircraft. There were few tanks on either side.

The siege itself began on October 30, when Manstein mounted the first effort to break through the well-fortified Soviet lines. After three weeks, the attack had barely penetrated the Soviet defenses and was halted. On December 17, the Germans launched a second and more intense attack that breached the three defensive lines and pushed to within five miles of the city. The Soviets, however, fought for every inch of ground. The rainy and cold weather became a serious problem for the Germans, who were ill-prepared in summer uniforms.

The fighting was bitter, and tunnels deep below ground helped the Soviets survive. On December 26, Soviet forces landed on the Kerch Peninsula to the east, diverting German troops. By mid-January, the Germans were again forced to discontinue the attack. For a few months that winter, the population of Sevastopol believed they had won the battle, and life in the city even began to return to some semblance of normalcy.

It was not to be. Stavka, the Soviet High Command, activated the Crimea Front under Major General D. T. Kozlov and ordered him to deploy three armies on the Kerch Peninsula, which was possible in winter when the Kerch Strait was frozen solid. When good weather returned in the spring, Manstein dealt with Kozlov, committing 5 German and 2 Romanian infantry divisions and a German panzer division against Kozlov's 21 infantry divisions and 4 tank brigades. A German amphibious landing unhinged Kozlov's defenders and led to the surrender of more than 170,000 Red Army troops. Manstein now returned to the conquest of Sevastopol, which Hitler insisted be taken.

On June 2, the Germans used 700 guns to begin the systematic reduction of the massive Soviet forts. The German artillery included some three dozen very heavy siege guns that had been specially developed to reduce the French Maginot Line, ranging in size from 280 mm to 800 mm (10.9 inches to 31 inches). The largest of these, the 800 mm Schwerer Gustav railway gun, was in fact the largest artillery piece of all time. It took 4,000 men five weeks to get the gun into firing position and had a firing crew of 500 men.

Manstein opened a third assault by four divisions from the north on June 7, but it failed to break through the defenders, who from tunnels and caves continued an effective resistance with small arms. On June 11, three German divisions attacked on the southeast but also made little headway. After two weeks of fighting, the Germans were on the shore of Severnaya Bay north of Sevastopol and at the Sapun Heights to the southeast. The last Soviet reinforcements arrived between June 22 and 26. Thereafter, the only links between Sevastopol and the outside world were by submarine and air. Waves of German bombers leveled the city and naval base, dropping some 50,000 bombs in one week.

A surprise German assault by boat across the bay on June 28 shattered the defenders, and beginning on the night of June 30, Admiral Oktyabrsky, Petrov, and a few hundred top Soviet military, party, and government personnel were evacuated by air. Fighting ended on July 4, 1942.

The Germans claimed 92,000 Soviet prisoners taken, along with 460 guns, but they suffered 24,000 casualties of their own in the June and July fighting alone. An overjoyed Hitler promoted Manstein to field marshal. Manstein had indeed achieved much, given the difficult terrain and weather and the defenders' determination. Hitler then transferred Eleventh Army north to Leningrad, a decision that adversely affected the German Army in its drive on Stalingrad later that year.

The Soviets retook Sevastopol in May 1944. Then the situation was reversed, with the German Seventeenth Army defending the city and the Soviets attacking. Although the Germans evacuated 38,000 troops by sea, the Soviets claimed 100,000 others killed and captured. After the long siege and this battle, little was left of Sevastopol itself.

Michael Share and Spencer C. Tucker

Further Reading
Erickson, John. *The Road to Stalingrad*. London: Weidenfeld & Nicolson, 1975.
Glantz, David, and Jonathan M. House. *When Titans Clashed: How the Red Army Stopped Hitler*. Lawrence: University Press of Kansas, 1995.
Manstein, Erich von. *Lost Victories*. Edited and translated by Anthony G. Powell. Chicago: Henry Regnery, 1958.
Ziemke, Earl F., and Magna E. Bauer. *Moscow to Stalingrad: Decision in the East*. Washington, DC: Center of Military History, 1984.

Siege of Singapore (February 8–15, 1942)

The siege of Singapore of February 8–15, 1942, saw Japanese forces besiege Singapore, the principal British military base in Asia. Simultaneous with their attack on the U.S. Pacific Fleet at Pearl Harbor, on December 8, 1941, the

Japanese struck Malaya from the air. Lieutenant General Yamashita Tomoyuki's Twenty-Fifth Army then landed undetected at Kota Bharu and at Singora and Patani in northern Malaya. Yamashita's 60,000 men, supported by artillery and tanks, consolidated their positions and then moved south, brushing aside the few British defenders and making their way toward their chief objective: Singapore.

The Japanese had to secure Singapore because it would pose a threat to their north-south supply lines to their principal goal of the vast natural resources (especially oil) of the Netherlands Indies. The Japanese also considered Singapore the key British defensive bastion guarding both the eastern approach to India and the northern approach to Australia. Throughout the campaign for Malaya and Singapore, Yamashita kept up the pressure and held the initiative. British commander Lieutenant General Arthur E. Percival had many more men—about 100,000—but he had anticipated Japanese attacks farther south and thus had the bulk of his defenders deployed there.

In early 1942, British forces were stretched thin, defending not only the British Isles but also the Mediterranean. Churchill also had to send supplies to the Soviet Union. There was a definite limit to what the British could do, and London expected Singapore to hold out until it could be relieved by naval units sent from Europe. Largely because Prime Minister Winston Churchill pressed for a show of strength, however, at the end of October 1941 the British Admiralty had ordered the new King George V–class battleship *Prince of Wales*, the old battle cruiser *Repulse*, the new aircraft carrier *Indomitable*, and four destroyers out to the Far East. The *Indomitable* ran aground near Jamaica and had to be left behind for repairs, but the remaining ships arrived at Singapore on December 2. They were entirely dependent for air cover on the few British land aircraft available.

On learning of the Japanese invasion of Malaya, British Eastern Fleet commander Admiral Tom Phillips immediately departed Singapore with Force Z, comprised of the two capital ships and several destroyers, to attack Japanese ships supporting the landings. Lacking reconnaissance aircraft, Phillips was unable to find the Japanese, however. Force Z was returning to Singapore when it was attacked on December 10 by at least 80 Japanese aircraft based in southern Indochina. Despite evasive tactics and antiaircraft fire, both ships were sunk by Japanese torpedo bombers. The Japanese lost only three aircraft. The British lost some 900 men killed, including Phillips; destroyers rescued the remainder.

Churchill later blamed Phillips for the disaster, claiming that he should not have attempted to intercept the Japanese invasion force. In fact, Churchill, Phillips, and the Admiralty had previously rejected the notion that battleships under way and firing antiaircraft guns could be sunk by air attack. The engagement demonstrated that battleships would need to have air cover of their own if they were to survive air attack. With the loss of the *Prince of Wales* and the *Repulse*, the Allies had no capital ships remaining in the Pacific except three U.S. aircraft carriers. The event also sealed the fate of Malaya and Singapore.

Singapore resembles a flattened diamond in shape; at its widest points it is some 27 miles east-west and 12 miles north-south. Singapore is joined to the Malay Peninsula to the north by a causeway just west of its northern apex. The colony's principal defenses were concentrated on the southern (seaward) side of the island. Three of the four British airfields were in the north and center and were highly vulnerable to land attack.

The great naval base of Singapore in the south, 20 years in the building and long touted for its supposed impregnability, now fell victim to British complacency and the failure to anticipate a northern overland attack. This "Gibraltar of Asia" had been built to withstand an attack from the sea rather than by land. Singapore boasted heavy coastal defense guns of up to the 15-inch type. Contrary to popular misconception, these did not just point toward the sea; most of the defending batteries were capable of 360-degree traverse. The problem lay in their ammunition. Large quantities of armor-piercing shell for use against ships were available, but there was little in the way of high-explosive projectiles for employment against troops.

In the north, moreover, virtually nothing had been done to prepare for a Japanese attack. Areas of beach there lacked even barbed wire or trenches. The defenders of Singapore, many of them Australian and Indian units, were poorly trained and lacked both antiaircraft and antitank guns. Modern aircraft were especially in short supply. The Japanese completely dominated the skies.

From February 3, the defenders of Singapore were subjected to Japanese artillery and air attacks. These intensified during the next five days, disrupting defensive communications and greatly affecting efforts to prepare Singapore to meet a Japanese assault. Despite this, the Japanese were actually greatly outnumbered (30,000 to 85,000 men); their ammunition was low, they had no reserves, and many of the men were sick. Percival was nevertheless unable to take advantage of this situation. Certainly, his defensive dispositions were faulty. Percival decided to defend the northern beaches, and the bulk of British forces were thus placed in unprepared forward defensive positions. British troops retreating from the mainland to Singapore made only an ineffectual effort to destroy the causeway.

Yamashita paused to make careful preparations. On the night of February 8, the Japanese launched their attack, crossing over to the island in collapsible boats and supported by artillery and air attacks. Unprepared for the speed and ferocity of the assault, many British officers ordered their men to withdraw prematurely, but there were no secondary positions or strong points north of the city on which to fall back. The Japanese also cut the water supply to Singapore Island, leaving the population there with only a few days' supply. Many of Percival's men actually deserted, including the engineers who were to destroy the naval dockyard.

Nonetheless, Yamashita and his staff were stunned by Percival's decision to surrender unconditionally on February 15. Percival did have the welfare of civilians to consider. For weeks, refugees had been pouring into the island from the Malay Peninsula. The Japanese took 70,000 prisoners and had only contempt for their captives who, they believed, had not shown proper martial spirit. Some of the British, including those already sick and wounded in Singapore's Alexandra Hospital, were simply massacred along with the medical staff. Others were imprisoned or shipped to various points in the Japanese Empire as slave labor for military construction projects. General Itagaki Seishiro explained sending British prisoners to Korea as necessary "to stamp out the respect and admiration of the Korean people for Britain and America and establish a strong faith in Japanese victory."

Malaya and Singapore had fallen in only 70 days. In the entire campaign, the British sustained 138,700 casualties, mostly captured; Japanese losses were trifling by comparison: only 9,824 men. The Japanese victory at Singapore opened the way for the Japanese to secure control of the natural resources of South Asia. British prestige in Asia never quite recovered from the shock. The Battle of Singapore signaled the end of the colonial era in Asia and is rightly considered Britain's greatest military defeat in its modern history.

Spencer C. Tucker

Further Reading
Falk, Stanley L. *Seventy Days to Singapore.* New York: Putnam, 1975.
Harries, Meirion, and Susie Harries. *Soldiers of the Sun: The Rise and Fall of the Imperial Japanese Army.* New York: Random House, 1991.
Roskill, Stephen. *Churchill and the Admirals.* London: William Collins, 1977.

Siege of Stalingrad (November 19, 1942–February 2, 1943)

The siege of the Soviet city of Stalingrad (today Volgograd), during November 19, 1942–February 2, 1943, was part of the wider World War II Battle of Stalingrad begun on August 23, 1942.

German chancellor Adolf Hitler rejected Field Marshal Erich von Manstein's call for the 1942 summer campaign in the East to be in mobile warfare in the center part of the front, believing that Soviet leader Josef Stalin would commit all possible resources to save Moscow and the Red Army might thus be destroyed. It would also have the Germans defending a more compact front. But Hitler placed major emphasis in the southern portion.

Hitler rejected this sound approach and divided his resources. In the north, he planned to take Leningrad, still under German siege. But the main effort would be Operation BLAU (Blue) in the south. Beginning on June 28, he sent Field Marshal Fedor von Bock's Army Group South from around Kursk to take Voronezh, which fell to the Germans on July 6. Hitler then reorganized his southern forces into two: Army Group A, the southern formation, under Field Marshal Siegmund W. List, and Army Group B, the northern formation, under Colonel General Maximilian von Weichs.

Hitler's original plan was for Army Groups A and B to secure the Don and Donets valleys and capture the cities of Rostov and Stalingrad, then move southeast to take the oil fields. On July 13, however, Hitler ordered a change, with the simultaneous capture of the Caucasus and Stalingrad. Dividing the effort placed further strains on already inadequate German resources and logistical support. On July 23, Army Group A captured Rostov. It then crossed the Don River, advanced deep into the Caucasus, reaching to within 70 miles of the Caspian Sea.

Hitler now intervened again, slowing the advance of General of Panzer Troops Friedrich Paulus's Sixth Army of Army Group B toward Stalingrad when he detached Colonel General Hermann Hoth's Fourth Panzer Army to join Army Group A. Hitler also ordered his sole strategic reserve, Manstein's Eleventh Panzer Army, north to reinforce at Leningrad, exacting a heavy toll on the German equipment.

Sixth Army reached the Volga north of Stalingrad on August 23. The major industrial center and key crossing point on the Volga River curved for some 20 miles along the high western bank of the river. Hitler's original intent was merely to control the Volga by gunfire and destroy the city's arms factories, notably the Tractor, Red October, and Barricades works, but now he demanded full occupation of the city in yet another example of his overconfidence in German abilities and underestimation of Soviet resources and resolve.

Stalingrad had great propaganda value to both sides, for it was Stalin's namesake city. Hitler proclaimed its population to be "thoroughly communistic" and "especially dangerous" and ordered that after its capture, all male citizens were to be killed and its women and children deported. Stalin, meanwhile, poured resources into the city.

To meet the German thrust toward Stalingrad, on July 12, the Soviet General Staff had formed the Stalingrad Front consisting of the Sixty-Second, Sixty-Third, and Sixty-Fourth Armies, all under Marshal Semen K. Timoshenko, who was replaced by Lieutenant General V. N. Gordov on July 27. The Twenty-First Army and the Eighth Air Army were also integrated into the Stalingrad Front. General Vasily Chuikov, a protégé of Marshal Georgii Zhukov, commanded the Sixty-Second Army, which held the west bank of the Volga.

On August 11, angry over the slow progress of the Sixth Army into Stalingrad, Hitler ordered Hoth's Fourth Army back from the Caucasus there, leaving a badly depleted Army Group A holding a 500-mile front and stalling the southernmost drive. Such wide-ranging shifts of German resources took a heavy toll on men but especially on equipment, consumed precious fuel, and stretched the German lines far beyond what was safe. German Army High Command Chief of Staff Colonel General Franz Halder and other generals pointed out to Hitler that the German Army in the Soviet Union now was forced to maintain a front of more than 2,000 miles. Between the two armies of Army Group B, a lone division held a 240-mile gap. North of Stalingrad, Romanian troops protected the single railroad bringing supplies to the Sixth Army. The possibilities open to the Soviets were enormous, providing they had the resources. Hitler claimed they did not. When Halder continued to express his concerns, Hitler sacked him. Hitler also relieved List, and 1,200 miles distant, took personal command of Army Group A himself. The irony is that the Germans might have taken Stalingrad in July had Hitler not diverted Hoth south.

Beginning on August 23, a costly battle of attrition raged for Stalingrad. Stalin refused to allow the evacuation of the civilian population, believing that this would force the defenders, especially local militia forces, to fight more tenaciously. Luftwaffe carpet bombing at the end of August killed some 40,000 people, but it also turned the city into defensive bastions of ruined buildings and rubble.

Siege of Stalingrad

Soviet snipers seeking out targets during the great German siege of the city of Stalingrad on the Volga River during November 19, 1942–February 2, 1943. (National Archives)

The ruined city posed a formidable obstacle. Germany's strength lay in maneuver warfare, but Hitler compelled Sixth Army to engage the Soviet strength of static defense. Stalin ordered the city held at all costs, and Soviet forces resisted doggedly. To make things as difficult as possible for German artillery and aviation, Chuikov ordered his troops to keep within 50 yards of the Germans. Zhukov, who had just been appointed deputy supreme commander—second in authority only to Stalin—arrived at Stalingrad on August 29 to take overall charge of operations.

Taking Stalingrad was unnecessary from a military point of view; the 16th Panzer Division at Rynok controlled the Volga with its guns, closing it to north-south shipping. But Hitler insisted the city itself be physically taken. For a month, the Sixth Army pressed slowly forward, but casualties were enormous on both sides. The battle disintegrated into a block-by-block, house-by-house—even room-by-room—struggle.

General Paulus has been blamed for refusing to disobey Hitler's order to stand firm and extracting his army before it was too late, but his and Hitler's greatest failing lay in not anticipating the Soviet encirclement. Nor did Paulus possess a mobile tank reserve to counter such a Soviet effort and keep open a supply corridor.

While feeding the cauldron of Stalingrad with only sufficient troops absolutely necessary to hold the city, Zhukov patiently assembled 1 million men in four fronts (army groups) for a great double envelopment. This deep movement, Operation URANUS, began on November 19, timed to coincide with the frosts that would facilitate Soviet cross-country tank maneuvers. For the northern pincer, the Soviets assembled 3,500 guns and heavy mortars to blast a hole for three tank and two cavalry corps and a dozen infantry divisions. The Romanian infantry divisions here fought bravely, but their 37 mm guns and light Skoda tanks were no match for the Soviet T-34s. The southern Soviet prong of two corps, one mechanized and the other cavalry, broke through on November 20 against two Romanian infantry divisions.

By November 23, URANUS had completely encircled the Sixth Army and had driven some units of the Fourth Army into the pocket. Hitler now ordered Manstein from the Leningrad Front, gave him a new formation—Army Group Don, drawn from Army Group A—and ordered him to rectify the situation.

Convinced that Sixth Army could be resupplied from the air, Hitler forbade withdrawal, no doubt misled by the Luftwaffe success the previous winter in supplying by parachute drops 5,000 German troops surrounded at Kholm and 100,000 men at Demyansk. This decision was, however, taken with the Soviets enjoying air superiority. By November 20, they had committed between 1,350 and 1,414 combat aircraft to Stalingrad. Luftflotte 4, flying in support of the Sixth Army, had only 732 combat aircraft, with but 402 operational. The Soviets used their air superiority to attack German Army positions and bomb the main Ju-52 base at Zverevo, where they destroyed a substantial number of these German transport aircraft. Worsening weather also impeded the relief effort, and much of the Luftwaffe's airlift capability was redeployed to resupply Axis troops in North Africa following the Allied landings there in early November.

Even in the best weather conditions, the Luftwaffe could only bring in one-tenth of the Sixth Army's requirements, and this fact condemned the German forces in the pocket to slow starvation and death. The final tally over a 72-day period was 8,350 tons with 488 aircraft and more than 1,000 aircrew lost. Then, on January 16, 1943, the Soviets took Pitomnik, the principal airfield within the Stalingrad pocket. Its loss was the death blow to the resupply operation. During the last days of the battle, supplies were dropped only by parachute, and many fell into Soviet hands.

Hitler refused to authorize any escape attempt by Sixth Army. He would allow only a linking up of a relief force, with none of the hard-won territory to be surrendered, but it was simply impossible for Sixth Army to accomplish this and not yield territory in the process. Paulus favored a breakout but was unwilling to disobey Hitler. Manstein's force of three understrength panzer divisions managed to reach within 35 miles of Sixth Army positions, and he urged a fait accompli on Paulus. The latter replied with a pessimistic assessment of his army's ability to close the short distance to reach Manstein's relief force. The relieving forces would have to come closer. No linkup was possible without shrinking the pocket, which Hitler expressly forbade.

In mid-December, the Volga froze, allowing the Soviets to use vehicles to cross the ice. During the next seven weeks, Zhukov sent 35,000 vehicles across the river along with 122 mm howitzers to blast the German defensive works. By then, seven Soviet armies surrounded the Sixth Army, and breakout was impossible. Even in this hopeless situation, Paulus refused to disobey Hitler and order a surrender. Hitler sought to stiffen his will by promoting Paulus to field marshal, noting that no Prussian or German field marshal had ever surrendered. Nonetheless, Paulus himself surrendered on January 31 (he maintained he had been "taken by surprise"), but he refused to order his men to do the same. The last German units capitulated on February 2.

As many as 294,000 men had been trapped at Stalingrad, including Hiwis (Soviet auxiliaries working with the Germans) and Romanians. Of only 91,000 men (including 22 generals) taken prisoner by the Soviets, fewer than 5,000 survived the war and Soviet captivity. The last were not released until 1955. Including casualties in Allied units and the rescue attempts, Axis forces lost upward of half a million men. The Stalingrad Campaign may also have cost the Soviets 1.1 million casualties, including more than 485,000 dead.

The effect of the Battle of Stalingrad on the German war effort has been hotly debated. It is often held to be the turning point in the European Theater, but militarily Stalingrad was not irredeemable. The German front lines had been largely recreated when the remnants of the Sixth Army surrendered. Stalingrad was more important for its psychological than its military value. If any single battle denied Germany victory, it was Kursk, six months in the future.

Spencer C. Tucker

Further Reading

Beevor, Antony. *Stalingrad: The Fateful Siege, 1942–1943*. New York: Viking, 1998.

Ellis, Frank. *The Stalingrad Cauldron: Inside the Encirclement and Destruction of the 6th Army*. Lawrence: University Press of Kansas, 2013.

Glantz, David M., and Jonathan House. *When Titans Clashed: How the Red Army Stopped Hitler*. Lawrence: University Press of Kansas, 1995.

Hayward, Joel S. A. *Stopped at Stalingrad: The Luftwaffe and Hitler's Defeat in the East, 1942–1943*. Lawrence: University Press of Kansas, 1998.

Seaton, Albert. *The Russo-German War, 1941–1945*. New York: Praeger, 1971.

Zhukov, Georgii K. *Marshal Zhukov's Greatest Battles*. Translated by Theodore Shabad. New York: Harper & Row, 1969.

Siege of Imphal and Kohima (April 4–May 31, 1944)

Defeat of the Japanese sieges of Indian Army and British forces at Imphal and Kohima in the spring of 1944 marked the turning point in the defense of India against Japanese invasion during World War II. The fierce fighting there has led the sieges to be referred to as "The Stalingrad of the East." Dates for the battle vary widely, depending on source, from March 15 to April 4 for the beginning and May 31 to June 22, 1944, for the end.

> *The Indian National Army (INA)*
>
> The Indian National Army (INA, Free Indian Army) was a military force formed by Indian nationalists during World War II to fight alongside the Japanese, with the goal of securing Indian independence from British rule. Established by Mohan Singh in 1942, the INA recruited Indian Army soldiers captured by the Japanese in the Malayan campaign and at Singapore. Differences with the Japanese, however, brought the INA to an end in late 1942, but it was revived in 1943 under Indian nationalist Subhas Chandra Bose as the military arm of his Provisional Government of Free India. The INA ultimately grew to some 43,000 men and included expatriate Indians as well as former prisoners of war of the Japanese.
>
> The INA was controversial, and a number of its members were later tried in India as war criminals. Although not a major factor in the war, the INA is thought to have furthered Indian nationalism and thus the end of British rule, especially in the publicity surrounding the postwar trials of some of its members.
>
> **Spencer C. Tucker**

Having secured Malaya and the great British naval base of Singapore, the Japanese repositioned their forces used in the descent on Malaysia and moved into Burma (today Myanmar). With its mountains and rivers running mostly north and south, Burma presented difficult topographical challenges for the Japanese advancing from east to west and for the British seeking to move in the opposite direction. Terrain, climate, and disease were also formidable obstacles.

Securing Burma would enable the Japanese to sever the chief land supply route to China, the so-called Burma Road. They also would gain Burma's resources, including oil, and they hoped to stir up nationalist opposition in India to British rule. India's location, vast population as a source for military manpower, raw materials, and manufactured goods made it critical to the Allied war effort.

The Japanese invaded Burma from Thailand beginning on January 20, 1942. The British were then stretched thin, and British, Indian, and Burmese forces suffered major defeats. On March 7, the British abandoned Rangoon (today Yangon). Nationalist Chinese forces, nominally commanded by U.S. Lieutenant General Joseph Stilwell, entered the fighting by the Burma Road to help the retreating British, and Lieutenant General William Slim arrived in Burma in mid-March and assumed command of the British units as both sides reinforced.

On April 29, the Japanese captured Lashio and cut the Burma Road to China. Slim continued to withdraw under heavy Japanese pressure until he reached the Indian border and Imphal, with the Japanese pursuit halting at the Chindwin River. Meanwhile, the Chinese Sixth Army largely disintegrated under Japanese attacks, and other Chinese forces withdrew into Yunnan.

The rainy season beginning in May 1942 brought a lull in operations for both sides. The Japanese now occupied four-fifths of Burma and sought to organize their vast gains, while the British worked to prepare the defense of eastern India against the expected Japanese invasion from Burma. Although it would be some time before enough trained troops and sufficient matériel would allow British and Indian forces to take the offensive in Burma, British commander in India General

A Sikh signaler (left) with a walkie-talkie relays to British officers information gleaned from patrols on Japanese positions on the Imphal Front during the Japanese siege of Imphal and Kohima in eastern India. (Library of Congress)

Sir Archibald Wavell worried about the effects of inaction on morale, and therefore mounted a limited offensive action during the 1942–1943 dry season. This took the form of a counterattack by the Indian 14th Division and British units against Arakan, but the Japanese were able to reinforce and the Allied troops were driven back to India by May.

The Japanese reorganized their forces in Burma. In March 1943, Lieutenant General Kawabe Masakazu had assumed command of the six Japanese divisions in Burma. Kawabe had direct supervision of the two divisions in southwest Burma; the other four divisions forming the Japanese Fifteenth Army were in the north under Lieutenant General Mutaguchi Renya. Well aware, that the Allies were planning a major offensive, Kawabe directed Mutaguchi to invade eastern India with three of his divisions. Toward that end, the Japanese amassed some 85,000 troops, along with some 7,000 Indian Nationalist Army auxiliaries.

The Japanese planned to forestall the Allied attack by seizing the Imphal-Kohima Plain of Manipur, the logical British staging area for an invasion of Burma from central India, and taking the vast supply depots being organized there. Their second major goal was to take and hold the rail line into Assam that passed through Manipur, along which flowed most of the supplies ferried into China as well as those destined for Stilwell's divisions in north Burma. The Japanese also held out hope that a successful attack would spark nationalist risings in India. In Japanese hands, Imphal could also be used as an air base from which to attack deep into India.

Located some 400 miles east-northeast of Calcutta, the city of Imphal was the capital of Manipur Province. Imphal is situated on the Imphal plain, a high plateau some 2,500 feet above sea level and surrounded by mountains. Kohima is 60 miles to northward. Imphal served as the base for the Lieutenant General Geoffrey Scoones's Indian Army IV Corps of the 17th, 20th, and 23rd divisions.

Because Slim was planning to take the offensive with his British Fourteenth Army soon, the IV Corps units were positioned forward almost to the Chindwin River and were widely separated. This made them vulnerable to being isolated and surrounded. In addition to the three Indian Army infantry divisions at Imphal, the Indian Army 254th Tank Brigade was south of Imphal and an Indian parachute brigade was north of it.

Mutaguchi began a broad-based advance across the Chindwin River on March 7. He sent two divisions against Imphal, and Lieutenant General Satō Kōtoku's 31st Division against Kohima. Aware that the Japanese intended an offensive, but not anticipating it until after March 15, Slim and Scoones positioned the three Indian Army divisions around Imphal, with the plan to mount a fighting withdrawal to Imphal where the decisive battle would occur. Only a small force of the 161st Indian Brigade was at Kohima.

Mutaguchi planned to cut the road running south from the supply depot at Dimapur through Kohima to Imphal, seize the major supply dumps at Imphal and, utilizing these for his own troops, drive farther west. The larger battle for both Imphal and Kohima began on April 4 and ended on June 22 when British and Indian troops from Kohima and Imphal linked up.

Were Kohima to fall, British units to the south would have been forced to withdraw. The 50th Indian Parachute Brigade delayed the Japanese arrival and, although the Japanese took Kohima Ridge that dominated the road, the 161st Indian Brigade there held and, the 2nd Infantry Division was sent by road and rail into Dimapur and then it and the 7th Division constituting Lieutenant General Montagu Stopford's XXXIII Corps pushed down the road toward Kohima. Its elements began arriving at Kohima on April 18. The Japanese initially held there, and heavy fighting ensued. Finally, on June 3, ignoring orders from Mutaguchi to stand to the last man, Satō withdrew what remained of his division. The fighting for Kohima was over and the XXXIII Corps could then push down the road to Imphal.

Meanwhile to the south, the Japanese offensive there opened in earnest on March 11–12 with Mutaguchi's 33rd Division feinting south of Imphal and cutting off the British outposts, although the forces there were able to fight their way out and withdraw back on Imphal just ahead of the arrival of the 15th Division. Mutaguchi then surrounded Imphal with his two divisions, cutting off supplies and laying siege to its British and Indian defenders. Slim had expected an attack but was surprised by the speed of the Japanese advance. He quickly organized the flying in to Imphal of ammunition, provisions, fuel, and, during March 19–29, the 5th Indian Division from Arakan to reinforce the defenders. The British also greatly benefited from having the 254th Indian Tank Brigade available. As the only armor in the battle, it played a decisive part in breaking the siege.

Although the Japanese nearly took Kohima in the course of several attempts, its defenders managed to hold out until the arrival of the relief column of the XXXIII Corps on April 20. The margin of victory was provided by U.S. Army Air Forces and Royal Air Force light bomber and fighter aircraft, which repeatedly attacked the Japanese troops.

At Imphal the defenders were greatly assisted by the arrival of additional aircraft, which enabled them to establish air superiority over the Japanese, a major factor in the ultimate victory. As at Kohima, Allied fighters and medium bombers savaged the Japanese positions. Allied air supremacy and the airstrip at Imphal also permitted aerial resupply and the addition of reinforcements. Efforts by the British XXXIII Corps to fight its way through at Kohima to relieve Imphal were, however, slowed by a tenacious Japanese defense.

Meanwhile, the airlifts had gradually increased the number of defenders at Imphal to some 100,000 men. In addition to ferrying in 12,000 reinforcements and evacuating some 13,000 wounded and 43,000 noncombatants, the U.S. and British transports brought to Imphal 14 million pounds of rations as well as ammunition, mail, cigarettes, and fuel. Several thousand mules helped move the supplies on the ground. Although the Japanese were able to repel initial counterattacks by the British, they had anticipated capturing supply dumps at Imphal. When this failed to occur, their own supply shortages, abetted by the onset of the monsoon on May 27, which added to the misery on both sides but weakened the Japanese to the point that Slim's XXXIII Corps was able to smash through the Japanese lines and enter the city on May 31. The siege had lasted 88 days.

Fighting continued, however. Finally, on July 8, with his supply situation now desperate, General Mutaguchi ordered his Fifteenth Army to withdraw back into Burma. Stubbornly resisting Allied land and Allied air attacks, the Japanese made their way back to the Chindwin Valley. Although Mutaguchi was able to maintain unit cohesion, his army had sustained some 53,000 casualties out of an original force of 85,000 men, ruining it as a fighting force. At 16,500 casualties (4,000 at Kohima and 12,500 at Imphal) of some 120,000 engaged, British and Indian Army losses were far less, with many of the Allied wounded and sick saved thanks to prompt air evacuation.

Supreme Allied Commander, South-East Asia Command, Admiral Louis Mountbatten later described the Allied victory there as "probably one of the greatest battles in history . . . in effect the Battle of Burma. . . . [It was] the British-Indian Thermopylae." The Japanese forces in Burma never recovered from their defeats at Imphal and Kohima and continued to be worn down thereafter as Slim took the initiative and launched his invasion of Burma that culminated in victory there the next year.

Spencer C. Tucker

Further Reading

Allen, Louis. *Burma: The Longest War, 1941–1945.* New York: St. Martin's Press, 1984.

Callahan, Raymond A. *Burma, 1942–1945.* London: Davis Poynton, 1978.

Callahan, Raymond A. *Triumph at Imphal-Kohima: How the Indian Army Finally Stopped the Japanese Juggernaut.* Lawrence: University Press of Kansas, 2017.

Connell, John. *Wavell, Supreme Commander, 1941–1943*. London: Collins, 1969.
Fay, Peter W. *The Forgotten Army: India's Armed Struggle for Independence, 1942–1945*. Ann Arbor: University of Michigan Press, 1993.
Franks, Norman. *Air Battle of Imphal*. London: William Kimber, 1985.
Latimer, Jon. *Burma: The Forgotten War*. London: John Murray, 2004.
Slim, William. *Defeat into Victory*. London: Cassell, 1956.

Siege of Budapest (November 3, 1944–February 13, 1945)

This long World War II siege during November 3, 1944–February 13, 1945 ended with the expulsion of German troops from Budapest by the Soviet Army. During this one battle, Soviet forces sustained half of all casualties suffered by them during the campaign in Hungary.

The city of Budapest stretches along both sides of the Danube River and consists of Pest on the east bank and Buda on the west bank. During the siege, there was heavy fighting for virtually every building. Hundreds of thousands of civilians were trapped in the city, unable to leave and soon were caught in the cross fire without food and bereft of essential services, such as electricity. The siege lasted 108 days, and for 52 of those days, the defending Germans were completely surrounded.

In September 1944, Soviet troops invaded Hungary from Romania. The Hungarian government was then desperately trying to leave the war, and on September 28, representatives of Hungarian Regent Miklós Horthy de Nagybánya were dispatched to Moscow. There, they signed a preliminary armistice agreement on October 11, which Horthy announced publicly four days later. This step led to the German Army's occupation of Budapest. Using his son as a hostage, the Germans forced Horthy to appoint Ferenc Szálasi, head of the German Arrow Cross (Fascist) Party, as "Leader of the Nation."

SS-Obergruppenführer Karl Pfeffer-Wildenbruch commanded the German defense of Budapest. He had at his disposal the 8th and 22nd SS Cavalry Divisions and elements of the 13th Panzer Division, the 60th Panzergrenadier Division, and the 271st Volksgrenadier Division. Some units of the Hungarian army under General Iván Hindy fought alongside the Germans. Altogether, the defenders numbered some 92,000 men. Adolf Hitler ordered that Budapest and Hungary be held at all costs. He needed Hungary for its agriculture and industry but also as a location from which to mount a future counterattack in the Carpathian Basin.

Josef Stalin's goal was to drive Hungary from the Axis alliance and introduce a Soviet-style political and social system as soon as possible. His plan to expand the Soviet sphere of interest was threatened by a British proposal to send forces to the Adriatic in autumn 1944 and from there perhaps move against the Carpathian Basin. Stalin was determined to forestall any British presence in the area, and on October 28, 1944, he ordered the capture of Budapest. He did not anticipate a lengthy battle for the city.

The Soviet 2nd Ukrainian Front (army group), commanded by General of the Army Rodion Y. Malinovsky, and the 3rd Ukrainian Front, commanded by Marshal of the Soviet Union Fedor I. Tolbukhin, now converged on the Hungarian capital. In all, the Soviets committed some 157,000 men, including a Romanian contingent, to the operation. Red Army troops first reached the east bank of the city (Pest) on November 3, 1944, but operations then halted.

Following several unsuccessful attempts, Soviet forces completed the encirclement of the city on December 25. On January 1, 1945, the Soviets took the first buildings in Pest proper, and by January 18, they had all of Pest under their control. Many civilians and defending army units escaped across the Danube to the Buda side, but before the evacuation was completed, all the bridges over the Danube connecting the two halves of the city were blown. Meanwhile, on December 24, 1944, fighting had begun in Buda on the west bank.

General Pfeffer-Wildenbruch wanted to break out with his forces on December 28 when the Soviet encirclement was still loose, but Hitler strongly opposed this and ordered his troops to stand fast. Hitler did attempt to relieve the German garrison, however. The first effort was made in early January 1945 by SS-Obergruppenführer Herbert Gille's IV SS Panzer Corps from Komárno, about 30 miles west of Budapest, but the attempt was unsuccessful. Gille then tried again from the vicinity of Lake Balaton to the southwest, but got no closer than 15 miles from the city.

Intense fighting continued, meanwhile, between German and Soviet forces in a small area of Buda, only some 3 miles by 4 miles in size. On February 11, 1945, Pfeffer-Wildenbruch authorized his remaining men to break out of the city westward through the Buda Hills to join up with other German troops just outside the Soviet encirclement. Only some 800 of these men succeeded. The Soviets declared Buda secure on February 13. Pfeffer-Wildenbruch was among those captured and remained a prisoner in the Soviet Union until 1955.

The fighting is estimated to have claimed the lives of 60,000 German troops. The Soviets lost 72,000 confirmed dead, with another 80,000 missing. Some 105,000 Hungarians, mostly civilians, were also dead. Among survivors of the siege were some 100,000 Jews who had managed to escape Arrow Cross roundups. The last German Army units did not leave Hungary until April 4, 1945.

Anna Boros-McGee and Spencer C. Tucker

Further Reading

Landwehr, Richard. *Budapest: The Stalingrad of the Waffen-SS*. New York: CreateSpace, 2012.

Ungváry, Krisztián. *The Siege of Budapest: 100 Days in World War II*. New Haven, CT: Yale University Press, 2006.

Ziemke, Earl F. *Stalingrad to Berlin: The German Defeat in the East*. Washington, DC: Center of Military History, 1984.

Siege of Bastogne (December 20–27, 1944)

The siege of Bastogne during December 20–27, 1944, was a key element of the wider Battle of the Bulge (the German Ardennes Offensive) of December 16, 1944–January 16, 1945.

By the autumn of 1944, Germany's fate was largely sealed. The Western Allies were driving on Germany from the west and the Soviets were closing from the east. German leader Adolf Hitler, however, rejected the rational course for his people of surrender. Deaf to all reason, his alternative was a desperate gamble. With the Eastern Front static for several months and the Allied offensive in the West gaining ground, in September 1944 German chancellor Adolf Hitler conceived of a sudden offensive there that would take the Allies by surprise, break their front, and recapture the important port of Antwerp. He hoped at the very least to buy three to four months to deal with the advancing Soviets. Western Front commander Field Marshal von Rundstedt believed the plan was unrealistic, as did other high-ranking officers. But Hitler refused to change his mind, and substantial German forces were transferred from the Eastern Front to the West for what would be the largest battle on the Western Front in World War II and the largest engagement ever fought by the U.S. Army.

The Germans began their counteroffensive, dubbed Operation WATCH ON THE RHINE after a patriotic hymn of that name, in the pre-dawn darkness and fog on December 16, 1944. Hitler could not have selected a better location than the Ardennes. Allied forces in the area were weak, as supreme commander of Allied Expeditionary Forces General Dwight D. Eisenhower had deployed most of his strength northward and southward. The German timing was also fortuitous, as bad weather restricted the use of Allied air power. In an exceptional achievement the Germans marshaled, without Allied knowledge, 250,000 men, 1,420 tanks and assault guns, and 1,920 rocket and artillery pieces, along with 2,000 aircraft.

Assuming that only they could launch an offensive, the attack took the Western Allies completely by surprise. Initially Lieutenant Generals Omar N. Bradley, commanding the 12th Army Group, and George S. Patton, commanding the Third U.S. Army, did not assess the offensive as major. Eisenhower, however, held it to be a major offensive effort rather than a spoiling attack, and on its second day he ordered the battle-weary 82d and 101st Airborne divisions out of a reconstitution camp at Reims, France, and to the front.

The German force of 24 divisions pushing against three divisions of Lieutenant General Courtney Hodges's First Army soon drove a "bulge" in the American defenses, which gave the battle its name. The German penetration eventually extended 50 miles deep and 70 miles wide.

Bastogne, Belgium, was a key German objective. Bastogne was an important transportation hub, as seven main roads, a railroad line, and several minor roads met there. Elements of the U.S. First Army had liberated Bastogne and the Ardennes area in September 1944. Taking Bastogne early on, along with the Allied fuel depots and the communications routes between it and Saint Vith were essential if the Germans were to reach Antwerp before additional Allied land and aircraft assets could be brought to bear.

General of Panzer Troops Hasso Eccard von Manteuffel commanding the German Fifth Panzer Army had given General of Panzer Troops Heinrich Freiherr von Lüttwitz's XLVII Panzer Corps the assignment of capturing Bastogne, which was only some 20 miles from the German line of attack. Bastogne was defended chiefly by the U.S. 28th Infantry Division, which had seen continuous fighting from July 22 to November 19, before being assigned to what was believed to be a relatively quiet area presumably facing only one German infantry division.

The Germans expected to occupy Bastogne no later than December 18, but the poor state of the roads from recent heavy rains, the need to build bridges over the Our River, American defenders, and misinformation provided by Belgians delayed their arrival. Meanwhile, the 101st Airborne Division arrived at Bastogne by truck near midnight on December 18. The first American units to reach the city, however, were elements of the 10th Armored Division, which had arrived there a few hours earlier.

Lieutenant General Fritz Bayerlein's Panzer Lehr Division reached Bastogne just after midnight on December 19. It immediately attacked the American positions, as Bayerlein was aware from radio intercepts that the 101st Airborne had been ordered there. The Americans beat back the German assault but were under constant German pressure from this point.

The defenders pressed numerous U.S. Army service troops into service as infantrymen, while a mobile force of 48 tanks was scraped together to act as a mobile "fire brigade" to be employed where needed. Three artillery battalions, each with 12 155 mm howitzers, provided heavy fire support for the defenders, although restricted in effectiveness by dwindling stocks of ammunition.

With the American defenses holding, Lüttwitz decided to encircle Bastogne and strike from the south and southwest, beginning the night of December 20–21. The Germans enjoyed initial success and nearly took the American artillery positions southwest of Bastogne before they were stopped. All the highways leading there had been cut by the Germans by noon on December 21 with Bastogne now completely surrounded. The Americans here were outnumbered some 5–1 and were lacking in cold-weather clothing, food, ammunition, and medical supplies, while poor weather conditions both prevented aerial resupply and tactical air support. With Bastogne completely encircled in a six-mile-diameter pocket, the Germans then brought up supplies and reinforcements. Ultimately, the battle would see some 22,800 Americans opposing some 54,000 Germans.

On December 22, four German soldiers, one carrying a white flag, walked toward an American outpost near Bastogne. They carried an ultimatum addressed to "the U.S.A. commander of the encircled city of Bastogne." The message informed the American commander of the situation and urged him to save his troops with an "honorable surrender." The response of Brigadier General Anthony McAuliffe, commanding the division in the absence of Major General Maxwell D. Taylor, was memorable: "To the German Commander: Nuts. The American commander." When the German officer receiving the message asked its meaning, he was told it meant "Go to Hell!"

Even though the Germans pressed their offensive all around Bastogne, they failed to take it. The Allied forces did not break, as elements of Patton's Third Army were rushing to relieve Bastogne from the south. Patton had told an unbelieving Eisenhower that he could wheel his army 90 degrees and strike north into the bulge with three divisions in only two days. He accomplished this feat in difficult conditions in what was one of the most memorable mass maneuvers of that or any war.

Soldiers of the U.S. Army's 4th Armored Division fire at German troops during the American relief of U.S. forces at Bastogne, Belgium, December 27, 1944. (National Archives)

Other Allied resources were also diverted to the Ardennes, and on December 23 a weather change moved over the front, clearing the sky and freezing the ground, making the terrain passable for armor. Allied planes filled the skies and transports dropped supplies to Bastogne, which was then down to only some 10 rounds per gun. On Christmas Day, the German panzers ground to a halt, out of fuel, while 2nd Armored Division gunners had a turkey shoot at Celles, almost at the Meuse, destroying 82 German tanks. Then, on December 26, Lieutenant Colonel Creighton Abrams's tanks of the 37th Tank Battalion of the 4th Armored Division arrived to lift the siege of Bastogne. Ground communication with supply dumps was effected on December 27, along with evacuation of the wounded.

Allied aircraft attacked the German armor without letup, destroying large numbers of tanks. The last major German attack on Bastogne occurred on January 4. Other smaller attacks took place until January 8, with the battle ending the next day. The fight for Bastogne had claimed about 3,000 German and 2,700 American casualties; 782 Belgian civilians also died.

Unfortunately, British field marshal Bernard Montgomery, commanding the British 21st Army Group on the Allied left flank, decided to stay on the defensive, overruling U.S. Army general J. Lawton Collins's plan to cut off the bulge by striking from each shoulder. Finally, the Allies attacked midway up the salient, passing up the chance to surround the Germans. Patton believed that timidity on the part of Eisenhower and Montgomery allowed most of the Germans to escape.

On January 1, 1945, the Germans mounted a surprise attack on Allied air bases in Belgium. Operation BODENPLATTE (base plate) destroyed 500–800 Allied aircraft, most of them on the ground, but it also resulted in about 300 German aircraft shot down and 214 trained pilots lost, many of these to German antiaircraft fire. The Allies could replace their losses; the Germans could not. The Battle of the Bulge dragged on to the middle of January. Prior to that point, Hitler ordered part of the panzer divisions transferred back to the East. Before the Germans could switch these resources, however, the Soviets launched their last great offensive.

The Battle of the Bulge had been fought and won largely by American forces. Montgomery later portrayed the Battle of the Bulge as an Anglo-American affair and implied that the British had saved the Americans. This caused something of an uproar, and Winston Churchill set this right in a speech to the House of Commons on January 18 when he said that "United States troops have done almost all the fighting, and have suffered almost all the losses."

By the end of January, the American First and Third Armies had reached the German frontier and reestablished the line of six weeks before. Of the 600,000 U.S. troops involved, 19,000 were killed, about 47,000 were wounded, and 15,000 were prisoners. Among 55,000 British engaged, casualties totaled 1,400, of whom 200 were killed. The Germans, employing nearly 500,000 men in the Ardennes battle, sustained nearly 100,000 casualties killed, wounded, and captured. Both sides suffered heavy equipment losses, about 800 tanks on each side, and the Germans lost virtually all their aircraft committed. But again, the Western Allies could quickly make good their losses, while the Germans could not. Hitler had also seriously weakened German defenses in the East. In effect Operation WATCH ON THE RHINE hastened the end of the war. Germany surrendered four months later.

Spencer C. Tucker

Further Reading

Cole, Hugh M. *The United States Army in World War II: The European Theater of Operations: The Ardennes: Battle of the Bulge.* Washington, DC: Government Printing Office, 1965.

Dupuy, Trevor N., David L. Bongard, and Richard C. Anderson Jr. *Hitler's Last Gamble: The Battle of the Bulge, December 1944–January 1945.* New York: HarperCollins, 1994.

Eisenhower, John S. D. *The Bitter Woods.* New York: G. P. Putnam's Sons, 1969.

Forty, George. *The Reich's Last Gamble: The Ardennes Offensive: December 1944.* London: Cassell, 2000.

MacDonald, Charles B. *A Time for Trumpets: The Untold Story of the Battle of the Bulge.* New York: William Morrow, 1985.

Marshall, S. L. A. *Bastogne: The Story of the First Eight Days.* Washington, DC: Infantry Journal Press, 1946.

Merriam, Robert E. *Dark December: The Full Account of the Battle of the Bulge.* Yardley, PA: Westholme Publishing, 2011.

Siege of Berlin (April 16–May 2, 1945)

The Soviet siege of Berlin (April 16–May 2, 1945) was the culminating land battle of the European Theater in World War II. Berlin, the capital of the Reich, was vital to the German war effort. German leader Adolf Hitler spent little time there during the war, but the city was the administrative center of the new German empire and powerhouse of the war effort, the greatest industrial and commercial city in Europe. Berlin was also a vital communications and transportation hub and a key production center, particularly for electrical products and armaments.

In August 1940, after the bombing of London, Bomber Command of the Royal Air Force (RAF) raided Berlin, but the city enjoyed a respite thereafter until March 1943; then there was another pause. The battle for the city began in earnest in November 1943 with the first in a long series of punishing Allied air raids, with particularly severe attacks in March 1944. Berliners managed to carry on amid the ruins.

Hitler returned to Berlin from the Alderhorst (Eagle's Nest), his retreat at Ziegenberg, by train on January 16, 1945, and as the war drew to a close, the city became the ultimate prize, at least for the Soviets. Soviet leader Josef Stalin wanted it desperately. So did British prime minister Winston L. S. Churchill, but he was overruled by U.S. leaders, who showed little interest in capturing the city, particularly after agreements setting up the postwar occupation placed Berlin deep within the Soviet zone. Supreme commander of Allied forces in the west, General Dwight D. Eisenhower, who was in any case distracted by a phantom Nazi Alpine "National Redoubt," said he had no interest in taking the city. High casualty estimates (Lieutenant General Omar Bradley posited a cost of 100,000 men) also deterred Eisenhower. Thus, although U.S. forces, including the 82nd Airborne Division, were readied for such an assault, the task was left to the Soviets. The major Western Allied contribution to the battle was the bombing of Berlin during 1945, halted only on April 20 when the Soviets were in the city.

Stalin deliberately concealed the U.S. ambivalence concerning Berlin from his front commanders, Generals Ivan S. Konev and Georgii K. Zhukov. By early February, Zhukov's 1st Belorussian Front and Konev's 1st Ukrainian Front had completed the initial phase of their advance into Germany. Zhukov's troops were across the Oder River, some 60 miles from Berlin. The Soviets had surrounded large German troop concentrations at Breslau and Posen. Meanwhile, Soviet forces carried out a horrible revenge on eastern Germany, in which tens of thousands of civilians were murdered. Total German casualties ranged into the millions.

Zhukov might then have pushed on to the capital in another several weeks had not Stalin ordered a halt, necessary because of logistical problems resulting from the vast distances the Soviet forces had covered to that point. Meanwhile, Konev's forces threatened the German capital from the southeast. In defense of Berlin, Hitler had only the remnants of his Third Panzer and Ninth Armies, now constituting Army Group Vistula. In March, however, he ordered that the city be held "to the last man and the last shot."

On March 8, alarmed by the American crossing of the Rhine the day before, Stalin summoned Zhukov to Moscow to discuss an offensive against Berlin. The now rapid progress of the Western Allies eastward set off alarm bells in Moscow, and Stavka (the Soviet High Command) rushed plans for an offensive to take the German capital. On March 31, Stalin ordered the offensive to begin.

Zhukov would make the principal drive on Berlin, while Konev supported him on the left flank and Marshal Konstantin Rokossovsky's 2nd Belorussian Front on the lower Oder moved on Zhukov's right flank. Altogether, the three fronts had some 1.5 million troops, 6,250 armored vehicles, and 7,500 aircraft. Opposing them, the German Ninth Army and Third Panzer Army had only 24 understrength divisions, with 754 tanks and few aircraft.

The siege or Battle of Berlin officially began on April 16 with troops of the 1st Belorussian Front assaulting the Seelow Heights, the last major defensive line outside the city. The Battle of the Seelow Heights, fought during April 16–19, was one of the last pitched battles of World War II and involved nearly 1 million Red Army soldiers and more than 20,000 tanks and artillery pieces against some 100,000 German soldiers with perhaps 1,200 tanks and guns. On April 19, Zhukov's forces broke through the German positions, having suffered about 30,000 dead, with 12,000 German soldiers dead. Only broken German forces now separated the Soviets from Berlin.

Meanwhile, on April 18, Stalin ordered Zhukov to proceed around Berlin from the north, while Konev encircled the city from the south. Hitler ordered his Ninth Army to stand fast on the Oder, thus facilitating Konev's move.

On April 20, Hitler's 56th birthday, artillery of the 1st Belorussian Front began shelling Berlin. That same day, Konev's tanks reached Jüterbog, the airfield and key ammunition depot south of Berlin. Also, on April 20, Hitler allowed those of his entourage who wished to do so to leave the city while announcing his intention to remain there.

The Soviets completed the encirclement of Berlin on April 25. Also, on that day, Soviet and U.S. forces met on the Elbe River. Hitler attempted to organize the Ninth Army as a relief force for Berlin, but it, too, was surrounded and soon destroyed. Although Lieutenant General Walther Wenck's Twelfth Army tried to reach Berlin from the west, it was too weak to accomplish the task.

Meanwhile, the defense of Berlin itself fell to the German troops unfortunate enough to be pushed back there and by old men and boys hastily pressed into service for the daunting task. On April 30, with the defenders' ammunition nearly depleted and the defenses fast crumbling and as Soviet troops took the Reichstag (Parliament) building, Hitler committed suicide in his underground bunker. On May 2, Lieutenant General Hans Krebs, chief of the German General Staff, surrendered Berlin.

Given their country's suffering in the war, Soviet soldiers hardly needed encouragement to destroy the German capital, the symbol of Nazism, and they proceeded to commit widespread atrocities in the city both during and after its fall.

Bradley's estimate of the cost of taking Berlin was, in fact, low. According to one source, the "Berlin Strategic Offensive" from April 16 to May 8, involving the 1st Belorussian, 2nd Belorussian, and 1st Ukrainian Fronts, produced a staggering total of 352,475 Soviet casualties (including 78,291 dead)—an average of 15,325 a day.

What is remarkable is how Berlin came back. It survived the destruction of the war and the building of the Berlin Wall in 1961, which divided the city into east and west portions. Today, it is again the capital of a united, economically powerful, but this time peaceful and democratic German state.

Spencer C. Tucker

Further Reading
Beevor, Antony. *The Fall of Berlin, 1945*. New York: Viking Penguin, 2002.
Hastings, Max. *Armageddon: The Battle for Germany, 1944–1945*. New York: Macmillan, 2004.
Read, Anthony, and David Fisher. *The Fall of Berlin*. New York: W. W. Norton, 1992.
Ryan, Cornelius. *The Last Battle*. New York: Simon & Schuster, 1966.

Berlin Blockade and Airlift (June 24, 1948–May 12, 1949)

The first serious crisis of the Cold War precipitated by the Soviet Union's attempt to cut off access to and absorb West Berlin, the Berlin Blockade, was not a military action, but the attempt to starve a population center into submission by cutting off its supply lines is a feature of a siege and for that reason it is included here.

West Berlin lay deep within Soviet-occupied eastern Germany. As part of the Potsdam Agreements, Germany and Berlin were divided into occupation zones by the victorious World War II Allies (the United States, the Soviet Union, France, and Great Britain), reaffirming principles laid out earlier at the Yalta Conference. Although the provisions of the agreement allocated occupation sectors of Berlin to the other three Allies, no formal arrangements had been made for access to Berlin via the Soviet zone.

After the war, the relationship between the Soviet Union and the West steadily deteriorated, as demonstrated by disputes in the United Nations, Winston Churchill's March 1946 "Sinews of Peace" speech (also known as the "Iron Curtain" speech), U.S. emphasis on Soviet containment, Soviet hostility toward the Marshall Plan, and a growing commitment on the part of the United States, Britain, and France to consolidate their occupation zones in western Germany. The Soviets, who had been invaded by Germany twice in the first half of the twentieth century, were alarmed at the prospect of a reunited, independent Germany, and they sought to take control of all Berlin, deep in their zone of occupation. Berliners did not want communism. They had jolted the Russians in October 1945 by giving the Social Democrats very nearly a majority (48.7 percent); whereas, the communist-sponsored Socialist Unity Party polled slightly less than 20 percent of the vote.

In late 1947, discussions on the fate of Germany broke down over Soviet charges that its former Allies were violating the Potsdam Agreements. On their part, the Western powers charged that they were being forced to subsidize the Soviets economically with a common currency in effect for all four zones of Germany as the Soviets dismantled and removed whole factories and virtually anything they could transport from their zone to the Soviet Union. After the decision of the Western powers that they would introduce a new currency in their three zones of

> **"Operation LITTLE VITTLES"**
>
> "Operation VITTLES" soon added a subset, "Operation LITTLE VITTLES." C-54 pilot U.S. Air Force Lieutenant Gail Halvorsen, encountered children behind a fence at Berlin's Tempelhof Airport and offered them some chewing gum, only to see them break it in small pieces and share it. Taken aback, he promised to drop candy in his next flight. When asked how they would know his plane, he said he would "wiggle his wings."
>
> Halvorsen, who became known as "Wiggle Wings" and the "Candy Bomber," lived up to his promise, then got other air crew to donate their candy rations and also drop them on handkerchief parachutes. Things grew from there, as more and more children showed up to catch his airdrops. Newspaper stories led to candy donations from the United States, supported by the Air Force because of the great propaganda value.
>
> "LITTLE VITTLES" was in effect from September 22, 1948, to May 13, 1949, and reportedly delivered 23 tons of candy on 23,000 parachutes.
>
> **Spencer C. Tucker**

Germany alone, on March 20, 1948, the Soviets withdrew from the Four-Power Allied Control Council, which controlled Berlin.

Beginning on April 1, 1948, The Soviets instituted a creeping blockade of Berlin. Little by little they cut off surface access to the city. First the key Elbe road bridge was closed, ostensibly for repairs. The Russians meant business but the Western powers were slow to react. They were focused on the introduction of the new currency and the restoration of a sound West German economy. On April 7, 1948, they announced the introduction of the new currency. This was the signal for the blockade to begin in earnest. On June 7, the Western powers announced their intention to proceed with the creation of a West German state. On June 15, the Soviets declared the Autobahn entering Berlin from West Germany closed for repairs. Three days later all road traffic from the west was halted, and on June 21 barge traffic was prohibited from entering the city. On June 24, the Soviets stopped all rail transportation between West Germany and Berlin, arguing that if Germany were to be partitioned, Berlin could no longer be the German capital. By August 4, 1948, the blockade was complete.

Located 110 miles inside the Soviet occupation zone, West Berlin from the start of the Cold War had been a Western outpost deep within the communist bloc, a hotbed of intelligence operations by both sides, and the best available escape route for East Germans fleeing communism and Soviet control. U.S. president Harry Truman was convinced that abandoning Berlin would jeopardize control of all of Germany. He further believed that the Soviets were determined to push the Western powers out of Berlin, thereby discrediting repeated American assurances to its allies and the rest of Europe that it would not allow Berlin to fall.

Direction of this first major battle of the Cold War fell upon the shoulders of General Lucius Clay, American military commander in Germany. Clay informed Washington that if West Berlin were abandoned, the Soviet Union would be emboldened by this display of weakness to try to seize the rest of Germany. He said, "If we withdraw, our position in Europe is threatened, and

Berliners watch a U.S. Air Force Fairchild C-82A Packet landing with supplies for the civilian population at the city's Tempelhof Airport during the 1948–1949 Berlin Airlift. (U.S. Air Force)

communism will run rampant." Clay informed Washington that there were three alternatives: withdraw from Berlin, attempt to push an armored column up the autobahn, and organize an airlift to try to supply the city by air. Truman's reaction was, "We shall stay, period." Mayor of West Berlin Ernst Reuter was skeptical about the airlift and favored the second choice, but Washington rejected this was as being too risky; it ran the high probability of a shooting war with the Soviets.

In mid-June, General Clay informed Reuter that the United States would begin an air-lift to supply the city. It would not be hard to supply Allied personnel by air but the prospect of providing for more than 2 million Germans in the Western zones of Berlin looked impossible. Initially, the assumption was that this would be a short-term measure lasting perhaps five to six weeks with Allied planes bringing in perhaps 500–700 tons of freight a day. In reality, what the Americans came to call "Operation VITTLES" began on June 26, 1948.

Aircrews from the U.S. Air Force, the British Royal Air Force, the French Air Force, the Royal Australian Air Force, the Royal Canadian Air Force, the Royal New Zealand Air Force, and the South African Air Force, all under the leadership of U.S. Air Force Lieutenant General Curtis LeMay, flew a total of 272,000 flights into West Berlin, delivering thousands of tons of supplies every day.

The situation in the summer and fall of 1948 became very tense as Soviet planes buzzed U.S. transport planes in the air corridors over East Germany, but the Allies only increased their efforts to resupply the German city once it became apparent that no resolution was in sight. The Soviets never attempted to shoot down any of the Western aircraft involved in the airlift, no doubt because such a provocation might well have resulted in war.

Hundreds of aircraft were employed to fly in a wide variety of cargo items, including more than 1.5 million tons of coal. Although the airlift was begun by the workhorse C-47 Skytrain with a 3-ton cargo capacity, the signature aircraft became the U.S. Air Force four-engine C-54 Skymaster, capable of handling 10 tons of cargo. The British employed the Lancaster, York, and Hasting, as well as Sunderland Flying Boats that utilized Lake Havel in Berlin.

By the fall, the airlift was transporting an average of 5,000 tons of supplies a day. At the height of the operation on April 16, 1949, an aircraft landed in Berlin every minute around the clock. The three main Berlin airfields involved in the effort were Tempelhof in the American sector, Gatow in the British zone, and Tegel in the French sector. The British even landed seaplanes on the Havel River.

The airlift gained widespread public and international admiration, and on May 12, 1949, the Soviets, concluding that the blockade had failed, reopened the borders in return for a meeting of the Council of Foreign Ministers, perhaps believing that they could have some influence on the Western Allies' proposed plans for the future of Germany. Even though the Soviets lifted the blockade in May, the airlift did not end until September 30 because the allies sought to build up sufficient amounts of reserve supplies in West Berlin in case the Soviets blockaded it again. In all, the United States, Britain, and France flew 278,118 flights transporting more than 2.3 million short tons of cargo. Thirty-one Americans and 39 British citizens, most of them military personnel, died in the airlift.

In the end, the blockade was not only completely ineffective but also backfired on the Soviets in other ways. The blockade provoked genuine fears of the Soviets in the West and introduced even greater tension into the Cold War. Instead of preventing an independent West Germany, it actually accelerated Allied plans to bring about that state. It also hastened the creation of the North Atlantic Treaty Organization (NATO), an American–West European military alliance.

James H. Willbanks and Spencer C. Tucker

Further Reading

Cherny, Andrei. *The Candy Bombers: The Untold Story of the Berlin Airlift and America's Finest Hour.* New York: G. P. Putnam's Sons, 2008.

Clay, Lucius D. *Decision in Germany.* Garden City, NY: Doubleday, 1950.

Collins, Richard. *Bridge across the Sky: The Berlin Blockade and Airlift, 1948–1949.* New York: Pan Macmillan, 1978.

Harrington, Daniel F. *Berlin on the Brink: The Blockade, the Airlift, and the Early Cold War.* Lexington: University of Kentucky Press, 2012.

Haydock, Michael D. *City under Siege: The Berlin Blockade and Airlift, 1948–1949*. London: Brassey's, 1999.

Schlain, Avi. *The United States and the Berlin Blockade, 1948–1949: A Study in Decision-Making*. Berkeley: University of California Press, 1983.

Tusa, Ann. *The Last Division: A History of Berlin, 1945–1989*. Reading, MA: Addison-Wesley, 1997.

Siege of Dien Bien Phu (March 13–May 7, 1954)

The March 13–May, 1954 siege of Dien Bien Phu was one of the most important battles of the entire twentieth century, signaling the end of the Indochina War and Western colonialism in Asia. The French refusal to reach accommodation with Vietnamese nationalism and efforts to restore their pre–World War II position in Indochina led to the beginning of fighting there in December 1946 between French forces and the Vietnamese nationalists, the Viet Minh, led by veteran communist Ho Chi Minh. The French soon restored control in the cities, but the Viet Minh took to the jungles and waged a growing guerrilla war. Despite increasing quantities of U.S. aid to the French, the Viet Minh steadily controlled more and more territory, especially Tonkin in the northern part of the country.

The war was lost for all practical purposes for the French in the autumn of 1949, when the communists triumphed in China. This provided the Viet Minh with both a sanctuary and a supply base. The French also lost the battle for the hearts and minds of the people by failing to grant genuine authority to their alternative "State of Vietnam."

In early 1954, Viet Minh commander General Vo Nguyen Giap prepared to invade Laos. French commander in Indochina General Henri Navarre's response was Operation CASTOR, which entailed the establishment of an air base in the village of Dien Bien Phu in far northwestern Vietnam. Navarre claimed that the base would serve as a blocking position astride the chief Viet Minh invasion route into northern Laos, but he actually hoped to use Dien Bien Phu as bait to draw Viet Minh forces into battle, whereupon he planned to destroy them with superior artillery and airpower.

Located in an obscure valley some 185 miles by air from Hanoi, Dien Bien Phu boasted a small airstrip. On November 20, 1953, 2,200 French paratroopers dropped into the valley and easily defeated the small Viet Minh garrison there. Navarre assumed that Giap would commit at most one division against Dien Bien Phu. Should this prove incorrect, the French commander was confident that the garrison could be evacuated. Leaving the Viet Minh in control of the high ground surrounding the base, however, was courting disaster.

Colonel Christian Marie Ferdinand de la Croix de Castries (promoted to brigadier general during the battle) commanded French forces at Dien Bien Phu. His men were entirely dependent on air supply by some 75 C-47s transports. The French could also call on 48 B-26 Marauder and PB4Y-2 Privateer bombers, 112 Bearcat and Hellcat fighter-bombers, and a few helicopters. After the battle, Navarre wrote in his memoirs, "The insufficiency of aviation was, for our side, the principal cause of the loss of the battle."

Siege of Dien Bien Phu

De Castries set up his central command post in the village itself. Around it he ordered the construction of a series of strong points: Beatrice, Gabrielle, Anne-Marie, Dominique, Huguette, Françoise, Elaine, and Isabelle (all reportedly named for his current mistresses). This last post was, unfortunately for the defenders, separated from the others some three miles to the south and easily cut off. Isabelle also tied down a third of the French forces.

By mid-March and the beginning of the siege, the French had nearly 11,000 men in the valley, a third of them ethnic Vietnamese. Ultimately the French committed 16,544 men to Dien Bien Phu. Fortifications were totally inadequate, as the French assumed that their artillery could quickly knock out any Viet Minh artillery.

Giap accepted the challenge of trying to dislodge the French at Dien Bien Phu, but there was strong political pressure on him to do so. A diplomatic conference of the great powers was set to begin in Geneva, and a major Viet Minh victory might bring negotiations there that would end the war. Giap committed not one but four divisions to the effort, assembling some 49,500 combat troops and 31,500 support personnel.

The siege opened on March 13, 1954, with a heavy Viet Minh bombardment. Although the French added 4,000 men during the battle, Giap more than offset this with manpower increases of his own; he also steadily improved his artillery. Tens of thousands of porters dragged the guns there. The Viet Minh actually deployed more artillery pieces (20–24 105 mm howitzers, 15–20 75 mm howitzers, 20 120 mm mortars, and at least 40 82 mm mortars, along with 80 Chinese-crewed 37 mm antiaircraft guns, 100 antiaircraft machine guns, and 12–16 six-tube Katyusha rocket launchers) than did the French (four 155 mm howitzers, 24 105 mm howitzers, and four 120 mm mortars). The Viet Minh also fired more artillery rounds than did the French.

On the very first night of the siege, March 13–14, the Viet Minh took Beatrice. Gabrielle fell two days later. The Viet Minh also shelled the airstrip, destroying or driving its aircraft away and knocking out its radio-direction beacon. C-47 transports still flew in supplies and took out wounded but at great risk. The last flight in or out of Dien Bien Phu occurred on March 27. During the battle, the Viet Minh shot down 48 French planes and destroyed another 16 on the ground.

Heavy casualties forced Giap to shift from costly human-wave tactics to classic siege warfare. The Viet Minh built miles of zigzag trenches that inched ever closer to the French lines. Their final assault occurred on May 6, and the last French troops surrendered the next evening. A plan to rescue the garrison or break out came too late.

The French sustained some 20,000 casualties in the battle (2,242 killed, 3,711 missing, and 6,463 wounded as well as 6,500 taken prisoner and forces lost in relief operations); the Viet Minh lost at least 22,900 (7,900 killed and 15,000 wounded). The Viet Minh sent their prisoners off on foot on a 500-mile trek to prison camps, from which fewer than half returned.

The outcome of the battle allowed French politicians to shift the blame for the defeat in Indochina to the French Army and extricate France from the war. The Geneva Conference did hammer out a settlement for Indochina, but the settlement proved to be only a truce. Within a few years the fighting resumed, but this time the Americans had taken the place of the French.

Spencer C. Tucker

Further Reading

Fall, Bernard. *Hell in a Very Small Place: The Siege of Dien Bien Phu*. Philadelphia: J. B. Lippincott, 1967.

Morgan, Ted. *Valley of Death: The Tragedy at Dien Bien Phu That Led America into the Vietnam War*. New York: Random House, 2010.

Navarre, General Henri. *Agonie de Indochine*. Paris: Plon, 1956.

Porch, Douglas. *The French Foreign Legion. A Complete History of the Legendary Fighting Force*. New York: HarperCollins, 1991.

Roy, Jules. *The Battle of Dienbienphu*. New York: Harper & Row, 1965.

Simpson, Howard R. *Dien Bien Phu: The Epic Battle America Forgot*. Washington, DC: Brassey's, 1994.

Windrow, Martin. *The Last Valley: Dien Bien Phu and the French Defeat in Vietnam*. London: Weidenfeld & Nicolson, 2004.

Siege of Khe Sanh (January 21–April 8, 1968)

The siege of Khe Sanh (January 21–April 8, 1968) was a bloody encounter between the Peoples' Army of Vietnam (PAVN, North Vietnamese Army, NVA) and the U.S. Marine Corps and supporting elements during the Vietnam War (1958–1975).

In late April and early May 1967, heavy fighting occurred near Khe Sanh in the Republic of Vietnam (RVN, South Vietnam). This strategically insignificant base with an air strip was located in western Quang Tri province about 6 miles east of Laos and 14 miles south of the Demilitarized Zone (DMZ) dividing North Vietnam and South Vietnam. Khe Sanh had been established to monitor PAVN infiltration through Laos down the so-called Ho Chi Minh Trail into South Vietnam. Military Assistance Command, Vietnam (MACV) commander General William Westmoreland hoped that an enlarged base there could enable monitoring such movements along Route 9 in Laos and perhaps serve as a jumping-off point for a future invasion of that kingdom.

In order to monitor nearby infiltration routes, the Marines were ordered to take three enemy-held hills. Fighting for these was intense, even hand-to-hand; but at the end of these so-called hill fights—later known as the First Battle of Khe Sanh (April 24–May 12)—the marines had suffered 160 killed and 746 wounded. They claimed 570 confirmed VC/PAVN dead and another 589 probable dead.

The First Battle of Khe Sanh was only one of many in PAVN commander General Vo Nguyen Giap's "peripheral campaign," designed to draw U.S. forces away from the population centers to terrain more suitable for PAVN operations. In September, PAVN forces crossed the DMZ to attack a U.S. Marine Corps outpost at Con Thien, and for the first time in the war PAVN forces used long-range guns and rockets to support an infantry assault. In just nine days, they fired 3,000 shells.

Westmoreland supported U.S. operations in I Corps with a bombing campaign planned by Air Force General William Momyer. Dubbed SLAM—for Seek,

Siege of Khe Sanh

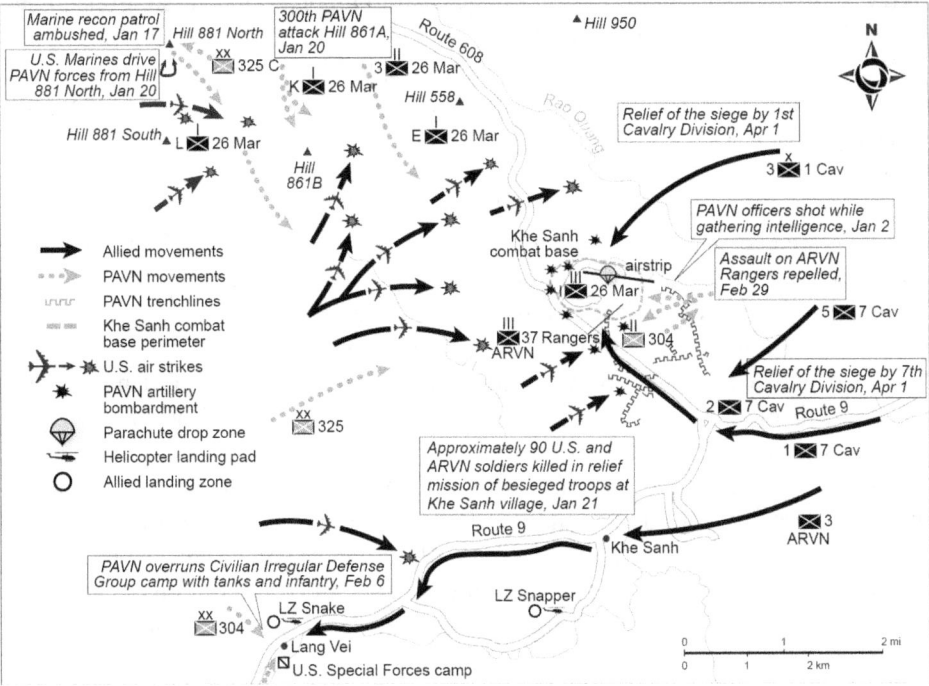

A diagram of the unsuccessful North Vietnamese siege of the U.S. Marine base at Khe Sanh in far northwestern South Vietnam during January 21–April 8, 1968. Each side saw the siege as an opportunity to inflict a major psychological defeat on their enemy. (ABC-CLIO)

Locate, Annihilate, and Monitor—the campaign was on a massive scale. At Con Thien alone, B-52s dropped 22,000 tons of bombs. This was in addition to ordnance delivered by fighter bombers, naval gunfire, and ground artillery. SLAM's success convinced Westmoreland that with adequate bombing and aerial resupply U.S. outposts could survive even when outnumbered. As Westmoreland said of Con Thien in reference to the 1954 French defeat in the siege of Dien Bien Phu, "It was Dienbienphu in reverse. . . . massed firepower [is] in itself sufficient to force a besieging enemy to desist."

In January 1968, attention turned again to the marine base at Khe Sanh, inspiring frequent comparisons to Dien Bien Phu. Although surrounded by hills and jungle that could conceal PAVN artillery, Khe Sanh was not in a bowl such as Dien Bien Phu; indeed, its location on a plateau gave the defenders the advantage of high ground against an assault.

For 77 days, from January 21 until April 8, 1968, some 20,000–40,000 PAVN troops in four divisions besieged the base at Khe Sanh and the high terrain around it. PAVN forces also employed a dozen or so PT-76 light amphibious tanks, one of only two such instances in which they used tanks prior to 1972.

The defenders were equally split between the base and the hill positions around it. The defense centered on 6,000 marines, supported by artillery and a small contingent of U.S. Army Special Forces. There was also an Army of Vietnam (ARVN, South Vietnamese Army) Ranger battalion, on which Westmoreland had insisted as a sign of Allied solidarity.

By mid-January, the marines were equally split between the main plateau and the four surrounding hills named for their heights: 950, 881, 861, and 558. Infantry at each garrison were supported by 105 mm howitzers and mortars.

At 5:30 a.m. on January 20, Captain William Dabney and 185 men of Company I launched a patrol from Hill 881 South to Hill 881 North. This resulted in heavy contact. By nightfall, Dabney's men were back on Hill 881S, and the Khe Sanh combat base was on maximum alert. (Years later, Dabney was awarded the Navy Cross for his heroic leadership.) That night, an apparent communist deserter revealed that a major attack was planned on 881S and 861 at 12:30 a.m. on the 21st. The marines brought up two Ontos assault vehicles capable of firing flechette rounds with thousands of steel darts. They also set out razor-sharp concertina wire, claymore mines, and trip flares.

PAVN forces attacked 861 on schedule using bangalore torpedoes. Although the attack was initially successful, at 5:00 a.m. in fierce fighting the marines counterattacked with success. Then at 5:30, PAVN forces began an intense rocket and artillery attack against Khe Sanh itself, hitting the main ammunition dump, which blew up in spectacular fashion and severely restricted the ammunition available for return fire.

That same afternoon six C-130 planes flew in and offloaded their 24 tons of cargo, consisting mostly of artillery shells, but Khe Sanh's commander Colonel David Lownds estimated he would need 160 tons of supplies per day. U.S. air power proved vital. C-130 and C-123 aircraft, along with Marine Corps CH-46 and Army CH-47 and UH-1E helicopters, ran a gauntlet of enemy antiaircraft fire to bring in supplies and evacuate wounded.

On February 10, a C-130 was destroyed while unloading fuel. After that C-130 landings were suspended, although the planes continued to resupply the base by parachute drops or a hook and line system for extracting pallets in flight (LAPES).

The first major PAVN ground attack against the base came on February 8 but was repulsed in heavy fighting at a cost of 150 PAVN and 21 Marine dead. During the next weeks, the attackers concentrated on a relentless artillery barrage from 82 mm and 120 mm mortars, 122 mm rockets, and 130 mm and 152 mm artillery pieces. PAVN forces fired an average of 2,500 rounds a week into an area barely 330 by 600 yards. This artillery fire, however, caused few casualties among the sandbagged and dug-in defenders. The last major land attack occurred over February 29 to March 1 and was directed principally against the ARVN 37th Ranger Battalion. With heavy supporting fire, the Rangers turned back three separate PAVN attacks.

Khe Sanh loomed large in American attention. This otherwise obscure fortress became the focus of daily newspaper and television reports amid fears of a repetition of Dien Bien Phu. U.S. president Lyndon Johnson, obsessed with the battle, even had a terrain model of the base erected in the White House "war room" and insisted that the Joint Chiefs of Staff sign a declaration stating their belief that Khe Sanh would hold.

Westmoreland was determined to do just that and saw the battle as a rare opportunity to inflict a major defeat on a massed enemy. Khe Sanh would be his victory and not that of Giap. He would destroy his enemy with air power. Westmoreland himself came up with the operation's name. As he put it, NIAGARA was "to invoke an image of cascading shells and bombs." Aided by electronic sensors, Operation NIAGARA was intended to destroy PAVN forces and interdict supply lines to the fortress. A wide range of tactical aircraft flew around the clock to provide air support, and the area around the base became one of the most heavily bombed targets in military history. The Seventh Air Force flew 9,961 sorties and dropped 14,233 tons of bombs. The 1st Marine Air Wing flew another 7,078 sorties and dropped 17,015 tons of ordnance, while the U.S. Navy flew 5,337 sorties and dropped 7,941 tons of bombs. This totaled one-fifth of all ordnance dropped by the United States in the Pacific Theater in all of World War II.

While tactical aircraft attacked to within 400 yards of the defender's positions, B-52s flying at 30,000 feet, which up to that time had always bombed targets only beyond 3,000 yards of friendly positions, now struck to within 1,000 yards. Some bombs came closer than that. Each B-52 could carry a payload of up to 108 500- and 750-pound bombs capable of producing craters up to 40 feet wide and 24 feet deep. The "Buffs" (Big Ugly Fat Fellow) flew 2,548 ARC LIGHT sorties (those directed against infiltration) and dropped 59,542 tons of bombs, turning the area around the base into something resembling the surface of the moon. B-52s also devastated PAVN staging areas and depots.

Although PAVN forces withdrew from the vicinity of Khe Sanh beginning on March 6, the siege was not officially ended until April 8 when, in Operation PEGASUS, Allied units pushed in by land and relieved the marine defenders. The official MACV casualty count for the siege of Khe Sanh was 205 Marines killed and more than 1,600 wounded, although base Chaplain Ray W. Stubbe placed the actual death toll closer to 475. This figure also does not include those killed in collateral actions, ARVN Ranger casualties on the southwest perimeter, 1,000–1,500 Montagnards who died during the fighting, or the 97 U.S. and 33 ARVN soldiers killed in relief efforts. MACV's official count of PAVN dead was 1,602, but the PAVN routinely removed their dead, and Westmoreland put the actual number killed at 10,000–15,000.

Both sides had seen the battle largely as a test of wills and the opportunity to inflict a major psychological defeat. But the true measure of Khe Sanh's strategic importance may be seen in the fact that U.S. forces abandoned the base in June 1968. John S. Carroll, an Associated Press correspondent who wrote about this, had his press credentials lifted.

Who won at Khe Sanh? Controversy still surrounds the battle there and what Giap intended there. Westmoreland believed that Giap wanted a repeat of Dien Bien Phu and that it had been an "abject failure" in this regard. As General Phillip Davidson noted, if the siege of Khe Sanh was a PAVN diversion, "military history provides few examples of one more expensive." Certainly, the PAVN paid a very heavy human cost in the battle, including a significant number of front-line troops.

Spencer C. Tucker

Further Reading

Davidson, Phillip B. *Vietnam at War: The History, 1946–1975.* New York: Oxford University Press, 1991.

Murphy, Edward F. *The Hill Fights: The First Battle of Khe Sanh.* New York: Random House, 2003.

Nalty, Bernard C. *Air Power and the Fight for Khe Sanh.* Washington, DC: U.S. Government Printing Office, 1973.

Pisor, Robert. *The End of the Line: The Siege of Khe Sanh.* New York: W. W. Norton, 1982.

Prados, John, and Ray W. Stubbe. *Valley of Decision.* Boston: Houghton Mifflin, 1991.

Shulimson, Jack. *U.S. Marines in Vietnam, 1966.* Washington, DC: U.S. Marine Corps, 1982.

Tucker, Spencer C. *Vietnam.* Lexington: University Press of Kentucky, 1999.

Siege of Beirut (June 14–August 21, 1982)

The siege of Beirut, Lebanon, during June 14–August 21, 1982, occurred during the Lebanon-Israeli War, also known as the Israeli Invasion of Lebanon and Operation PEACE FOR GALILEE, of June 6–September 1982, when Israeli defense minister Ariel Sharon, acting in accord with instructions from Prime Minister Menachem Begin, ordered Israel Defense Forces (IDF) into southern Lebanon to destroy the Palestine Liberation Organization (PLO) there. The PLO had moved its headquarters to Beirut in the early 1970s and became a major force in the Christian-Muslim conflict in Lebanon during 1975–1976, which gave the Syrian government the excuse to intervene. In the next years, both the PLO and Syria increased their influence, with the central Lebanese government unable to curtail their actions that included heightened PLO attacks on northern Israel. Begin, the first Israeli prime minister from the right-wing Likud Party, was determined to maintain Israeli hold over the West Bank and Gaza, which had been secured in 1967, but he also had a deep commitment to Eretz Israel, the ancestral homeland of the Jews that embraced territory beyond Israel's borders into Lebanon and across the Jordan River. Sharon shared Begin's ideological commitment to Eretz Israel and played an important role in expanding Jewish settlements in the West Bank and Gaza. Sharon also took a hard-line approach toward the Palestinians, endeavoring to undermine PLO influence in the West Bank and Gaza.

In June 1978, under heavy pressure from the United States, Begin withdrew Israeli forces that had been sent into southern Lebanon in the Litani River operation carried out the previous March. The United Nations Interim Force in Lebanon (UNIFIL) then took up position in southern Lebanon, charged with confirming the Israeli withdrawal, restoring peace and security, and helping the Lebanese government reestablish its authority there.

Israeli bombardment on June 17, 1982, of a Palestine Liberation Organization (PLO) position on the Lebanese coast during the siege of Beirut. (Clandestine Immigration and Naval Museum)

UNIFIL proved incapable of preventing the PLO from establishing bases in southern Lebanon and using these to attack Israel, bringing Israeli reprisals. The ensuing fighting killed civilians on both sides of the border as well as some UNIFIL personnel. Israel, meanwhile, provided weapons to a pro-Israeli Christian militia in southern Lebanon later known as the South Lebanon Army and led by Major Saad Haddad that operated against the PLO.

Although Lebanese-American diplomat Philip Habib brokered a cease-fire, the PLO repeatedly violated it, and major cross-border strikes resumed in April 1982. By that time, the PLO presence in south Lebanon had grown to some 6,000 men, and their rocket and mortar attacks regularly forced thousands of Israeli civilians into bomb shelters.

On June 3, 1982, three members of a Palestinian terrorist organization connected to Abu Nidal attempted to assassinate Israeli ambassador to Britain Shlomo Argov in London. Although Argov survived, he remained paralyzed until his death in 2003. Begin used this attack as the excuse to bomb Palestinian targets in West Beirut and other targets in southern Lebanon during June 4–5, 1982. The PLO responded by attacking Israeli settlements in Galilee with rockets and mortars. It was this PLO shelling of the settlements rather than the attempted assassination of Argov that led to the Israeli decision to invade Lebanon.

Operation PEACE FOR GALILEE began on June 6, 1982. Israel ultimately committed to it some 76,000 men, 800 tanks, 1,500 armored personnel carriers (APCs), and 364 aircraft. Syria committed perhaps 22,000 men, 352 tanks, 300 APCs, and 96 aircraft, while the PLO had about 15,000 men, 300 tanks, and 150 APCs.

The Israeli operation had three principal objectives. First, destruction of the PLO in southern Lebanon; second, eviction of Syrian forces from Lebanon and removal of its missiles from the Bekaa Valley; and third, Israel hoped to influence Lebanese politics in an alliance with the Maronite Christians led by Bashir Jumayyil (Gemayel), the leader of the Phalange (al-Kata'ib) and head of the unified command of the Lebanese Forces. As with the Israelis, Jumayyil was strongly opposed to the Syrian presence in Lebanon.

The Palestinian militias were then well established in West Beirut, but the Israeli cabinet was opposed to placing its troops into an urban combat situation that was bound to bring heavy civilian casualties and incur opposition from Washington and western Europe. Thus, Begin and Sharon informed the cabinet that the goal was merely to break up PLO bases in southern Lebanon and push back PLO and Syrian forces some 25 miles, beyond rocket range of Galilee. The IDF invasion was a three-pronged affair. One force proceeded up the coastal road toward Beirut; a second moved to cut the Beirut-Damascus road; and a third proceeded into Lebanon along the Syrian border to prevent interference from Syria.

Once the operation began, however, Sharon quickly changed the original plan by expanding the mission to incorporate Beirut. This was well beyond the 25-mile mark, and many in the cabinet now believed that Begin and Sharon had deliberately misled them.

Tyre and Sidon, two cities within the 25-mile limit, were both heavily damaged in the Israeli advance. Rather than standing their ground and being overwhelmed by the better equipped Israelis, the Palestinian fighters withdrew back on West Beirut. The IDF reached the outskirts of Beirut within days. Indeed, the siege of the city began on June 14. Sharon now argued in favor of a broader operation that would force the PLO from Beirut, and for some 10 weeks Israeli guns shelled West Beirut, killing both PLO and civilians alike.

Fighting also occurred with Syrian forces in the Bekaa Valley. Unable to meet Israel on equal footing and bereft of allies, Syria did not engage in an all-out effort. Rather, much of the battle was waged in the air. By June 10, the Israeli Air Force had neutralized Syrian surface-to-air missiles and had shot down dozens of Syrian jets. (Some sources say the ultimate toll was as many as 80 Syrian aircraft.) The Israelis employed helicopter gunships to attack and destroy dozens of Syrian armored vehicles and tanks. The Israelis also trapped Syrian forces in the Bekaa. Israel was on the verge of severing the Beirut-Damascus highway on June 11 when Moscow and Washington brokered a cease-fire.

Meanwhile, Sharon hoped that Jumayyil's Lebanese Forces would bear the brunt of the fighting in West Beirut, but Jumayyil was reluctant to do so, afraid that such a move would harm his chances to become the president of Lebanon.

Sharon wanted to send Israeli forces into the city, but Begin's cabinet refused to approve an assault on West Beirut because of the likelihood of high casualties. Some parties threatened to leave the coalition should this be carried out. Meanwhile, the United States had been conveying ambiguous signals regarding its position in the conflict, but in a phone conversation with Begin, President Ronald Reagan condemned the civilian casualties that were occurring. International criticism of the Israeli government encouraged PLO head Yasser Arafat to entrench himself and the PLO in West Beirut.

Sharon disregarded cabinet opposition and placed the western (predominantly Muslim) part of the city under a siege from air, land, and sea that cut off all food and water supplies to the city. He hoped that this might convince the citizens to turn against the PLO. By the end of the first week in July some 500 buildings in the city had been destroyed. The bombing and shelling brought mostly civilian casualties, however, bringing denunciations of Israel in the international press. Efforts by the Israelis at targeting Arafat himself failed.

The PLO believed that it could hold out longer under siege than the Israelis could under international pressure, leading Israel to intensify its attacks on Beirut in early August. Now convinced that a full-scale assault was impending, on August 18 the PLO consented to a UN-brokered arrangement whereby American, French, and Italian peacekeeping forces, known as the Multinational Force in Lebanon, would escort the PLO fighters out of Lebanon by the end of the month. Habib also assured the PLO that the many refugees in camps in Lebanon would not be harmed.

Some 350 French paratroopers arrived in the city on August 21, joined by 800 U.S. marines and Italian Bersaglieri. Ultimately, there were 2,130 international peacekeepers in Beirut to oversee the removal of the PLO by sea. A total of 850 PLO, including the leadership, went to Tunis and some 2,500 others ended up in other Arab countries.

On August 23, 1982, Jumayyil was elected president of Lebanon. He was dead within two weeks, assassinated on September 14, 1982, by a member of the pro-Damascus National Syrian Socialist Party for his cooperation with the Israelis.

Following the assassination of Jumayyil, Israeli forces occupied West Beirut. This was in direct violation of the UN agreement calling for the evacuation of the PLO and protection of the Palestinian refugees who remained behind. With the PLO removed, the refugees had virtually no defense against the Israelis or their Christian allies.

Once Israel had control of the Palestinian refugee camps, in September 1982 Sharon invited members of the Phalange to enter the camps at Sabra and Shatila to "clean out the terrorists." The Phalange militia then slaughtered more than 1,000 refugees in what he claimed to be retaliation for Jumayyil's assassination.

Estimates of casualties in the Lebanon-Israel War vary widely, although the numbers may have been as high as 17,826 Lebanese killed and approximately 675 Israelis. The cost for Lebanon had been high. Much of Beirut lay in ruins, with damage estimated as high as $2 billion, and the tourist industry was a long time in recovering.

Israel achieved a short-term victory. It had expelled the PLO from Lebanon and temporarily destroyed its infrastructure. It also had weakened the Syrian military, especially its air assets, and Israel had strengthened the South Lebanon Army, which would help control a buffer, or security zone, in the south.

These gains were short-lived. An agreement between Israel and Lebanon for a staged Israeli withdrawal fell apart on Syrian pressure. Although in January 1985, Israel began a unilateral withdrawal to a security zone in southern Lebanon, completed in that June, not until June 2000 did Israel finally withdraw all its forces from southern Lebanon.

Rather than producing a stable, pro-Israeli government in Beirut, the Israeli operation intensified the turmoil in Lebanon. Sharon was forced to resign as minister of defense, and Begin's political career also suffered greatly. He resigned as prime minister in 1983 and withdrew entirely from public life. Finally, whether true or not, decades later Osama bin Laden cited the siege of Beirut as one of the reasons for the September 11, 2001, attacks on the United States.

Spencer C. Tucker

Further Reading

Davis, M. Thomas. *40 km into Lebanon*. Washington, DC: National Defense University Press, 1987.

Friedman, Thomas. *From Beirut to Jerusalem*. New York: Anchor Books, 1995.

Gabriel, Richard. *Operation Peace for Galilee: The Israel-PLO War in Lebanon*. New York: Hill and Wang, 1984.

Rabil, Robert G. *Embattled Neighbors: Syria, Israel and Lebanon*. Boulder, CO: Lynne Rienner, 2003.

Rabinovich, Itamar. *The War for Lebanon, 1970–1985*. Rev. ed. Ithaca, NY: Cornell University Press, 1986.

Siege of Vukovar (August 25–November 18, 1991)

The siege of the city of Vukovar in Croatia carried out by the Yugoslav People's Army (Jugoslovenska narodna armija, JNA) and Serb militia units against Croat forces, during August 25–November 18, 1991, was a central event of the Croatian War of Independence (1991–1995).

The state of Yugoslavia was established as a consequence of World War I. Serbia—one of the victorious powers—engineered a union with the Kingdom of Montenegro at the end of that conflict and then achieved its war aim of adding substantial Slavic territories taken from the former Austria-Hungary. Overrun in 1941 by the Axis, the Kingdom of Yugoslavia reemerged at the end of the war, but the communists, led by Josip Broz, known by his nom de plume of Tito, soon took power.

During the period of the Cold War, although Serbia dominated, Yugoslavia's multinational, multiethnic, multicultural, and multireligious population inhabited six different republics (Bosnia and Herzegovina, Croatia, Macedonia, Montenegro, Serbia, and Slovenia) and two autonomous regions (the Vojvodina and Kosovo). As long as Tito lived, he held Yugoslavia together, but decentralization introduced in the 1960s saw the republics gain increased autonomy, abetted by the rise of nationalism. All this worked against a unitary state. Yugoslavia's 1974 constitution was designed to provide political stability by addressing ethnic concerns, but it included the right of the republics to veto federal legislation, which further loosened central authority. Worsening economic conditions also plagued the national government.

Tito died in 1980 and with him went the strong leadership necessary to hold the country together. The new system of a collective rotating leadership that replaced Tito's rule could not cope with a deteriorating situation. Serbian president Slobodan Milošević greatly contributed to tensions by pushing Serbian nationalism, stockpiling weaponry under Serbian control, and abolishing the autonomous provinces. All of this seemed to presage a Greater Serbia.

The long-dreaded breakup of Yugoslavia began on June 25, 1991, when both Slovenia and Croatia declared their independence. Unwilling to recognize the secession of these republics, that same day Milošević directed the JNA, dominated by Serbs, to subdue the breakaway republics by force. This began the civil war (the Croat and Slovene Wars of Independence).

Fighting between Serbia and Slovenia ended in July. The most northern of the Yugoslav republics and removed geographically from Serbia, Slovenia had few Serbs within its borders. In August 1991, a Serbian Autonomous Region in Western Slovenia was established and the Yugoslav Army pulled out of Slovenia.

This was not to be the case with Croatia, where President Franjo Tuđman had actively promoted Croatian nationalism. Located south of Slovenia, Croatia was bordered to the east by the Vojvodina, which was controlled by Serbia, to the east and south by Bosnia Herzegovina, to the far south by Montenegro, and to the west by the Adriatic. Unfortunately for Croatia, it contained a large and vocal Serb minority concentrated in eastern Croatia. Indeed, in mid-1990, before Croatia's declaration of independence, the Serbs of Croatia had reacted to Tuđman's nationalist statements and policies by establishing militia units loyal to Serbia. Clandestinely armed by the Serbian government, they had seized control of much of the Serb-populated areas of Croatia. On April 1, Serb villagers around the city of Vukovar and other towns in the Croatian region of eastern Slavonia began erecting barriers to block roads, and fighting there began the next month, with the JNA intervening.

In August 1991, following Croatia's declaration of independence, the JNA invaded eastern Slavonia in force with the avowed aim of occupying all Croatia and forcing its political leadership to rejoin the rest of Yugoslavia. This soon changed, however, with much of the JNA won over to the concept of a Greater Serbia. The centerpiece of the Serb-Croat struggle became the city of Vukovar.

Located in eastern Slavonia at the confluence of the Vukar and Danube Rivers, Vukovar was Croatia's largest river port. Its 1990 population was some 45,000 people, of whom 47 percent were Croats, 32 percent Serbs, and the remainder other minorities. All had lived together in relative harmony until the beginning of the war.

The siege of Vukovar began on August 25, 1991, and by the end of September the city was almost completely surrounded. The JNA would commit to the battle some 36,000 men, tanks, heavy artillery, and rockets, as well as aircraft and naval vessels in the Danube. JNA chief of staff general Života Panić had command.

The Croatian Army was still in the process of formation when the siege began, but the initial 1,800 or so self-organized defenders (some 100 of them Serbs) armed with hunting rifles and light infantry weapons and commanded by former JNA officer Milo Dedaković would grow to some 20,000 men, supported by tanks, artillery, and aircraft. The Croatians also adopted several Antonov AN-12 biplanes to drop supplies by parachute but also to drop improvised bombs on the Serb positions.

The siege of Vukovar has been likened in its intensity and destruction to the World War II Battle of Stalingrad, for the fighting was street-by-street and building-by-building. During the height of the battle, Vukovar was subjected to some 12,000 rockets and shells daily. The city was all but destroyed in what has been characterized as the heaviest fighting in Europe since World War II.

On November 3, the JNA mounted an amphibious assault across the Danube and finally took possession of the city on November 18, 1991. Among prisoners taken by the JNA were some 400 people who had taken refuge in the ruins of the city hospital. Two hundred of them were arbitrarily separated and taken to nearby Ovčava Farm. There they were summarily executed in what is known as the Vukovar Massacre. A number of other individuals simply disappeared, while thousands were removed to Serb prison camps in harsh conditions. According to Croat figures, 879 Croat fighters died and 770 were wounded, with 1,131 civilians dead and another 22,000 fleeing. Serb losses were more than 1,100 killed and 2,500 wounded. Vukovar was then integrated into what became the self-proclaimed Serbian-controlled Republic of Serbian Krajina (RSK).

The JNA secured about a third of Croatia. Attempts by the European Community to arrange a peace settlement failed, and the Serbs remained in occupation. A cease-fire went into effect in January 1992, and both sides entrenched. Following deployment to Croatia of the United Nations Protection Force (UNPROFOR), which replaced the JNA in the Serb-occupied areas, there was only intermittent fighting.

In August 1995, however, the Croatian Army, having received new weaponry and U.S. training, launched a surprise lightening offensive that quickly overran the areas conquered earlier by the Serbs and ended the war in its favor. Rightly fearing retaliation, a number of Serbs fled, and the RSK was reintegrated into Croatia. The last UNPR area, including Vukovar, was restored in 1998 under the Dayton Peace Accords.

Like much of Croatia, Vukovar has been rebuilt, although it has yet to regain its former prominence and its population is only somewhat more than half what it had been in 1990. The ruined Vukovar water tower, pockmarked by shell holes, has been preserved in its damaged state as a symbol of the battle.

A number of individuals, both Serb and Croat, were brought before the International Criminal Tribunal for the Former Yugoslavia (ICTY), but in 2015 the International Court of Justice dismissed claims of genocide brought by both Croatia and Serbia against the other. The court recognized that crimes against civilians had occurred but that these did not constitute genocide.

This was not the end of fighting in the former Yugoslavia, however, as warfare spread to Bosnia. By the time the Bosnian state led by Alija Izetbegović received international recognition on April 6, 1992, Serbs and Croats living there had established satellite states under a secret agreement struck by Milošević and

Tuđman. Serbia and the JNA supported the Republika Srpska led by Radovan Karadžić, while Croatia supported Bosnia and Herzegovina. A three-sided ethnic war ensued, and by the end of 1992 the Serbs controlled about 70 percent of Bosnia and laid siege to the Bosnian capital city of Sarajevo for three years, carrying out ethnic cleansing and torturing and murdering thousands of people in concentration camps, with the most notorious incident occurring at Srebrenica in July 1995 when Serbs massacred more than 8,000 Bosniak men and boys. Croatian forces launched a war against the Muslims in May 1993 and laid siege to the city of Mostar. Peace in Bosnia was finally secured in the Dayton Accords of November 21, 1995. The peace was enforced by 60,000 UN troops, reduced to a 24,000-strong international Stabilization Force (SFOR) in 1997.

Fighting also occurred in Kosovo in 1999. Responding to Serbian suppression and atrocities against its 90 percent Albanian majority, the North Atlantic Treaty Organization (NATO), led by the United States, undertook air strikes during March–June 1999 that targeted the Serbian military and infrastructure, including strikes against Belgrade itself. Milošević finally accepted a peace plan on June 3, 1999, that created yet another international protectorate in the Balkans for Kosovo.

The name "Yugoslavia" officially disappeared from the map on March 14, 2002, when the two remaining republics of the Federal Republic of Yugoslavia voted to rename it Serbia and Montenegro. Despite Serbian threats, Montenegro seceded from that union in 2006.

Spencer C. Tucker

Further Reading

Boduszyński, Mieczysław P. *Regime Change in the Yugoslav Successor States: Divergent Paths toward a New Europe*. Baltimore, MD: Johns Hopkins University Press, 2010.

Cohen, Lenard J. *Broken Bonds: Yugoslavia's Disintegration and Balkan Politics in Transition*. 2nd ed. Boulder, CO: Westview, 1995.

Doder, Dusko, and Louise Branson. *Milosevic: Portrait of a Tyrant*. New York: Simon & Schuster, 1999.

Lampe, John R. *Yugoslavia as History: Twice There Was a Country*. 2nd ed. Cambridge, UK: Cambridge University Press, 2000.

Naimark, Norman M., and Holly Case, eds. *Yugoslavia and Its Historians: Understanding the Balkan Wars of the 1990s*. Stanford, CA: Stanford University Press, 2003.

U.S. Central Intelligence Agency, Office of Russian and European Analysis. *Balkan Battlegrounds: A Military History of the Yugoslav Conflict, 1990–1995*. Vol. 1. Washington, DC: Central Intelligence Agency, 2000.

West, Richard. *Tito and the Rise and Fall of Yugoslavia*. New York: Carroll and Graf, 1994.

Siege of Aleppo (July 19, 2012–December 22, 2016)

The siege of Aleppo, during July 19, 2012–December 22, 2016, occurred during the Syrian Civil War (1911 to the present). In it, Syrian government and rebel forces fought to control what was the largest city in Syria with a population of some 2.5 million. The repeated efforts by international relief agencies to provide aid to civilians or facilitate evacuation were routinely disrupted by continued combat and mistrust on both sides. UN attempts to end the carnage saw the Syrian government turn down plans that would grant eastern Aleppo autonomy, and the battle settled into a struggle of attrition ultimately decided by force of arms on December 22, 2016.

Nationwide protests in Syria against the regime of President Bashar al-Assad began in mid-March 2011, part of the so-called Arab Spring throughout much of the Arab world that demanded an end to corruption and more democratic governments. Aleppo, known as a multicultural city, remained largely unaffected by these developments and indeed was generally supportive of the Syrian government until the beginning of large-scale protests there in May 2012. Then on July 22, rebel fighters opposing the Assad regime entered Aleppo from neighboring communities. The government response was heavy-handed and indiscriminate.

Initial rebel strength was perhaps 6,000–7,000 men, with the largest contingent being the al-Tawhid Brigade and the most prominent the Free Syrian Army (FSA), which was largely composed of men who had deserted from the regular Syrian armed forces. Although most of the initial anti-government forces were drawn from the immediate Aleppo countryside, they were later joined by Islamic extremists and foreign fighters, many of whom had taken part in the ongoing insurgency in neighboring Iraq. The long battle that followed pitted the FSA and other Sunni Muslim groups such as the Levant Front and the Al Qaeda-affiliated Al-Nusra Front, but also the Kurdish People's Protection Units (YPG) against the Syrian government armed forces, supported by Hezbollah (Shia Muslims from Lebanon), various Shia Muslim militias, Iran, and then Russia. Russian air strikes, which began in late September 2015, were key in turning the battle in the government's favor.

Late in the battle, Syrian president Assad likened the fighting in Aleppo to that of Stalingrad during World War II and, in the destruction wrought, there certainly is a parallel. Government forces, having lifted the rebel siege of Aleppo in October 2013, continued their offensive in 2014. This culminated in their capture of the Sheikh Najjar industrial district north of Aleppo and the raising on May 22, 2014, of the rebel siege of Aleppo Central Prison, where government soldiers had held out since 2012.

The battle was largely a stalemate for its first four years with the government controlling west Aleppo and opposition forces holding much of east Aleppo. This phase ended in July 2016 when, greatly aided by Lebanese Hezbollah Shiite militiamen, heavy Syrian artillery, and indiscriminate Syrian government air strikes allowed Syrian government forces to seal off east Aleppo, closing the last rebel supply lines into the city and essentially trapping there some 250,000 civilians, a third of them children.

In early August, the rebels led by Jabhat Fateh al Sham, formerly the al Nusra Front (which had only two weeks before broken its long-standing ties with Al Qaeda in order to build closer alliances with other jihadist and rebel groups) opened an offensive and seized a government military complex in the Ramouseh district, securing the weaponry stored there. This success did not

Destruction in the old city area of Aleppo on October 2, 2013. Part of the ongoing Syrian Civil War, this protracted battle left the nation's largest city in ruins. (Richard Harvey/Dreamstime.com)

take. Other rebel offensives in September and October failed. Syrian government forces, again greatly aided by Russian air strikes, turned back the rebel attacks and then began a major offensive operation of their own that ultimately brought victory.

The fighting saw widespread atrocities against civilians, with the targeting of clearly marked hospitals and schools by both the Syrian and Russian air forces as well as extensive artillery shelling of civilian areas, the indiscriminate use of anti-personnel "barrel bombs" and cluster munitions by the Syrian and Russian air forces, as well as residual air strikes designed to target rescue workers after a first strike. There were also charges that the Syrian government had employed chemical weapons. Improvised and wildly inaccurate artillery employed by the rebel forces also resulted in civilian casualties.

On December 13, following two weeks of steady government advances and with only some 5 percent of the city still in rebel hands, a cease-fire agreement was reached following talks between Assad's main ally Russia and Turkey, a leading backer of the rebels. After some hitches and a resumption of shelling by the government side, on December 22 the evacuation of tens of thousands of civilians and fighters from the remaining rebel-held areas of Aleppo came to an end, leaving what remained of the city in government hands.

Although certainly Assad's biggest victory in the civil war to date, much of Aleppo lay in ruins, with some 33,500 buildings demolished. A third of the Old City of Aleppo, a UNESCO World Heritage site, had been destroyed. Some 31,000 people had died in the fighting, two-thirds of them civilians, including a large number of children. Hundreds of thousands of city residents were also displaced. Whether this marked a turning point in the long-running Syrian Civil War remained unclear.

Spencer C. Tucker

Further Reading

The Battle of Aleppo: The History of the Ongoing Siege at the Center of the Syrian Civil War. Waltham, MA: Charles River Editors, 2016.

Beehner, Lionel, and Mike Jackson. "What the Siege of Sarajevo Can Teach Us about Aleppo." *Washington Post,* May 9, 2016.

Dehghanpisheh, Babak, and Liz Sly. "Iran Pledges Support for Syria as Battle Rages for Aleppo." *Washington Post,* August 7, 2012.

Hubbard, Ben. "Turning Point in Syria as Assad Regains All of Aleppo." *New York Times,* December 22, 2016.

Sorenson, David S. *Syria in Ruins: The Dynamics of the Syrian Civil War.* Santa Barbara, CA: Praeger Security International, 2016.

Siege of Kobanî (September 27, 2014–January 26, 2015)

The siege of Kobanî, during September 27, 2014–January 26, 2015, was a key battle in the fight against the Islamic State of Iraq and Syria (ISIS). After having already taken much of northern Syria in the ongoing Civil War there (2011 to the present) and most of Anbar Province in Iraq in which it had displaced a half million Iraqis, in early June 2014 ISIS launched a major offensive in northern Iraq. ISIS fighters seized Iraq's second largest city of Mosul and also captured Tikrit, displacing another half million Iraqis, then advanced south toward Baghdad. By June 22, they were only some 60 miles from the Iraqi capital city. These territorial acquisitions accompanied by widespread ISIS atrocities—including the summary execution of non-Muslims refusing to convert to Islam, the raping and enslavement of women, and the beheading of hostages—prompted the formation of a broad-based international coalition headed by the United States to defeat and indeed destroy ISIS.

Then beginning on September 17, ISIS launched a major offensive to capture the important largely Kurdish town of Kobanî (also known as Kobanê or Ayn al-Arab), located in northern Syria on the border with Turkey and a major crossing points into that country. The ISIS offensive included tanks and artillery. By the beginning of October, ISIS fighters had taken some 350 Kurdish villages and towns in the Kobanî vicinity; displaced some 150,000 Kurds, most of whom sought refuge in Turkey; and were attacking Kobanî itself.

This presented the Turkish government with a dilemma, and on September 30 Turkish soldiers and tanks took up position along the border with Syria as the government debated whether to intervene militarily. Meanwhile, on September 27, U.S. and coalition air strikes targeted ISIS positions near Kobanî for the first time.

On October 2, the Turkish parliament voted 298–98 to authorize military force against ISIS. Although Turkish president Recep Tayyip Erdoğan had been outspoken in his insistence that Syrian president Bashar al-Assad must be removed from power and had urged the establishment of a no-fly zone over portions of Syria, he was also reluctant to intervene in Kobanî. With Turkish tanks and troops remaining in place, on October 8, ISIS fighters commenced a siege of Kobanî.

Turkey's failure to act brought rioting by that country's Kurdish minority, in which at least nine protests, organized in part by the pro-Kurdish Peoples' Democratic Party, occurred across Turkey and in several foreign cities. Since 1984 some 40,000 people had been killed in clashes between Turkish government forces and its Kurdish minority, led by the Kurdistan Workers' Party (PKK), which sought greater rights for the Kurds. In March 2013, however, imprisoned PKK leader Abdullah Ocalan had called for a cease-fire, and PPK fighters had withdrawn to the Iraqi mountains and the beginnings of a peace process had emerged. The Turkish failure to intervene to aid Kobanî, and indeed its turning back of Turkish Kurds wanting to fight for the city, fueled Kurdish anger anew. Ankara feared the establishment of an independent radical Kurdish state that would seek a larger Kurdistan to include the Kurdish portions of Turkey. Nonetheless, in a statement from prison, Ocalan warned that "the reality of Kobanî and the peace process are not separable." On October 12, however, Ankara announced it would permit the United States and other coalition forces battling militants in Syria and Iraq to use some of its bases, which would make it easier for coalition air forces to assist the Kobanî defenders. However, the next day, Turkish warplanes attacked not Kobanî but PKK positions in southeastern Turkey.

Meanwhile, the battle for Kobanî raged on and intensified as the United States and other coalition forces continued air strikes in support of the Kurds. If ISIS were to capture Kobanî, it would control three official border crossings between Turkey and Syria and some 60 miles of their common frontier.

On October 19, for the first time in the coalition campaign against ISIS, U.S. military aircraft airdropped weapons provided by the Iraqi government to the Kurdish fighters in Kobanî as well as ammunition and medical supplies. Then the next day the Turkish government announced that it would allow some Kurds to cross the Turkish border into Syria to join the fight for Kobanî, but only those from Kurdistan and not those from Turkey itself. This decision opened a corridor to Syria for the Peshmerga fighters. The semi-autonomous northern region of Iraqi Kurdistan was one of Turkey's major security allies and a principal exporter of oil to Turkey. Indeed, in June Turkey signed a 50-year energy pact with the Kurdistan Regional Government. Iraqi Kurdistan had also been at odds with the PKK and its affiliates in Syria.

The struggle for control of Kobanî raged on but by mid-January 2015, the national army of Syrian Kurdistan, known as the People's Protection Units (YPG), supported by the Peshmerga, other Kurdish volunteers, and members of the FSA, had turned back a number of ISIS assaults.

Finally, on January 26, 2015, the YPG and its allied fighters drove the last ISIS units from the city. The Battle of Kobanî reportedly resulted in the deaths of more than 1,000 ISIS fighters and 324 YPG, as well as 12 allied rebels. Reportedly hundreds of other ISIS militants died in the U.S.-led coalition airstrikes on the city and surrounding countryside.

For some time thereafter, however, most of the villages in the Kobanî Canton remained under ISIS control. Kurdish forces supported by allied Arab armed groups and aided by coalition air strikes, then made rapid advances. By early February, ISIS fighters had been driven some 15 miles from the city and by the end of April almost all of the villages in the canton captured earlier by ISIS had been retaken. Although the fight against ISIS continues, the Battle of Kobanî is considered by many analysts to have been a turning point in the fight against the Islamic State.

In late June 2015, ISIS again attacked Kobanî, killing some 233 civilians.

Spencer C. Tucker

Further Reading
Abdulrahim, Raja. "Islamic State, Rival Al Nusra Front Each Strengthen Grip on Syria." *Los Angeles Times*, November 28, 2014.
Cloud, David, and Brian Bennetan. "U.S., Allies Rush Heavy Weapons to Kurds to Fight Militants in Iraq." *Los Angeles Times*, August 11, 2014.
Khalilzad, Zalmay. "To Fight the Islamic State, Kurdish and Iraqi Forces Need Expedited Aid." *Washington Post*, August 13, 2014.
"La France renforce son dispositif militaire en Irak avec trois Rafale." *Le Monde*, October 8, 2014.
"Military Airstrikes Continue Against ISIL in Syria and Iraq Supporting Operation Inherent Resolve." U.S. Central Command, January 14, 2015.
Rush, James. "Isis Air Strikes: US Brings in Apache Helicopters as British Jets Target Militants in Iraq." *The Independent*, October 8, 2014.

Siege of Mosul (October 17, 2016–July 9, 2017)

In Operation WE ARE COMING, NINEVEH, during October 17, 2016–July 9, 2017, Iraqi forces, supported by their allies, battled to retake the Iraqi city of Mosul from the Islamic State of Iraq and Syria (ISIS). The attacking forces consisted of troops of the Iraq Army, Shiite and Sunni militias, Kurdish Peshmerga fighters, and international forces, to include extensive coalition air support (largely from the United States, United Kingdom, and France) as well as from Iran and Hezbollah (based in Lebanon). The October 2016 offensive followed unsuccessful Iraqi attempts in 2015 and earlier in 2016 to retake the city. The battle is held to be the largest attack on a city in several generations.

During June 10–14, 2014, as sectarian violence raged largely unchecked in Iraq, ISIS militants mounted a lightening offensive that overran and seized control of Mosul, Iraq's second largest city with a mostly Sunni population of some 1.5 million. ISIS also secured much of former president Saddam Hussein's hometown of Tikrit. Hundreds of thousands of Iraqi civilians fled the area, prompting a major refugee crisis. There were widespread reports of Iraqi security forces simply throwing down their weapons, shedding their uniforms, and fleeing, or even rallying to the Islamists. In Mosul, ISIS seized vast caches of weaponry and military supplies. There were fears, unrealized, that Baghdad would also fall.

ISIS then made Mosul its capital in Iraq. ISIS leader Abu Bakr al-Baghdadi addressed his followers and announced from inside the city's historic twelfth-century Grand al-Nuri Mosque the establishment of an Islamic caliphate.

A U.S. Army M109A6 Paladin howitzer at Qayyarah Airfield West in Iraq supporting the drive of Iraqi government forces on Mosul, October 17, 2016. This began the siege of that city, which was held by the Islamic State of Iraq and Syria (ISIS). (Army photo by Spc. Christopher Brecht)

ISIS retained its firm grip on the city until the fall of 2016. Following the recapture of Fallujah in what was the third battle for that city during May 23–June 28, 2016, liberating Mosul became the Iraqi government's declared next goal. Mosul was near to major Iraqi oil fields, as well an oil pipeline that serviced Turkey. Securing these fields could bolster Iraq's economy and would certainly adversely affect ISIS finances in a meaningful way, as ISIS had sold oil illegally to fund its operations. Securing the safety of Mosul Dam, Iraq's largest dam and briefly held by ISIS, was also a vital goal. Certainly, the ISIS capture of Mosul in 2014 had been a major embarrassment for the Iraqi government, one that it was anxious to reverse.

Iraqi Lieutenant General Abdul Amir Rashid Yarallah had command of Operation WE ARE COMING, NINEVEH, in what was the largest Iraqi military operation since the end of the Iraq War in 2011. Coalition forces numbered as many as 108,000 men. In preparation for the offensive, U.S. forces in the country were increased in July 2016 to 4,647 personnel, although the vast majority of these remained in a training role rather than directly supporting the operation.

Haqqi Esmaeil Owaid (a.k.a. Abu Ahmed) was governor of Mosul, and Ahmad Khalaf al-Jabouri was the city's military commander. ISIS fighters defending Mosul numbered only 8,000–12,000 men, however, with ISIS air support limited to a few drones.

Before the offensive began, Iraqi and coalition forces endeavored to seal off Mosul in the Nineveh Governorate, preventing ISIS resupply and support. U.S. and British drones and manned aircraft struck identified ISIS targets in and around the city, including ammunition stockpiles, rocket launchers, artillery pieces, and mortar positions. Three days before the beginning of the ground offensive, leaflets dropped on the city called on noncombatants to try to leave and young males to rise up against ISIS.

Iraqi prime minister Haider al-Abadi announced the start of the offensive on October 16, 2016, although the first ground assaults of towns surrounding the city did not occur until the next day. The assaulting forces first focused on the eastern districts of the city before moving against the narrow streets of the Old City in the west.

On October 21, dozens of ISIS fighters attacked Kirkuk, targeting four police stations and Kurdish security offices in an apparent effort to divert Iraqi forces from the effort to retake Mosul, 109 miles to the northwest. ISIS militants also struck a government building in Dibis, a town some 25 miles northwest of Kirkuk.

During October 21–22, ISIS executed 284 men and boys as coalition forces closed in on Mosul. Those killed had reportedly been used as human shields in southern parts of the city. ISIS militants used a bulldozer to dump the corpses in a mass grave at the scene of the executions. ISIS fighters had reportedly taken more than 500 families from villages around Mosul as human shields.

With Mosul finally largely isolated, early on November 1, Iraqi Special Operations Forces entered the eastern part of the city. Heavy fighting ensured. Well aware of the oft-stated Iraqi determination to retake Mosul, ISIS fighters had made extensive preparations. The Iraqi Army advance was slowed by elaborate defenses, booby traps, tunnels that connected ISIS positions and also permitted escape, and by the goal of trying to minimize civilian casualties. On January 24, 2017, the Iraqi government claimed that eastern Mosul had been liberated. Iraqi troops began their offensive to recapture western Mosul on February 19, 2017.

On June 29, 2017, al-Abadi announced that Iraq forces had recaptured the Al Nuri Grand Mosque in Mosul, but only rubble remained, as the iconic structure had been blown up by ISIS on June 20 after having remained unscathed since the twelfth century.

The campaign lasted far longer than expected and took a far heavier toll than predicted. After eight and a half months of combat, al-Abadi traveled to Mosul on July 9 and declared victory, although there was still some fighting in a small area in the city suburbs. Initially the Iraqi government set casualties in the battle at as many as 11,000 ISIS fighters killed, along with some 1,000 Iraqi soldiers were killed and 6,100 were wounded. Two U.S. military personnel were also killed, as were three Iranians. Civilian casualties were originally set at 1,266 killed. In mid-December, however, these figures were revised sharply upward, based on morgue count, to 9,606 civilians killed, with many more still buried in the rubble. Nearly a third of the deaths were attributed to air strikes by the U.S.-led coalition or shelling by Iraqi forces, another third died in ISIS's final frenzy of violence. The remainder of the dead could have been killed from actions by either side.

The physical destruction was immense. At least six of western Mosul's 44 districts had been largely leveled, with air strikes, fierce house-to-house combat, and attacks by suicide bombers having obliterated crucial infrastructure such as roads, bridges, the water works, and the electricity net. Homes, schools, and hospitals were destroyed. UN officials estimated that $1 billion and more than a year would be required for the restoration of only basic services such as water, sewage, electricity, schools, and medical facilities. Long-term rebuilding would be much more costly and take far longer. Certainly, the level of destruction severely complicated the return of the Mosul residents who had fled the fighting, as more than 900,000 former inhabitants had been displaced and were living with other family members or in refugee camps. For the vast majority, a lengthy stay in a refugee camp lay ahead and, were this poorly managed, it could well feed radical sentiment.

Spencer C. Tucker

Further Reading

Arango, Tim. "Tal Afar, West of Mosul, Becomes Center of Battle for Influence in Iraq." *New York Times*, October 29, 2016.

George, Susannah. "IS Attack Underscores Fragility of Iraqi Security Forces." *Washington Post*, July 6, 2017.

Hennessy-Fiske, Molly. "New Phase Begins in Offensive to Drive Islamic State out of Key City of Mosul." *Los Angeles Times*, December 29, 2016.

Kesling, Ben. "ISIS Herds Civilians to Mosul as Human Shields." *Wall Street Journal*, October 28, 2016.

King, Laura. "Iraqi Forces Launch Assault on Mosul." *Los Angeles Times*, November 1, 2016.

Michaels, Jim. "U.S. Aircraft to Block ISIL Militants Fleeing Mosul in Ira." *USA Today*, October 31, 2016.

Specia, Megan, and Rik Gladstone. "Iraq Recaptures Mosque in Mosul, but Only Rubble Remains." *New York Times*, June 30, 2017.

About the Author and Contributors

AUTHOR

Dr. Spencer C. Tucker graduated from the Virginia Military Institute and was a Fulbright scholar in France. He was a U.S. Army captain and intelligence analyst in the Pentagon during the Vietnam War, then taught for 30 years at Texas Christian University before returning to his alma mater for 6 years as the holder of the John Biggs Chair of Military History. He retired from teaching in 2003. He is now Senior Fellow of Military History at ABC-CLIO. Dr. Tucker has written or edited 68 books, including ABC-CLIO's award-winning *The Encyclopedia of the Cold War* and *The Encyclopedia of the Arab-Israeli Conflict* as well as the comprehensive *A Global Chronology of Conflict*.

Among honors he has received for his publications are two John Lyman Book Awards from the North American Society for Oceanic History (1989 and 2000), the Rear Admiral Ernest M. Eller Naval History Prize for best article in naval history (2000), the Theodore Roosevelt and Franklin D. Roosevelt Prize for best book in naval history (2004), three Society for Military History awards for best reference work in military history (2008, 2010, and 2014), and four American Library Association RUSA Outstanding Reference Source awards (2009, 2010, 2014, and 2015).

CONTRIBUTORS

Marcia Schmidt Blaine earned her PhD at the University of New Hampshire and is a professor of American history and chair of the Department of History and Philosophy at Plymouth State University.

Anna Boros-McGee, earned her PhD at the Hungarian National Defense University, now merged with the National University of Public Service in Budapest and is employed by the U.S. government.

Timothy C. Dowling is professor and holder of the Burgwyn Chair in Military History at the Virginia Military Institute. A specialist in German and Russian history, in which he is widely published, he earned his PhD from Tulane University.

Richard M. Edwards is senior lecturer of philosophy at University of Wisconsin Colleges, Sheboygan. He received his PhD from the University of Wales, Lampeter in Historical and Philosophical Theology.

C. J. Horn is a retired U.S. Army colonel and director of the College of Information and Cyberspace of the National Defense University. He earned his PhD at Ohio State University.

Jerry Keenan is retired from the book-publishing business and a widely published author on the history of American Indian Wars.

Dorothy A. Mays is head of public services for Olin Library at Rollins College and an associate professor there. She holds an MA in history from the University of Virginia and has published widely in women's history.

Alexander Mikaberidze is the Sybil T. and J. Frederick Patten Professor of History at Louisiana State University in Shreveport. He holds a degree in international law from Tbilisi State University and a PhD in history from Florida State University. He has published widely in European and Middle Eastern history.

Nathan Schumer, PhD, earned his doctorate through the Department of Religion at Columbia University, New York, NY.

Michael Share, PhD, is a professor on the Faculty of the World Economy and International Affairs at the University of Macao and specializes in Chinese-Russian relations.

Grant T. Weller, PhD, is an associate professor of history at the U.S. Air Force Academy. He earned his doctorate at Temple University.

James H. Willbanks, PhD, is retired from teaching but held the General of the Army George C. Marshall Chair of Military History at the U.S. Army Command and General Staff College. A retired army officer and author of many books, he earned his doctorate in history at the University of Kansas.

Bradford A. Wineman, PhD, is a professor at the U.S. Marine Corps University and an adjunct assistant professor for the Center for Security Studies at Georgetown University. Specializing in early U.S. military education, he earned his doctorate at Texas A&M University.

David T. Zabecki, PhD, is a retired U.S. Army major general. He earned his doctorate at Cranfield University in Britain. A widely published military historian, Zabecki has written seven books and numerous articles and encyclopedia entries.

Index

Note: Page numbers in *italics* indicate photos and maps.

Abbasid Caliphate, 45–46
Adrian I, Pope, 36–37, 38
Aerial resupply, 211
Alexander II of Russia, 178–179, 180
Alexander the Great, 11–14, 80
American Civil War, 160, 162, 167
    Bermuda Hundred Campaign, 167–168
    "Dictator" (Union 13-inch iron mortar), 168
    Lee's surrender at Appomattox Courthouse, 171
    Overland Campaign, 164, 167
    See also Siege of Fort Sumter (December 26, 1860–April 14, 1861); Siege of Petersburg (June 15, 1864–April 2, 1865); Sieges of Vicksburg (May 18–July 4, 1863) and Port Hudson, Louisiana (May 21–July 9, 1863)
American Revolutionary War, 109, 113, 115, 117, 120, 126, 199
    Battle of Biggin Bridge, 123
    Battle of Bunker Hill, 111
    Battle of Chelsea Creek, 110
    Battle of Oriskany, *114*
    Battle of Sullivan's Island, 112, 121
    Battles of Lexington and Concord, 109
    Second Battle of the Chesapeake, 128
    See also Siege of Boston (April 19, 1775–March 17, 1776); Siege of Charles Town (Charleston), South Carolina (March 29–May 12, 1780); Siege of Fort Stanwix, New York (August 2–23, 1777); Siege of Gibraltar (June 21, 1779–February 6, 1783); Siege of Yorktown (September 28–October 19, 1781)
Arab-Byzantine Wars, 32. *See also* Siege of Damascus (634–635?)
Austro-Prussian War, 152

Balloon incendiaries, 149, 151
Basilisks, 63
Battering ram, 26
    naval battering rams, 13
    siege machines equipped with, 19
    used at siege of Carthage (149–146 BCE), 19
    used at siege of Jerusalem (April 14–September 8, 70 CE), 26
    used at siege of Masada (72–73), 28
    used at siege of Paris (November 25, 885–October 886), 39
    used at siege of Plataea (428–427 BCE), 7
    used at siege of Tyre (332 BCE), 13
Battle of Agincourt, 52
Battle of Ascalon (Askelon), 42
Battle of Barrosa, 141
Battle of Berlin. *See* Siege of Berlin (April 16–May 2, 1945)
Battle of Bicocca, 65
Battle of Biggin Bridge, 123
Battle of Boydton Plank Road, 171
Battle of Britain, 227
Battle of Bunker Hill, 111
Battle of Burma, 247
Battle of Cannae, 14
Battle of Cape St. Vincent, 118
Battle of Chaffin's Farm, 170
Battle of Chelsea Creek, 110
Battle of Cold Harbor, 167
Battle of Ctesiphon, 212

Battle of Custoza, 150
Battle of Fair Oaks and Darbytown Road, 170
Battle of Five Forks, 171
Battle of Gravelotte-St. Privat, 173
Battle of Hatcher's Run, 171
Battle of Hattin, 43
Battle of Inkerman, 153
Battle of Jerusalem Plank Road, 169
Battle of Kobanî. *See* Siege of Kobanî (September 27, 2014–January 26, 2015)
Battle of Ky Hoa, 158
Battle of Madrid, 219
Battle of Majuba Hill, 194
Battle of Marathon, 6
Battle of Mohács, 71
Battle of Novara, 150, 152
Battle of Omdurman, 184
Battle of Oriskany, *114*
Battle of Pavia (October 28, 1524–February 24, 1525). *See* Siege and Battle of Pavia (October 28, 1524–February 24, 1525)
Battle of Peebles' Farm, 170
Battle of Quebec (June 26–September 13, 1759). *See* Siege and Battle of Quebec (June 26–September 13, 1759)
Battle of Quiberon Bay, 105
Battle of Sedan, 174
Battle of Sevastopol (October 30, 1941–July 4, 1942). *See* Siege of Sevastopol (October 17, 1854–September 9, 1855)
Battle of Singapore, 239
Battle of Sluys, 50
Battle of Stalingrad, 239, 243, 272, 274. *See also* Siege of Stalingrad (November 19, 1942–February 2, 1943)
Battle of Sullivan's Island, 112, 121
Battle of Szigeth (August 6–September 8, 1566). *See* Siege of Szigetvár (August 6–September 8, 1566)
Battle of Taginae, 32
Battle of Tel-el-Kebir, 181
Battle of the Adda, 29
Battle of the Bulge, 249, 253. *See also* Siege of Bastogne (December 20–27, 1944)
Battle of the Crater, 169
Battle of the Nile, 133
Battle of the Plains of Abraham. *See* Siege and Battle of Quebec (June 26–September 13, 1759)
Battle of the Seelow Heights, 255
Battle of the Sontius (Isonzo), 29
Battle of the Takir Ridge, 154
Battle of the Wilderness, 167
Battle of the Yellow Sea, 202
Battle of Tours, 36, 57
Battle of Trafalgar, 136
Battle of Valmy, 175
Battle of Verona, 29
Battle of Vienna (July 14–September 12, 1683). *See* Siege and Battle of Vienna (July 14–September 12, 1683)
Battle of Zama, 17
Battles of Lexington and Concord, 109
Berlin Blockade and Airlift (June 24, 1948–May 12, 1949), 256–260
aftermath, 259
Clay, Lucius, and, 257–258
Operation LITTLE VITTLES, 257, 258
starvation into submission used at, 256–258
U.S. Air Force Fairchild C-82A Packet landing with supplies, *258*
"Big Bertha" (420 mm German siege howitzer), 204, 205
Black Death (bubonic plague), 52, 96, 135
Boer War (South African War), 193. *See also* Siege of Mafeking (October 13, 1899–May 17, 1900)
Bubonic plague (Black Death), 52, 96, 135
Buchanan, James, 159, 160
Burghers of Calais, The (Rodin), 50

Caesar, Julius, 22–24, 89
Cannibalism, 22, 35, 92, 233
Catapults, 13, 15, 18, 19, 53
Celtiberian Wars, 20
Charlemagne (Charles the Great), 37
education and the arts under, 37
leadership and temperament, 37
siege of Pavia (September 773–June 774), 36–38
Charles I of England, 79, 81
Charles II of Spain, 86, 90
Charles III (Charles the Fat, king of West Francia), 38–40
Charles III of Spain, 106–107
Charles V, Duke of Lorraine, 88–89
Charles V of Spain, 65, 67, 68, 69

Charles VII of France (Charles the Well-Served), 52–55
Charles VI of France, 52
Cholera, 151, 152, 153, 210
Churchill, Winston, 222, 224–225, 227, 229, 237, 253, 254, 256
Circumvallation walls, 21, 23, 28
Claws (grapples), 15, *16*
Cold War, 256, 257, 259, 270
Constantine the Great, 34
Constantine XI, 55–57
Contravallation walls, 21, 23
Cornwallis, Lord, 124, 126–129
Cortés, Hernán, 60, 62–63
Cretan War of 1645–1669, 83. *See also* Siege of Candia (May 1, 1648–September 27, 1669)
Crimean War, 152, 154, 178, 180. *See also* Siege of Sevastopol (October 17, 1854–September 9, 1855)
Crusades
    First Crusade, 40–41
    Fourth Crusade, 83
    Third Crusade, 43–44
    See also Siege of Acre (August 28, 1189–July 12, 1191); Siege of Jerusalem (June 7–July 18, 1099)
Cuitláhuac, 62
Cyrus the Great (Cyrus II of Persia), 4–5
    capture of Jerusalem, 5
    death of, 5
    legacy of, 5
    permission given for Jews of Babylon to return to Jerusalem, 5
    siege of Babylon (539–538 BCE), 4–5
    strategy of trenches and ditches, 4–5
    toleration and benevolence of, 5

Darius III of Persia, 12, 14
Defense of Sevastopol (October 30, 1941–July 4, 1942). *See* Siege of Sevastopol (October 17, 1854–September 9, 1855)
Dutch War of 1672–1678 (Franco-Dutch War), 84, 85, 88. *See also* Siege of Maastricht (June 13–30, 1673)
Dutch Wars of Independence, 73, 76. *See also* Siege of Antwerp (July 1584–August 17, 1585); Siege of Breda (August 28, 1624–June 5, 1625)

Earthworks, 70, 121, 141, 179
Edward III of England, 50–52

Elephants, war, 14, 16, 19, 21, 158
Explosive shell, 64, 106, 118, 119

Fatimid Caliphate, 42
First Battle of Deep Bottom, 169
First Battle of Manila Bay. *See* Siege and First Battle of Manila (May 1–August 14, 1898)
First Battle of Petersburg, 168
First Battle of Tobruk, 227
First Jewish-Roman War, 24, 27. *See also* Siege of Jerusalem (April 14–September 8, 70 CE); Siege of Masada (72–73)
Franco, Francisco, 214, 216, 217, 218, 219, 220, 221
Franco-Dutch War (Dutch War of 1672–1678), 84, 85, 88. *See also* Siege of Maastricht (June 13–30, 1673)
Franco-German War, 158
François (Francis) I of France, 65–67
Franco-Prussian War, 171, 175, 210. *See also* Siege of Metz (August 19–October 27, 1870); Siege of Paris (September 19, 1870–January 28, 1871)
French and Indian War, 96, 98, 102, 105, 106–107, 115. *See also* Siege of Fort William Henry (August 3–10, 1757); Siege of Havana (June 6–August 13, 1762); Siege of Louisbourg (June 8–July 26, 1758)
French Revolution, 130, 132, 143, 148, 155, 194, 213–214, 224
Furius Philus, Lucius, 21

Gallic Wars, 23. *See also* Siege of Alesia (July–October 52 BCE)
Genghis Khan, 46, 47
Giambelli, Federico, 74
Godfrey of Bouillon, Duke of Lorraine, 41, 42
Gothic War, 30. *See also* Siege of Rome (March 2, 537–March 12, 538)
Grant, Ulysses S., 164–165, 167–171
Grapples (claws), 15, *16*
Greco-Persian Wars, 6
Greek fire, 35
Greek War of Independence, 142, 143. *See also* Third Siege of Missolonghi (April 15, 1825–April 23, 1826)
"Guerrilla," origin of the term, 137

Gunpowder
- cannon, 49
- harquebus and, 65
- heavy siege artillery, 26
- invention of, 34
- small arms, 65

Hannibal Barca, 14, 17
Hannibalic War (Second Punic War), 14, 17–18, 20
Harquebus (arquebus), 62, 65, 66
Herod the Great, 27
Hitler, Adolf, 214
- siege of Bastogne (December 20–27, 1944), 250, 253
- siege of Berlin (April 16–May 2, 1945), 253–254, 255
- siege of Budapest (November 3, 1944–February 13, 1945), 248, 249
- siege of Dunkirk (Dunkerque) (May 26–June 4, 1940), 222, 224
- siege of Leningrad (July 10, 1941–January 27, 1944), 231, 232, 233, 234
- siege of Leningrad (July 10, 1941–January 27, 1944), 233, 234
- siege of Malta (June 11, 1940–November 20, 1942), 226
- siege of Sevastopol (October 17, 1854–September 9, 1855), 235, 239
- siege of Stalingrad (November 19, 1942–February 2, 1943), 239–243
- siege of Tobruk (April 10–December 5, 1941), 228

Hoplites (armed foot soldiers), 8, 9, 12, 17, 19
Hulegu Khan, 45–46
Human wave assaults, 57, 62, 261
Hundred Years' War, 50, 52, 54–55. *See also* Siege of Calais (September 4, 1346–August 3, 1347); Siege of Orléans (October 12, 1428–May 8, 1449)

Iliad (Homer), 3
Imjin War, 76
Indochina War, 260. *See also* Siege of Dien Bien Phu (March 13–May 7, 1954)
Investment fortifications, 87, 115, 202
Iraq War, 279
Israeli Invasion of Lebanon, 266, 269. *See also* Siege of Beirut (June 14–August 21, 1982)

Israeli War of Independence, 29
Italian War of 1521–1526, 65

Jeanne d'Arc (Joan of Arc), 52–54
Justinian I, 30–31, 32

King George's War, 99
Kitchener, Herbert, 197
Kitchener, Horatio, 184
Knights of St. John (Hospitallers), 63–64, 69–70, 133
Kublai Khan, 47, 48

Ladders, 7, 15, 16, 42, 54
Lebanon-Israel War, 266, 269. *See also* Siege of Beirut (June 14–August 21, 1982)
Lee, Robert E., 167–171
Leo III the Isaurian, 34, 35–36, 38
Lincoln, Abraham, 159, 160–161, 166, 167
Lusitanian War, 20

McKinley, William, 187, 189, 192, 193
Mehmed II (Mehmed the Conqueror), 55–57, 63
Metellus Macedonicus, Quintus Caecilius, 20
Mines, 68, 87, 108, 139, 141, 144, 169, 186, 202, 216
- claymore mines, 264
- countermines, 64
- fake land mines, 196
- land mines, 183

Ming dynasty, 76
Möngke Khan, 46, 47, 48
Mortars, early, 106
Muhammad XI of Granada, 58–59

Nabonidus of Babylonia, 4–5
Napoleon Bonaparte, 140, 148–149
- siege of Acre (March 17–May 20, 1799), 45, 133–135
- siege of Toulon (September 18–December 19, 1793), 131–132
- sieges of Zaragoza (June 15–August 17, 1808; December 20, 1808–February 20, 1809), 136–139

Napoleon III of France, 150, 154, 175
- siege of Metz (August 19–October 27, 1870), 172–173, 174
- siege of Saigon (March 1860–February 1861), 155–156

Napoleonic Wars, 143, 148, 224
  Peninsular War, 136, 137, 139
  See also Sieges of Zaragoza (June 15–August 17, 1808; December 20, 1808–February 20, 1809)
Numantine (or third Celtiberian War), 20. *See also* Siege of Numantia (Numancia) (134–133 BCE)

Ögödei Khan, 47
Operation BATTLEAXE, 229. *See also* Siege of Tobruk (April 10–December 5, 1941)
Operation BLAU, 239. *See also* Siege of Stalingrad (November 19, 1942–February 2, 1943)
Operation BODENPLATTE, 252. *See also* Siege of Bastogne (December 20–27, 1944)
Operation BREVITY, 229. *See also* Siege of Tobruk (April 10–December 5, 1941)
Operation CASTOR, 260. *See also* Siege of Dien Bien Phu (March 13–May 7, 1954)
Operation CRUSADER, 230. *See also* Siege of Tobruk (April 10–December 5, 1941)
Operation DYNAMO, 222. *See also* Siege of Dunkirk (Dunkerque) (May 26–June 4, 1940)
Operation HERKULES, 226. *See also* Siege of Malta (June 11, 1940–November 20, 1942)
Operation LITTLE VITTLES, 257, 258. *See also* Berlin Blockade and Airlift (June 24, 1948–May 12, 1949)
Operation NIAGARA, 265. *See also* Siege of Khe Sanh (January 21–April 8, 1968)
Operation PEACE FOR GALILEE, 266, 267
Operation PEDESTAL, 226. *See also* Siege of Malta (June 11, 1940–November 20, 1942)
Operation PEGASUS, 265
Operation SPARK, 234. *See also* Siege of Sevastopol (October 17, 1854–September 9, 1855)
Operation TORCH, 226. *See also* Siege of Malta (June 11, 1940–November 20, 1942)
Operation URANUS, 242. *See also* Siege of Stalingrad (November 19, 1942–February 2, 1943)
Operation WATCH ON THE RHINE, 250, 253
Operation WE ARE COMING, NINEVEH. *See* Siege of Mosul (October 17, 2016–July 9, 2017)
Opium War of 1840–1842, 197
Oxen, 31–32, 112

Peninsular War, 136, 137, 139
Philippe VI of France, 50–52
Philippine-American War, 193
Pius IX, Pope, 150

Queen Anne's War (War of the Spanish Succession), 88, 90, 93, 117
Quinqueremes (banks of oars), 15, 17, 18

Redoubts, 107, 126, 128, 158, 254
Richelieu, Cardinal (Armand Jean du Plessis), 14, 78–81
Roman First Triumvirate, 22
Roosevelt, Theodore, 188
Rosetta Stone, 133
Russo-Japanese War, 200, 206. *See also* Siege of Port Arthur (February 8, 1904–January 2, 1905)

Sambucas (ships mounted with scaling ladders), 15
Sappers (military engineers), 11, 138
Saps (small trenches), 186
Scaling ladders, 7, 15, 16, 42, 54
Scorched-earth strategy, 23
Second Battle of Deep Bottom, 169
Second Battle of El Alamein, 226, 231
Second Battle of Petersburg, 168
Second Battle of Reams Station, 169–170
Second Battle of the Chesapeake, 128
Second Opium War, 156
Second Peloponnesian War (431–404 BCE)
  siege of Plataea (428–427 BCE), 6–7
  siege of Syracuse (415–413 BCE), 8–10
Second Punic War (Hannibalic War)
  Battle of Zama, 17
  siege of Carthage (149–146 BCE) and, 17–18
  siege of Numantia (Numancia) (134–133 BCE) and, 20
  siege of Syracuse (213–212 BCE), 14–17

Seminole Wars, 146
Sertorian War, 22
Seven Years' War, 96, 98, 102, 105, 106–107, 115. *See also* Siege of Fort William Henry (August 3–10, 1757); Siege of Havana (June 6–August 13, 1762); Siege of Louisbourg (June 8–July 26, 1758)
Shrapnel, 74, 118, 120
Shrapnel, Henry, 118, 120
Siege and Battle of Pavia (October 28, 1524–February 24, 1525), 65–67
   aftermath, 66–67
   Charles de Bourbon and, 66
   deaths and casualties, 66
   François (Francis) I of France and, 65–67
   Habsburg victory, 66
   harquebus (arquebus) used at, 65, 66
Siege and Battle of Quebec (June 26–September 13, 1759), 102–105
   aftermath, 105
   Amherst, Jeffery, and, 103
   British victory, 104–105
   The Death of General Wolfe (Benjamin West), *104*
   deaths and casualties, 105
   Montcalm, Marquis de, and, 103–104
   Pitt, William, and, 103
   Stobo, Robert, and, 103
   Wolfe, James, and, 103–104
Siege and Battle of Vienna (July 14–September 12, 1683), 88–90
   aftermath, 89–90
   Christian victory, 89
   Kara Mustafa and, 89
   Louis XIV of France and, 88
   Mehmed IV and, 88
   Sobieski, King John III, and, 89
   Starhemberg, Ernst Rüdiger von, and, 88–89
Siege and First Battle of Manila (May 1–August 14, 1898), 187, 190–193
   aftermath, 193
   American-Filipino victory, 193
   Dewey, George, and, 190, 191–192
   Greene, Francis V., and, 190–193
   MacArthur, Arthur, and, 190, 192–193
   Merritt, Wesley, and, 190, 191–193
   Montojo, Patricio, and, 187, *191*
   Reina Christina, *191*

Siege engines and machines
   claws (grapples), 15, *16*
   crow (barbed hook), 13
   with inflammatory devices, 44
   mounted on towers, 21
   sand and, 13
   used at siege of Acre (August 28, 1189–July 12, 1191), 44
   used at siege of Baghdad (January 29–February 10, 1258), 46
   used at siege of Constantinople (August 15, 717–August 15, 718), 34
   used at siege of Jerusalem (June 7–July 18, 1099), 41
   used at siege of Numantia (Numancia), 21
   used at siege of Paris (November 25, 885–October 886), 38, 39
   used in Sieges of Tyre and Gaza (332 BCE), 12, 13
   See also Battering ram; Catapults; Siege towers; Trebuchets
Siege of Acre (August 28, 1189–July 12, 1191), 43–45
   aftermath, 44–45
   Crusader victory, 44
   Frederick Barbarossa (Frederick I) and, 44
   Guy, king of Latin Kingdom of Jerusalem, and, 43–44
   Henry of Troyes, Count of Champagne, and, 44
   Philippe II Augustus of France and, 44
   Richard I (the Lion-Hearted) of England and, 44
   Saladin and, 43–44
   siege towers used at, 44
   surrender of Acre, 44, *45*
   trebuchets used in, 43, 44
Siege of Acre (March 17–May 20, 1799), 133–136
   aftermath, 135
   Anglo-Ottoman victory, 135
   capture of Alexandria, 133
   deaths and casualties, 134, 135
   French force, 133
   Jessar Pasha and, 134, 135
   Napoleon Bonaparte and, 45, 133–135
   Smith, Sydney, and, 134, 135
Siege of Aleppo (July 19, 2012–December 22, 2016), 273–276
   aftermath, 275–276
   Assad, Bashar, and, 274, 275

destruction in old city area of Aleppo, *275*, 275–276
displaced persons, 275–276
Jabhat Fateh al Sham and, 274
Syrian Army and allied victory, 275
Siege of Alesia (July–October 52 BCE), 22–24
   aftermath, 23–24
   Caesar, Julius, and, 22–24
   circumvallation wall, 23
   contravallation wall, 23
   Labienus and, 23
   Roman victory, 23
   Vercingetorix and, 23
Siege of Antwerp (July 1584–August 17, 1585), 73–74
   aftermath, 74
   Farnese, Alessandro, and, 73–74
   Philippe de Marnix and, 73
   siege devices used at, 73–74
   Spanish victory, 74
Siege of Babylon (539–538 BCE), 4–6
   Books of Daniel and Jeremiah (Hebrew Bible) on, 4, 5
   Cyrus the Great (Cyrus II of Persia) and, 4–5
   differing accounts of siege, 4–5
   exile of Nabonidus, 5
   Herodotus on, 4
   Nabonidus of Babylonia and, 4–5
   onset and timing of, 5
   Persian victory, 5
   strategy of trenches and ditches, 4–5
   towers made from palm trees, 5
Siege of Baghdad (January 29–February 10, 1258), 45–47
   Abbasid Caliphate and, 45–46
   aftermath, 46
   death of al-Mustasim, 46
   deaths and casualties, 46
   destruction of Baghdad, 45–46
   Hulegu Khan and, 45–46
   Mongol victory, 46
Siege of Bastogne (December 20–27, 1944), 249–253
   aftermath, 253
   American victory, 252–253
   deaths and casualties, 252–253
   Hitler, Adolf, and, 250, 253
   Operation BODENPLATTE, 252–253
   Operation WATCH ON THE RHINE, 250, 253
   U.S. Army's 4th Armored Division, *252*
Siege of Beirut (June 14–August 21, 1982), 266–270
   aftermath, 269–270
   Arafat, Yasser, and, 269
   Begin, Menachem, and, 266, 267, 268, 270
   Israeli bombardment of Palestine Liberation Organization position, *267*
   Israeli bombardment on June 17, 1982, *267*
   Operation PEACE FOR GALILEE, 266, 267
   Palestine Liberation Organization (PLO) and, 266–270
   Sharon, Ariel, and, 266, 268–270
Siege of Berlin (April 16–May 2, 1945), 253–256
   aftermath, 255–256
   Battle of the Seelow Heights, 255
   Bradley, Omar, and, 254, 255
   deaths and casualties, 255
   Hitler, Adolf, and, 253–254, 255
   Soviet victory, 255
   Stalin, Joseph, and, 254–255
Siege of Boston (April 19, 1775–March 17, 1776), 109–113
   aftermath, 113
   American victory, 112–113
   Clinton, Henry, and, 11, 110, 112
   Gage, Thomas, and, 109–111
   Greene, Nathanael, and, 111, 113
   Howe, William, and, 110, 111, 112–113
   Prescott, William, and, 110–111
   Ward, Artemas, and, 109, 110–111
   Washington, George, and, 111–113
Siege of Breda (August 28, 1624–June 5, 1625), 76–78
   aftermath, 78
   Mansfeld, Peter Ernst von, and, 77
   Maurice of Nassau and, 76–77
   Spanish victory, 78
   Spinola, Ambrosio de, and, 76–77
   The Surrender of Breda (Diego Velázquez), *77*
Siege of Budapest (November 3, 1944–February 13, 1945), 248–249
   aftermath, 249
   Allied victory, 249
   Gille, Herbert, and, 249
   Hindy, Iván, and, 249
   Hitler, Adolf, and, 248, 249
   Pfeffer-Wildenbruch, Karl, and, 248, 249

Siege of Cádiz (February 5, 1810–August 24, 1812), 139–142
  aftermath, 142
  Battle of Barrosa, 141
  Coalition victory, 142
  deaths and casualties, 141
  Marmont, Auguste, and, 142
  Soult, Nicolas Jean-de-Dieu, and, 139, 141, 142
  Victor-Perrin, Claude, and, 139–140, 141–142
  Wellington, Viscount, and, 139–140, 142
Siege of Calais (September 4, 1346–August 3, 1347), 50–52
  aftermath, 52
  The Burghers of Calais (Rodin), 50
  Edward III of England and, 50–52
  English force, 51
  English victory, 51–52
  French force, 51
  Jean de Vienne and, 51
  ouches inutiles (useless mouths) and, 51
  Philippe VI of France and, 50–52
  starvation into submission used at, 51
Siege of Candia (May 1, 1648–September 27, 1669), 83–84
  aftermath, 84
  Ahmed Köprülü, Fazil, and, 84
  Knights of Malta and, 83
  Louis XIV of France and, 84
  Morosini, Francesco, and, 84
  Ottoman force, 83
  Ottoman victory, 84
Siege of Cartagena de Indias (March 9–May 20, 1741), 93–96
  aftermath, 96
  deaths and casualties, 96
  geopolitical significance of Cartagena, 95
  Spanish victory, 95
  Vernon, Edward, and, 93–96
  Washington, Lawrence, and, 96
  Wentworth, Thomas, and, 94, 95
Siege of Carthage (149–146 BCE), 17–20
  aftermath, 20
  "Carthaginian Peace," 20
  Himilco Phameas and, 19
  Mancinus, Lucius Hostilius, and, 19
  Masinissa of Numidia and, 17–18
  Piso Ceasonibus, L. Calpurnius, and, 19
  Roman victory, 19–20
  Scipio Aemilianus and, 19–20
  siege machines equipped with battering rams, 19
Siege of Charles Town (Charleston), South Carolina (March 29–May 12, 1780), 120–125
  aftermath, 124
  Arbuthnot, Mariot, and, 121
  British victory, 124
  Clinton, Henry, and, 121, 123–124
  deaths and casualties, 124
  Ferguson, Patrick, and, 123
  Lincoln, Benjamin, and, 121, 123–124
  parallel trenches used at, 123
  Scott, William, and, 124
  Tartleton, Banastre, and, 123, 124
Siege of Constantinople (April 6–May 29, 1453), 55–57
  aftermath, 57
  Constantine XI and, 55–57
  Golden Horn (natural harbor), 56–57
  Hagia Sophia and, 57
  map, 56
  Mehmed II (Mehmed the Conqueror) and, 55–57, 63
  Ottoman naval force, 55–56
  Ottoman victory, 57
Siege of Constantinople (August 15, 717–August 15, 718), 34–36
  aftermath, 36
  Byzantine victory, 36
  geopolitical significance of Constantinople, 34
  Golden Horn (natural harbor), 34, 35
  Greek fire used at, 35
  Leo III and, 34, 35–36
  Maslama (brother of Suleiman) and, 35–36
  Omar II and, 35–36
  Suleiman and, 34–35
  Terbelis, king of the Bulgars, and, 35
Siege of Damascus (634–635?), 32–34
  Abu Bakr and, 33
  aftermath, 34
  Byzantine forces, 33
  deaths and casualties, 34
  Heraclius and, 33
  Khalid ibn al-Walid and, 33–34
  Mansur Ibn Sarjan and, 33
  Rashidun forces, 33
  Rashidun victory, 33
  Thomas (son-in-law of Heraclius) and, 33

Siege of Dien Bien Phu (March 13–May 7, 1954), 260–262
  aftermath, 261–262
  de Castries, Christian Marie Ferdinand de la Croix, and, 260, 261
  deaths and casualties, 261
  geopolitical significance of Dien Bien Phu, 260
  Giap, Vo Nguyen, and, 260, 261
  Viet Minh victory, 261
Siege of Dunkirk (Dunkerque) (May 26–June 4, 1940)
  aftermath, 223–224
  Churchill, Winston, and, 222, 224–225
  escape of British Expeditionary Force, 222–224, *223*
  Göring, Hermann, and, 222
  Hitler, Adolf, and, 222, 224
  Operation DYNAMO, 222–223
Siege of Fort Stanwix, New York (August 2–23, 1777), 113–117
  aftermath, 116–117
  American victory, 116
  Arnold, Benedict, and, 116–117
  Carleton, Guy, and, 114
  deaths and casualties, 116
  Herkimer, Nicholas, and, 115–116
  investment fortifications, 115
  map, *114*
  Schuyler, Philip, and, 115, 116
  St. Leger, Barrimore (Barry), and, 114–117
  Willet, Marinus, and, 115, 116
Siege of Fort Sumter (December 26, 1860–April 14, 1861), 159–162
  aftermath, 162
  Anderson, Robert, and, 161, 162
  Beauregard, Pierre G. T., and, 160, 161
  Confederate victory, 162
  depiction of bombardment of Fort Sumter (Currier & Ives), *161*
  Fox, Gustavus V., and, 161, 162
Siege of Fort William Henry (August 3–10, 1757), 96–98
  aftermath, 98
  deaths and casualties, 97, 98
  French victory, 98
  Loudoun, Lord (John Campbell), and, 96
  Monro, George, 97
  Montcalm, Marquis de, and, 97–98
  Webb, Daniel, and, 97

Siege of Gaza (332 BCE). *See* Sieges of Tyre and Gaza (332 BCE)
Siege of Gibraltar (June 21, 1779–February 6, 1783), 117–120
  aftermath, 120
  British victory, 119–120
  Darby, George, and, 118
  Eliott, George Augustus, and, 118
  floating batteries and, 118–120
  geopolitical significance of Gibraltar, 117
  military innovations at, 118–120
Siege of Granada (Mid-April 1491–January 2, 1492), 57–60
  aftermath, 59
  Ferdinand and Isabella of Spain and, 58–59
  Muhammad XI and, 58–59
  Spanish forces, 59
  Spanish victory and terms of surrender, 59
Siege of Havana (June 6–August 13, 1762), 105–109
  aftermath, 109
  British victory, 108–109
  de Hevia, Gutierre, and, 106, 107, 108
  de Prado, Juan, and, 106, 107–108
  Family Compact and, 107
  geopolitical significance of Havana, 106
  Pocock, George, and, 107
  Velasco, Luis Vicente de, and, 107–108
Siege of Imphal and Kohima (April 4–May 31, 1944), 243–248
  aftermath, 247
  airlifts, 247
  British victory, 247
  Mutaguchi Renya and, 245, 246, 247
  Sikh signaler, *245*
Siege of Isfahan (March–October 23, 1722), 91–93
  Afghan victory, 92
  aftermath, 92
  Mahmud and, 92
  Safavid dynasty and, 91–92
Siege of Jerusalem (April 14–September 8, 70 CE), 24–27
  aftermath, 26
  battering ram used at, 26
  capture of Antonia Fortress, 26
  capture of John of Gischala and Simon bar Giora, 26
  deaths and casualties, 26

Siege of Jerusalem (*Continued*)
  destruction of the Second Temple, 26
  diagram, *25*
  Eleazar Ben Simon and, 24
  factionalism and, 24
  John of Gischala and, 24, 26
  Josephus and, 26
  Roman victory, 26
  sack of Jerusalem, 26
  Simon bar Giora and, 24, 26
  Tiberius Julius Alexander and, 24
  Titus and, 24, 26
Siege of Jerusalem (June 7–July 18, 1099), 40–43
  aftermath, 42–43
  Crusader victory, 42
  deaths and casualties, 42–43
  Godfrey of Bouillon, Duke of Lorraine, and, 41, 42
Siege of Khartoum (March 13, 1884–January 26, 1885), 181–184
  aftermath, 184
  Dervishes and, 182–184
  Gladstone, William, and, 182, 183, 184
  Gordon, Charles George, and, 182–184
  Mahdist victory, 183–184
  Wolseley, Garnet, and, 181, 183
Siege of Khe Sanh (January 21–April 8, 1968), 262–266
  aftermath, 265–266
  First Battle of Khe Sanh, 262
  Giap, Vo Nguyen, and, 262m 265
  map, *263*
  Westmoreland, William, and, 262–265
Siege of Kobanî (September 27, 2014–January 26, 2015), 276–278
  aftermath, 277–278
  Erdoğan, Recep Tayyip, and, 276
  Islamic State of Iraq and Syria (ISIS) and, 276–278
  Rojava Federation victory, 277
Siege of Kut (December 7, 1915–April 29, 1916), 210–213
  aftermath, 213
  damage to interior of bazaar at Kut, *212*
  first aerial resupply, 211
  Ottoman victory, 213
  Townshend, Charles V. F., and, 211–213
Siege of La Rochelle (August 1627–October 28, 1628), 78–81
  aftermath, 81
  Charles I of England and, 79, 81
  deaths and casualties, 79, 81
  Edict of Nantes and, 78, 79, 81
  floating wall of chained ships used in, 81
  French victory, 81
  Louis XIII and, 78, 80
  Richelieu, Cardinal (Armand Jean du Plessis), and, 78–81
Siege of Leningrad (July 10, 1941–January 27, 1944), 231–234
  aftermath, 234
  Hitler, Adolf, 233, 234
  Hitler, Adolf, and, 231, 232, 233, 234
  Leeb, Wilhelm R. von, and, 231–232
  map of disposition of forces, *232*
  Meretskov, Kirill A., and, 233, 234
  Soviet victory, 234
  Stalin, Joseph, and, 232, 233, 234
Siege of Liège (August 5–16, 1914), 203–206
  aftermath, 206
  assassination of Franz Ferdinand and, 203
  "Big Bertha" (420 mm German siege howitzer) used at, 204, 205
  geopolitical significance of Liège, 204
  Leman, Gérard Mathieu, and, 204, 205
  Ludendorff, Erich, and, 205, 206
  Moltke, Helmuth von, and, 204
Siege of Louisbourg (June 8–July 26, 1758), 98–102
  aftermath, 102
  Amherst, Jeffery, and, 100–102
  Boscawen, Edward, and, 100, 101
  British force, 100
  British victory, 101–102
  deaths and casualties, 102
  Hardy, Charles, and, 100
Siege of Maastricht (June 13–30, 1673), 84–88
  aftermath, 87–88
  artillery used at, 87
  deaths and casualties, 87
  French victory, 87
  investment fortifications, 87
  Louis XIV of France and, 84, 86
  parallel trenches used at, 87
  Vauban, Sébastien Le Prestre de, and, 85, 86–87
Siege of Madrid (November 6, 1936–March 31, 1939), 217–221
  aftermath, 220–221
  bombing, 219
  Casado López, Segismundo, and, 220

Franco, Francisco, and, 217, 218, 219, 220, 221
   notable events outside Madrid, 219
   Republican counteroffensive, 219–220
Siege of Mafeking (October 13, 1899–May 17, 1900), 193–197
   aftermath, 197
   Baden-Powell, Robert S. S., 195–197
   British victory, 197
   Cronjé, Piet A., and, 195–196
   deaths and casualties, 196–197
   Mahon, Bryan T., and, 196
Siege of Magdeburg (November 20, 1630–May 20, 1631), 81–83
   aftermath, 83
   Catholic forces, 82
   Catholic victory, 83
   deaths and casualties, 83
   destruction of Magdeburg, 83
   geopolitical significance of Magdeburg, 81–82
   Pappenheim, Gottfried H. zu, and, 82, 83
   Tilly and, 82–83
Siege of Malta (June 11, 1940–November 20, 1942), 224–227
   aftermath, 226
   Allied victory, 226
   deaths and casualties, 226
   geopolitical significance of Malta, 224, 225
   Hitler, Adolf, and, 226
   Operation HERKULES, 226
   Operation PEDESTAL, 226
   Rommel's assessment of importance of Malta, 225
Siege of Malta (May 18–September 8, 1565), 69–71
   aftermath, 70
   Christian victory, 70
   deaths and casualties, 70
   Knights of St. John (Hospitallers) and, 69–70
   Ottoman force, 70
   Suleiman I, the Magnificent, and, 69, 70
Siege of Masada (72–73), 27–29
   aftermath, 28–29
   battering ram used at, 28
   deaths and casualties, 28
   definition of "masada," 27
   Flavius Silva, Lucius, and, 27
   geopolitical significance of Masada, 27
   Jewish defense forces, 27
   Josephus on, 28
   Roman forces, 27
   ruins of, *28*
Siege of Metz (August 19–October 27, 1870), 171–175
   aftermath, 174–175
   Battle of Gravelotte-St. Privat, 173
   Battle of Sedan, 174
   Bazaine, François Achille, and, 172–175
   Canrobert, François Certain, and, 173
   German victory, 174
   MacMahon, Patrice, and, 173, 174, 175
   Moltke, Helmuth von, and, 172, 173–174
Siege of Mosul (October 17, 2016–July 9, 2017), 278–281
   aftermath, 280–281
   al-Abadi, Haider, and, 280, 281
   allied victory, 280
   Baghdadi, Abu Bakr al-, and, 278
   displaced persons, 281
   Islamic State of Iraq and Syria (ISIS) and, 278–281
   U.S. Army M109A6 Paladin howitzer, *279*
Siege of Numantia (Numancia) (134–133 BCE), 20–22
   aftermath, 22
   cannibalism and, 22
   circumvallation wall, 21
   contravallation wall, 21
   deditio (complete submission) and, 21
   escape of Rhetogenes, 21
   geopolitical significance of Numantia, 20
   Mancinus, Gaius Hostilius, and, 21
   Roman victory, 21–22
   Scipio Aemilianus and, 21–22
   siege engines used in, 21
Siege of Odawara Castle (May–August 4, 1590), 74–76
   aftermath, 76
   Hideyoshi, Toyotomi, and, 75–76
   Hideyoshi victory, 75
   Hōjō forces, 75
   unification campaigns and, 74–75
Siege of Orléans (October 12, 1428–May 8, 1449), 52–55
   aftermath, 54–55
   Charles VII of France and, 52–55
   French victory, 54
   Jean Dunois, Comte de Longueville, and, 53
   Jeanne d'Arc (Joan of Arc) and, 52–54
   scaling ladders used at, 54

Siege of Paris (November 25, 885–October 886), 38–40
   aftermath, 40
   battering rams used at, 39
   Charles III (Charles the Fat, king of West Francia) and, 38–40
   Frankish victory, 39–40
   geopolitical significance of Paris, 38–39
   Henry, Count of Saxony, and, 39
   Odo (Eudes), Count of Paris, and, 39, 40
   Viking force, 39
Siege of Paris (September 19, 1870–January 28, 1871), 175–178
   aftermath, 177–178
   Bazaine, François Achille, and, 176–177
   French defense force, 176
   Gambetta, Léon, and, 175, 176–177
   German victory, 177
   Moltke, Helmuth von, and, 176
   Treaty of Frankfurt, 177–178
Siege of Pavia (September 773–June 774), 36–38
   Adelchis and, 37
   aftermath, 38
   Charles the Great (Charlemagne) and, 36–38
   Desiderata, wife of Charles the Great, and, 36–37
   Frankish victory, 37–38
   Pope Adrian I and, 36–37, 38
Siege of Peking (Beijing) (June 20–August 14, 1900), 197–199
   aftermath, 199
   allied victory, 199
   Chinese nationalist societies and, 198
   deaths and casualties, 199
Siege of Pensacola, West Florida (March 9–May 10, 1781), 125–126
   aftermath, 126
   arrival of Spanish reinforcements, 125
   Campbell, John, and, 125, 126
   Franco-Spanish victory, 126
   Gálvez, Bernardo de, and, 125
Siege of Petersburg (June 15, 1864–April 2, 1865), 167–171
   aftermath, 171
   Battle of Boydton Plank Road, 171
   Battle of Chaffin's Farm, 170
   Battle of Cold Harbor, 167
   Battle of Fair Oaks and Darbytown Road, 170
   Battle of Fort Stedman, 171
   Battle of Hatcher's Run, 171
   Battle of Jerusalem Plank Road, 169
   Battle of Peebles' Farm, 170
   Battle of the Crater, 169
   Battle of the Wilderness, 167
   Beauregard, Pierre G. T., and, 167–168
   First Battle of Deep Bottom, 169
   First Battle of Petersburg, 168
   Grant, Ulysses S., and, 167–171
   Lee, Robert E., and, 167–171
   Second Battle of Deep Bottom, 169
   Second Battle of Petersburg, 168
   Second Battle of Reams Station, 169–170
   Sheridan, Philip H., and, 169, 171
   Union victory, 171
Siege of Plataea (428–427 BCE), 6–7
   aftermath, 7
   Archidamos of Sparta and, 6–7
   battering rams used at, 7
   deaths and casualties, 7
   escape of Plataeans, 7
   initial Spartan attack, 6
   Plataean defense forces, 6
   Plataean wall defenses, 7
   Spartan denial of Plataean request for truce, 6
   Spartan palisade and embankment, 7
   surrender of Plataeans, 7
   Thebes and, 6, 7
   Thucydides on, 6
Siege of Pleven (July 19–December 10, 1877), 178–181
   aftermath, 180–181
   Alexander II and, 178, 179, 180
   Gourko, Ossip, and, 180
   Mehemed Ali and, 179
   Osmān Pasha and, 179, 180
   Russian-Romanian-Bulgarian victory, 180
   Todleben, Franz Eduard Ivanovich, and, 180
   Treaty of Berlin, 180–181
   Treaty of San Stefano, 180
Siege of Port Arthur (February 8, 1904–January 2, 1905), 200–203
   aftermath, 203
   deaths and casualties, 201, 203
   investment fortifications, 202
   Japanese victory, 202–203
   Makarov, S. Ossipovitch, and, 202
   Nogi Maresuke and, 202

Oku Yasukata and, 202
Stoessel, Anatoli M., and, 202
Tomgom Heihachirom and, 201
wrecked Russian warships in Port Arthur, *201*
Siege of Port Hudson. *See* Sieges of Vicksburg (May 18–July 4, 1863) and Port Hudson, Louisiana (May 21–July 9, 1863)
Siege of Przemyśl (September 16, 1914–March 22, 1915), 208–210
aftermath, 209–210
Conrad von Hštzendorf, Franz, and, 209–210
Russian victory, 209–210
Siege of Puebla (September 14–October 12, 1847), 146–148
aftermath, 148
Childs, Thomas, and, 146, 147, 148
deaths and casualties, 146–147, 148
Franco-Imperial victory, 148
Lane, Joseph, and, 147–148
map, *147*
Rea, Joaquín, 146–147, 148
Santa Anna, Antonio López de, and, 146, 147–148
Siege of Qingdao (August 23, 1914–November 7, 1914), 206–208
aftermath, 208
Anglo-Japanese victory, 208
Meyer-Waldeck, Alfred, and, 207, 208
Plüschow, Gunther, and, 207, 208
Siege of Ravenna (Autumn 490–February 27, 493), 29–30
aftermath, 30
capture of Rimini, 30
deaths and casualties, 30
murder of Odoacer, 30
Odoacer of Italy and, 29–30
Ostrogoth victory and terms of surrender, 30
Theodoric the Great and, 29–30
Siege of Rhodes (July 28–December 21, 1522), 63–64
aftermath, 64
explosive shell, 64
geopolitical significance of Rhodes, 63
Knights of St. John (Hospitallers) and, 63–64
Ottoman victory, 64
Suleiman I, the Magnificent, and, 63–64

Siege of Rome (March 2, 537–March 12, 538), 30–32
aftermath, 32
Belisarius, Byzantine general, and, 30–32
John "the Sanguinary" and, 32
Justinian I and, 30–31, 32
murder of Theodatus of Amalasuntha, 30–31
Ostrogoth forces, 31
oxen used at, 31–32
Roman victory, 32
Theodebert of Austrasia and, 32
Vitiges, king of the Ostrogoths, and, 31–32
Siege of Saigon (March 1860–February 1861), 155–158
aftermath, 158
Battle of Ky Hoa, 158
French victory, 158
Tu Duc, Emperor of Japan, and, 158
Vietnamese defense force, 158
Siege of Santiago de Cuba (July 1–17, 1898), 187–190
aftermath, 190
American-Cuban victory, 190
Cervera, Pascual, and, 187–188, 189
Roosevelt, Theodore, and, 188
Sampson, William T., and, 188
Shafter, William, and, 188–189
Siege of Sevastopol (October 17, 1854–September 9, 1855), 152–155
aftermath, 155
allied victory, 154
Battle of the Takir Ridge, 154
Canrobert, François Certain, and, 153, 154
cholera and, 153
Commencement of the Siege of Sebastopol (Thomas Packer), *153*
deaths and casualties, 154
Hitler, Adolf, and, 235, 239
Kingdom of Sardinia's entrance into the war, 153–154
Treaty of Paris and, 154–155
Siege of Sevastopol (October 30, 1941–July 4, 1942), 234–236
aftermath, 236
Axis victory, 236
deaths and casualties, 236
Manstein, Erich von, and, 235–236

Siege of Singapore (February 8–15, 1942), 236–239
  aftermath, 238–239
  deaths and casualties, 238
  Japanese victory, 238
  Percival, Arthur E., and, 237, 238
  Yamashita Tomoyuki and, 237, 238
Siege of St. Augustine (November 10–December 29, 1702), 90–91
  aftermath, 91
  Daniel, Robert, and, 90–91
  Moore, James, and, 90–91
  Spanish victory, 91
  Zúñiga y la Cerda, José de, and, 90–91
Siege of Stalingrad (November 19, 1942–February 2, 1943), 239–243
  aftermath, 243
  Hitler, Adolf, and, 239–243
  Operation URANUS, 242
  Soviet snipers seeking out targets, *241*
  Soviet victory, 243
Siege of Syracuse (213–212 BCE), 14–17
  Archimedes and, 15
  Carthaginian expeditionary force, 16
  claws (grapples) used in, 15, *16*
  death of Archimedes, 17
  Epicydes and, 14, 15, 17
  geopolitical significance of Sicily, 14–15
  Himilco Phameas and, 16
  Hippocrates and, 14–15, 17
  Marcellus, Marcus Claudius, and, 14–17
  Roman surprise attack, 16
  sambucas used in, 15
  tolleni (assault machines with boom and basket) used in, 15
  war elephants used in, 14, 16
Siege of Syracuse (415–413 BCE), 8–10
  aftermath, 10
  Alcibiades and, 8
  Athenian naval force, 8
  deaths of Nicias and Demosthenes, 9
  Demosthenes and, 9
  first Athenian expedition, 8–9
  Gylippus and, 8–9
  Lamachus and, 8, 9
  Nicias and, 8, 9
  second Athenian expedition, 8–9
  Spartan intervention, 8–9
  Spartan victory, 9–10
  surrender and enslavement of Athenians, 9
  three Athenian generals, 8
  Thucydides on, 8, 9
Siege of Szigetvár (August 6–September 8, 1566), 71–73
  aftermath, 72
  death of Suleiman, 72
  Ottoman victory, 72
  Sokollu Mehmed Pasha and, 72
  Suleiman I, the Magnificent, and, 71–72
  Zrínyi, Miklós, and, 71–72
Siege of Tenochtitlán (May 26–August 13, 1521), 60–63
  aftermath, 63
  Cortés, Hernán, and, 60, 62–63
  Cuitláhuac and, 62
  deaths and casualties, 63
  geopolitical significance of Tenochtitlán, 60
  map, *61*
  Montezuma and, 60, 62
  Spanish and Tlaxcallan victory, 62–63
  Spanish force, 60, 62–63
Siege of the Alcázar at Toledo (July 21–September 27, 1936), 213–217
  aftermath, 216
  deaths and casualties, 216
  execution of Moscardó, 215
  Franco, Francisco, 214, 216
  Moscardó Ituarte, José, and, 215, 216
  Nationalist victory, 216
Siege of Tobruk (April 10–December 5, 1941), 227–231
  aftermath, 231
  Allied victory, 230–231
  deaths and casualties, 230–231
  Hitler, Adolf, and, 228
  Morshead, Leslie, and, 229
  O'Connor, Richard N., and, 227, 228–229
  Rommel, Erwin, and, 228–230
Siege of Toulon (September 18–December 19, 1793), 130–132
  aftermath, 132
  Carteaux, Jean François, and, 131–132
  French Republican victory, 132
  Hood, Alexander, and, 130–131
  Howe, Richard, and, 130
  Napoleon Bonaparte and, 131, *131*, 132
Siege of Troy (1194–1184 BCE), 3–4
  Achillles and, 3
  Aeneas and, 3

archaeological evidence, 3
economics and, 3
geopolitical significance of Troy, 3
great fire as end of, 3
Greek victory, 2–3
Hector and, 3
Iliad (Homer) and, 3
trade and, 3
Trojan horse used in, 3–4
Ulysses and, 3
Siege of Tuyen Quang (November 24, 1884–March 3, 1885), 184–187
aftermath, 186–187
Black Flags and, 184–186
deaths and casualties, 186
French victory, 186
Siege of Veii (404–396 BCE), 10–11
aftermath, 11
Camillus, Marcus Furius, and, 11
geopolitical significance of Veii, 10
pillage and sack of Veii, 11
Roman control of Juno (deity), 11
Roman occupation of the north, 11
Roman victory, 11
Siege of Venice (August 1848–August 27, 1849), 148–152
aftermath, 152
Austrian naval blockade, 151–152
Austrian victory, 152
balloon incendiaries and, 149, 151
Five Days of Milan and, 149
Manin, Daniele, and, 150–152
Risorgimento and, 148, 152
Siege of Vienna (September 24–October 14, 1529), 67–69
aftermath, 68
Ferdinand, Archduke of Austria, and, 67, 68
Habsburg victory, 68
Ottoman force, 68
Suleiman I, the Magnificent, and, 67–68
Siege of Vukovar (August 25–November 18, 1991), 270–273
aftermath, 272–273
deaths and casualties, 272–273
geopolitical significance of Vukovar, 271
Yugoslav victory, 272
Siege of Xiangyang (March 1267–March 14, 1273), 47–49
aftermath, 49
Duzong (Song emperor) and, 49
Kublai Khan and, 47, 48

Lü Wenhuan and, 48, 49
Möngke Khan and, 47, 48
Ögödei Khan and, 47
Song dynasty and, 47–49
starvation into submission used at, 48
trebuchets used in, 48–49
Yuan dynasty and, 48–49
Yuan force, 48
Yuan victory, 49
Siege of Yorktown (September 28–October 19, 1781), 126–130
Abercrombie, Robert, and, 128–129
aftermath, 129
Cornwallis, Lord, and, 126–129
de Grasse-Tilly, Comte, and, 126–128
de Rochambeau, Comte, and, 127
deaths and casualties, 129
depiction of British surrender (John Trumbull), *129*
Franco-American victory, 129
Graves, Thomas, and, 128
Lafayette, Marquis de, and, 126–127
redoubts used at, 128–129
Washington, George, and, 126–127, 129
Siege towers, 3–4, 12, 13, 31, 42, 44
Sieges of Tyre and Gaza (332 BCE), 11–14
aftermath and legacy, 14
Alexander the Great and, 11–14
Batis (governor of Gaza) and, 13, 14
battering rams used at, 13
deaths and casualties, 13, 14
Dyadis the Thessalian and, 12, 13
geopolitical significance of Tyre, 12
Macedonian victory at Gaza, 14
Macedonian victory at Tyre, 13
Sieges of Vicksburg (May 18–July 4, 1863) and Port Hudson, Louisiana (May 21–July 9, 1863), 162–167
Banks, Nathaniel P., and, 165–166
deaths and casualties, 165–166
Gardner, Franklin, and, 165–166
Grant, Ulysses S., and, 164–165
Pemberton, John C., and, 164–165
siege of Port Hudson, 165–166
siege of Vicksburg, 162–166
Sieges of Zaragoza (June 15–August 17, 1808; December 20, 1808–February 20, 1809), 136–139
deaths and casualties, 137, 138–139
The Defence of Saragossa (David Wilkie), *138*

Sieges of Zaragoza (*Continued*)
  first siege of Zaragoza, 136–138
  geopolitical significance of Zaragoza, 136
  Junot, Jean-Androche, and, 138
  Napoleon Bonaparte and, 136–139
  second siege of Zaragoza, 138–139
  Verdier, Jean Antoine, and, 137–138
Silverius, Pope, 31
Sino-French War, 184, 185. *See also* Siege of Tuyen Quang (November 24, 1884–March 3, 1885)
Song dynasty, 47–49
South African War (Boer War), 193. *See also* Siege of Mafeking (October 13, 1899–May 17, 1900)
Spanish American War, 190. *See also* Siege and First Battle of Manila (May 1–August 14, 1898)
Spanish Civil War, 213–214, 217, 220, 221. *See also* Siege of Madrid (November 6, 1936–March 31, 1939); Siege of the Alcázar at Toledo (July 21–September 27, 1936)
Stalin, Josef, 232, 233, 234, 235, 239, 240, 241, 248, 254–255
Stephen III, Pope, 36
Suleiman I, the Magnificent
  siege of Malta (June 11, 1940–November 20, 1942), 69, 70
  siege of Rhodes (July 28–December 21, 1522), 63–64
  siege of Szigetvár (August 6–September 8, 1566), 71–72
  siege of Vienna (September 24–October 14, 1529), 67–68
Syrian Civil War, 273, 276. *See also* Siege of Aleppo (July 19, 2012–December 22, 2016); Siege of Kobanî (September 27, 2014–January 26, 2015)

Taiping Rebellion, 182, 184
Third Punic War, 18. *See also* Siege of Carthage (149–146 BCE)
Third Siege of Missolonghi (April 15, 1825–April 23, 1826), 142–146
  aftermath, 145
  "Greece Expiring on the Ruins of Missolonghi" (Eugène Delacroix), 145
  Mahmud II and, 143–144
  Muhammad Ali of Egypt and, 143–144
  Ottoman-Egyptian victory, 145
  Reşid Mehmed Pasha and, 143, 144, 145
Thirty Years' War, 76, 81, 82. *See also* Siege of Breda (August 28, 1624–June 5, 1625); Siege of Magdeburg (November 20, 1630–May 20, 1631)
Thucydides
  on siege of Plataea (428–427 BCE), 6
  on siege of Syracuse (415–413 BCE), 8, 9
Todleben, Franz Eduard Ivanovich, 152, 153, 180
Tolleni (assault machines with boom and basket), 15
Trebuchets, 43, 44, 48–49
Trenches, 44, 97, 101, 107, 121, 191–192
  parallel trenches, 85, 87, 123, 144
  semi-circular and circular trenches, 4, 183
  snaking trenches, 186
  zigzag trenches, 127, 144, 166, 261
Triremes (war galleys with three banks of oars), 8, 9, 12, 17, 19

Umayyad Caliphate, 36
Urban II, Pope, 40–41
Urban VII, Pope, 83

Valois-Habsburg Wars, 66. *See also* Siege and Battle of Pavia (October 28, 1524–February 24, 1525)
Vauban, Sébastien Le Prestre de, 85, 86–87
Vietnam War, 262. *See also* Siege of Khe Sanh (January 21–April 8, 1968)

War galleys, 17
  effectiveness of, 17
  quinqueremes (galleys with four or five banks of oars), 15, 17, 18
  triremes (galleys with three banks of oars), 8, 9, 12, 17, 19
War of Devolution, 85
War of Jenkins' Ear, 93. *See also* Siege of Cartagena de Indias (March 9–May 20, 1741)
War of the Austrian Succession, 93. *See also* Siege of Cartagena de Indias (March 9–May 20, 1741)
War of the First Coalition, 130. *See also* French Revolution

War of the League of Augsburg, 85, 88
War of the Spanish Succession (Queen Anne's War), 88, 90, 93, 117. *See also* Siege of St. Augustine (November 10–December 29, 1702)
Ward, Artemas, 109, 110–111
Watchtower, 27
World War I, 168, 178, 181, 187, 206, 208–209, 210
   state of Yugoslavia and, 270
   See also Siege of Kut (December 7, 1915–April 29, 1916); Siege of Przemyśl (September 16, 1914–March 22, 1915); Siege of Qingdao (August 23, 1914–November 7, 1914)
World War II, 178, 224, 227, 231, 235, 243, 248, 250, 253
   Battle of Britain, 227
   Battle of El Alamein, 231
   Battle of Stalingrad, 239, 243, 272, 274
   Battle of the Bulge, 249, 253
   Battle of the Seelow Heights, 255
   First Battle of Tobruk, 227
   Indian National Army (INA) and, 244
   Spanish Civil War and, 221
   See also Siege of Bastogne (December 20–27, 1944); Siege of Berlin (April 16–May 2, 1945); Siege of Budapest (November 3, 1944–February 13, 1945); Siege of Dunkirk (Dunkerque) (May 26–June 4, 1940); Siege of Imphal and Kohima (April 4–May 31, 1944); Siege of Leningrad (July 10, 1941–January 27, 1944); Siege of Malta (June 11, 1940–November 20, 1942); Siege of Sevastopol (October 17, 1854–September 9, 1855); Siege of Stalingrad (November 19, 1942–February 2, 1943); Siege of Tobruk (April 10–December 5, 1941)

Yellow fever, 95, 106, 107, 108, 210
Yuan dynasty, 48–49